Managing Growing Organizations

A New Approach

Managing Growing Organizations

A New Approach

Theodore D. Weinshall
Faculty of Management
Tel Aviv University

and

Yael-Anna Raveh
Department of Business Administration
University of Haifa

JOHN WILEY & SONS
Chichester · New York · Brisbane · Toronto · Singapore

Library of Congress Cataloging in Publication Data:

Weinshall, Theodore D.
  Managing growing organizations.

  Includes index.
  1. Management. 2. Organization. II. Raveh, Yael-
  Anna. II. Title.
HD31.W416   1983   658.4'06   82-21967

ISBN 0 471 90116 4

British Library Cataloguing in Publication Data:

Weinshall, Theodore D.
  Managing growing organizations.
  1. Management
  I. Title   II. Raveh, Yael-Anna
  658.4   HD31

ISBN 0 471 90116 4

Typeset in Great Britain by
Pintail Studios Ltd, Ringwood, Hampshire
Printed by The Pitman Press, Bath, Avon

This book is dedicated to the memory of John Desmond Glover. Jack Glover was a great man, intellectual, and humanist. He was a dear and unforgettable friend to us.

TDW and YAR

Contents

Preface

One may say that this book has been written by the first author for over 20 years, and by the second author since 1972, when the dialogue between us about the dynamics of the Total Organizational System (TOS) commenced. These past 10 years have not always been a continuous period of harmony and consensus as to the TOS. Nevertheless, we feel that it has been a worthwhile discussion, debate, and analysis. We hope that the readers will concur when they have finished the book.

We present the dynamics of organizations from the time they are conceived and created by entrepreneurs. This book follows the organizational development, as the organizations grow through advancing technology, product/service diversity, and geographical dispersal, and in the way that their managements run them, whether in entrepreneurial, functional, decentralized, or, finally, federated structures. Management of growing organizations is presented by way of a TOS analysis. In developing the TOS, we have drawn upon some of the principal contributors to organizational theory. We believe that the TOS which emerged is unique in encompassing all types of organizations, the principal systems which affect management in running them, and the various stages through which organizations pass when they grow.

We would like, therefore, to thank all those from whom we learned, and those whose scientific contributions helped us to develop the TOS. They are personally mentioned throughout the book. Within this context we would like to thank each other for what we have learned from one another, and the consequent contributions to the TOS which emerged from our common work. We are indebted to our many students, from whom we probably learned even more than from our teachers and from one another.

Finally, we would like to thank those who have helped us directly in writing this book. The writing itself has been done in three main places (apart from planes and trains, in which part of the first author's writing has been performed). The mimeographed draft of the last chapter (7) about helping organizations was written in the London Business School in 1978; we are grateful to the school and our friends there for their inspirational environment, including the view of London's Regents Park. A major part of chapters 4, 5, and 6 was written in the house and garden of our dear friends Woolf and Helene Marmot, in the beautiful suburb of Paris, Le Vesinet; we are very grateful for their hospitality, kindness, and patience. The remainder of the book, chapters 1, 2, and 3, was written in our homes in Haifa; we are most grateful to our family, especially to Yonna Weinshall and Yaacov Raveh, for having sacrificed their time and encouraged us to continue with our work. Our gratitude is also extended to Michal and Jonathan Raveh, and to Talia and Howard Brodsly, for being helpfully 'around'.

We are very grateful to two of Teddy Weinshall's collaborators at Tel Aviv University—Orna Posner and Nancy Bennett—who have been a tremendous help to us over and beyond their line of duty. We are also grateful to all those in Tel Aviv University who contributed towards the mimeographed editions of chapters 4, 5, and 6, which appeared separately in the Faculty of Management Working Paper series.

Last, but not least, we thank most heartily our friend and tutor Theodore (Ted) Lang, who has devotedly and relentlessly corrected our English, edited our writing, and advised us as to its contents. Those readers who feel that the book is easily readable should give the credit mainly to Ted, not to us.

TDW and YAR

Haifa,
Israel
March 1982

Abbreviations and Glossary

Where abbreviations and terms appearing in the definition are themselves defined elsewhere in this glossary, they are printed in *italic*.

BCS
: BRITISH CHAIN STORES, a fictitious name for the *organization* in which Raveh's doctoral research was carried out.

BOD
: BASE ORDINANCE DEPOT, the depot described in the Army Logistics organizational example.

BP
: BRITISH PETROLEUM, a large, British-based multinational corporation. BP is also Business Policy, part of which is business strategy, to which we refer as organizational strategy (*OS*).

CE or CEO
: CHIEF EXECUTIVE or CHIEF EXECUTIVE OFFICER, the head of the *management*. He is the highest ranking person in the formal hierarchy of the *managers* (i.e. the general manager or *president* appointed by the board of directors) and of the shareholders. If he is the chairman, or another member of the board of directors, he has to devote enough time to the *organization* to be able to run its *management*. This would mean at least half of his time; he could be the CE of two organizations if he divides all of his time between their two managements.

Communicogram
: A technique for describing, analysing, and feeding back oral interactions for therapeutic and corrective purposes. It is usually based on a two-weeks' self-recording study carried out among about 30–50 managers who record their interactions from memory. The interactions are subsequently matched and the results are fed back to the participants.

DM
: DECISION MAKING, the totality of the decisions taken by the members of the *organization*.

DMP
: DECISION-MAKING PROCESS, the ways in which human beings conduct their *decision making* (*DM*).

EVP
: EXECUTIVE VICE PRESIDENT, the senior among the *VP*s (usually in an American corporation) who is meant to replace the *president* in case of his absence.

FDM

FACTOR/S OF DECISION MAKING, the human factors which take part in the *decision making*, namely the human groups into which all the members of the *organization* are divided according to their *TOS* roles (i.e. according to their roles in the organizational input–output system) and their effects on organizational survival. The FDM in industrial and business organizations include: *managers, workers*, trade unions, bankers, shareholders, suppliers, customers, and governments. In other types of organizations the names of the FDM may be different.

Formal grid

A matrix indicating the formal location of every member of the *operating organization*. The columns of the formal grid are the formal units of the *organization* (divisions, departments, sections, etc.) while its rows are the formal levels used in the *organization* (e.g. governmental or academic ranks), or salary brackets. The formal grid is used for the visual chart presentation of a *communicogram* or a *formalogram* or an *informalogram*.

Formalogram

The formal or required interpersonal relationships as perceived by all the *managers*, and sometimes *workers*, participating in the Formalogram, presented in chart or table form.

General Manager

The formal head of the managers.

GIGO

'GARBAGE IN—GARBAGE OUT'. This sarcastic term has to do with the lack of usefulness and inadaptability to the real situation of certain data-processing systems. In such cases the data input fed into the computer, and the output coming out of it, could be considered as GIGO.

GFA

GROUP FEEDBACK ANALYSIS. A method for acquiring responses to closed, mainly sealed, questionnaires in a group session of the respondents; and subsequently feeding back the averages and distributions of the group's results. The feed-back session serves for training and research purposes, by way of conducting a discussion within the same group as to the meanings and reasons for the averages and distributions of the results. The GFA was devised by Dr. Frank Heller of the Tavistock Institute of Human Relations in London.

HBS

HARVARD BUSINESS SCHOOL.

IBM

INTERNATIONAL BUSINESS MACHINES, the large multinational corporation, which deals primarily with all kinds of data-processing equipment.

IMEDE

International Management Development Institute, Lausanne, Switzerland.

Immediate environment

The environment in which organizations compete with each other for the *FDM*.

Informalogram	Informal diagram, chart of the *MPWR* among all the *managers* (and sometimes workers, too) participating in the Informalogram. Also the technique for establishing the *managerial structure* (*MS*), on the basis of the informal *MPWR*, on the one hand, and the formal relationships based on the *organigram* and on the *formal grid*, on the other hand.
INSEAD	European Institute of Business Administration in Fontainebleau.
ITT	INTERNATIONAL TELEPHONE AND TELE-GRAPH, an international conglomerate which started in the 1920s in telephone and telegraph material and equipment, and diversified into many different product and service lines. Probably the first supranational (the third and most important aspect of an *MNC*) organization in the world, except for the *RCC*.
Management	Usually refers to the totality of *managers* in one *organization*, but sometimes refers to the 'managerial class', i.e. the management of all the organizations of one country, or in the entire world.
Manager	Any member of the *operating organization* whose main role is in guaranteeing the continued cooperation with the *organization* of at least one other member of the *organization*. Thus, a supervisor guarantees the continued cooperation with the *organization* of his *manager* or worker subordinates. A salesman guarantees the continued cooperation of the customers, a buyer guarantees the continued cooperation of the suppliers, etc.
MD	MANAGING DIRECTOR. Originally that member of the board of directors in the UK who was responsible for the liaison between the board and the *management*. However, over the years the British MD has spent more and more of his time working for the organization and has gradually taken over from the *general manager* as the *CE*. Therefore, nowadays in UK managing director is more or less synonymous with a US *president*.
MBA	MASTER OF BUSINESS ADMINISTRATION, the second university degree usually granted to management graduates.
MC	MANAGERIAL CHARACTERISTICS, the interpersonal characteristics (leadership, followership, and others) of *managers*. A manager relates best to other people and to his work when his role in the *managerial structure* (*MS*) is suited to his MC, and when the *MS* is the proper one for the organizational *scope of decision making* (*SDM*).

MNC   MULTINATIONAL CORPORATION, or multi-national. This term has been used quite loosely for all kinds of international, transnational, joint (national) ventures, and other types of organizations operating in more than one country. An MNC is an *organization* operating in two or more countries in which all considerations related to its growth process and its survival are based wholly on the interests of the *organization* itself, national pressures having no influence, except in so far as constraints are imposed by the countries within which it functions. The more an *organization* is a multinational, the less it carries with it the constraints of one country to other countries.

MPWR   MUTUALLY PERCEIVED WORKING RELATION-SHIPS. These are based on the answers of *managers* when responding to the question, 'Please list the people with whom you generally work most closely, regardless of their position in the *organization*.' The MPWR represent the informal relationship structure, while the formal relationships of the *organization*, or the position in the *formal grid*, represent the formal relationship structure. Together they constitute the *managerial structure (MS)* as established by the *informalogram*.

MS   MANAGERIAL STRUCTURE, the actual relationship structure of the *management*, which indicates the way in which the managers are directed by the person who is at their head. When the MS is of a whole *organization*, we find the *CE* at the head of the MS. In order to encompass and manage the growing *organization*, *management* has to adapt its structure to the *SDM* from time to time. The main MS in which managements are structured when the *organization* grows over time are: entrepreneural structure (informally centralized), functional structure (formally centralized), product/service line structure, and area structure (the latter two are formally decentralized).

OAPEC   ORGANIZATION OF ARAB PETROLEUM EXPORTING COUNTRIES. The majority of the *OAPEC* countries, with an overwhelming share of the *OPEC* oil reserves, are Arab countries. Two of the *OAPEC* members, Algeria and Indonesia, are non-Arab but exclusively Muslim countries.

OB   ORGANIZATIONAL BEHAVIOUR, a behavioural academic discipline which deals with the behaviour of the *TOS*, as well as the behaviour of individuals and of small and larger groups within them. It is a distinct and separate

	behavioural discipline along with sociology, psychology, anthropology, political science, education, etc.
OD	ORGANIZATIONAL DEVELOPMENT, a method for adapting the *managers* to the required MS by way of training.
OPEC	ORGANIZATION OF PETROLEUM EXPORTING COUNTRIES, the members of which were, in 1973: Algeria, Ecuador, Gabon (associate), Indonesia, Iran, Iraq, Kuwait, Libya, Nigeria, Qatar, Saudi Arabia, United Arab Emirates, and Venezuela. The majority of these belong to *OAPEC*.
Operating organization	*Management* (the *managers*) and the *workers*. These are all the employees of the *organization* who spend a substantial portion of their time in the *organization* and are remunerated by it by salaries and wages.
OR	OPERATIONS RESEARCH, quantitative techniques and models applied to managerial problems.
Organigram, or organizational chart	The way that formal interpersonal relationships are perceived by someone at the top of the *MS*, usually the *CE*.
Organization	From among the many definitions of organization, we prefer that of Chester Barnard (*The Functions of the Executive*, Harvard University, Cambridge, Mass., 1938, p. 81): 'A system of consciously coordinated activities or forces of two or more persons.' These persons or members of the organization are not only the *managers* and *workers* (whom we refer to as the *operating organization*) but also persons—for example, the customers—belonging to any of the *factors of decision making* (*FDM*) without the cooperation of whom the organization cannot survive.
OS	ORGANIZATIONAL (or OPERATIONAL) STRATEGY which the *management* undertakes for the *organization* to perform. It is the *what* (product/service line), *how* (the technology), and *where* of the *organization*. OS is analogous to business strategy, namely the objectives which *management* spells out for the *organization* within its business policy.
PDG	PRÉSIDENT DIRECTEUR GÉNÉRAL, the French manager who is simultaneously the chairman ('président' in French) and *general manager* ('directeur général'). When used in its wider sense in France and generally in Europe, it means a *CE*.
PERT	PROJECT EVALUATION AND REVIEW TECHNIQUE, also referred to as critical path analysis. It is a planning and control method which is best suited for pro-

jects and tasks with which there has been little or no previous experience or in which it is difficult to predict with a reasonable degree of accuracy the length of the different stages, phases, and operations of the task.

PR   PUBLIC RELATIONS; in the USA and elsewhere sometimes nicknamed 'Madison Avenue'.

President   An American term describing the head of the *management*. The term is used in most of the industrial and highly industrial countries, as well as in the *MNC*s. It is usually assumed that the president is the *chief executive (CE)* of the *organization*, which is not necessarily the case.

RCC   ROMAN CATHOLIC CHURCH, usually referred to as the Catholic Church.

RR   ROLLS-ROYCE, a British manufacturer known for its high-quality motor cars and aircraft engines.

SDM   SCOPE/S OF DECISION MAKING, the total physical amount and complexity of the managerial DM, which the *management* undertakes in order to ensure the continued cooperation of the *FDM* so that the *organization* may survive. The SDM is a function of the competition of other organizations for the different *FDM* in the *immediate environment*. The intensity of the competition is determined by the conditions existing in the *wider environment*.

SOE   STATE-OWNED ENTERPRISE/S, the economic organizations owned by the state. The degree to which the state is actually involved in managing the SOE may vary in a way similar to the involvement of the shareholders and their boards of directors in managing the organizations. There is, however, one important difference between an SOE and a non-SOE. The shareholders and the government in an SOE are one and the same *FDM*.

T-groups   TRAINING GROUPS are therapy groups led by a 'trainer'. They are an offspring of the Group Dynamics school in *OB*. Closely related to them are other types of therapy groups such as encounter groups, sensitivity training groups, role-playing groups, and all kinds of other human 'laboratories' or 'workshops'.

TOS   TOTAL ORGANIZATION SYSTEM is a set of interrelated organizational systems presenting the coningency dynamics of the *organization* over time, navigated by *management*. It serves primarily analytical purposes and leads to a better understanding and evaluation of the state of an *organization* at a given point in time. Its other contribution is in permitting the strategic planning of all its component systems and their effect on each other. The

TOS is composed of two main system groups and six principal systems which are interrelated in different ways. The *decision-making* main system is composed of the *immediate* and *wider environment* systems, as well as the *organizational strategy* (*OS*) and the *scope of decision making* (*SDM*) principal systems. The *management* main system consists of the *managerial structure* (*MS*) and the *managerial characteristics* (*MC*) systems.

VP — VICE PRESIDENT, the deputy of the *president* in business corporations. It usually refers to the heads of the functions, i.e. engineering, research and development, finance, manufacturing, marketing, personnel, purchasing, etc. In the UK, where the head of the *management* is nowadays usually a *managing director*, the VPs are referred to as 'directors', e.g. engineering director, financial director, etc. In France, the equivalent to the VP is a 'directeur'.

Wider environment — One of the six principal systems of the *TOS* and one of the four principal systems of the main system of *decision making* in the *TOS*. It is composed of five environmental systems—the employment market, the capital market, the consumer market, the technological–scientific system, and the socio-cultural system. Together with the *MC* it is one of the two principal systems of the *TOS* which are independent of other principal systems.

Workers — Those members of the *operating organization* who are not *managers*. That is to say, all those employees who do not have managerial responsibility, i.e. who are not responsible for the continued cooperation of one or more other members of the *organization*, and whose work is directed and supervised by the *managers*.

Introduction

The Total Organizational System (TOS)

WHAT THIS BOOK IS ABOUT

This book tells what organizations must do to survive, what they must do to avoid stagnation and collapse. The dynamics of management and organizations over time are described and analysed by way of the TOS (Total Organizational System). This notion of a total organization system assumes a dynamic relationship between management of the organization and the environment, both of which are affected by changing conditions of size, place, and human nature. Any change in one part of the total system affects the other parts and the survival of any organization is continually threatened by the changes brought about by growth, which in itself is essential for survival.

The TOS (see Figure 1) is composed of the immediate environment, the wider environment, the organizational strategy, the scope of decision making, the managerial structure, and the managerial characteristics. The immediate environment includes the organizations competing for the organizational cooperation of the human factors of managers, workers, trade unions, bankers, shareholders, suppliers, customers, government, etc. The wider environment includes the systems of the employment market, money market, supply of and demand market for materials and products, as well as the technology and socio-cultural systems. The scope of decision making is the total amount and complexity of the decisions imposed upon the management by their own organizational strategy, influenced by both the immediate and wider environments. Managerial structure refers to the *actual* way in which the decision making is carried out, formally or informally. The managerial characteristics are the leadership and followership characteristics of managers, from the chief executive down.

Consequently, organizational systems are actually contingency systems; that is to say that the different components are contingent upon each other. A major change in one subsystem may not only affect what is happening in other subsystems, but may also alter the rules by which these systems are governed. It will be shown, therefore, that principles which, until quite recently, have governed management education, its teaching and writing, are based on false assumptions.

1

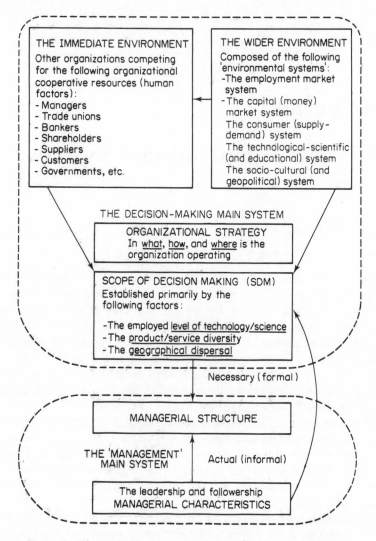

Figure 1   Two main systems and six principal systems of the TOS

Thus, all of the following principles turn out to be *absolutely wrong*:

—there exists a 'good' and desirable organizational structure in which an organization should operate at all times;
—there are good and bad managers, i.e. a good manager will always be good and a manager who has completely failed in one organization or another could never succeed in the same or in any other organization;
—it is desirable to have people continue to work in the organization as long as possible, and the organization should do whatever it can to hold on to employees who are doing very well today;
—there are rules which should govern the establishment of organizational

structures. One of these rules is the so-called 'span of control'; it represents the number of subordinates that a manager can control.

FOR WHOM THE BOOK IS INTENDED

This book is meant for three different types of population. First, it is for practising executives, namely all those upon whose shoulders lies the responsibility of organizations and their successful operation, whether they call themselves managers, executives, administrators, or directors. The second population includes the students of management and administration. Third, it is also meant for organizational scientists, researchers, teachers, and consultants. Different parts of the book may serve one population of readers better than another. Thus, for example, the references to other sources and readings are meant primarily for the scholar and researcher, rather than for the ordinary practitioner. This is why such references, or any other elaborations of the text, appear in notes at the end of each chapter. We also suggest that the practitioners, rather than the scholars, should now stop reading this introduction, resuming it on page 8. All readers are advised not to study the Abbreviations and Glossary at the outset, and only refer back to the beginning of the book whenever they need to while reading.

SOMETHING ABOUT THE AUTHORS AND THEIR RELATION TO THE TOS

We have always found it helpful to know something of the background of the authors we read, particularly their conceptual framework. To know that Frederick Taylor was an engineering foreman who turned into a management consultant; that Frank Gilbreth was originally a bricklayer; that Chester Barnard was a chief executive of a telephone company and that Fritz Roethlisberger had studied engineering and administration at MIT and at Harvard before joining Elton Mayo in the Hawthorne studies; all this seemed to help us, and increased our pleasure in studying their work.

We would like to help the readers of this book by providing them with some additional insight into the concept of the TOS. The first author, Teddy Weinshall, came to the fields of general management and organizational behaviour from industrial engineering, where he acquired first-hand experience in organizations as a conventional management consultant. Most of what he learned in industrial engineering and management consulting came from Professor Julius F. Cahen, who introduced organizational efficiency into some of the major industrial and governmental organizations in Holland in the 1920s, 1930s, and 1940s, before doing the same in Israel in the 1950s, 1960s, and 1970s.

Weinshall's exposure to organizational behaviour took place at the Harvard Business School in the late 1950s. At that time the disciplines of human relations, business policy, organizational environment, formal organizations, and organizational behaviour, were more or less integrated and cross-fertilized each other. So did the professors who taught, examined, and supervised him: Professors John D. Glover, C. Roland Christensen, Abraham Zaleznik, Fritz J.

Roethlisberger, Richard S. Merriam, George F. Lombard, and Paul Lawrence. Weinshall's ideas have been strongly influenced by these great teachers. His final doctoral dissertation was presented in 1960 and is described in the Devon Corporation following chapter 3*.

Chester Barnard's *Functions of the Executive* and Fritz Roethlisberger's and Dickson's *Management and the Workers* influenced his work significantly. This is probably why, when he first thought about this book, he wanted to call it 'Back to Barnard and Hawthorne'. What he meant to imply by that was that, although more than 40 years have elapsed since Mayo, Roethlisberger, and Barnard first appeared with their organizational behaviour findings, their approaches and conclusions are still valid.

The second author, Yael Raveh, came to the TOS through her initial studies in the behavioural sciences—psychology, sociology, and anthropology—and her subsequent graduate studies in organizational behaviour. Despite her long relationship with the first author, she was exposed to his TOS as a graduate student only in 1972. Subsequently, Raveh utilized the TOS as one of the models according to which she tested the relationships among the variables she studied in her doctoral work, supervised by Derek Pugh. Raveh's doctoral research and its findings, presented in her 1976 thesis, are described in the British Chain Stores (BCS) organizational example at the end of chapter 4*. Yael Raveh, like Teddy Weinshall, has used the TOS as the basis on which she has been teaching and performing her action research. However, she has contributed to the TOS partnership some socio-psychological elements on the one hand and, on the other, strengthened the algorithmic relationships of the TOS, while still maintaining its contingency approach, which evolved out of her work with Derek Pugh.

ON CONTENTS AND PRESENTATION

The construction and elaboration of the TOS has evolved through our own research, that of others, and the feedback we have received from the thousands of students in our classes in various countries.

Because our greatest strength is as teachers, we have presented the TOS in much the same way as we have in the classroom, i.e. alternating and interweaving ideas with organizational examples.* Also, we have included various descriptions of the Total Organizational System—its two main systems: the decision-making and the management systems; and its six contingent components: the immediate and wider environments, the operational strategy, the scope of decision making, the managerial structure, and the managerial characteristics. This repetition of the elements of the TOS is considered necessary for a better comprehension and integration of the TOS by the reader.

The most important aspect of the presentation of material is the level of

---

* Each of the seven chapters is followed by short descriptions of a few organizational examples which serve as illustrations, mainly in that chapter. These same organizational examples will appear in our forthcoming book: *Management in Practice—Eighteen Organizational Examples of Managing Growing Organizations Throughout the World.*

abstraction. For all reader populations, the same level of abstraction has been chosen and applied throughout the book, both for the conceptual material and for the organizational examples.

One may detect contradictions among the concepts, hypotheses, and findings of the different contributions to organizational theory.[1] This does not necessarily mean that many of these concepts, hypotheses, and findings were or are incorrect. One of our most important teachers[2] used to say that 'most theories are correct, if tested within the limits where they are applicable'. This is indeed true; we consider all the contributions mentioned in this book as important, novel (in their time), and, needless to say, conceptually and factually correct. One has to add to this the words 'within the limits where they are applicable'. These limits may be wider or narrower, depending on the level of abstraction on which the phenomena were studied and conceptualized, and the degree of culture-boundedness of the concepts and findings. Let us consider separately each of these constraints as they affect the degree of generalization and coverage of conceptual schemes and theories.

Level of Abstraction

It is clear that the higher the level of abstraction, the wider the coverage. On the other hand, the higher the level of abstraction, the less a conceptual scheme becomes applicable to actual life situations. This means that if one wishes to have as wide a coverage as possible and yet to have 'practical' theories in organization and management, one has to lower the level of abstraction until one reaches that level which seems wide enough in coverage and yet applicable enough in its current contributions to organization and management.

Degree of Culture-boundedness

In this case one moves down the ladder of generalization from universal to culture-bound organizational and managerial phenomena.[3] Here again, a narrow cultural coverage would be at the expense of wider use of the concepts, and vice versa.

An additional price to be paid for a higher level of conceptualization is the difficulty in carrying out rigid statistical research. The utilization of the Total Organizational System makes it necessary to fill the gaps between bits of foolproof statistical research by clinical research, in which one accepts the 'again and again and again' proof: namely that when a phenomenon occurs repeatedly in the same fashion, without ever occurring to the contrary, it may be accepted as axiomatic.[4] It is clear that when only a few variables are part of a low-level conceptualization, it is relatively easy to construct a model for foolproof statistical research. However, when one tries to encompass as many as possible of the variables of organizational phenomena, one cannot construct a realistic model integrating all organizational behaviour. Therefore, the higher the level of conceptualization, the more heuristic elements in the system, and the fewer the algorithmic elements.

The level of conceptualization of the TOS is higher than that of any of the other systems which will be mentioned in this book, both in terms of the level of abstraction and in the degree of culture-boundedness. It is not, however, too high to destroy its usefulness in teaching and research.

The level of abstraction, applied to both the concepts and the organizational examples, sometimes makes it necessary to ignore factors and details for the sake of simplicity. This, however, is unavoidable in such a presentation of the TOS.

A special effort has been made to utilize simple language and to avoid unnecessary academic jargon. Nevertheless, here and there, the daily spoken language did not provide the special term required in the context. Thus a glossary of special terms, with their definitions, has been provided.

Last, but not least, we would like to stress that this book is about and is meant for women as much as men. There are very few, if any, roles that women cannot fill as employees of the organization. Management is definitely not one of them. Therefore, if not explicitly referring only to men, whenever we say 'he', 'him', 'his', and 'himself', we also mean 'she', 'her', 'hers', and 'herself'.[5]

HOW THIS BOOK DIFFERS FROM OTHERS THAT DEAL WITH ORGANIZATIONAL SYSTEMS

'System' is one of those words which is used loosely in different disciplines and has recently penetrated the fields of organization and management.[6] The systems, as used in organization and management, are either 'descriptive' or qualitatively analytical, on the one hand, and 'modelistic' or quantitatively analytical, on the other.[7] The operations research scientists have been using exclusively 'modelistic' systems, while the organizational scientists have, on the whole, been using descriptive systems, but with some distinct exceptions.[8]

The TOS is definitely not a quantitative model. Indeed, we do not believe that, in the foreseeable future, a useful quantitative model for the TOS could or would be developed. The reason for this is that the effect of many variables in the TOS cannot, in the present state of the art, be quantitatively incorporated in an overall model.

A mathematical model usually indicates that its validity is conditional upon the assumption that specified variables, not included in the model, are not part of it and appear under the encompassing caption, 'all other things being equal'.

The validity of a quantitative model is in direct proportion to its explanatory share of the variables included in the model, and should be reasonably high. Otherwise, the usefulness of the model quickly diminishes. If a quantitative model can explain, say, 80 per cent or more of the phenomena it claims to describe, then one may consider it to be within the realm of usefulness. If, on the other hand, a model explains only up to, say, 20 per cent of the phenomena, it should be scrapped.

Unfortunately, an enormous wastage of effort and means is invested in constructing models of the latter type. Such resources are vainly invested in collecting, processing, interpreting, and even acting upon data and conclusions which have been worthless right from the outset. To this one should add the investment in human and physical resources of constructing the model, and the electronic data processing of the input, which is of the 'garbage in–garbage out' type.

It is indeed the level of abstraction of operations research models which accounts for the usefulness of using mathematical models. In those systems where one usually concentrates on only a small part of one component of the TOS to the exclusion of the rest of the total phenomena, one could easily reduce the explanatory share of the variables covered in the model to 20 per cent, 10, 5, or even to 1 per cent.

The boundaries of this limited domain are considered, in a dangerously self-deceiving way, to be isolated from the effects of other phenomena. However, only within such defined boundaries of the problem can the quantitative model aspire to become useful by increasing its explanatory share to, say, at least 80 per cent.

Let us take, for example, the operations research models in the area of inventory management. Such models usually assume no changes in the selling behaviour of the firm. However, even when one attempts to incorporate into the inventory model the changing patterns of sales, such a model would still exclude other important determinants affecting inventory management. The new inventory model would still not include variables such as the availability and cost of capital, energy, labour, materials, supply, etc., let alone the incorporation of the personal characteristics of the managers, who could unpredictably change the role and degree of importance of any of the variables included in the model, or excluded from it, and fit them to their own personality needs. All such inventory models fail to incorporate all the variables affecting the phenomena of the TOS. Nevertheless, whenever possible and plausible, quantitative measurements and ratios will be presented in describing the components of the TOS, their interrelationships, and their implications regarding total organizational behaviour.

Up to now we have compared the TOS with other systems, based primarily on a modelistic system. This includes operations research systems primarily, but a few organizational systems as well. The following is a presentation of the bulk of organizational systems, those which are, to a large extent, descriptive, though they may use, in varying degrees, quantitative techniques, primarily in correlating their variables with one another.

The TOS is different from such systems in several ways. First, the TOS level of abstraction is higher than that of other organizational systems, enabling it to widen its coverage, i.e. to encompass more subsystems.[9]

Second, the study of the various subsystems is based on the data from within those subsystems. This is in addition to the way these subsystems are perceived by the people inside the operating organization, i.e. management and the workers. Other organizational systems are usually studied through the perceptions of the people in operating organizations only, in some cases based on how one or a few people at the top view the situation.[10]

Third, along with the relatively higher level of abstraction, the establishment of the relationships within and among the components of the TOS requires only a limited number of measurements. In other organizational systems the quantification of organizational and managerial concepts in contingency conditions sometimes results in misleading deductions from measurements.[11]

Fourth, some organizationalists overlook the very dominant effect of the contingency of organizational systems. In doing so they generalize the implications of their findings, though important within the limits of that developmental stage of the organization, to all organizations, anywhere, any time.[12]

Fifth, the high level of abstraction of the TOS enables the integration of the major variables affecting the phenomena with the tools with which its components are measured. In other systems, the tools by which the components are measured may use much more sophisticated quantitative techniques, but sometimes exclude important variables without which the measured phenomenon emerges partially and sometimes wholly distorted.

Now that the advantages of the TOS have been demonstrated, we would not like to finish this section before emphasizing two important advantages of other organizational systems when compared with the TOS.

The higher level of abstraction of the TOS and the wider range of subsystems encompassed within it have their shortcomings. The TOS cannot incorporate variables of a lower level of abstraction which other organizational systems are able to include. For the same reason, the TOS does not lend itself to 'rational' quantitative research. This deprives the TOS of the distinction of standing up to the rigours of scientific proof, which is the 'halo' of systems applying mathematics in their research.

All the other organizational systems which are referred to in this book, whether they preceded the development of the TOS (i.e. before 1960) or have coincided with it, have contributed to the TOS. Without them the development of the TOS would have been impossible.

MANAGING GROWING ORGANIZATIONS

Finally, let us present the essential elements of the TOS which the management of growing organizations must follow. Figure 1 schematically describes the composition of the two main systems and the six components of the TOS, and the interrelationships between them. This book is all about the dynamics of these interrelationships, and how they affect the organization over time. The book is divided into seven chapters which may be divided into three different groups. The first three chapters introduce the readers to the various aspects of the TOS. The following three chapters include more fundamental and advanced analyses of the TOS. The final chapter discusses ways for helping organizations overcome the pitfalls of their contingency and their dynamics. Let us consider their summary contents chapter by chapter.

The first chapter discusses the human resources (managers, workers, customers, bankers, etc.) who make up the organization and its decision-making process. The second chapter describes how the organizational strategy attracts pressures and competition from both immediate and wider environments; these pressures and competition form the basis of the scope of decision making (SDM) imposed upon the management. These interorganizational and environmental pressures and competition bring about the inevitable growth in SDM over time.

Chapter 3 shows how the management has to structure itself differently at different stages of growth; it also deals with two ingredients of managerial structure—degrees of autonomy and formal clarity—and how to measure them.

Chapter 4 discusses the main aspects which affect SDM: the number of managers, the organizational strategy, the degree of customer involvement, and the type of managerial culture. It also analyses the structural and contextual reasons for organizations moving from one managerial structure to another.

Chapter 5 discusses the dominant effect of the managerial characteristics on the managerial structure. These characteristics include leadership, followership, and other interpersonal relationships of the chief executive and other key position managers. The chapter presents advanced managerial structures for complex and large scopes of decision making.

Chapter 6 is devoted to the multinationals; it first describes the nation state environments in which multinational corporations operate, and then analyses the development of multinationals and their contribution to the human race.

Chapter 7 deals with ways in which outsiders could help managements run organizations. The first section compares the ways in which pathologists and other doctors try to learn about human beings in order to fight disease, with the ways in which managerial scientists may do the same about organizations. The second section analyses three ways in which outsiders have tried to help organizations: (a) by changing managerial characteristics; (b) by innovating managerial structures; (c) by consulting, through giving straightforward advice and recommendations. The third section discusses ways by which *all* organizations may be helped to follow and survive the path of growth, and other aspects of the dynamics of the TOS.

THE DYNAMICS OF ORGANIZATIONS—FROM ENTREPRENEURIALS TO MULTINATIONALS

There are several points to bear in mind when reading this book. The primary one is that, in the long run, all organizations have to grow. There is hardly any organization which has been with us for, say, at least a quarter of a century which has not grown over its lifetime. It has not always been so. Until the eighteenth century, there were many organizations which survived for long periods of time without growing at all.

The second point to consider is that an ever-growing part of the world cannot exist in its accustomed way without being served by large organizations in areas such as manufacturing, retailing, communication, and power. Any major organizational collapse which would disrupt such things as telephones, mail or telex, electric power or oil supply, food distribution, etc., would bring our lives to a standstill. All these things are maintained only by way of the smooth operation of the organizations which provide them.

Last, but not least, one has to bear in mind constantly that growing organizations require different types of management.[13] As long as organizations remained static, they could do with a simple type of managerial structure. When humanity

10

was not completely dependent on those organizations, it did not suffer to any large extent if they failed, as it does nowadays. Management was much simpler and less crucial to humanity until the nineteenth century.

Today, management has to function in ever-changing patterns and ways in order to catch up with the ever-growing organizations. While it does so, the eyes of humanity are upon it and, indeed, managers perform the central role among human beings, enabling organizations to survive. All other people comprising the organizations—the workers, owners, customers, suppliers, etc.—would have torn apart their organizations by pulling them too much in their own directions. In other words, if it were not for the managers keeping organizations intact, the whole world we have built around us would have collapsed.

The origin of the concepts presented in this book may be traced back to the clinical research carried out by Elton Mayo and Fritz Roethlisberger at Hawthorne, around 1930, and to Chester Barnard's service as the president of the New Jersey Bell Corporation, in the late 1930s and early 1940s.[14] However, the actual concepts of this book have been put forward by us in an integrated form, similar to the way in which they are presented here, ever since 1960.[15]

The purpose of the first three chapters of the book is to present these concepts in such a way that they will become a living reality in the reader's mind, based on his own organizational experience, as wide or as narrow as it may be. This would require overcoming two obstacles. First, to encompass all the chief systems which have an effect on the operation and management of the organization, and to relate them to one another in a comprehensive way. Secondly, to present them in such a way that will bring them to life; this necessitates the utilization of real-life organizational examples which conclude each chapter.

The best example of an organization is a family, which is the oldest and most basic form of organization. It is also the organization in which we have the most experience. We shall compare, therefore, organizations to individual human beings and use terminology which is generally applicable to them (e.g. 'birth', 'living', and 'death'). This we shall do especially when discussing the development of organizations from their creation, through their existence and until their collapse. The last chapter of the book discusses the role of outsiders who, like doctors, try to help organizations overcome their ailments.

In this book we shall follow organizations along their growth path. We shall see that, like the growth of human beings, organizational growth is manifested in two main things: the changes in the things they do and the parallel changes in the structure, namely the changing framework by which they accommodate themselves to their changing environments.

NOTES

1 Let us take, for example, one of the earliest efforts to include, within the same framework, contributions in many areas of organizational behaviour. This was the *Organizations* of March and Simon (1958). When one compares the algorithms scattered throughout the book, one can easily point out many inconsistencies in their

assumptions and findings. A more recent effort to include different organizational systems in one book (Kast and Rosenzweig, 1970) leaves the different subsystems in separate chapters and does not try to integrate different system approaches into the same subsystem.

2   Professor Jules Cahen's industrial engineering contributions from the late 1920s to the 1940s in Philips, Eindhoven, and in Holland in general, were of a pioneering nature. After the Second World War he was the pioneer of teaching, research, and consulting in the field of industrial engineering in Israel, until his death in 1979.

3   The situation is, however, basically different between the 'level of abstraction' and the 'degree of culture-boundedness' in the area of availability of learning material— research, text, case studies, etc. While there is a lot of material for the managers operating at the lower levels of abstraction, at the functional and subfunctional levels, there is relatively little material on the total organizational level. On the other hand, most of the literature available on the effects of culture on management assumes universally bound conditions; relatively little research and writing have been devoted to culture-bound organizational and managerial phenomena (Weinshall, 1977, pp. 7–9).

4   Weinshall's first major research in the TOS was his doctoral thesis research (1960). It was not under Fritz Roethlisberger's supervision or with his close direction; it was very much influenced by him, though, through the three professors with whom Weinshall did work closely and who were at one time or another close to Roethlisberger. Fritz Roethlisberger was Weinshall's teacher in the doctoral instruction group on administrative practices and in a reading seminar on organizational behaviour. All this increased Weinshall's acquaintance with Roethlisberger's work and especially the pioneering research at Hawthorne, the cornerstone of organizational behaviour ever since the early 1930s. Probably Weinshall's strongest identification with Roethlisberger has been in his clinical approach to organizational research (Roethlisberger and Dickson, 1939). Fritz Roethlisberger used to say that there was no need to undertake a voluminous statistical research into a phenomenon which had repeated itself 'again and again and again' without ever occurring to the contrary.

5   The present book is a joint product of a woman and a man. So was the first book one of us participated in writing; it was about the role of women in managerial positions, explored in Israeli organizations and based on the research of Miriam Barad (Barad and Weinshall, 1965). Barad and Weinshall pointed out that the condition of Israeli women in 'the Israeli setting is far from equalling that of men', and that 'the advancement of a professional woman in Israeli industry was slower than that of a man with a comparable training' (Weinshall, 1976b, pp. 967–971).

6   Let us consider some definitions of a 'system' from the days before it penetrated the fields of organization and management, coming from a 1947 edition of a Webster's dictionary:

'1. A combination of parts into a whole, as, the bodily *system*, a railroad *system*, the solar *system*;
'2. Orderly arrangement, as 'you need more *system* in your work';
'3. Physics: a group or series of bodies moving about each other in space;
'4. A set of principles or a method, as 'my system dictates the play'.

'Synonyms: order, arrangement, method'.

7   We are using the words 'descriptive' and 'modelistic' rather than such terms as 'administrative', 'analytic', 'managerial', 'problem solving', and 'rational' because the latter terms have been loosely used by scientists who are initially qualitative, and those who are predominantly quantitative.

8   The renowned exceptions are probably Herbert A. Simon and the chain of his
    collaborators: James G. March with Simon (1958), Richard M. Cyert with March
    (1963), and W. H. Starbuck (Cyert, March, and Starbuck, 1961). Simon started as a
    disciple of Chester Barnard (1938) and his first major publication, *Administrative
    Behavior* (1947), was his own presentation and interpretation of Barnard. Although
    Simon tried to convey Barnard to his readers, the book already shows traces of the
    later Simon and his followers. Barnard himself may be considered, however, as one
    of the two first descriptive system scientists, the other being Fritz Roethlisberger
    (Roethlisberger and Dickson, 1939). Chester Barnard is indeed the pioneer of the
    Total Organizational System, a point made earlier in the Introduction.
9   A comparison of the TOS with other organizational systems is presented in a paper
    on which, to a large extent, we based this last part of the Introduction (Weinshall,
    1976a, p. 82).
10 Thus, for example, Lawrence and Lorsch (1968) studied the organizational environ-
    ment within the operating organization only, without exploring the way that the
    immediate environment (customers, suppliers, shareholders, bankers, government
    officials, etc.) perceives its role in the organization. Nor did they measure the systems
    of the wider environment (the manpower market, the money market, the consumer
    supply/demand market, and the systems of technology and socio-culture) surround-
    ing their organizations. These additional reflections on the organization could serve
    as checks and balances, enriching their important findings. Another example is that
    of the Aston group research (Pugh and Hickson, 1976). It was based, to a large
    extent, on the assumption that quantitative measures are 'objective', and that the data
    collected in an organization are often provided only by the chief executive. This,
    incidentally, does not undermine the importance and contribution of the Aston
    research, which demonstrated the significant relationships among organizational
    variables, and the contingency character of these relationships.
11 One of the measurements used by the Aston research group represents an example of
    drawing the wrong conclusions from relating a quantitative measurement to
    organizational phenomena. It compares the number of written reports in an organiza-
    tion to the degree of formalization of the organization (Pugh and Hickson, 1976).
    This relationship is based on one of the main characteristics of a bureaucratic
    organization as defined by Max Weber (1947), namely that the more the communica-
    tion occurs in writing, the more bureaucratic or formalized the organization. This,
    however, does not take into account the contingency of this Weberian principle upon
    the stage of organizational development. The principle holds true after the organiza-
    tion has already reached a certain degree of bureaucratization, or formalization.
    However, if the organization is still in an informal stage, operating in a managerial
    structure which we refer to in this book as the entrepreneurial structure, things are
    quite different. When the organization grows in an entrepreneurial structure and
    requires more formalization, the entrepreneur tries to introduce more and more
    written reporting, data processing, management science, etc. All these management
    controls are, to a large extent, ignored in the actual running of the organization and it
    becomes more and more informal and, alas, confused.
12 Probably the best known and most important of these generalizations is found in the
    degree of *participation* of the subordinate levels in the decisions of their manager.
    Findings of a large number of organizational scientists—e.g. Coch and French
    (1948), McGregor (1960), and Heller (1971)—led to the conclusion that the more
    participative the decisions, the better the whole decision-making process, both in its
    efficiency and in its effectiveness. These findings, however, emerged from research
    carried out in larger organizations which had come into being some time before and
    which were already formalized to a certain degree. They had a greater number of
    people with more education and different backgrounds. However, if we consider an
    organization at the stage of its creation, only an entrepreneurial structure, strongly

informal and centralized, could make it come into being. If it were not for this structure, hardly any progress through new ventures, innovations, and organizations could come about. The entrepreneur and many of the people one finds in newly born organizations neither need nor want to operate in a more participative structure. It is wrong to deduce findings from the established, larger, and more formalized organizations and generalize them to the earlier stages of the organization in which everything is contingent upon the entrepreneurial success.

13   Some of the organizational systems research projects which required the establishment of the actual managerial structure of the organizations under study assumed that the organizational chart represented the actual organizational structure (Woodward, 1958; 1965); (Stopford, 1968); (Stopford and Wells, 1972). The managerial structure is composed of both the formal and informal structure; the organizational chart describes only how the formal structure is perceived at the top, and not the degree of formalization through the management structure. Consequently, the scientists who used the organizational chart had to disregard a certain number of organizations which they encountered in their samples. They had no organizational charts, nor were they able or willing to prepare such charts. These were usually organizations run in an entrepreneurial structure, that is to say, a predominantly informal structure. However, even in more formalized structures, the organizational chart should be considered only as an approximation to the actual managerial structure.

This is not to belittle in any way the important contributions of the research of Joan Woodward or John Stopford who established the managerial structure by way of organizational charts. On the other hand, though not encompassing all the components of the TOS, the studies of Woodward and Stopford did not confine themselves to the traditional variables of one component only. Thus, Joan Woodward tried to correlate the managerial structure with additional variables to those traditionally considered as indicating the 'size' of the organization (e.g. number of employees, sales turnover, capital investment). Among the additional variables she introduced was technology, which eventually she found to be the only factor which correlated with structure in her study (Woodward, 1958; 1965).

Stopford introduced additional factors to those of Woodward when he tried to correlate the managerial structures of the organizations he studied with a variety of variables. Stopford's background, in economics, international business, and business strategy, was completely different from that of Joan Woodward's, who was an industrial sociologist. His organizations, which were multinational corporations, had more environmental factors affecting them than Woodward's organizations which operated in the same region of one country, usually within the same product group. Thus, Stopford found that, in addition to technology, the managerial structures of his multinational corporations correlated also with product/service line diversity and with geographical dispersal (Stopford, 1968). In a way he reiterated what Alfred Chandler had discovered about the relationship between strategy and structure in his historical studies of organizations, such as Du Pont, General Motors, Sears, Roebuck & Company, and Standard Oil of New Jersey (Chandler, 1962).

14   The Hawthorne experiments were carried out between 1928 and 1932. They were based on an integration of Elton Mayo's conceptualization (Mayo, 1933) and Fritz Roethlisberger's research approach (Roethlisberger and Dickson, 1939). The story of Fritz Roethlisberger, his life and achievements, was told in a book prepared by his lifelong collaborator at the Harvard Business School, George Lombard (Roethlisberger and Lombard, 1977). Chester Barnard is described by the publisher of *The Function of the Executive* (Barnard, 1938) as follows:

Mr. Barnard has had many years of experience in several types of organization— business, educational, governmental, philanthropic—during which he has observed closely the processes of other individuals and executive groups. He has correlated this practical knowledge with a thorough study of the theoretical aspects of human organization.

Everyone who has made major contributions to the 'theoretical aspects of human organization', which led to the understanding of what is referred to in this book as the TOS, has had, like Barnard, practical or clinical experience in several types of organization. In addition to Mayo, Roethlisberger, and Barnard, this includes others like Frederick Taylor (1911); Carl Rogers (1942), and Joan Woodward (1965). It also includes other prominent contributors to the theoretical aspects of human organizations in the first half of the twentieth century who are not mentioned elsewhere in the book, such as Frank and Lillian Gilbreth (Gilbreth, 1911; Gilbreth, 1914); Mary Follett (1941); Henri Fayol (1949), and George Homans (1951). Unlike other fields of knowledge, in which major contributions predominantly originated in theoretical work or laboratory studies, most of the significant contributors to the TOS or the theoretical aspects of human organization were made by people with rich knowledge and experience in real organizations.

15   The first basis for the concepts of the TOS was Weinshall's doctoral research at the Devon Corporation which is described in an organizational example at the end of Chapter 3. The following quotation from the foreword to this dissertation explains who the people were who directly influenced his doctoral studies and research (1960):

> This study could not have been made but for the active support and inspiration I received from the members of my thesis committee at the Harvard Business School. Professor John D. Glover, my supervisor, and Professors C. Roland Christensen and Abraham Zaleznik. I am also deeply indebted to my other teachers in the Harvard Business School: to Professor Fritz J. Roethlisberger, who first introduced me to the field of organizational behavior; to Professor Richard S. Merriam, who contributed to my knowledge and insight in the field of general management, where my practical experience was gained by working for many years under Professor Julius F. Cahen of Haifa, Israel; and to Professor George F. Lombard, who taught me how to look at and listen to individuals in organizations.

SELECTED BIBLIOGRAPHICAL SOURCES

Barad, M., and Weinshall, T. D., 1965. *The Status of Women in Managerial Positions in Industrial and Other Organizations in Israel*, The Israeli Management Centre (Hebrew), Tel Aviv.

Barnard, C. I., 1938. *The Functions of the Executive*, Harvard University Press, Cambridge, Mass.

Chandler, A. D., Jr, 1962. *Strategy and Structure, Chapters in the History of Industrial Enterprise*, MIT Press, Cambridge, Mass.

Coch, L., and French, R. F., 1948. 'Overcoming resistance to change', *Human Relations*, 1 (4), pp. 512–536.

Cyert, R. M., and March, J. G., 1963. *A Behavioral Theory of the Firm*, Prentice-Hall, Englewood Cliffs, NJ.

Cyert, R. M., March, J. G., and Starbuck, W. H., 1961. 'Two experiments on bias and conflict in organizational estimation', *Management Science*, 7, 254–264.

Fayol, H., 1949. *General and Industrial Management*, Pitman, London.

Follett, M. P., 1941. 'Individualism in planned society' and 'The psychology of control', in H. C. Metcalf and L. Urwick (eds), *Dynamic Administration*, Management Publications, London.

Gilbreth, F. B., 1911. *Motion Study*, D. Van Nostrand, New York.

Gilbreth, L. M., 1914. *The Psychology of Management*, Sturgis & Walton, New York.

Heller, F. A., 1971. 'Group feedback analysis as a change agent', *Human Relations*, **23** (4), pp. 319–333.

Homans, G. C., 1951. *The Human Group*, Routledge & Kegan Paul, London.

Kast, F. E., and Rosenzweig, J. E., 1970. *Organization and Management, A Systems Approach*, McGraw-Hill, New York.

Katz, D., and Kahn, R. L., 1966. *The Social Psychology of Organizations*, Wiley, New York.

Lawrence, P. R., and Lorsch, J. W., 1967. *Organization and Environment*, Division of Research, Graduate School of Business Administration, Harvard University, Boston, Mass.

March, J. G., and Simon, H. A., 1958. *Organizations*, Wiley, New York.

Mayo, E., 1933. *The Human Problems of an Industrial Civilization*, Macmillan, New York.

McGregor, D. M., 1960. *The Human Side of Enterprise*, McGraw-Hill, New York.

Pugh, D. S., and Hickson, D. J., 1976. *Organizational Structure in its Context: The Aston Programme I*, Saxon House, Aldershot, Hants.

Roethlisberger, F. J., and Dickson, W. J., 1939. *Management and the Workers*, Harvard University Press, Cambridge, Mass.

Roethlisberger, F. J., and Lombard, F. F., 1977. *The Elusive Phenomena*, Harvard University Press, Boston, Mass.

Rogers, C. R., 1942. *Counseling and Psychotherapy*, Houghton Mifflin, Boston, Mass.

Simon, H. A., 1947. *Administrative Behavior*, Macmillan, New York.

Stopford, J. M., 1968. 'Growth and organizational change in the multinational firm', unpublished doctoral dissertation, Harvard University.

Stopford, J. M., and Wells, L. T., 1972. *Managing the Multinational Enterprise*, Basic Books, New York.

Taylor, F. W., 1911. *Scientific Management*, Harper, New York.

Vernon, R., 1971. *Sovereignty at Bay: The Multinational Spread of U.S. Enterprises*, Basic Books, Longman, London.

Weber, M., 1947. *The Theory of Social and Economic Organization*, translated by A. M. Henderson and Talcott Parsons, Oxford University Press.

Weinshall, T. D., 1960. 'The effects of management changes on the organizational relationships and attitudes', unpublished doctoral dissertation, Harvard University.

Weinshall, T. D., 1976a. 'The total organizational system (TOS) and the interdisciplinary approach in management and organization', in P. Verburg, P. C. A. Malataux, K. T. A. Halbertsma, and J. C. Boers (eds), *Organisatiewetenschap en Praktijk* (*Organization Science and Practice*), Stenfert Kroes, Leiden, Holland, pp. 55–106.

Weinshall, T. D., 1976b. 'The industrialization of a rapidly developing country—Israel', in R. Dubin (ed.), *Handbook of Work, Organization and Society*, Rand McNally College Publishing Company, Chicago, Ill.

Weinshall, T. D. (ed.), 1977. *Culture and Management*, Penguin Books, London.

Woodward, J., 1958. *Management and Technology*, HMSO, London.

Woodward, J., 1965. *Industrial Organizational Theory and Practice*, Oxford University Press.

Chapter 1

The Decision Making Process (DMP) and its Human Resources

Organizations can be perceived as input–output systems of resources.[1] Resources such as capital, manpower, raw materials, equipment, water, electricity, etc., flow into these systems, while finished products and services flow out of them, to be acquired and used by customers and clients. The latter provide the organization with the current funds necessary for recycling. However, not only the customers but *all the other resources* necessary for the functioning of the organization happen to be *human* factors.

No resource can come forward on its own, without the human factor which provides it. The creation of the finished product or service of an organization requires the contribution of *all* the resources necessary for the functioning of the organization, by the various human factors, including the customers.

This notion traces back to Chester Barnard,[2] who pointed out that the weight and value of the customers of an organization is not different from that of its workers. If one of these human factors withdraws from the organization, the final effect will be the same: the organization will not be able to go on functioning and existing.

This chapter discusses every one of the principal human factors forming the organization. On the input side we find the workers, who provide the labour; the suppliers providing the raw materials, the equipment and the different services (water, gas, electricity, or the human services, like management consultants); and the bankers and shareholders providing the capital. On the output side we find the customers who receive the goods and services produced by the organization, and they return money to the system.

In addition to those human groups which directly manipulate resources of the organization, we find a few additional groups which, over the years, have acquired the necessary power to make the organization dependent on them for its functioning and existence. These latter human factors for the most part include local and central government and the trade unions. All these have the same effect on the organization as the other, directly contributive factors (i.e. management, workers, bankers, shareholders, suppliers, and customers).

16

The first two sections of this chapter are devoted to discussing the different human factors comprising the organization. The third section deals with the dynamics of the contribution of these groups to the organization, and the process by which the organization can be managed within its dynamic environment.

The order of presentation of the different human factors in sections 1.1 and 1.2 is roughly that in which they first appeared in organizations, as factors dominantly affecting organizational success and survival, or, sometimes, unfortunately, failure and collapse. Section 1.1 presents the human factors of management and workers; people belonging to these two groups spend most of their active hours within the organization.

In section 1.2 we discuss the remaining human groups comprising the organization: customers, suppliers, bankers, shareholders, government, and trade unions. The contacts of people in these groups with the organization are less frequent than those of management and the workers, and usually take only a small part of their active time.

Section 1.3 introduces the reader to the issue of interorganizational relationships. Interrelationships among organizations are created through the human factors comprising the organizations. It is the competition among organizations for the same human factors which creates the dynamic nature of the organizational decision making. A discussion of the responsibility of managers towards their organizations throughout this process of interorganizational turbulence and change follows.

Finally, within section 1.3, we review the consequences of organizational strategy, i.e. the what, how, and where of the organizational operations, and its environmental competition and pressures, as well as the role and responsibility of managers in this dynamic process.

1.1 THE OPERATING ORGANIZATION

The operating organization is the term used in this book for that part of the total organization which includes its management and workers.[3] These two groups are presented in the following two sections. This presentation takes the form of a historical discussion of the process by which these groups took the form, the nature, and the role they maintain today.

The last subsection deals with the form in which management has assumed power through specialization.

1.1.1 The Manager-Owner

Present-day operating organizations are relatively complex systems in which management and workers fulfil different functions to reach their common goals. Past organizations, however, were very different from the present-day form.

Until the eighteenth century, an organization was a relatively simple unit, headed by one manager, who was also the owner of the business. We label him the 'manager-owner'. The manager-owner had a number of workers working for him. He had absolute power within his little 'kingdom'. The structure of this simple organization is described in Figure 1.1, presenting organizational charts of pre-Industrial Revolution manufacturing.[4] When the organization grew in size, the manager-owner instituted foremen, or bosses as they were referred to in the USA, between himself and the workers. Each boss had a number of workers under him, and had absolute power to make all the decisions regarding his workers.

This was the state of affairs until almost the end of the eighteenth century, when the Industrial Revolution began. Until then the production energy had come directly from natural sources: manual and animal power, the power of the wind and the water. The invention of the steam engine started the energy revolution in that it introduced power only indirectly derived from nature. Water was heated by coal, thus creating steam which made the engine move.

This fundamental change had far-reaching consequences as far as the actual human organization was concerned. We shall first study the effects of the Industrial Revolution on the workers, and subsequently consider its effects on the managers.

1.1.2 The Workers

Until the Industrial Revolution each worker himself performed all the tasks and jobs necessary for manufacturing a complete and final product. If we take as an example a shoe-manufacturing operation, a worker in such an organization would

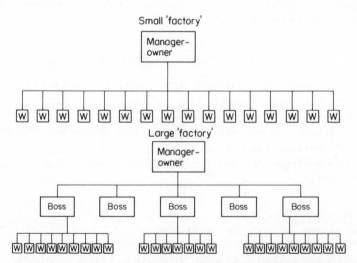

Figure 1.1 Organizational charts of pre-Industrial Revolution manufacturing illustrating the manager-owner managerial structure. Every worker (W) performs all the required manufacturing operations to produce a product. The manufacturing by every worker is performed either in the worker's home or in a 'factory'

perform by himself all of the following operations: walk over to the storeroom to collect the necessary leather (or directly to the leather supplier, if he worked at home and there was no factory or storeroom), then cut the leather with a pair of scissors and/or a knife, sew the leather with needle and thread, nail it with a hammer, etc. He would carry out all these operations at his worktable in the workshop, or at home.

The most drastic consequence of the Industrial Revolution at the workers' level was the division of labour, i.e. the specialization of the workers' tasks. Every worker, instead of doing the whole job from beginning to end, now carried out only one or a few operations, constituting just one stage within the whole production process.

In our shoe factory, one worker would bring the leather from the storeroom, another would cut it with a guillotine (or cutting machine). A third worker would sew the material using a sewing machine, the next would nail it with a nailing machine, etc. In this fashion the product is transferred from one worker to another during the manufacturing process.

The division of labour was *not* a direct result of the introduction of the steam engine and the equipment and machinery which was powered by it. Specialization could have been introduced and could have achieved even better results before the Industrial Revolution. Had the division of labour been adopted earlier in the eighteenth century it would have increased the productivity of manual operations to an even greater extent than the machine operations of the skilled workers did. Therefore, the introduction of the division of labour following the Industrial Revolution was prompted by a reason other than specialization.

The main reason for the division of labour was the desire to utilize to the maximum the highest cost factor in the manufacturing process. Before the Industrial Revolution, the main worry of the manager-owner was how to make the most of his labour, as this was his highest cost factor. The cost of the equipment at that time was comparatively cheap. The same simple tools, such as files, hammers, needles, scissors, etc., were sometimes used by a worker over his entire working life. So, although labour was very cheap at the time, the equipment was even cheaper. The main managerial consideration was, therefore, how to utilize to the utmost the time of the worker while he performed an operation with a specific tool.

The Industrial Revolution altered this balance between labour and equipment. From then on the full utilization of the equipment became the dominant factor, labour becoming a secondary aspect. It was very much more important to consider exploiting to the utmost the machinery, rather than the workers.

The division of labour was, therefore, a direct result of this major change in the relative cost of the industrial factors. In order to exploit the machines it was necessary to assign a worker to each machine. It was believed, at first, that if every worker were to be assigned to a specific machine, this would make all the machines run at full volume all the time. That notion was, obviously, mistaken. The coordination among the various machines producing different parts of, or performing different operations on a particular product at different speeds meant that even though every machine had a worker attached to it, this would not prevent idle machine time.

Worker specialization led, eventually, to another inevitable consequence. Every worker developed a specific skill in the particular task to which he was assigned. This sort of skill, in which he was usually trained by the foreman, acquired by endless repetition and practice, made him a valuable asset to the firm. It was now difficult to replace him quickly, perhaps in some cases he would be almost indispensable. It also gave him enormous power, because he became a link in a chain which could not operate without all the links being intact.

1.1.3 Management

The Industrial Revolution brought about vast changes in the structural functioning of management. The most drastic change that took place at the managerial level, as a result of the industrial changes, was the specialization of their roles. The need for managers to specialize was directly caused by the introduction of more highly powered equipment into the manufacturing process.

Machines increased productivity to such a degree that the nature of the decision-making process (DMP) of the organization had to take a drastic turn. The new problems faced by management grew both in quantity and in quality. Each one of the human factors which the organization now required for its functioning demanded much more attention from the managers. Let us consider the problems faced by management regarding, for example, the customer population after the Industrial Revolution, in comparison with that before it. Formerly, marketing just did not trouble the manager at all as the market was a 'sellers' market'; one could sell as much as one produced. Every firm had its own customers and would produce according to the specific demands of each customer. For instance, a cobbler produced hand-made shoes.

The Industrial Revolution launched manufacturing on a much larger scale. Much larger quantities of output were now involved; selling ceased to be on a person-to-person basis. One had to market specific models, in specific sizes and colours. Production had now to be carried out on a standard basis. Consequently, it was necessary to carry out some form of market research in order to find out what would sell. Management had to determine the range, qualities, sizes, and measurements of the products they were to manufacture. Another new problem which emerged as a result of the larger and more varied customer population was that of marketing channels. It was now necessary to develop an appropriate framework within which the customer could come into contact with the vast variety of standardized products and be able to purchase them.

As the reader can undoubtedly see, customers and selling became a very important and time-absorbing issue for the manager of a firm. Following the Industrial Revolution he had to deal with a whole set of problems which did not exist at all, or existed to a much smaller extent, before the nineteenth century.

Let us now turn to another human factor in the organizational decision-making process: the suppliers. Here, too, the manager of a manufacturing firm faced new issues which were not crucial before the Industrial Revolution. In order to maintain production at full volume, so as to utilize the machinery to the utmost, it was vital that the new materials should arrive at the site at a certain rate. The particular qualities of the raw materials had to be ascertained, otherwise difficulties in processing them through the machine might arise, and the finished products might not sell. These problems, new to management at the onset of the nineteenth century, were not the sort of issues to be solved and then put aside. They had to be given constant attention to ensure the survival of the organization.

The customers and the suppliers are only two of the human groups comprising the organizational DMP. Another group is made up of the individual owners and, later, the shareholders. This group had now to be persuaded to invest in the firm large amounts of money in order to finance the big enterprises that were born of the Industrial Revolution. Large capital had to be raised to invest in plant and equipment. Similarly, large inventories of raw materials, work in progress, and finished products had to be maintained. Thus, ever-growing funds for both fixed and working capital were required.

Another set of decisions which had now to be faced regarding investments was related to profitability forecasts. Management now had to decide among alternative investments in plant and capital.

The employees are another human group without whose cooperation the organization cannot survive. As in the case of the customers, suppliers, and investors discussed above, after the Industrial Revolution the employees created a major source of problems that management was forced to deal with. As a result of the growth and expansion in industry, and of the process of workers' specialization that accompanied it, it was now necessary to recruit different types of workers, in terms of variability in skills as well as variance in competence. Recruitment and training now became problems in their own right. Whereas in the past craftsmanship was passed down from father to son, after the eighteenth century it became the firm's responsibility to train the workers. The new manufacturing firms employed different kinds of managers. They also had to be recruited and trained. Another crucial problem to be solved was the basis of payment for all employees, workers as well as managers. The old system of paying by unit of production was no longer valid.

These are some of the many problems faced by the management of firms as a direct result of using much faster equipment in the production process. For a time, managers continued to function in the ways to which they had become accustomed before the Industrial Revolution, although needs had drastically changed. A transformation in the approach to management was vital.

The first person who systematically dealt with the formal structure in industry at the time, as related to the needs of the period, was Frederick Taylor. He introduced specialization at the management level in industry. One manager could no longer deal with all the problems regarding every different human factor necessary for organizational survival. The management role had to be divided and distributed among several managers. Management became a strong human group, comprising an ever-growing number of people. Each manager had a different set of responsibilities, dealing with the various problems of one or more human groups, within the total organization.

1.2 THE TOTAL ORGANIZATION: ADDITIONAL HUMAN FACTORS

Subsection 1.1 dealt with two human groups within the organization: the management and the workers, who together make up the operating organization only. The total organization includes, additionally, any human group whose cooperation is essential for the survival of the organization. Figure 1.2 is a schematic representation of the total organization, presenting the more important groups which play a part in most organizations.

1.2.1 Trade Unions

When workers first became a factor in the DMP, the manager-owners were extremely displeased to see some of their power fall into the hands of the workers. The manager-owners attempted to compromise the division of labour which was, in fact, the source of power of the workers. Instead of the system in which each worker would specialize and carry out one task only, management trained teams of workers to carry out a variety of tasks in various parts of the production line. This enabled the manager-owner to substitute workers who made demands

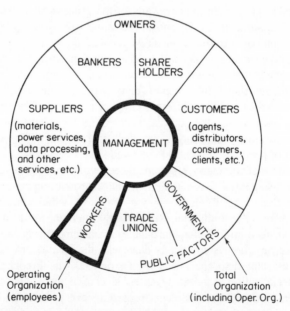

Figure 1.2   Factors of decision making (FDM): human factors comprising the organizational decision-making process (DMP)

upon management as a result of the power which they had acquired. Individual workers no longer acted as a 'bottleneck' in the total manufacturing process.

A second step taken by the manager-owners against the rising power of the workers was to unite and take measures against the pressures which workers exerted upon them. Most of the firms at the start of the Industrial Revolution were concentrated in one geographical area around Yorkshire in the north of England, and they were all in the textile business. This facilitated coordination among manager-owners. They agreed among themselves not to accept workers who had been dismissed from neighbouring firms, nor those who had left freely, thus diminishing to a great extent the demands and the threats of the workers.

This attempt of the manager-owners to win back power without giving way to the workers did not remain unanswered; the workers profited from the experience of their managers. They decided that 'what *they* can do, *we* can do better'. They began to unite in organized groups, according to trades.

England was a pioneer in trade unionism, with the emphasis on 'trade', and remains foremost in this field to this day. She is paying a high price for having been the first in unionization. Often unions have only a limited view of their trade without understanding the issues and problems characterizing the various industries, such as the textile industry versus the metal industry. These unions certainly have difficulty in understanding the situation of the individual firm. Thus it is possible, for example, for a union of machinists to have members working not only in different organizations, but also in a variety of industries such as textiles, machinery, construction, or metal working. The union cannot possibly recognize the conditions in each individual organization or industry as separate business areas. When such a union calls for a strike on the basis of its particular interests, it might cause the downfall of the firm, rather than achieving whatever benefits or goals it was aiming for.

As the notion of unionization took form in other countries, they profited from the early experience of labour organizations in England. They organized themselves in such a way that they could achieve the maximum for themselves, without damaging their source of income by pulling the rug from under their feet. Thus unions in countries such as Holland, Belgium, France, Italy, and Israel have been organized into federations. One federation could, in this way, represent all the workers of a particular firm. Thus, if workers in one trade are applying pressure on the federation to alter their working conditions in a particular organization or group of organizations, the federation can say to them: 'if we go along with your proposition, we would end up ruining your organization or harming the conditions of workers in other trades, who are also members of our federation'.

The next step in the development of unionization of workers was the organization of not only national federations of various industries, but also all the unions within one industry only, e.g. all car industry workers, or textile workers.

The advantage of this system of unionization was the ability of the union to specialize in the problems of a particular industry. Different industrial areas can be subject to different economic and social influences. It is not enough to have knowledge of the relationships among the various trades within the federation.

The union must recognize specifically the main issues and problems of a whole industry before it can try to improve the working conditions of its workers. Unions organized by industries or by areas of activities operate in the USA and in Germany.

The final development in the organization of workers' unions was the creation of one union for all the employees of an organization. Such unions are found in Japan. The large Japanese conglomerates, called zaibatsu, have an industrial type of union federation which is exclusive to the zaibatsu as a whole. In this way, the union includes trade unions of the various areas of activity of Mitsubishi, such as Mitsubishi Bank, Mitsubishi industry, Mitsubishi shipping, etc.

It is quite possible to assume that one of the factors influencing the economic success of a country is the form in which its workers organize themselves. It is not coincidental that in countries such as Japan, the USA, and Germany, which have some of the most successful economies in the world, unionization is more advanced than in other countries. It is also no coincidence that the workers in Germany and the USA are known to be not only efficient, but also comparatively satisfied with their work and their standard of living. As far as the total organization is concerned, there are fundamental differences between the workers and the unions in the organizational DMP. Each one of these factors is often found to take different and even opposing sides in conflicts and struggles among the various human groups in the organizational DMP. One of the major differences between the workers and the unions associated with the organization is the way in which they participate in its DMP. Whereas the participation of the unions is carried out on a formal basis, the workers' participation is on an informal one. The form of participation and contacts of union members with management are decided and agreed upon in advance, and are a basis for future negotiations between unions and management. As for the workers, nothing is decided in advance as to when and how this or that group of workers will confront management with various demands, and in what way they could pressure management to obtain them.

1.2.2 Bankers

At a certain stage of growth in manufacturing organizations, following the Industrial Revolution, the manager-owners found themselves in a position where they could no longer supply the growing appetite of their firms for investment and working capital. The private capital of the manager-owners, which enabled them to introduce the fruits of the Industrial Revolution into their factories, came originally from their profits as traders in the colonies and the empires of their countries, or from profits of small industrial firms which they owned and managed before the revolution. In both cases, these sums of money lasted only a short period of time after the Industrial Revolution.

The first source of capital to which they turned were the banks. Banks had already existed for several centuries. Up until that time they had made use of their capital for loans to business fields other than industry, mainly in commerce and areas related to it, such as navigation, as well as personal loans. On the whole, the banks participated, then as now, in an informal way in the DMP of the organizations with which they did business. The only formal aspect of their association with the organization was the loan contract and the written conditions of repaying the loan and the interest. Thus, for example, no formal arrangements existed for the organization to report regularly to the bank on the way in which they were using the money; nor on how the projects financed by these loans were progressing. What is more, there were no previously defined periodic controls of the collateral given by the borrowers to the bank. The fact that banks were, on the whole, an informal factor in the DMP of the organization often caused much unnecessary friction between the organization and the banks. There were even cases which led to the unnecessary downfall of banks.

1.2.3 Shareholders

The financial resources that the banks could offer organizations were soon found to be insufficient for the increasing appetite of organizations for investment and working capital. Organizations initiated the idea of turning straight to the public as an additional source of capital. Public money was, until that time, invested only in banks. Whoever thought of this option probably understood that the general public would not give their money directly to industrial firms, even though they would be offered a higher interest than organizations paid the banks (which was higher than that paid by banks to the investors). The consequences of industrial development and its potential were hardly understood; besides, the banks had the public's confidence which had been acquired over the years. Placing money in the hands of those who would 'make use' of it, rather than the banks who 'guard' it, seemed to be an unnecessary risk.

Business managements arrived at a solution by which they gave depositors a double offer that would tempt them to give their money directly to business organizations. First, investors were offered ownership, or partnership in ownership. Not only would they invest their money and be able to take it back whenever they wished by selling their stock, but the value of their stock would depend on the degree of success of the firm, increasing as a result of the growth in profitability, or vice versa. Banks, on the other hand, return only the deposit; they invest directly in organizations which provide them with a continuous rise in the value of the investment, providing the value of their shares increases also.

The second 'bait' intended to attract potential investors directly to business organizations was access to a formal control system built into the deal and attached to the ownership. As owners, management offered the investors a hierarchy of control, complete with defined institutions, as described in Figure 1.3. An annual meeting of shareholders was decided upon. The number of votes in this meeting was equivalent to the shares represented by the people participating in the meeting. This meeting elected the board of directors, which was the highest institution standing between the shareholders and management. The board of directors elected its chairman, and the chairman together with the board selected the heads of management.

Historical developments have slightly altered the procedures by which

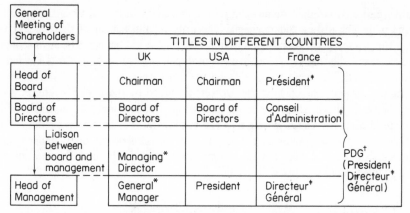

Figure 1.3   The hierarchy of formal participation of the shareholders in the organization (and the titles of the formal heads of the board of directors and of management in different countries)

* Until the Second World War; then the Managing Director became the Head of Management instead of the General Manager.

† In France the managerial power is generally concentrated in the hands of one person whose title is PDG. The managerial power of a PDG is similar to that of what we refer to as Chief Executive (CE), or Chief Executive Officer (CEO). A definition of the latter is 'the highest ranking member of the hierarchy of management and the shareholders, who actually controls the management'. (If it is someone of the shareholders' hierarchy, the chairman, the managing director, or another director, it usually means that he has to devote at least half of his time to the organization.)

‡ Similarly spelt words in English may have different meanings in French (referred to by the French as 'les petits faux amis'). Thus a 'president' in French is a chairman, rather than an executive president; the French 'administrateur' is a director, rather than the Anglo-Saxon administrator; and the French 'directeur' is a senior manager rather than the British–American member of the board.

shareholders have participated in organizations in various countries, and from one period to another. The most important factor has been defining the head of the organization, who directs and controls the actions of its management. In Britain, for example, before the Second World War, the organization was headed by a general manager who was nominated by the board of directors, but was not one of them. Boards of directors in Britain during the nineteenth century, and up to the Second World War, were composed mainly of members of the nobility. The boards eventually felt that they were losing contact with what was actually going on within the firm. Consequently, they appointed one of their members to act as a managing director, whose role was to liaise between the management and the board.[5] The MD involved himself gradually more and more with the problems of the firm, to the point where the person who nowadays heads the management is called the Managing Director. His subordinates, who were previously the production manager, the financial manager, the marketing manager, etc., also preferred to be called 'directors'. Thus, as they were inducted into the board, their titles became Production Director, Marketing Director, etc.

We also know of many cases where the chairman of the board of directors *actually* heads the management of his organization, thus turning the MD and the

GM (in Britain) or the president (in the USA) into his subordinates. As a result of this, we find it essential to name and define the role of the head of the organization, be his title that of chairman, or MD, or GM, or president. We shall call him the Chief Executive (CE) or Chief Executive Officer (CEO).

The CE of an organization is defined as the actual head of an organization and the highest ranking member of the managerial and ownership hierarchy who devotes as much time to the organization as is required to assume the overall responsibility and control for its running and survival.[6]

The body that steers the organization must be regarded as its management. Historically, the separation of management from ownership is considered to have taken place at the time when the shareholders joined the organization. The participation of the shareholders in the DMP of organizations is formal (see Figure 1.3), and takes place according to the different institutions which report one to the other within their hierarchy of control.

1.2.4 Suppliers

As long as raw materials were in abundance, the managements of organizations could more or less dictate to suppliers the quantities, qualities, prices, and supply dates of their goods. As soon as organizations started to compete among themselves for supplies and services, the suppliers were, from that moment, able to make it clear to organizations that they would no longer be dictated to in such a manner. They could now insist that over the matter of quantities, qualities, prices, and delivery dates, they would participate in the decision-making process of managements. In fact, towards the end of the nineteenth century, when shortages first appeared, followed by interorganizational competition over suppliers, the latter became involved in the DMP of organizations.

At that time, the suppliers' participation in the DMP was informal. As in other cases of informal participation, it could well be predicted that eventually suppliers would organize themselves to enforce their participation in the DMP in a formal way. In fact, around the beginning of the 1970s, suppliers entered the DMP of almost every organization for the first time, through the formal organization of the oil suppliers in OPEC (Organization of Petroleum Exporting Countries). It may well be assumed that over the years more groups of suppliers of materials and services will organize themselves in such a way that their influence over the DMP of organizations will become much more effective than it has been so far.[7]

1.2.5 Customers

The customers, as in the case of the suppliers, first appeared as participants in the DMP of organizations as a result of competition for the customer's market. As long as the market was a sellers' market, organizations could dictate the quality, the price, and the availability of products and services to the customers. As soon as the customer was given the choice between products and services of different organizations, he entered the DMP of organizations as a participant of great influence.

28

As we have already mentioned, from time to time the relative weight and influence of the human factor changes in the organizational DMP. It is affected by the prevailing conditions in the wider environment of the organization (to be discussed in chapter 2). However, if we study the events since the First World War, when customers were first introduced as factors in decision making in organizations, we can undoubtedly comment that, on the whole, they influenced the developments in organizations more than any other factor. During the 1920s and 1930s in the USA it was generally known that the 'marketivity' of an organization was more important than its production output. Its organizational strategy as to the what, how, and where of the organization was geared mainly towards the customers.

One of the main reasons for the breakdown of organizations nowadays is probably related to this inability to adjust themselves to the needs of actual or potential customers. The organizational example of Rolls-Royce at the end of this chapter points out that the straw that probably broke the camel's back was their incompetence in finding customers for their products at competitive prices.

The participation of customers in the DMP is informal. As in the case of other human factors, however, it can be assumed that more and more formalized customer organizations, for industrial as well as consumer products, will eventually be formed.[8] Such organizations have already begun for consumer products, mostly in the USA, and for industrial products, as a response to the formal organization for suppliers, such as OPEC.[9]

1.2.6 Government

The first phenomenon of government intervention in industrial organizations took place as early as the nineteenth century as a result of developments that followed the Industrial Revolution. After the establishment of the trade unions in Britain, the British Government came out with a programme of social legislation regarding the employment of women and children, the issue of individual safety, etc. Compared with government intervention in business organizations today, these early legislative activities in Britain seem negligible.

Massive government intervention in organizations operating in their countries began only after the First World War, and was completed after the Second World War. We are excluding from our remarks any intervention that took place during periods of emergency and war.[10]

The first country which maximized its government's participation and intervention in the DMP of industrial and business organizations was Russia. The regime which followed the October Revolution of 1917, which brought the Communists to power, fundamentally changed the DMP of organizations. Intervention in the USSR was so great that, in fact, the major part of the DMP of organizations was taken over by the centralized government of the country.

A few years later, with the rise of the Fascist regime in Italy in the early 1920s, the Italian Government also centralized the DMP of Italian organizations in a totalitarian manner.

The year 1933 became the year in which the governments of two of the most industrialized countries in the world entered the DMP of their organizations. Nazi Germany formed a regime similar to that of Fascist Italy. On the other side of the Atlantic, the 'New Deal' came into being following the inauguration of Franklin Delano Roosevelt as president of the USA.

These were the first countries in the world in which governments joined the DMP of organizations within their midst. After the Second World War, governments all over the world joined the DMP of organizations operating in their countries. No country today, be it small or large, idealistic or capitalistic, industrialized or developing, is free of governmental intervention and participation in organizational DMP.

1.3 ORGANIZATIONAL SURVIVAL

Sections 1.1 and 1.2 shed light on the process of change that took place in organizations over the past two centuries and especially following the Industrial Revolution. There developed a need for the organization to respond actively and continuously to its immediate environment. In fact, organizations could no longer view themselves as only comprising the people and the activities taking place within the four walls of the enterprise. Certain activities involving relationships with human factors other than managers and workers became part of the organization itself. We referred to this wider concept of an organization as the 'total organization'. The continued cooperation of the human factors with the organization is a necessary condition of organizational survival. Thus, for example, an organization cannot survive without the cooperation of its employees and of the customers purchasing its products. Similarly essential for its existence are the incoming raw materials and services from its suppliers, without which its products could not be manufactured. The organizations would be totally paralysed without a source of capital: its shareholders. These are just a few examples of the organization's dependence on its human factors. Some organizations are more dependent on the cooperation of some human factors than others.[11] For each organization, whether it is a manufacturing firm, a service organization, a voluntary or a military one, there are a number of human factors, the list slightly differing from case to case, without which the organization could not continue to exist. The relative degree of importance of the different human factors depends to a large extent on the conditions of the organization which are its *secondary objectives*, namely in what, how, and where it chooses to operate. The secondary objectives of its organizational strategy are relatively flexible and adaptive to its *primary objective*: organizational survival. In order to attain this primary objective, the organization must ensure the continued cooperation of all the essential human factors. This continuous effort of relating to customers, employees, suppliers, bankers, owners, etc., in a particular way, referred to by us as the organizational strategy, is discussed in the following chapter.[12]

The struggle for survival basically means the ability to compete successfully with other organizations over the same human factors. Thus organizations become interlinked through mutual interests. Interorganizational relationships in this sense are discussed in subsection 1.3.1. Subsection 1.3.2 is devoted to the responsibility of the management of the organization for the effort of its survival. Subsection 1.3.3 deals with the implications of the decision-making process for the clarity of managerial responsibility as well as for the adaptation of organizational strategy to the environment within which the organization operates.

The best managerial policy for handling the pressures and demands of various factors of decision making (FDM) is to compensate each factor at the lowest acceptable level. That is to say, workers, customers, shareholders, etc., should be compensated at the minimal level at which they are willing to cooperate fully with the organization. Offering one FDM more than the minimum they require may leave less than the minimum for other FDM, thus endangering their continued cooperation with the organization. One can visualize the total amount of resources of an organization as one whole cake, which has to be divided somehow among the various FDM. If management does not follow the policy of compensation at the minimal level, it will consume the organizational 'cake' by compensating some FDM at too high a level and be left with no more 'cake' for other FDM. For a better understanding of this notion, see the organizational example on Israeli Cinemas at the end of chapter 2.

1.3.1 Interorganizational Links

There are several basic resources that enable the organization to survive. Manpower is one of them. Manpower is supplied to the organization by its workers and management. Another essential resource is investment and working capital. These are supplied by the bankers and shareholders. Another resource, the purchasing power of the market, is supplied by its customers. Availability of machinery and tools, of materials as well as of services, such as electricity, water, computers, and expertise, are taken care of by the various suppliers of the organization.

The basic notion to be imparted in this section is that organizations inevitably become interlinked and involved with each other, through their mutual interests in the very same human factors.

In the continuous battle for survival, organizations have had in many cases to change their secondary objectives in order to survive. This happens when customers refuse to continue purchasing, or the suppliers cannot or will not continue supplying, or because of any of the other FDM. Hence organizations have had to switch to another technology, product, or geographical area. This in turn means profound changes in the organization itself in terms of the different human groups included in its DMP. An example of such a case is provided by the organization of Henry J. Kaiser, which shifted after the Second World War from shipbuilding to car manufacturing, then in the early 1950s moved away from car production to become a conglomerate of construction, aluminium, etc.[13]

Each and every human group taking part in the DMP of the total organization is, actually or potentially, part of the total organization of other organizations as well. Let us consider, for example, a shoe factory. The customers of this firm, who purchase their shoes, are actually or potentially customers at other shoe factories in the district, or even out of it or abroad. The suppliers of this firm, who supply the leather, the machinery, and the tools, may supply these same things to other leather-producing industrial firms, as well as to other manufacturers. Those firms which could use the materials that the suppliers can provide, but are not doing so at a particular time, are, in fact, potential purchasers of these goods. Unless our shoe factory satisfies the demands of its suppliers, and vice versa, those suppliers might turn to the other potential purchasers in the district. The employees working in our shoe factory could also, under certain conditions, turn to other leather-producing firms, as well as to different places of employment altogether.

In other words, an organization must never take for granted the cooperation of one or more human factors in its DMP. It has to compete constantly with many of the organizations in its immediate environment in order to ensure the continuing cooperation of these factors. This competition is not, as is widely accepted, over the customer population only. The organization also competes for its suppliers, its employees, its bankers, its shareholders, as well as for the acceptance and cooperation of institutions such as the government and trade unions. We refer to all these various human groups as factors of decision making.[14] Figure 1.4 presents the immediate environment of a chocolate factory in the London area. We see that organizations in the immediate environment are not necessarily in the geographical vicinity of the organization. They are 'immediate', rather, in the sense that they are of immediate concern to it. At every point in time the various FDM are exerting pressures on the organization according to the competition in

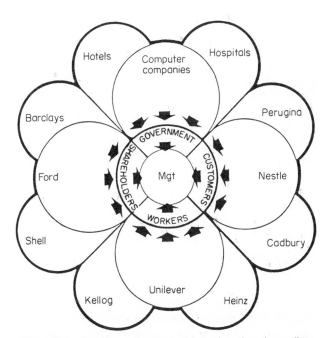

Figure 1.4 Results of competition in the immediate environment: several links between a chocolate factory in the London area and other organizations through its factors of decision making

32

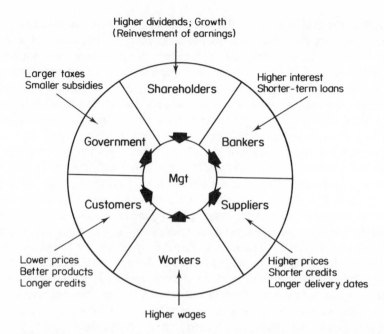

Figure 1.5   Some pressures exercised on management of the chocolate
factory by factors of decision making

the immediate environment. Figure 1.5 presents some of the possible demands on management. The shareholders may push for higher dividends and growth; the workers want higher wages, better working conditions, and other motivational inducements; suppliers strive for higher prices, shorter credits (i.e. faster payment) and further delivery dates; bankers may demand higher interests and shorter-term loans, etc.

Let us assume that at a particular time the organization has arrived at a certain balance with its FDM. The pressures from the FDM are momentarily satisfied. At this point, what could disrupt and disturb this peace? What could push a worker to demand more pay? What could make a supplier raise his prices?

The answers are to be found somewhere outside the organization itself; elsewhere in its immediate environment. As soon as a significant change, which positively affects certain FDM, takes place in one organization, the same FDM in other organizations are also affected. Whether the organization in which the change occurred tries to attract FDM of other organizations or not, other FDM, learning of the change, will begin to put pressure on their own management to obtain comparable conditions. Thus, through those same FDM, be they workers, customers, shareholders, suppliers, etc., every organization is interlinked with every other organization in the immediate environment. For example, the customers of similar products or services compare the conditions of their sale and supply in one organization with those of another. Similarly, investors, or brokers acting on behalf of other investors, would transfer their investment from organization to organization according to the conditions for the shareholders' FDM prevailing in the different organizations. Likewise, the workers in one organization compare themselves with other workers in the wider environment, i.e. the socio-cultural-economic environment.

1.3.2 Managerial Responsibility

In all the dynamics of the decision-making process described in the previous sub-section, the special role of management is to ensure the continued cooperation of the human FDM with the organization, so that organizational survival is secure. Hence, the definition of a *manager* is, any employee whose main role in the organization is that of ensuring the cooperation with the organization of one or more persons belonging to one or more FDM. In this sense, a foreman is categorized as a manager; he is responsible for the continued cooperation of a number of workers. A salesman is a manager, despite the fact that he may have no subordinates, since he is responsible for the continuing cooperation of clients or customers. A person responsible for contacts with government offices is a manager because he is the one who ensures the continued cooperation of the government with the organization.

The management group, owing to its special role in the organization, is basically different from all the other human groups participating in the DMP. We have seen that each of the other FDM has its own reference group composed of its own kind of people, constituting parts of other organizations. They do not compare themselves with other FDM in their own organizations. On the contrary, each FDM in an organization tries to get out of it at least as much as its peer groups in other organizations are obtaining in return for their cooperation with those other organizations. Every one of the FDM, except the management, treats the organization in what seems to be an 'egoistic', self-centred way.

Management is the only group among the FDM whose reference group is not only managers in parallel positions outside their own organizations. Their pride lies not only in the fact that they receive higher salaries, but mainly in that they belong to an organization which has successfully coped with its environmental pressures and competition. In other words, they are proud of their success in having secured the cooperation of all the FDM, so that the organization survives. Their attitudes, therefore, seem to be altruistic, for the benefit of all the other FDM.

We have to realize, however, that while customers, for example, compare themselves with other customers, priding themselves on having found an organization from which they can buy better quality products at cheaper prices and more convenient delivery terms, managers, on the other hand, when compar-ing themselves to other managers, pride themselves on belonging to an organiza-tion which is more successful than other organizations and which has survived while others have been collapsing.

Thus, while all the FDM, including the managers, compare themselves with their FDM peers in other organizations,[15] the role of the managers regarding sur-vival is cardinally different from that of the other FDM. We can regard the role of managers as *altruistic*. They are responsible for the survival of the organization.

The rest of the FDM are egoistic. They would switch over to another organization whenever the return for their cooperation is, or appears to be, significantly larger there.

In order to cope effectively with the demands and pressures from the various FDM, management must safeguard its neutrality. Joining or allying itself with another FDM would disrupt the management's ability to regard the demands of the other FDM in an objective and balanced way. For example, it would not be generally advisable for the managers to be substantial shareholders of the organization. Such a situation might impair their independent judgement when it comes to compensating the owners as compared with compensating the demands of other FDM.[16] Similarly, another severe burden on management's ability to fulfil its duties efficiently is the introduction of 'worker participation in management', or 'industrial democracy' as the accession of worker representation to management is termed.[17] This measure is sometimes taken by management as a safety valve against continuous pressure from workers' groups, but more often it is the result of mistaken political views and governmental legislation as to what is good for the organization, the economy, and the country.

Let us consider what happens when workers are made to participate in management, as in Germany, where the law decrees that they are part of a 'managerial board'. The first possibility is that worker representatives may turn out to be good managers, that is, they will learn to regard the workers and their demands on the organization in the right perspective, in terms of the total pressures on the organization. In such a case they may eventually have to face the workers with the unfortunate news that not all of their demands can be fulfilled, although they may well be legitimate. The workers are eventually bound to view such representation as treacherous. Their dissatisfaction may increase as well as their pressure on management for higher compensation. Such workers who have managerial capacities should have been picked up by management to become managers; their initial accession to management as worker representatives makes things difficult for them as managers.

Another possible result of worker participation in management is that these workers may, in fact, fight only for the workers' demands. If they are powerful enough, they may make the organization compensate the workers at much more than their lowest acceptable level. This could well leave the organization with too small a cake, or no cake at all, out of which to reward the other FDM.

A third possibility is that the workers' representatives may be present at management meetings, but assume a passive role, refraining from influencing them in any significant way. This is what usually seems to happen when workers are put on managerial boards. In any case, if the organization is to survive, it is important to help management be as independent as possible from the interests of any other integral FDM. The consequence of all this is that sometimes neither trade unions nor the workers themselves aspire to participation in management. They feel in many cases that such participation would limit or even rob them of their ability to fight freely, strongly, and independently for their rights.[18]

1.3.3 Implications for the Dynamics of the DMP

The competition from other organizations in the immediate environment, and the pressures from the wider environmental system, which we shall describe in more detail in the next chapter, are at the source of the dynamics of the decision-making process. We have observed earlier in this section the meaning of the interorganizational links. A change in one factor of decision making may affect the concerned members of the organization: employees, customers, suppliers, shareholders, etc. They, in turn, transmit the knowledge of the effects of the changes in better remuneration for employees, lower prices to customers, better payment conditions to suppliers, higher financial returns to shareholders, etc., to their reference groups, i.e. to the employees, customers, etc., in the environments of the organization. Through these populations the knowledge of the newly created conditions is transmitted to members of other organizations. They, in turn, put pressures on their managements for better conditions in return for their continued cooperation. These dynamics are what we mean when we speak about organizations competing with each other for their employees, customers, shareholders, etc.

These turbulent interorganizational competitions and pressures have completely changed managerial responsibility. No longer are managers responsible exclusively to the owners, by way of ensuring financial growth and profitability. If they were to continue with this undivided loyalty to shareholders and bankers, they would have led their organizations to inevitable collapse. They are now responsible to all the FDM for the safeguarding of the survival of the organization; this we see clearly in the experiences of Rolls-Royce and Swissair, whose organizational examples appear at the end of this chapter, as well as of the Israeli Cinemas, mentioned at the end of chapter 2.*

The conclusion of these turbulent dynamics in the decision-making system is that the only way in which management can carry out effectively its managerial responsibility for the survival of the organization is by rewarding each FDM at the lowest level acceptable for its continued cooperation. In order to be able to carry out this responsibility in the best possible way, management should be as independent as possible from the other FDM. This independence should be both practical and ideological. The moment that key position managers have vested interests in one or more of the other FDM, or they identify ideologically with one or more of the FDM, they will no longer be able to carry out their managerial responsibility as they should, even when they are suitable for the managerial structure in which the organization should be run.

The second main implication of the dynamics of the TOS is its resulting growth in the scope of decision making (SDM), dealt with in chapter 2. This growth in the organizational SDM leads to the second major problem in TOS survival, the first being the maintenance of the balance within the main system of decision making

* These examples are dealt with in our forthcoming book *Management in Practice* (in preparation).

illustrated in Figure 2.5. This problem is in the need to keep the managerial structure in line with the SDM. The ever-growing organization requires more frequent changes in its managerial structure, which is only possible if there is interorganizational or intra-organizational mobility of key position managers. Chapters 3 and 5 deal with this aspect of the TOS dynamics in more detail.

1.4   SUMMARY

This opening chapter first introduces the various human factors in the organizational decision-making process: workers and management, as well as trade unions, bankers, shareholders, suppliers, customers, and government. We see that the members of each of these and other factors of decision making are equally important for organizational survival. The reason for this is that any FDM without the cooperation of which the organization cannot survive, is neither more nor less important than any other such FDM.

Section 1.3 discusses the role of management in ensuring the organizational survival. In this the managers are unique when compared with other FDM, each of whom try to get as much as possible out of the organization. The management, in contrast, is trying to keep them all together, by way of rewarding the FDM as little as possible for their cooperation with the organization.

The main points are illustrated by the two following organizational examples.

Rolls-Royce (RR)

This is the story of the bankruptcy of RR at the end of the 1960s. When planning major organizational changes, management has to be aware of their implications for all the factors of decision making. Otherwise, while trying to solve crucial problems involving one or more factors of decision making, it may create serious problems in the cooperation of other factors with the organization.

The main reason why the owners did not insist on a profitable management of RR much earlier was that the British Government had gradually become RR's major shareholder. As such, it was predominantly concerned with its vested national interests, rather than its owner's interests.

The last point emphasized in this example is the inevitable need to grow in terms of what the organization is doing and not to put 'all the eggs in one basket'. This is illustrated by the consequent complete collapse of scores of small manufacturing firms which had been producing only one product or product line and were captive suppliers of RR. Had these firms diversified with other products and widened their customer market over and beyond RR, they would have considerably reduced the risk of their collapse.

Swissair (SA)

This example is in a way similar to that of RR in that the management was being made to neglect the competition from other organizations for several of its decision-making human factors. While in RR the main neglected factor was the interests of the owners, in SA it was the other way around. Through an instruction from the board of directors, representing the shareholders, the management was made to pursue a policy mistakenly meant to defend the owners. Actually, if this policy had been pursued for too long, the management of SA could not have secured the continued cooperation of all the factors necessary for its survival.

NOTES

1 The notion of the organization being an input–output system has been well described by Dan Katz and Bob Kahn (1966).
2 Chester Barnard was a practising manager, like Frederick Taylor and Frank Gilbreth, the US 'time and motion' pioneers, and like Henri Fayol, the French formal organization pioneer, who preceded him in the earlier part of this century. However, while the latter three were part of the Scientific Management movement (Fayol was one in spirit rather than in formal affiliation), Barnard was one of the pioneers who took management out of it. His *The Functions of the Executive* (Barnard, 1938) is one of the two books which could be considered as the basis of modern managerial and organizational theory.
3 *Management and the Workers* (Roethlisberger and Dickson, 1939) is the second book from which modern managerial and organizational theory started. We shall elaborate upon the contribution of the two books mentioned in this note and in note 2. Barnard, Roethlisberger, and the others will be discussed in chapter 4.
4 A more detailed description of this structure appears in an industrial presentation of the TOS (Twiss and Weinshall, 1980, pp. 11–16).
5 A popular joke of the time was as follows:

   Q: Who is the Managing Director?
   A: That member of the board who knows where the factory is.

(This appeared in Nigel Balchin's book, *How to Run a Bassoon Factory*, the publisher and the publication date of which we could not obtain.)
6 As a rule, we can assume that if a chairman or managing director (i.e. a member of the board who is responsible for the connection of the board with the organization) devotes at least one half of his time to the organization, he can be considered its chief executive (CE). Thus, if a man devotes all his working time to being the chairman of boards of directors and, as such, acts as the chairman of two boards, he is, in fact, the CE of two organizations. But if he acts as chairman of three boards or more, he has no time to take full control of the managements of their organizations.
7 Attempts by suppliers of materials such as sugar, cocoa, copper, and other commodities, to organize themselves have been made. However, unlike the case of oil, 80 per cent of which is produced in countries which are culturally homogeneous, the above suppliers found it hard to communicate (Sampson, 1975; Servan-Schreiber, 1980).
   On the other hand, we can find in various countries quite effective organizations of suppliers and services such as chartered accountants, management consultants, lawyers, etc. These suppliers determine between themselves the quantity, level, and price of their services.
8 Ralph Nader is one of the better known people, who started his consumer movement regarding safety devices for cars in the USA. He then moved on to other fields in other countries.
9 The organization of the oil-consuming countries aims not only to protect the individual consumers (for heating their homes and running their cars), but mainly to

protect their industries, including the energy industries within each of the countries which is taking part in the confrontation with OPEC.

10   We refer not only to the mobilization of all resources during wartime, but also to emergencies of a different nature. Thus, for example, we know that at the time of the great famine in ancient Egypt, the government interfered in the production and distribution of the crops of all the feudal lords who headed the organizations of the time. This was the basis of the biblical story of Joseph, who imposed levies on wheat so as to accumulate during the seven 'fat' years sufficient wheat to distribute to the population during the seven 'lean' years.

11   We refer to human factors—the cooperation with the organization of which is more problematic, causing the managerial scope of decision making to be invested in them to be larger than with other human factors—as *bottleneck factors*. A partial discussion of the conditions in which a human factor turns out to be a bottleneck factor appears in Weinshall (1973). The effects of the 'environmental system' on the appearance or disappearance of bottleneck factors throughout the wider environment are discussed in section 2.2 of chapter 2.

12   The choice of specific organizational strategies (i.e. secondary objectives) so as to ensure organizational survival (the primary objective) has been a subject of study by many writers and consultants who have dealt with business strategy. The field of business strategy started with, and was initially developed by, people like Ed Learned (1951), Jack Glover (1954), and Chris Christensen (1953) and others of the Harvard Business School (HBS). It was later formalized by Igor Ansoff (1965). The above mentioned business policy pioneers were likewise succeeded by another group of the HBS in the 1960s and 1970s. Most of them had been followers of Alfred Chandler (1962) and his 'strategy and structure'. (We shall refer to them in more detail in chapter 4.)

    On the consulting side, probably the best-known two organizations are the Boston Consulting Group and Strategic Planning Institute, both based in Boston, Massachussetts which developed ways for establishing different strategic policies for organizations, according to their needs and environments.

13   The reasons for these two drastic changes in organizational strategy, in technologies, product lines, and geographical areas, were different. Kaiser produced in his shipyards the 10 000 ton 'Liberty' ships during the Second World War. They said he produced them faster than the German U-boats could sink them. However, when the war was over, nobody needed Liberty ships.

    The reason for abandoning car manufacture was, however, somewhat different. In this case it was an example of moving too early to innovated products, rather than reaching the saturation of the product curve which then suddenly (though expectedly) collapses (Twiss and Weinshall, 1980, pp. 30–31). In both the Kaiser and the Citroën cases, the organizations came out with product strategies which were not accepted by the customers of the time.

14   By definition, the immediate environment of an organization is composed of all the organizations which are actually or potentially competing with the organization for its integral FDM (integral FDM are those without the cooperation of which the organization cannot survive).

15   A sort of 'workers of the world, unite', a consumer solidarity, suppliers informally cartelizing their prices, shareholders driving to achieve the best rate on the stock exchange for their shares, etc.

16   One of the historical achievements of organizations was the separation of management from ownership. Indeed, it was considered at the time, about 100 years ago, as a remedy for all organizational problems of survival, granting organizations an eternal life. We have learned since then that the owner participation in management is just one of several grave diseases which can be fatal for organizations.

    We have to realize, however, that entrepreneurs who start organizations are more often than not motivated by the fact that their own money is invested and that they own them. Indeed, we know now that when a small organization is run by its owners it is more successful than small organizations run by non-owner managers. This situation is reversed, however, in large organizations, which are much more successful when run by non-owner managers (Zwerman, 1970).

17　Worker participation in management is not an 'industrial democracy', but rather an 'industrial autocracy', because the workers are the only FDM represented in management. If it happens in the spirit in which it is intended, the workers may well sway the whole DMP in their favour, causing the collapse of the organization. The whole question of worker participation in managerial decisions, rather than their cooperation in the organization as workers, is discussed in more detail in Twiss and Weinshall (1980, pp. 157–166).

18　Let us consider France as an example. When Charles de Gaulle wanted to introduce worker participation in management in France in the 1960s, the more politically inclined to the left the unions were, the greater their opposition to worker participation in management. Thus, the CGT, the trade union federation linked to the communists, were the most extreme in their opposition to worker participation in management.

SELECTED BIBLIOGRAPHICAL SOURCES

Ansoff, I., 1965. *Corporate Strategy*, McGraw-Hill, New York.

Balchin, N., *How to Run a Bassoon Factory*.

Barnard, C. I., 1938. *The Functions of the Executive*, Harvard University Press, Cambridge, Mass.

Chandler, A. D., Jr, 1962. *Strategy and Structure—Chapters in the History of Industrial Enterprise*, MIT Press, Cambridge, Mass.

Christensen, R. C., 1953. *Management Succession in Small and Growing Enterprises*, Division of Research, Graduate School of Business Administration, Harvard University, Boston, Mass.

Glover, J. D., 1954. *The Attack on Big Business*, Division of Research, Graduate School of Business, Harvard University, Boston, Mass.

Katz, D., and Kahn, R. L., 1966. *The Social Psychology of Organizations*, Wiley, New York.

Learned, E. P., 1951. *Executive Action*, Division of Research, Graduate School of Business, Harvard University, Boston, Mass.

Roethlisberger, F. J., and Dickson, W. J., 1939. *Management and the Workers*, Harvard University Press, Cambridge, Mass.

Sampson, A., 1975. *The Seven Sisters—The Great Oil Companies and the World They Made*, Hodder & Stoughton, London.

Servan-Schreiber, J. J., 1980. *Le Defi Mondial*, Librairie Artheme Fayard, Paris.

Twiss, B. C., and Weinshall, T. D., 1980. *Managing Industrial Organizations*, Pitman, London.

Weinshall, T. D., 1973. 'A study of organizational size and managerial structure', in Desmond Graves (ed.), *Management Research—A Cross-cultural Perspective*, Elsevier, Amsterdam.

Zwerman, W. L., 1970. *New Perspectives on Organization Theory*, Greenwood Publishing, Westport, Conn.

Chapter 2

The Dynamics of Decision Making

Before the Industrial Revolution, there was little interaction and interconnection among organizations. Each organization operated quite independently. Few changes occurring in one organization had any effect on others. Hardly any decisions regarding events happening outside the organizations were taken.

Following the Industrial Revolution, as the size and numbers of FDM grew, the interorganizational links became increasingly closer. Organizations were forced to be aware and involved with each other as they were becoming more and more mutually dependent and hence required cooperation. Without this constant awareness of changes taking place in organizations within the local environment, they might lose the cooperation of their FDM and eventually die.

This interorganizational competition compels organizations to grow in order to succeed. Organizational growth is the topic of the first section of this chapter. Growth is, in fact, the product of the dynamics of decision making of organizations in their immediate environments. The immediate environment may be viewed as the arena where the struggle for survival takes place.

The DMP of organizations must relate not only to events taking place in its immediate environment, but also to changes occurring in its wider environment. Section 2.2, on organizational maintenance, refers to the five systems of the wider environment, and their influence on the organization. In order to adjust adequately to its immediate and wider environments, the organization must define and redefine its strategy periodically. Organizational strategy, the response of the organization to the demands of its environment, is discussed in section 2.3.

2.1 ORGANIZATIONAL GROWTH

Organizations have had to develop and grow continuously over the last three centuries, in order to survive. An organization that has remained in one place in its development in real terms, has in relative terms become smaller and taken a big step towards failure. Other organizations competing for its employees, its customers, its sources of funding (stockholders and bankers), etc., have continued growing and pulling these FDM with them, thus leaving behind the organization that could not follow fast enough.

Growth takes place through changes in the scope of decision making of the organization. Competition from other organizations for human factor resources leads to expansion in the scope of decision making (SDM).

These changes take place through one or more of the following three dimensions:

(a) the level and variety of the technology employed by the organization;
(b) the variety of its products or services;
(c) the geographical dispersal of the organization
    (for further discussion see section 2.3).

Let us take, for example, an industrial firm producing blades. When this firm was small, it produced blades for knives only, employing a comparatively simple technological process. The firm operated in one plant, and catered for a market limited to a small district. By now the firm has grown in all three criteria listed above. It employs a much more complex technology for some of its products, but still utilizes simple technologies for others, thus increasing both the level and the variety of technologies employed. It is producing a large variety of blades and knives for industrial and domestic use, and lately has entered into the production of blades for jet planes. The organization is widely dispersed, operating in six production plants all over the district and catering for large markets in the country and abroad.

Organizational size, as the concept is used in this book, relates to all three criteria of level of technology, variety of products, and geographical dispersal. It is not the function of what is widely accepted as the number of employees, the volume of sales, etc. These could be limited indicators of organizational size in some cases, but they cannot be universally used for measuring the size of organizations.

The meaning of size for an organization is, in fact, its scope of decision making. A higher level of technology, a larger variety of products and services, and a greater geographical dispersal, all make its SDM more complex.

Scope of decision making is, therefore, a synonym for organizational size. Organizational growth expresses itself directly in an increase in the SDM.

Immediately after the Industrial Revolution, organizational growth came through increased levels of technology employed, and contributed to the introduction of great masses of machine-made products into the market. But at the time, each organization still produced one line of products, within one physical location.

At the beginning of the twentieth century, and especially after the First World War, it was discovered that it is too risky to place all one's eggs in one basket. Technological developments enabled the use of the same basic machinery for the production of a variety of products. Organizations began expanding by increasing their variety of products.

The technological developments, reflected in better communications within and among different countries, enabled the geographical dispersal of the various plants of one organization. With good communications and transportation facilities, organizations could now locate their plants according to availability of a cheap labour market and/or nearness to sources of raw materials.

This dynamic activity of continuous increase in SDM of organizations takes place within the *immediate environment* of the organization. Each specific organization has its own immediate environment composed of those organizations which actually or potentially compete for its own FDM. The immediate environment is, therefore, an organizational and not necessarily a geographical environment.

We now turn to an analysis of several aspects of organizational growth. Subsection 2.1.1 is devoted to the human factor: those groups or individuals with whom the various FDM identify themselves. Subsection 2.1.2 presents the competitive growth pressures as a result of the human factors involved in the various FDM. Subsections 2.1.3 and 2.1.4 study trends of organizational growth over time (2.1.3) and in different business areas (2.1.4).

2.1.1 Human Factors

We mentioned elsewhere that whereas the managers are responsible for the survival of their organization, the other human factors with whom they come into contact are interested only in gaining the most for themselves. They compare the benefit from their relationship with the local organization with possible benefits from similar relationships with competitive organizations. Their reference populations are, therefore, other employees, suppliers, customers, bankers, etc., fulfilling similar roles in the functioning of other organizations.

The responsibility for organizational growth lies, therefore, solely with management. The workers, customers, trade unions, government, etc., will cooperate and go along with the changes necessary for progress and growth only if they are adequately compensated.

2.1.2 Competitive Growth Pressures

Changes occurring in any organization create a kind of competition, whether they involve the human factor resources or not. Thus any specific change in any other organization could constitute competition for one's own employees, or for the shareholders, suppliers, or any other human factor of the specific organization. The change can take the form of a pay rise to the workers, a high dividend distribution, the introduction of some innovation to the traditional product for the same price, or an additional product or service line.

As soon as the change has been introduced by one organization, competition forces the making of comparisons by members of one or more of the FDM of other organizations within the same immediate environment. Such a comparison reveals that members of the reference population belonging to the first organization have improved their position as a result of the change occurring within it.

The changes in the originating organization constitute an expansion in its SDM. The competitive challenges of these changes, through the human factor resources, lead to the expansion of the SDM in other organizations, because their managements are put under pressure from *their* human factors to improve their lot. In this way organizational growth takes place.

The rate of growth of organizations varies from one business area to another, and from one organization to another within the same field. It is now clear that organizations must grow and progress continuously in order to survive. But they must grow at a pace that is within an acceptable framework in their business area. An organization may be a leader within its field, or a follower. If it progresses too quickly, or grows too slowly, it may lead to the decline and fall of the organization. For example, an organization may have developed a very sophisticated tool, much beyond the level of the basic tool produced at the time, but if it markets this tool too soon, it is bound to fail. Henry J. Kaiser, for example, started a car industry in the USA after the Second World War. He produced a car the qualities of which were too advanced for its time. It could not sell and the organization eventually had to abandon car manufacturing and move to other product lines, in order to survive.

Leaders are those organizations within their business area which keep one step ahead of their contemporaries. The other organizations within the same field must grow at a pace that would enable them at least to follow the leaders.

Let us imagine an example of an airline that decided to build a few of its own hotels, thus adding another line of service to the organization. Other airlines would be compelled to follow in the leader's steps. This same thing happens when one airline company decides to expand by adding some of its own tourist coaches and travel agencies. Other airlines are then forced to follow suit in order to stay in the field and survive.

2.1.3 Total Innovation Rate

For centuries after the appearance of the human race and until the nineteenth century, the rate of innovation was negligible. Technological innovations were not understood and were considered unnecessary to the physical and mental survival of *homo sapiens*. Consequently, many innovations were labelled as witchcraft, and their originators burned at the stake.

Suddenly, towards the middle of the nineteenth century, the rate of innovations started to grow at an exponential rate (see Figure 2.1), and the attitudes towards the innovators changed completely. The dynamics of the theoretical approach developed in this book—the Total Organizational System—provide a possible explanation for the survival of individuals, dependent on the maintenance of the industrial and business organizations which they had created. Therefore, threats to organizational survival put enormous pressures on organizations to incorporate the innovations of others.

The 'rate of innovations' is a good and convenient measure of organizational growth, as it directly reflects the technological and scientific growth of organizations and indirectly influences the other two aspects of growth: geographical dispersal and variety of product lines. The curve of the total innovation rate

44

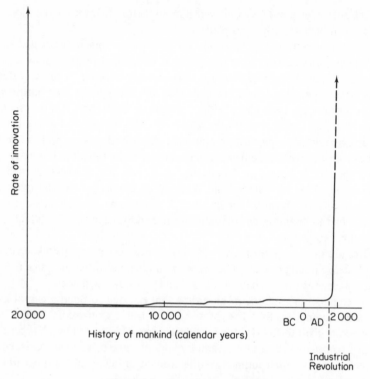

Figure 2.1   Total innovation rate

(Figure 2.1) is therefore an indication of the curve of organizational growth. It shows clearly how organizations started to grow at an exponential rate during the Industrial Revolution. This growth demanded additional innovation and development in order to continue.

The human race can no longer exist without organizations. They have thus become like gods to whom the human race must continue to offer sacrifices in the form of innovations. The trend of innovation and change will continue in spite of the natural resistance of human beings to change.

2.1.4   Organizational Growth in Different Business Areas

The curve of the innovation rate described in Figure 2.1 is, in fact, a summary or a mean of the rates of innovation in the various fields of business and industry. Some areas have developed at a lower rate, whereas in others changes have been taking place rapidly.

Figure 2.2 describes the rate of growth of a few business areas in the last few decades. Business areas that have developed at the highest rate are, in most cases, those that depend more than others on technological developments. Those areas tend to be new ones. They tend to be mobile and transferable geographically.

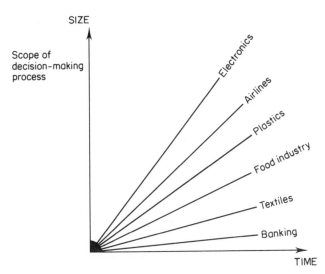

Figure 2.2 Organizational growth in different business areas

There are also those which are interlinked more often with a variety of branches of industry than with other business areas.

These qualities of fast-growing areas of industry and service explain why electronics is one of the fastest growing fields of business, whereas banking, which has been around for a long time and has therefore developed gradually over the centuries, has one of the lowest rates of growth in terms of what we call the SDM.

2.2 ORGANIZATIONAL MAINTENANCE

The continuing struggle of organizations for survival *vis-à-vis* other organizations in their immediate environments takes place within a larger environment which we shall label the wider environment. The process of relating to the changes occurring in the wider environment, in order to survive, is termed organizational maintenance.

The wider environment affects all the organizations located geographically within it. Factors, such as the economy of the country, the culture of the district, or the general technological level of the Western world, must be considered by each and every organization.

We view the wider environment as consisting of five environmental systems: the employment market system, the money market system, the consumer supply–demand system, the technology and education system, and the socio-cultural system. Pressures of the environmental systems lead to shortages and abundances in human factor resources, affecting the SDM of organizations. The boundaries for the wider environment are for some environmental systems along national, political, and economic lines. For other environmental systems, the wider environment is confined within areas of similar cultural and ethnic origins.

46

Organizations must respond to the changing conditions within their wider environments. These changes can explain and help to predict much of the volatility that is to take place within the immediate environments. This notion is graphically described in Figure 2.3. The dynamics of the organizational DMP, regarding the never-ending changes of the immediate environment, take place within the various systems of the wider environment, whose conditions are more stable. It is important to be well aware of these changes. The wider environment dictates the prevailing rules and conditions for the competition of organizations over the FDM.

The different environmental systems are presented in the following five subsections.

2.2.1 The Employment Market System

The employment market system dictates for the organization the state of the resources of manpower: managers as well as workers. This is a 'pendulum'

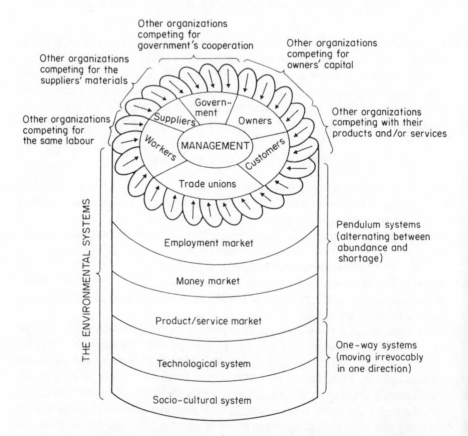

Figure 2.3   The total organization within its immediate and wider environments

system. It moves from shortage to abundance of the employment resource. An organization can be charted at one point in time, on a scale of shortage–abundance of manpower. The employment market system therefore moves from underemployment, or 'unemployment' which is characterized by abundance in the manpower market.

The state of the employment market system has a deep effect on the organizations within it. It affects the conditions of its competition for manpower with other organizations in its immediate environment. When the system is in a state of underemployment, there is little competition for employees. When the system is in a state of overemployment, there is keen competition over the labour force in the immediate environment.

2.2.2 The Money Market System[1]

The state of the employment market system is related to that of the money market and the consumer supply–demand systems. The money market system represents the relative access of individuals and organizations to money in the wider environment to which the organization belongs. This is a 'pendulum' system which moves from shortage conditions in the owners/human factor resource (shareholders, bankers, and other creditors) to abundance of money and of actual and potential shareholders, bankers, etc.

When the money market is tight, i.e. in a state of shortage, there is keen competition by the affected organizations to retain their position with respect to shareholders and bankers. The organization must impress them that it is successful and is bound to succeed in the future despite the unfavourable economic conditions. At such times organizations find it much harder to grow and develop, as they have to exploit their limited resources for short-term operations. Many small organizations close down, not being able to compete for the limited resources of money available.

In a state of abundance, on the other hand, there is little competition among organizations, within the same immediate environment, over the resources of capital and ownership. They can flourish and grow as there is comparatively little difficulty in obtaining the necessary capital.

The money market system is regulated primarily by government agencies. This is done by introducing political and economic controls in the wider environment within which the organizations operate.

2.2.3 The Consumer Supply–Demand System[1]

This system defines the purchasing power of the consumer population in the particular economy. Shortage and abundance in this system are closely related to shortage and abundance in both the money market and the employment market systems. That is to say, during an abundance in the consumer supply–demand system where the purchasing power of the consumers is high, one may generally expect to find an abundance in the money market system.

Organizations, therefore, have to fight hard to retain their customers in times of
rtage of demand in the consumer supply–demand system. The delicate balance
veen maintaining a satisfactory quality level and keeping the lowest possible
es must be guarded in order to be in a position to compete with other
nizations catering for the same market.

he prevailing conditions in the consumer supply–demand system, as in the
iey market and employment market systems, depend to a large extent on
iitical and economic policies of the governing authorities in the wider environment.

2.2.4 The Technology and Education System[1]

The level of technology of a specific wider environment is the point at which it
cannot absorb organizations operating in more advanced technologies. This level
of technology is, therefore, related to a great extent to the scientific and technical
level of a trained workforce.

While the employment market system is primarily a quantity system, the
technology system is a quality system. It deals with the more educated manpower
with respect to its technical and scientific orientation. Therefore, the technology
system is closely linked to the level of the educational system, making them one
and the same.

The level of the technology and education system at a particular time forces
organizations to change and advance by the introduction of technologies and
newly trained, high-level personnel, in order to be able to maintain the accepted
standard and variety of their products or services.

The technology and education system is, therefore, not a pendulum system like
the previous three systems. It does not change from a state of high-level
technology to that of low-level technology and vice versa, over time. In spite of
periods of short setbacks in the level of the technology system, it moves in the
long run in one direction. It advances continuously to higher and higher
technological levels. Organizations must have a built-in capability to keep changing and advancing in order to survive.

2.2.5 The Socio-cultural System

This system includes the social structure of the people, their values and mores. It
is linked to the political system in the wider environment, as well as to the geographical system, within which it exists physically.

The socio-cultural system is related in many ways to the technology and education system. The more the technology system advances, the more the socio-
cultural system adapts itself to it. The socio-cultural system, like the technology
system, is not a pendulum system. Thus, outdated and abandoned social
structures, moral values, and mores do not usually reappear.

Organizations must adapt their policies to the general trends in the socio-
cultural system, in order to survive. All aspects, such as managing personnel,

dealing with customers, with suppliers, and, for that matter, with all FDM—individuals as well as groups or organizations—must be carried out in a fashion that more or less conforms to the socio-cultural atmosphere.

There have been numerous cases of multinational organizations that have attempted to expand into foreign countries, but have not succeeded in their operations there. When a firm is not flexible enough in its policies and operation in adjusting to different socio-cultural systems, it often confronts great difficulties in its everyday running, and cannot possibly survive within the new system.

The state of the socio-cultural system, as well as that of the other four systems of the wider environment, must therefore be constantly kept in mind by management. It is those systems which define the conditions and the rules of competition of organizations within their immediate environments.

2.3 ORGANIZATIONAL STRATEGY

Organizational strategy is, in general terms, the form that the organization takes and the way it operates in practice. It is the answer to three basic questions about the organization: *What* does it attempt to achieve? *How* (by which means) does it set out to reach this goal? *Where* does it intend to do it?

By answering these three questions, the organization automatically defines the limits and characteristics of its immediate and wider environments. These to a large extent will dictate the future organizational DMP.

The specific way in which the organizational strategy is defined and carried out is therefore influenced by the nature of the immediate and wider environments. On the other hand, it is also largely affected by the managerial characteristics of the CEO (chief executive officer) and his team. We can now graphically relate the strategy of the organization to its environment, on one hand, and to the individuals who manage it, on the other. These relationships are presented in Figure 2.4.

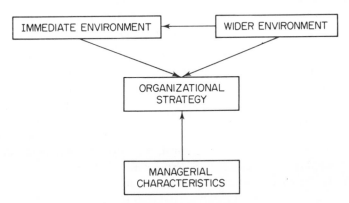

Figure 2.4   Factors   influencing   organizational   strategy   from within and without the organization

The nature of the immediate and wider environments and their effect on the organizational DMP have already been discussed in chapter 1 and the first two sections of chapter 2. Managerial characteristics and their positive influence on the organizational growth and development are discussed in chapter 4.

The present section is devoted to the notion of organizational strategy (or business strategy, as it is often termed) and the scope of decision making (SDM). The three factors affecting the SDM—the employed level of technology, the product/service diversity, and the geographical dispersal of the organization—are discussed, in turn, in subsections 2.3.2 to 2.3.4.

2.3.1 Business Strategy and the SDM

The terms 'business strategy' and 'organizational strategy' are used interchangeably in this text. They indicate that strategy is the sum of the operating policies of an organization looking towards the future. Strategy is, however, used by other types of organizations, e.g. military, correctional, or other government operated organizations in which shareholders do not participate. Furthermore, the traditional use of the terms 'business policy' and 'business strategy' is usually limited in its coverage. Many graduate schools of business administration offer programmes in business strategy as part of business policy. Such programmes deal almost exclusively with the effects of the immediate environment, usually neglecting the effects of the wider environment, especially those of the leadership and followership characteristics of the managers. Nevertheless, the term 'business strategy' is used interchangeably in this text with that of organizational strategy, for two reasons. First, the great majority of organizations in the Western world are business organizations in which shareholders or partners participate. Second, the term 'business strategy' may also be interpreted as organizational strategy in which the management of a non-business organization is operating as if it were a business organization. A business strategy contains three elements:

—*What* is the organization in? (And what is it going to be in?)
—*How* (with what means) is it operating? (Or is it going to operate?)
—*Where* is it operating? (Or is it going to operate?)

The business strategy describes the consequences of the pressures of the immediate environment and the constraints of the wider environments in the different geographical areas in which the organization operates. The business strategy—i.e. the what, how, and where—therefore establishes the organizational scope of decision making. The more competition there is for the various human factors in the organizational DMP, and the more constraints there are imposed on the organization by its wider environment, the larger is the amount and complexity of its DMP. The same factors also determine the time that management has to secure the continued cooperation of all the factors in the DMP, without which the organization cannot survive. That is to say, the more heterogeneous the business strategy in its what, how, and where, the larger its scope of decision making.

2.3.2   The Employed Level of Technology

As the level of technology rises and becomes more diverse, the SDM becomes larger. There are more problems, and more time is invested by management in maintaining the necessary continued cooperation of the essential factors of the DMP. Thus, the higher the level of technology, the more complex the problems the organization faces: with managers becoming more professional; with workers having more responsibility for maintaining larger technical systems; with suppliers assuring a steady flow of materials of uniform quality; with customers whose continuing needs for the products or services must be kept in mind; with bankers by securing larger-scale and longer-range loans; with shareholders, trade unions, government, etc.

2.3.3   The Product/Service Diversity

The larger the product/service diversity, the more management has to deal with different types of populations. Thus, going into new and different kinds of product/service lines means that the management should become more knowledgeable about the additional subgroups of the various human factors without the cooperation of which one or more of the different product/service lines cannot be successful. Adding a completely new and different product/service line could therefore mean that the management has to deal with completely different populations of workers having different skills, suppliers dealing in different materials, and customers purchasing different products or services. It would affect investors investing in different capital ventures with different rates of return and payback periods, and also government officials, etc.

2.3.4   The Geographical Dispersal

The more the organization moves to different countries, with different cultural and behavioural patterns, the larger the SDM of its management, because management has to secure the continued cooperation of additional employees, customers, bankers, shareholders, trade union and government officials, and the like. In dealing with the different types of these human factor resources, the management has to acquaint itself with the laws and habits of every country in which the organization operates.

2.4   SUMMARY

This chapter deals with the dynamics within the *decision-making main system*. We first discussed the competitive pressures from other organizations which lead to organizational growth in the *immediate environment*. Subsequently, the need for organizational maintenance in the *wider environment* was discussed, stressing the pressures which determine the factors of shortage and abundance in the immediate environment. Finally, we described the *organizational strategy*, and

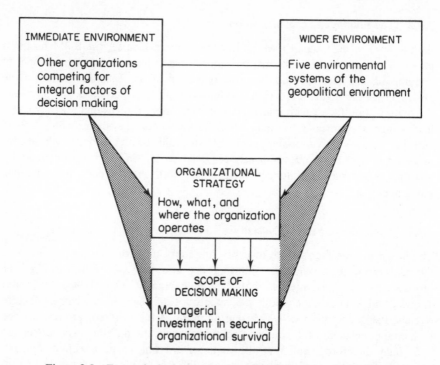

Figure 2.5   Four principal systems of the decision-making main system

how it affects, and is affected by, the competititon and pressures in the immediate and wider environments.

Figure 2.5 presents the four principal systems of the decision-making main system. We shall proceed with the analysis of the scope of decision making (SDM) system in the following chapter, and see how it links the decision-making main system with the management system, primarily with the managerial structure of the organization.

The ensuing descriptions include the salient features of two organizational examples.

Israeli Cinemas (IC)

This is a story about an announcement by a Ministry of Finance official that the prices of cinema tickets in Israel would be reduced by way of a substantial cut in government taxes on such tickets. This announcement caused the employees, the owners and the film suppliers to demand, separately and independently of each other, that the prices should *not* be reduced, so that each party could benefit from the additional returns. If not for the hurried announcement by the Ministry of Finance that the original announcement was a mistake, the Israeli cinemas would have confronted a major crisis, being unable to withstand the pressures of employees, owners and suppliers, and their appetites.

This example is similar to the two examples of chapter 1, Rolls-Royce and Swissair, in demonstrating that when one wants to introduce major changes in organizations, one should first ascertain their implications on all the human factors.

In the Israeli Cinemas case, the major change was introduced neither by the management nor by the board of directors through management. It was the government which gave up part of the cake, so that the customers could get a larger share of it. Furthermore, this change did not evolve from the dynamics of the IC organization; it was imposed by a government agency, unrelated to the survival needs of IC.

The Mafia

The main purpose for the inclusion of the Mafia example is that it illustrates the role of the five systems of the wider environment. We realize that the competition among organizations in the immediate environment is directed by the wider environmental systems. This is manifested by the Mafia gaining the upper hand over other organizations, mainly because it evades four of these environmental systems, the pressures of the employment, money and consumer markets, and the socio-cultural system of the wider environment. The fact that the Mafia cannot evade the fifth environmental system, the technological-scientific system, makes us predict that it will disappear within two generations, after having survived for over 800 years.

NOTES

1   We have permitted ourselves some terminological flexibility in the text. Thus the capital market system is also referred to as the money market system; the consumer supply-demand system may alternatively appear as the consumer market system; and in place of the technological-scientific system, we may use the technology and education system.

Chapter 3

The Dynamics of Managerial Structure and Scope of Decision Making (SDM)

In chapter 2 we learned that organizations must grow continually in terms of their factors of decision making (FDM) in order to survive the competition with other organizations in their immediate environments. The process of organizational growth is understood in terms of an expansion in its scope of decision making (SDM).

The flow of work in organizations is organized according to a particular accepted set of rules. The fashion in which work is organized within the operating organization is called the managerial structure. In order to expand effectively, the structure of an organization must be altered from time to time. An organization that has grown beyond a particular size can no longer operate in the fashion that it did when it was just established. When it has a varied and complex technology, when the number of product/service lines increases, and when it is located in more than one small plant or office, its managerial structure must be adapted to suit its size and complexity, and to suit its immediate environment.

Research has, in fact, shown the clear-cut relationship between organizational structure and organizational size in terms of its SDM: the level of the employed technology, the diversity of product/service lines, and the geographical dispersal. Joan Woodward studied 100 industrial organizations in the north of England. She paid particular attention to organizational size excluding geographical dispersal and number of product lines, as all researched organizations operated only one plant each and produced one line of products. They did not, therefore, vary on these two measures of size. She also measured the managerial structure of the firms in her sample. A clear-cut relationship was found between the way the management was structured and the level of technology employed in the organization.

John Stopford studied 170 multinational business organizations centred in the USA which operated in at least six other countries. He checked every organization at two points at which they went through structural transition. He tested the stage of development of the organization while it was moving from structure X to structure Y. These stages were measured in terms of a large number of indices of size. Two main findings were reported in this study. Stopford found a clear chronological order to managerial structures through which organizations proceed as they grow. He then tested the relationships between the scale of managerial structures and the different measures of organizational size. He found that structure related to three measures of organizational size: level of technology, diversity of product lines, and geographical dispersal—in short, the SDM.

It is clear, therefore, that organizations must change their structure as they grow in order to adapt it to their expanding SDM. The dynamics of this process constitute the issues of this chapter.

The chapter is divided into four sections. Section 3.1 presents and discusses three basic managerial structures and the processes which organizations go through as they move from one structure to another. Section 3.2 discusses the rate of growth in SDM and its relationship to the managerial structure. Two parameters of managerial structure are dealt with in section 3.3. Section 3.4 summarizes the whole chapter.

3.1 THREE BASIC MANAGERIAL STRUCTURES

Most organizations go through an orderly sequence of managerial structures during the course of their lives. An organization just established may be very small, but developing fast. In order to survive this difficult but exciting stage of its 'childhood', it must be managed in an informal, centralized fashion. This structure is called an entrepreneurial structure and is typical of new organizations in their first stage of development. Subsection 3.1.2 presents the nature of this managerial structure. When organizations grow beyond a particular size they can no longer function effectively within this structure. They must go through a major transformation in terms of the whole set of rules by which the work is managed and carried out in order to cope with the growing quantities of product and services, their variety, and the complexity of the organization. This second structure, called the functional structure, is the topic of subsection 3.1.3. The formalized and centralized nature of the functional structure must, at a certain stage of growth of the organization, give place to the decentralized structure, if the organization is to survive. As described in subsection 3.1.4, devoted to the two possible structural solutions for a decentralized management system, organizations cannot function effectively within a functional structure beyond a particular SDM.

This section is devoted to the discussion of these three basic managerial structures. We shall describe these structures as a function of the size of the organization, in terms of their SDM. The graph presented in Figure 3.1 will help us to visualize the development of organizations in these terms. The graph presents three variables—time, structure, and SDM. Time is measured in years and indicates the age or lifespan of the organization. Managerial structure is the ratio of the formal to the informal structure, i.e. the ratio of the structure that *actually* exists to the structure that *should* exist at the particular stage of development of the organization. Managerial structure is, therefore, not that which is described in

56

the organizational chart hanging in the chief executive's office. Nor is it the informal set of working relationships among the various managerial groups and individuals of the organization. The managerial structure appearing in Figure 3.1, therefore, is something midway between these two.

The third variable taken into account in this graph is organizational size.[1] It is the hardest one to measure. We have shown, on the basis of past research, that it comprises three factors: level of technology employed, diversity of products/services, and geographical dispersal. The larger the organization in these terms, the heavier the burden on the various managerial functions. We therefore assume that the larger the organization, the larger the number of managers it employs. The number of managers within an organization is, for our purposes, a rough measure of organizational size, i.e. its SDM. This measure has its limitations. By employing it, we are assuming that the organization is functioning effectively, that all its managers are fully occupied so that there is no underutilization of managers. The measure is, however, a good indicator of the SDM when the organization is relatively young and small. As the organization grows, various managerial functions of coordination among its departments and branches are formed. The total number of managers thus becomes a less accurate measure as the size and complexity of the organization increases. Nevertheless, we employ this measure to give some indication of the size of an organization at a particular point in its life.

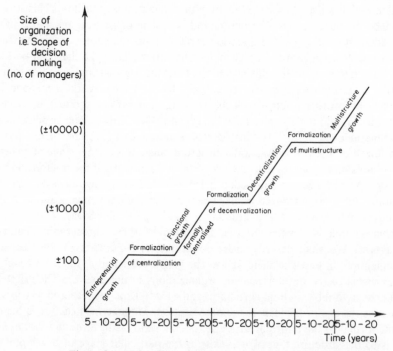

Figure 3.1   The effect of size on the managerial structure

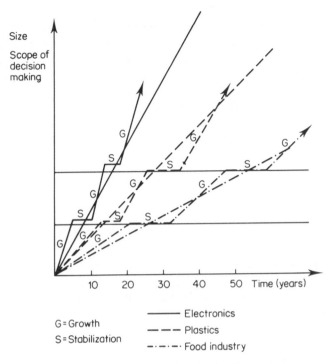

Figure 3.2 Schematic example of periods of growth and of stabilization (structural changes) in various fields of activities

Figure 3.2 presents a schematic description of how organizations grow. Their growth does not take place at a steady pace. There are periods of relatively fast development and periods of decline in the pace of growth. At a certain phase of development an organization is confronted by certain signals that indicate the necessity for a structural change. These signals relate to organizational phenomena that are a result of the changes that take place in the SDM of the organization. The size of the organization, measured by the number of managers employed in it, gives us some idea of critical points for structural changes. The organizational phenomena that alert the system of a need for such a change are discussed in subsections 3.1.2 to 3.1.4.

Different organizations in different business areas arrive at the size level that demands a structural change at different intervals of time. A fast-growing electronics organization in its entrepreneurial stage will reach the size of about 100 managers in a shorter period of time than a textile industrial firm established at the same time. Thus, the electronics company will have to consider switching into a functional structure several years before the textiles manufacturer (see Figures 2.2 and 3.2). The graph in Figure 2.2, therefore, describes average slopes of growth for several types of business organizations.

The period of time in the life of an organization from the point when a structural change takes form until it is finally established is called a formalization period. During these periods the organization reduces its pace of growth. It cannot keep up its former pace and go through a structural change at the same time. In some cases growth is stopped altogether for a period of a few years. In others, the size of the organization, the range of activities, geographical dispersal, etc., are slightly reduced, to enable it to reorganize itself.

The lines parallel to the time axis in Figure 3.1 describe the average organization which halts its development during periods of formalization of a new structure. The issue of formalization versus relaxation in management is dealt with in subsection 3.1.5.

Before turning to the discussion of the actual basic structures and the signals within an organization calling for a change, let us remind ourselves once again who, precisely, are the managers within the organization.

3.1.1 Who is a Manager?

The definition of a manager has altered over the years, and it has had to be adapted since the beginning of the twentieth century to embrace new human factors which have appeared in the organizational DMP. At present, the only suitable definition is: 'Managers are those members of the operating organization who are responsible for the continued cooperation of members of the human factors of the organizational DMP, without whom the organization cannot survive.'

This definition includes salesmen (responsible for the cooperation of customers), buyers (responsible for the cooperation of suppliers), and foremen (responsible for the cooperation of workers). It might also include senior secretaries, where they fulfil managerial roles, i.e. are responsible for contacts with various members of the organizational FDM. A secretary who not only types letters but also drafts them, who not only accepts phone calls and dials people she is told to phone but also initiates contacts, is a manager and not a worker in the organization.

When evaluating the SDM of an organization, reflected in the amount of managerial work that is carried out in the organization, all managers including those in seemingly non-managerial occupations must be counted.

3.1.2 The Entrepreneurial Structure

All organizations have been created by one person. For every organization there was at one point one man who visualized it and gave it the first push. He might have been aided by others, but the pusher of an idea can be a single individual only, an entrepreneur.

Entrepreneurs tend to have a set of typical traits. They are, in most cases, extremely hard-working people, pushing themselves as well as their subordinates and co-workers. They are in many cases restless and very mobile people. Most entrepreneurs believe that in order to succeed, as they did, one must go through the same course of occupational life. An entrepreneur will rarely accept the fact that his success was inspired by his own special character.

Entrepreneurs are usually extremely charismatic in nature. They are highly admired, though the admiration of those closely associated with them tends to be mingled with fear and sometimes even with deep hatred.

Entrepreneurs are manipulators, primarily of people but also of other resources. Therefore, in order to achieve their ends they manipulate employees, suppliers, customers, bankers, shareholders, as well as governments and trade union officials. They may regard regulations and laws of state and other organizations, even those of their own organization, as constraints and obstacles to the achievement of their objectives. Such regulations and laws are observed if they do not stand in their way, but are ignored and bypassed if they do. This is why, most probably, there are so many entrepreneurs and their aides to be found in prisons. The leadership of organized crime organizations is always composed of entrepreneurs and their aides.

On the other hand, if it had not been for entrepreneurs, no new organizations, technologies, standards of living, etc., could have been realized. It seems, therefore, that society has been judging these irregularities in observing laws and regulations by managers in entrepreneurial organizations by two different moral codes.

The typical characteristic of the entrepreneur can be seen in the way he manages his organization and the people working for him. The management style of the entrepreneur is extremely *centralized* and *informal*. He organizes the work in the organization in a manner similar to the way a soccer coach works with his team. The players stand in a circle, and the coach places himself in the middle, as described in Figure 3.3. The coach throws the ball to one of the players, without telling him what to do with it. The player decides to whom to pass it. Meanwhile, the coach can throw another ball to another player. He can demand the first ball back whenever he wishes. The result is that everyone plays with everybody else. But the coach initiates, pushes, and directs the game. This is the nature of the centralized, informal style of management of the entrepreneur.

Let us consider an example of a small furniture manufacturer. Its managing director goes on a tour abroad and visits an exhibition. He sees there a new aluminium chair. He picks up a catalogue describing the chair and takes it home. He turns to Mr Smith, the man in charge of the production of chairs, and asks him

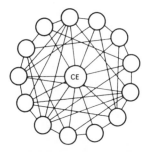

Figure 3.3   The entrepreneurial managerial structure is informal and centralized

60

to look into the possibility of making such a chair in their firm. Mr Smith brings Mr Fletcher, a machinery expert, into the project and Mr Lane, who sells chairs, and they work on it together.

Six months later the managing director once more travels abroad. Eyeing such a chair already on display in a shop, he buys it and brings it back home. He meets Mr Lane in the yard and asks him to look into the possibilities of the chair being produced there. The manager has, by now, forgotten to whom he turned over this project in the first place. Mr Lane takes the chair, and Smith, Fletcher, and Lane, continue to work on it.

The style of management described in this example can work, and does so successfully, as long as the *size of the firm* is limited to between 50 and 500 managers (order of magnitude of 100 managers).

If the firm had around 1000 managers, it is quite reasonable to assume that the managing director, after returning from his second trip, would not have met Smith, Fletcher, or Lane, but could well have turned to Mr. Grove, who may have had some past experience in working with aluminium. Grove could then have turned to Black (area salesman), etc., thus forming a completely new project team working on the new aluminium chair. Beyond a particular size range, two such groups could have worked side by side without one having any idea of the existence of the other.

A style of management that can work for a firm of 50 to 500 managers becomes disastrous within a firm of about 1000 managers. For such an informal but centralized management style to be productive, one has to know all the other managers working in the firm. Thus, every manager must be familiar with what his co-managers are doing, the projects they are working on, etc. In such a case, Mr Grove would immediately have pointed out to his managing director that another group, consisting of Smith, Fletcher, and Lane, was already working on the project of the aluminium chair. The firm being relatively small, he would be familiar with what is happening in every part of it.

The limitation of the informal, centralized style of management to not more than 50 to 500 managers is dictated by the innate limitations of the memory of the human brain. There is a large variance among individuals in the capacity of their memory bank. Generally, though, most people can manage a close and fundamental acquaintanceship with between 50 and 500 people. Beyond this number, the next critical size is that of 500 to 5000 people. We cannot remember much about every person out of a thousand. When we are surrounded by such a large number of managers in the firm we work for, we are not likely to remember what each of them is working on at a particular time, or even the department or section to which each of them is posted.

The next critical size is found in the group 5000 to 50 000. When it comes to such a large number of individuals one cannot remember the names of all those people. One can just about 'relate a face to a place'. This is the case when meeting a familiar face in the street and having to make a mental effort to remember where we met this person.

Organizations consist of people. People construct them, run them, and develop them. The structure of organizations must, therefore, be adjusted to the nature and limitations of the human being of which they consist. One of these limitations is related to the scope of our memory bank, as we have just seen.

The effectiveness of an informal, centralized structure is dependent on a close acquaintance of the managers with each other, and on the entrepreneur's ability to control them. As soon as the size of the organization grows beyond the possibility for this close acquaintance and centralized control, the organization, if it is still run in an entrepreneurial fashion, will cease to function effectively. The entrepreneur will lose control over his managers and the entrepreneurial structure will face the possibility of chaos. It will not be able to cope with internal and external pressures as they develop. Development and long-range planning will be replaced with a tendency to concentrate on present crises and 'extinction of fires'. In short, the organization will begin to deteriorate.

Before these difficulties arise, organizations must start the process of altering the structure by which the work is managed. Figure 3.1 describes this organizational change as a function of organizational size. The organization was established, run, and developed in an entrepreneurial structure, the only management structure possible for the initial growth of an organization. However, when the scope of decision making grows and, correspondingly, managers increase in number to about 100, steps must be taken to formalize the centralized management. A formalized, centralized management structure is, in fact, the second managerial structure in the organizational lifespan. It is described in subsection 3.1.3.

3.1.3 The Functional Structure

When the entrepreneur can no longer control the growing number of managers, and when it is no longer possible to trust the memory of the managers concerning the many details of the work of their fellow managers, two steps must be taken:

(a) The number of managers directly controlled by the CE (chief executive) must be reduced.
(b) The individual managers must be put into 'boxes'. Their jobs are *defined* as to who does what, when, and with whom. This enables people to trace each manager, according to his defined role in the organization, whenever he is needed.

The structural answer to these two steps, which are essential for the effective functioning of the growing organization, is the formal hierarchy. When the SDM of the organization increases to the dimension of about 100 managers, the organization must formalize its structure. The reader will remember that the nature of the entrepreneurial structure was informal, though it was centralized.

During the time that an organization is going through this transformation from an informal to a formal system, the rate of growth will decrease or even stop. The

62

structural change is a deep and fundamental one, involving a change of personnel, and a change of working techniques and communication channels. The process by which this change takes place is called formalization of centralization and it can take one or several years to carry out. Only when the structure is introduced and accepted by all the managers in the organization can the organization turn to another stage of growth within this structure (see Figure 3.1).

A formal, centralized managerial structure is called a functional one. The CE directly controls the various functional heads, such as those of Production, Marketing, Procurement, Personnel, Finance, etc. The functional structure is presented in Figure 3.4.

In a functional structure, none of the subordinates of the CE (the functional heads) is free to carry out a complete project on his own. They are all interdependent. The work flows from one function to another. In a typical industrial organization, Procurement and Engineering pass on plans and materials for Production. Production turns the finished goods over to Marketing. All functions are dependent on Personnel and Finance for the human and financial resources needed to run them. The process of the flow of resources from one function to another is rarely a smooth one. When difficulties and conflicts arise among the various organizational units, the problems are pushed upwards in the hierarchy. The head of the organization, the CE, thus centralizes them.

The independence of the different functions in a functional structure is, therefore, limited. In most organizations, those functions are independent for a period of up to one week, terminated by the weekly meeting of all functional heads or representatives with the CE. An independent period of more than a week—e.g. of one month—is extremely unlikely in a functional structure. Production, for example, would have to be capable of holding raw materials for a month, and to maintain a spare workforce and a storeroom that could hold all the finished goods produced in one month, etc. All of this is hardly possible. Most functional structures are organized in such a way that their units are independent for up to one week only.

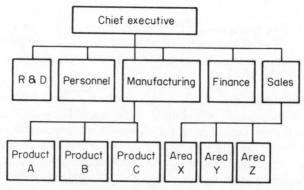

Figure 3.4   The functional managerial structure is formal and centralized

The dependence of the various functional heads on each other for the inflow and outflow of resources has its defects. Managers tend to avoid accepting responsibility. Success will always have many 'fathers' or claimants, but failure will be 'fatherless'. If, for example, a customer complains that the product was unsatisfactory, Production will try to avoid blame by putting it on other functions. They might blame Procurement for not having provided the appropriate materials; they might throw the blame on the plans handed over to them from Engineering; they might even throw it onto Marketing, claiming that they were pushed to hurry the production procedures in order to have the products ready earlier than had been planned, because of special requests from the customers.

The functional structure, on the other hand, has its advantages. It enables specialization within the functions, as well as having the 'advantage of size'. As the organization grows, the number of products and services grows and the geographical dispersal increases. The functional structure makes possible centralized purchasing for the whole organization, thus obtaining higher quality goods at lower prices. A large marketing function can afford to employ experts in a variety of fields, such as market research, advertising, marketing channels, transportation, etc. The advantages versus disadvantages of the functional structure are especially interesting when compared with those of the decentralized structures discussed in subsection 3.14. They might become crucial factors to be taken into consideration when an organization has grown to such dimensions as to require a decision concerning the optimal time for undergoing a structural change (see discussion at the end of subsection 3.1.4).

As the organization grows, the number of managers employed in it grows as well. The number of hierarchical levels in the functional organization thus increases, even though the number of functions, obviously, does not. However, as the organization expands, more units and roles are created within each function. The functional structure becomes increasingly complex and, gradually, ineffective.

Let us turn to our example of the furniture manufacturing firm (from subsection 3.1.2). We will first look up our people, Smith, Fletcher, and Lane. They are now somewhere at the bottom of the functional hierarchy, let us say at the sixth level from the top. Let us assume they are assigned the project of introducing a new product, e.g. an aluminium chair. Within the functional structure, each one of them belongs to a different branch. Smith is in charge of chair production (see Figure 3.5); Fletcher, a machinery expert, is in Engineering; and Lane, who sells chairs, is located somewhere in the Marketing branch of the hierarchy. In order for these three men to be able to work as a team on the new project they are temporarily pulled out of their units and put into a committee assigned to look into the possibility of making and selling the new chair. They work on this new product. Towards the end of the project, when they are about to reach a final decision, each one of them will find it hard to take the full responsibility for his decision, as he is 'only' a middle manager in his firm. This phenomenon is bound to happen. Each one of them will secretly or openly turn to his superior if only to 'keep him in the picture'. The superior will probably turn to his own superior, etc. The final decision is thus postponed. The issue is pushed upwards in the hierarchy.

64

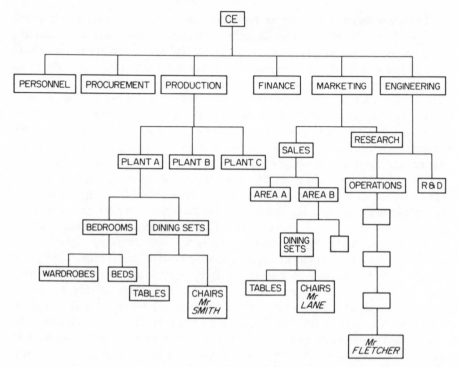

Figure 3.5   The furniture manufacturer at an advanced stage within the functional
structure

Time is wasted unnecessarily by managers throughout the organization. Work becomes extremely ineffective. The creation of such blockages as the one described here is due mainly to the fact that we, in the West, cannot accept bypassing. We will not stand being bypassed, and will, therefore, hesitate to bypass our own superiors. Although, as in the example of the project of the aluminium chair, it would be effective and efficient to reach the final decision within the committee as quickly as possible, it is generally passed straight on to the executive in charge. The experts assigned to the project were intimidated by the importance of their decision, by the possible reaction of their superiors to the fact that they took such a major decision, as well as by their reluctance to take on the sole responsibility for their decision. This last factor is inherent in the nature of the functional structure and is dealt with in the following subsection.

In other words, the functional structure is a suitable and effective managerial structure for an organization at a particular stage of its development. Beyond a certain size, or SDM, the functional hierarchy becomes a bulky, ineffective, and inflexible monster, paralysed by its own dimensions. The only way to avoid this is to restructure the organization and divide it not by functions, but by either product or service lines or by areas.

3.1.4 The Product/Service Line or Area Structures

As a result of expansion in the SDM into new product/service lines or new areas, the number of managers grows far beyond the number which can be effectively and efficiently operated in a functional structure. This happens at an organizational size of about 1000 (500 to 5000). Figure 3.1 shows that, at this stage, the organization must slow down its growth and allow for the introduction of a new, formal, decentralized structure.

The necessity of abandoning the functional structure is not only due to the increase in the size of the organization, in terms of the number of managers employed in it, but also to the nature of its SDM. If, for example, an organization has by now expanded into three completely different fields, e.g. insurance, banking, and industry, there is no longer any point in keeping them all running within a functional structure. Decentralization of the managerial structure is the appropriate way to deal with the new dimensions and nature of the organizational SDM.

The decentralization of the new managerial structure, appropriate to the new dimensions of the organization, can be carried out according to product/service lines or according to areas. The basis for the decentralization depends on the main development of the organization. In organizations which have units which are widely scattered, it is usually more sensible to decentralize them according to areas. Otherwise, and unless the area factor plays a major role in the nature of the production process, organizations must be decentralized by product or service lines, depending on whether the organization is basically a manufacturing or service company, or both. Figure 3.6 describes the two decentralized structural options.

Within a decentralized managerial structure, the formal heads of the product or service lines, in structure A, or the areas, in structure B, are directly responsible to the CE. Each area head or line head is responsible for a whole set of functions of his area or line. He has a production unit, a finance unit, a marketing unit, etc. All the unit heads are managers responsible to the line or area head only. The line or area head is, therefore, fully responsible, in a decentralized structure, for the fate of that line of products, or that area of which he is in charge.

Let us try and locate the managers of our furniture plant within a decentralized formal structure. The line of chairs might, by now, have grown into an independent line. Mr Smith, Mr Fletcher, and Mr Lane would now all be functional unit heads, all reporting to one line head. Figure 3.7 describes this situation.

In the case of an attempt to introduce a new product, such as the already familiar aluminium chair, all the functional units belonging to the line of chairs will be assigned to look into the project. No committees will be necessary. The units will naturally be centralized, if necessary, by their line head, who is also the person to whom they will submit their individual reports regarding the project.

The different lines or areas within the decentralized structure are, thus,

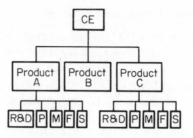

Structure A: decentralized by product line

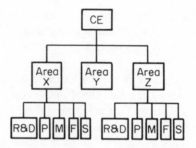

Structure B: decentralized by geographical area

Figure 3.6   Two formal decentralized managerial structures

independent units, as compared to the various functions within a functional structure. The period of independence of each unit varies from one organization to another. In most cases, an organization that has recently decentralized allows its units periods of one month of independent activities. Within this period the unit head (line or area head) is free to run his unit without any interference from the head office. At the end of each monthly period the unit head must file a full report to the CE describing the activities of the unit during that period.

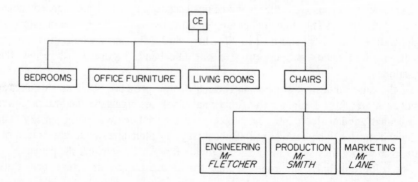

Figure 3.7   The furniture manufacturer decentralized by product lines

A larger decentralized organization can work on longer periods of autonomy, three months, six months, or one year, depending on the size of the organization. These periods run parallel to financial periods and require the filing of reports. The heads of the decentralized units (product/service, or area units) are, therefore, initially given complete independence for one month. For that period of time they are allowed to run all functions as they see fit. As the organization develops and the decentralized structure is shown to run smoothly, the length of the decentralized period is extended to three months, to six months, and finally to one year. Let us consider, as an example, the function of Personnel. In a one-month decentralized organization the personnel manager of each decentralized unit is allowed to handle workers only. He is fully responsible for the recruitment, training, managing, and firing of workers employed in the unit. Managers, including the level of foremen, are not his responsibility. They are responsible to the central personnel function at the head office. If a new foreman, for example, must be appointed within the month, either a worker is appointed temporarily until the end of the one-month period, or a special authorization is issued from the head office. In a three-month decentralized organization, a unit personnel manager handles foremen as well as workers. A personnel manager of a six-month decentralized unit is responsible for all the low-level managers in the unit, as well as the foremen and workers employed in it. In a unit which is decentralized for a whole year, the unit head would be fully responsible for all the employees of that unit, managers and workers, excluding himself.

In order to find out the period of decentralization of an organization, we can, therefore, go down to the decentralized units and investigate the extent of independence of their functional heads in carrying out their jobs. The unit procurement manager, for example, has the authority to make all purchases of less than a specific amount without having to get permission or submit himself to any form of control from the head office. We then measure the length of time for which this sum is normally sufficient—larger purchases can normally be postponed until the end of the period. We might find then that a one-month decentralized unit will be authorized a sum of $10 000 per purchase; a three-month decentralized unit will be authorized a sum of $50 000, etc. If, sometime within a period, the unit is in a position which necessitates an expense larger than the maximum sum allowed per period, the procurement manager can either divide the expense into two purchases, or apply for special permission from the head office to carry out the purchase.

The main advantage of the decentralized managerial structure lies in the full responsibility given to the decentralized unit head. This structural trait allows the unit head a feeling of high motivation, which is found to filter down to his senior management group. The sense of high job satisfaction is due to the fact that the consequences of one's acts lie on one's own shoulders only. For example, if the furniture manufacturing unit (Figure 3.7) has succeeded in turning out the aluminium chair, has marketed it, and has altogether profited on this achievement, no other manager in the company would be able to take this success away. It would lie solely on the line head, the head of the chairs department. If the unit head is capable of sharing the general feeling of well-doing and success with his staff, the sense of all-round satisfaction might even affect the general atmosphere, or 'morale', of the unit. High morale, in turn, tends to produce a positive trend in people to do well in the future, and especially for their unit head who makes them feel good and useful whenever he can (see organizational example of British Chain Stores at the end of chapter 4). Research has shown that these chain effects tend to take place in small organizational units, rather than large ones. Small units are characterized by a potential 'family feeling', which is one aspect of morale, typical of small units. This family sensation is possible when the unit is small enough to enable the attitude of the unit head to filter down and affect the whole unit. A newly decentralized organization should have units small enough to be subject to this phenomenon.

In any case, the motivation and satisfaction of the unit head in a decentralized managerial structure is far greater than that of a function head within a functional managerial structure. This comparison is a relevant and crucial one to remember. A functionally structured organization may have grown to such an extent that it can already operate within a decentralized structure but can still be relatively efficiently run within the functional structure for another few years. In other words, organizations often find themselves in a position where they can see the necessity of having to restructure themselves in the foreseeable future, but they question themselves as to the optimal time to carry out the structural change.

Whereas the decentralized structure has its advantages in the motivation of its managers, the functional structure has the advantages of size and specialization (subsection 3.1.3). A small, newly decentralized unit cannot afford the benefits of specialization. Since it is completely independent of other units and controls its own functions, the possibility of bulk purchasing, with the benefits and conditions it offers, are non-existent within the decentralized structural system. The management of an organization standing on the threshold of a structural change from a functional to a decentralized structure, will have to consider the advantages of taking immediate steps to begin the change versus delaying the change for a few years, thereby gaining more time for bulk purchasing and high-level specialization within the firm. The decision must always depend solely on the nature of the SDM of the company concerning its day-to-day operations, its product/service diversity, and its geographical dispersal.

Another option presents itself which appears to embrace the advantages of both structural systems. We will call it the 'mixed structure'. Let us return to our furniture manufacturer (Figure 3.7). We will assume a situation in which the price of wood has recently risen. The general management of the now decentralized structure decides that, due to the present price increases in the main raw material, it is necessary to centralize the function of procurement, in order to capture the advantages of purchasing in large quantities. The new organizational structure of the furniture manufacturer is shown in Figure 3.8.

Let us study the nature of this mixed structure. Does it, in fact, combine the advantages of the functional and decentralized structures? The answer is, 'No!'

In order to pin down the basic nature of an organization structure, the *first question* one must ask oneself about the organization is: What is the period of

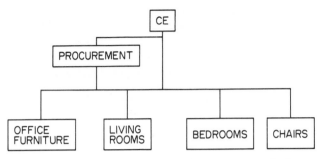

Figure 3.8   The   new   managerial   structure   of   the
furniture factory

time within which the direct subordinates of the CE achieve complete independence in managing their units?

The mixed structure, when studied from the point of view of this question, evidently leaves a short independence period (probably one week) for each of the unit heads. The fact that only one function has been taken away from them makes them no less dependent than if all functions had been centralized.

Our mixed structure has, therefore, none of the advantages of the decentralized structure. It has the advantage of the functional structure with respect to one function only, procurement.

In order to verify this conclusion, we must ask ourselves the *second question*, which points out the basic characteristics of the managerial structure: At the end of the decentralized period (one month, three months, etc.) if one of the units shows a profit, will the head of this unit be able to take all the credit for it? Similarly, in the case of a loss, will he have to take the blame or will he be able to throw the blame on somebody else in the organization? The answer is obvious in the case of the mixed structure. The procurement manager will always be able to take credit for the success of any unit. An unsuccessful unit head can also put the blame for his misfortune on the organization procurement manager.

The conclusion is straightforward. What we termed a 'mixed structure' is simply an ineffective and useless one. It has the disadvantages of both the functional and the decentralized structures. Centralizing one function within a decentralized system is a useless structural option.

Decentralizing a function within a functional structure is another matter altogether. Let us study a manufacturing organization, the plants of which are widely dispersed over the country, such as the one presented in Figure 3.4.

The organization is functionally structured. The centralized personnel function has been having great difficulties in operating in the various districts in which the plants are situated. Management arrived at the practical solution of delegating this function to the individual plants. Each plant manager is no longer responsible solely for production within his plants. He is also responsible for recruitment, training, etc., of his employees to the level of foremen. This solution enjoys the full benefits of size and specialization of the centralized functional structure as well as the benefits of specialization within the particular boundaries of the one function

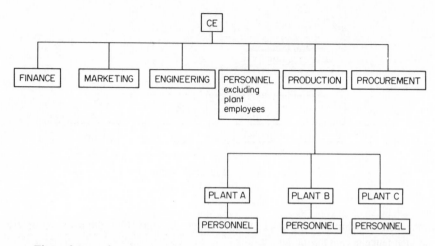

Figure 3.9   A functional structure of which one function has been decentralized

that has been delegated to the plants. This particular form of a functional structure is presented in Figure 3.9.

The nature of a managerial structure can thus be determined by a single measure: the actual length of time that the managers, who are directly responsible to the CE, are completely independent in their organizational units. When coming to assess the structure within which any organization operates, one must never be led astray by an organizational chart hanging on the CE's office wall, or by actual declarations or perceptions of individual managers within the firm. Their perceptions may be based on misjudgements on their part, or a subjective sense of independence, which might be a pleasant and motivating factor in itself, but does not alter actual structural facts within the firm. They might be led to feel free to initiate and internally to manage their units as they see fit (which is an achievement in itself) yet, actually, they are operating within a formalized functional structure.

3.1.5.   Formalization and Relaxation in Managerial Structure

The transfer of an organization from one structure to another is a deep and sometimes traumatic change for the organization and its members. It requires much managerial time, and a certain rigidity in the implementation of the new structure.

A structural change cannot be carried out while the organization is in the process of growth. As we shall see in more detail in chapter 5, such a change requires the replacement of people in key positions in the organization. These are the head of the organization and other managers capable of aiding in the imposition of the new structure. The need to replace these managers is due to the fact that people who are capable of managing the change have different personality characteristics than do people who manage the organization in periods of growth. At times of change the organization needs strong leaders who will insist on carrying out the various aspects of the needed change in all parts of the organization. They will see to it that the new structure is implemented exactly as planned. In other words, during times of change, the organization must be run very formally. Every procedure must be carried out precisely as described in the written regulations. This method of introducing a structural change is the only way of ensuring that the organization is, in fact, converted to a new structure. The people put at its head to carry out the change must, therefore, be those stiff and rigid personalities who are capable of pursuing the fine details of a programme for change, but lack the flexibility to work outside the dictates of structural details. Only such leaders can overcome the natural resistance of all members of the organization to any change whatsoever. The dislike and distrust of change is a human trait which we all have, some of us to a larger extent than others.

This natural resistance becomes especially acute when the change is not initiated by us, but rather imposed on us by others. The process of formalization of the structural change cannot be carried out in days, or weeks, or even months. This process can last several years and is equivalent to the length of time of the periods of growth. The nature of the change periods, and the character of its leaders, are such as to inhibit natural growth and development. During these times the scope of decision making does not, in most cases, change. It can expand to a limited extent or even shrink somewhat, to enable the change to come to pass. On the whole, though, the SDM during the formalization periods is more or less stable. This fact is described in the graph in Figure 3.1 by lines, parallel to the time axis, for each formalization period.

In the formalized organization, growth can hardly take place. Organizational growth requires a certain flexibility which cannot exist while the formal details of the structure are blindly followed, which is essential during formalization periods. The concept of growth in the SDM, therefore, contradicts that of formalization.

After the required structure has been introduced and put into operation, it is time to continue the organizational growth, in order to keep up with overall growth in the SDM within a particular field. To enable the organization to turn from formalization to growth, few managers occupying key positions in the organization must be replaced. These positions are to be filled with managers whose managerial qualities fit the new structure, but who are also less bureaucratic and more flexible than their predecessors. This will enable them to coordinate the various organizational units, and carry out the necessary activities during the period of growth lying ahead, within the general framework of the new managerial structure.

3.2 RATES OF GROWTH IN SDM (AND THE RELEVANT MANAGERIAL STRUCTURE)

It has been pointed out and discussed at length previously in this book that the managerial structure of an organization at a particular point in its life must be suited to the scope of its decision making (DM) at that time. The scope of DM (SDM) is assessed by establishing three organizational factors: level of technology, the product/service diversity, and the geographical dispersal (see section 2.1). Sometimes, by establishing only two aspects of organizational strategy, one can decide which managerial structure is most suitable for the management to run the organization efficiently.

The present section goes into these issues in detail. Whereas chapter 2 deals with basic definitions and concepts regarding organizational growth and organizational strategy, this part of the book attempts to reveal the processes and rationale behind these concepts. Subsection 3.2.1 is devoted to the issue of the assessment of the SDM. Subsection 3.2.2 examines the various stages of growth and discusses which managerial structure suits which organizational SDM. Finally, subsection 3.2.3 discusses management and organizational problems that arise in activity areas which are fast growing, as compared with areas that develop more slowly.

3.2.1 Assessment of the SDM

The scope of DM (SDM) is the main indicator of what managerial structure is necessary for an organization at a particular point in its life. The question of that element by which we can measure the SDM thus becomes a basic and crucial one.

The SDM is, on one hand, the totality of managerial problems that require decisions to be made so that the organization will be able to continue its existence. On the other hand, it is essential to discover some measure that will clearly give us the organizational SDM that will indicate when the managerial structure should be altered.

As to the totality of problems, it is evident that as the integral factors of the DMP grow, they will lead to growth in the number of workers, the number of managers, the numbers of customers, suppliers, etc. In turn, the overall activity in the organization regarding the factors of wages, sales, investments, etc., leads to the expansion of the SDM. But this view is rather simplistic. The growth in the integral factors may theoretically point to organizational growth, but actually, as is revealed in research, managerial structures are not related to those factors. In other words, growth in the integral human factors cannot be that significant change in the SDM which we are looking for, that factor whose change indicates that the structure must be altered.

Logically, it is quite clear that there is no need for a different structure when no factor within the total organization changes except the number of employees, i.e. when more employees now carry out the same jobs in the same locations. The type of problems that the organization now copes with has not changed.

The research of Joan Woodward and John Stopford, in the organizational examples of the South Essex Industry (at the end of Chapter 4), and on multinational organizations (at the end of Chapter 6), indicates that the only factors that relate significantly to the managerial structure of the organization are its level of technology, the diversity of its product or service lines, and its geographical dispersal. In other words, the need for a change in the structure of an organization arises, as a rule, when at least one of these three factors grow to a significant extent.

The research of Woodward and Stopford was carried out in such a way that there is little doubt as to the reliability of their results. Both studied a large number of organizations of various structures. They tried to correlate the structure with a large number of organizational factors. In fact, any factor that could possibly influence the need for a structural change was measured and included in their computations.

Measures of the size of the business in terms of the various integral factors included in the total organization, as well as accepted measures of organizational size, such as number of employees, sales volume, overall investments, etc., were among the many factors included in these studies. But, as previously mentioned, only the three factors of level of technology, product/service diversity, and geographical dispersal actually correlated with the managerial structure of the organization. These are, therefore, the three factors that determine the SDM of an organization.

These findings point out that the generally accepted size indicators, such as the total number of employees, are not universal to all organizations, though some research on a limited range of organizations does point at their significance in determining organizational size. We believe that, instead of classifying organizations in national and industrial statistics according to the number of employees, the sales volume, and the overall investment, etc., as is done today, it would be more meaningful and therefore advisable to classify them first of all according to their technological levels, their product diversity, and their geographical dispersal.[2]

The first step in the assessment of SDM, is the identification of the technology, the product/service lines and the geographical areas in which the organization operates. The second step, of establishing what the SDM is, could be performed in a similar way to that in which Joan Woodward assessed the technological levels and in which John Stopford assessed the product/service and geographical diversity (i.e. the geographical dispersal)[3].

3.2.2 Which Managerial Structure Suits which Organizational SDM?

The managerial structure of an organization must accord with its SDM at a particular point in time. It has been shown that the SDM is a function of three main factors, the level of technology, the product/service diversity, and the geographical dispersal. Let us now study the state of the organization in terms of these factors and the suitable managerial structures for possible variations or combinations of these factors.

When an organization is created it usually has one product or service line and operates only in one area. Only through an entrepreneurial structure can an organization be created and operated. Until it is finally and firmly established it has to continue to be operated in this structure. If the organizational level of technology is relatively low and not too sophisticated, and the organization is still producing one product line within a limited area, then its DMP should continue to be managed in an entrepreneurial structure.

This structure, however, ceases to be suitable when the level of technology is high and the equipment is effectively utilized. In such cases the organization should abandon the initial entrepreneurial structure and turn to a functional structure. In other words, organizations must operate within a functional structure if they produce one line of products in one location, but which have a high technological and scientific level which requires specialization and a linkage of particular experts to particular machinery and areas of activity.

As the organization grows and diversifies into two or more distinctly different product or service lines, its managerial structure should once again be adjusted to its enlarging SDM. The structure of an organization producing two or more distinctly different product lines should be decentralized by product line. However, when the organization moves to one or more additional areas in which the DMP conditions are different, it would be better to operate in a decentralized area structure.

Finally, when an organization is operating in a variety of countries that differ from one another in their natural culture, it must operate in a multistructure. This last structure is a federation of the three basic structures and will be described and discussed in chapter 5.

Thus, different scopes of DM correspond to different sized organizations and require different managerial structures to be able to operate efficiently and effectively, and thus to survive.

3.2.3 Rates of Expansion in SDM in Different Activity Areas (and Corresponding Periods of Stability in Managerial Structure)

We have already seen (section 2.1) that the rates of expansion in different business areas vary. Areas such as electronics, aeronautics, and the petrochemical industries grow at a much faster pace then the government and banking areas, for example (see Figure 2.2). The rate of the SDM expansion is reflected in the comparative length of each stage of expansion in the organization. Consequently, an organization in a business area with a slow rate of SDM expansion will operate for longer in one managerial structure than will an organization with a much faster rate of SDM expansion. Thus, for example, it may be 20 years before a banking organization reaches the SDM which requires its decentralization into a product/service line or an area structure. On the other hand, an electronics organization may only operate for 5 years in a functional structure before being obliged to decentralize. The banking organization would thus have longer periods of stability of its structure. Within these periods the managers holding the key positions, who have replaced the formal-type managers of the previous stage in the structural development, can establish themselves and help expand the organizational SDM gradually.

Organizations operating in fast-growing business areas cannot afford the same relaxed pace of change. Following a formalization period, in which a new managerial structure has been introduced, the new managers must be able to integrate themselves into their new jobs within the new structure, while at the same time monitoring the ever-changing SDM expansion. The fast pace of growth of the total field does not allow the gradual entrance of new managers into key positions at the beginning of each formalization period. Growth and expansion must continue with the gradual adjustment of managers to their new roles, and of subordinates to their new superiors. Most persons have a natural resistance to change, especially to frequent change. We need a certain length of time to adjust to new situations. This resistance comes into conflict with the ever-growing pace of development and expansion of organizations in the electronics, aeronautics, and other such areas of business and industry. The fast expansion in SDM demands frequent structural changes and, thus, very short periods of formalization and stability in the structure. Frequent changes in managerial personnel become necessary. This chain of events is very difficult for an organization to cope with. We have shown that, in order to ensure the continuity of growth of an organization so that it will be able to survive in its field, its managerial structure must be adjusted to its ever-expanding SDM. The difficulties in carrying out the necessary structural changes are, therefore, inevitable. They must be met if the organization is to ensure its continued growth and survival.

3.3 THE TWO PARAMETERS OF MANAGERIAL STRUCTURE

This section summarizes the discussion of the three basic forms of managerial structures: the entrepreneurial structure and the functional and decentralized structural alternatives. It defines these structures along two parameters: the degree of autonomy and the degree of formal clarity. This analysis brings us to a fourth form of managerial structure, which is presented in the second subsection.

Subsection 3.3.3 is devoted to a presentation of the informalogram—a specific tool for measuring the structure within which an organization operates. The structure which is 'visually apparent', or that which is declared by one or more managers in the organization to be the current managerial structure, is not necessarily the structure by which the organization is actually run. The informalogram is an integrative measure for establishing the actual structure within the management.

Subsection 3.3.4 presents examples for the use of the informalogram.

3.3.1 The Parameters of Autonomy and of Formal Clarity

The three basic forms of managerial structure were discussed at the beginning of this chapter: the entrepreneurial structure, the functional structure, and the area and product/service lines decentralized structures. These structures can be defined and measured along two dimensions, or parameters. The first parameter is the degree of autonomy allowed to the subordinates of the head of the organization, the CE.

Thus, the subordinates of the entrepreneur perceive themselves to be autonomous for up to one day only, the subordinates of a CE of a functional structure are usually independent up to a week, and the subordinates of a CE of a product/service line or area structure could be completely autonomous for one month, three months, six months, or one year. The degree of autonomy parameter, therefore, measures managerial structure all the way from a very centralized structure to a very decentralized one. Thus, the amount of decentralization of subordinate units is not measured in the number of functions they control, but rather in the length of time that they control all the functions which are essential for their autonomous operation.

The second parameter of managerial structure is that of the degree of formal clarity, or the degree of formalization. Its scale stretches from the very informal structure to the very formal one. Within an informal structure, in its extreme, sometimes the only formally clear thing is the identity of the CE. On the other hand, the formal relationships and procedures, the communication lines and associations among the managers within a very formal structure, are well defined and quite clear-cut.

Each of the managerial structures can be seen as either formal or informal and also either centralized or decentralized. Table 3.1 shows a two-by-two matrix within which the three basic structures fall. The entrepreneurial structure is thus a basically informal and centralized structure. The degree of informality and centralization obviously varies from one entrepreneurial organization to another.

The functional structure is formal but still centralized in nature, and the area and product/service line structures are both formal and decentralized. The organization, therefore, starts its life as a centralized and informal organization, and moves as its DMP expands to a formal and centralized structure. Only at a later stage in its growth does it move on to a decentralized structure, but still a formal one. Only small organizations can afford an informal structure. Large ones can be run and controlled only within a formal structure.

The direction of development of the organizational structures from a small, informal, centralized one to a large, formal, decentralized one is indicated by arrows in the matrix in Table 3.1. This matrix presents the extreme cases of the two parameters of autonomy and formal clarity. Clearly, varying degrees of autonomy and of formal clarity would produce different types of managerial structure. The basic forms of structure, though, remain the informally centralized (entrepreneurial), the formally centralized (functional), the formally decentralized

Table 3.1 The basic structures according to the two parameters of managerial structure

| Degree of autonomy | Degree of formal clarity (formalization) | |
	Informal	Formal
Centralized	Entrepreneurial structure →	Functional structure
Decentralized	Anarchic structure	↓ Product/service ↓ Area structure

(product/service or area), and the informally decentralized. This last variation is discussed in the following subsection.

3.3.2 The Missing Basic Managerial Structure in the Matrix of Autonomy and Formal Clarity

The fourth basic structural option in the autonomy and formal clarity matrix is that which is characterized as informal and decentralized. In order to visualize its form let us start with the informal centralized, or entrepreneurial, structure. The interrelationships and communications among its managers are based on no rules whatsoever, and resemble a relationship between a coach and his football team (see subsection 3.1.2).

In order to turn this structure into a decentralized yet still informal one, we will now omit the presence of the CE, the entrepreneur, as shown in Figure 3.10. The result is the anarchic structure. There is no leader heading it. Its members act on their own behalf and do as they wish. This structure is dysfunctional. It has not, therefore, been included in the three basic structures through which organizations may pass when their scopes of DM grow.

Every organization has its periods of anarchy. They may happen at times of change of the head of the organization, or during a long absence due to an accident or illness, for example. During these times, until the CE returns to function as the head, or until the new CE learns the job to the extent that he can assume the responsibility of heading the organization, the managers who are his direct subordinates must carry on their work without his leadership.

Such incidents in the life of an organization are equivalent, in fact, to periods of anarchy. The organization has no head to guide, coordinate, and centralize its activities.

Anarchic phases in organizations occur in entrepreneurial and in functional structures. These structures are centralized. Within them subordinates of the CE

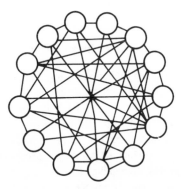

Figure 3.10   The derivation of the anarchic structure (informal, decentralized) from the entrepreneurial one

78

are, therefore, autonomous for up to one week only. The lack of a central management for a period of a few weeks may possibly cause anarchic effects. But a month's absence of the CE in a decentralized organization, even a small one, is not critical. His subordinates are completely autonomous for at least one month. The CE's absence cannot have a significant effect on their activities.

Decentralized organizations are, therefore, less likely to find themselves in a situation of anarchy. Any new CE or a replacement can usually take over the reins within a month. In centralized organizations, though, short periods of anarchy do occur whenever the head of the organization gives his place to another. These periods may be dangerous to the members of the organization as well as economically dangerous. They should, therefore, be made as short as possible.

Some organizations, though, function in an anarchic structure for long periods of time, sometimes for months or even years. One example of such an organization is the Students for a Democratic Society (SDS). This organization fought for some time in the USA against the Vietnamese War. How did it work? A member of the organization would organize an activity, e.g. a demonstration in Washington, with a few other members from all over the USA. A day and a time would be set. The information would be communicated to the other members of the organization through an informal network, i.e. it would be passed on from one member to another. Surprisingly, on the day of the demonstration, hundreds of thousands of people would arrive in Washington. The results were always extremely effective, despite the informal fashion in which such affairs were organized.

An anarchic organization, though, is not a typical form of structure. It lacks all the typical qualities of an organization which were discussed above. The main organizational attribute lacking in an anarchic organization is its internal drive to continue its existence, to survive. There is no central figure within it to say: Now we shall stop demonstrating and start another activity. After its goal is achieved, the anarchic organization ceases to exist.

3.3.3 The Informalogram—a Tool for Establishing Managerial Structure

One of the most important factors when studying an organization is the prevailing managerial structure within it. Scientists, students, and particularly researchers and consultants, are in need of a tool to help them describe and diagnose managerial structures. The informalogram is a comparatively simple tool developed by the first author over years of research and consulting.

The methodology of the informalogram is based on the responses of the managers of the organizations themselves to two simple requests: 'List the names of the people with whom you generally work most closely, regardless of their position in the organization.' (After the respondent has given a list of names:) 'Describe their job in a word or two.'

The responses of all the managers of the organization provides the informal relationship structure prevailing within the organization, i.e. the communication patterns that, in fact, exist there. The informal structure differs, in the majority of cases, from the formal structure within a particular organization. The informal structure is the *actual* structure, as perceived by its participants. It includes relationships which constitute part of the formal structure. In most cases it may be said that the clearer the formal structure, the weaker the informal activity, and vice versa.[4]

The informalogram question measures the informal activity within an organization. The responses to these requests form the basis for arriving at the informal structure of the organization, as compared to the organizational chart.

The informalogram methodology attempts to establish the managerial structure of the organization in terms of the two parameters discussed in the previous section—the degree of clarity of the formal structure and the degree of autonomy of the subordinate units to the CE. The informalogram tool indicates the basic structure within which an organization is operating at a particular point in time. The variety of modifications and combinations of the basic structures are also measurable by this tool.

The informalogram is a sociometric research technique, as it measures the interpersonal relationships based on the perceptions of the managers involved. The responses of all the respondents are matched in order to provide the mutually perceived working relationships (MPWR), i.e. the relationships between managers who mention each other in response to the above-mentioned requests. It is on the basis of these MPWR that the managerial structure is established by way of the informalogram.

Let us turn to the sociometric measurements of the two structural parameters of formal clarity and autonomy, which form the basis of the informalogram technique. Before describing the measurements, the two structural parameters should be operationally defined.

Formal clarity The formal relationships are the required relationships for the effective operation of the organization for achieving its explicit objectives. The formalization is the expression of the clarity of vertical and horizontal hierarchical relationships in which the perceived position of every person is in terms of reporting to one another; this makes formalization a simple, measurable parameter. The relation between the formal clarity and the informal activity in terms of the perceived working relationships, regardless of hierarchy, could be expressed as follows: the higher the degree of formal clarity, the lower the informal activity, and vice versa.

Autonomy The degree of autonomy is conceptually and actually expressed by the length of time during which the heads of the units could be or are held fully accountable for their activities; in other words, the length of time during which they have both the responsibility and the full authority and means for independently performing their activities, i.e. independently of other main units, be they so-called 'line', 'staff', 'functional', or any other type of units.

The above definitions of the structural characteristics of management enable us to translate them into measurable parameters. There are four 'structural measurements' which have been used in order to measure these two parameters of formal clarity and autonomy. These four 'structural measurements' are defined as follows:

Informal activity The average number per person of mutually perceived working relationships (MPWR). As we have already indicated, the informal activity is in inverse proportion to the formal clarity.

Formal–informal coverage The percentage of all the organization chart's required relationships which are covered by the informalogram MPWR. The organization chart's required relationships include both the vertical 'subordinate–superior' relationships (including specified relationships with additional superiors) and the horizontal relationships between peers (i.e. all the subordinates reporting to the same direct superior).

This is an additional measurement for the degrees of formalization and should be used as a complementary measurement to the informal activity.

Individual autonomy Managerial independence from the chief executive. The managerial dependence is measured by way of the number of participants directly connected to and once removed from the CE by MPWR. This is a measurement for determining the autonomy through the degree of centralization of the management organization by the CE. It measures, to some extent, the formal clarity, too, because when penetration of the CE into the management is high, it is indicative of an entrepreneurial structure, highly *centralized* and *informal*.

Interunit independence The ratio of MPWR within units to MPWR between units. This measurement is indicative of the autonomy of the units, because a high degree of autonomy in a decentralized structure would mean that the units are self-sufficient and, therefore, they have relatively more MPWR within each unit and relatively fewer MPWR between units.

Figure 3.11 is a convenient summary table on which calculations of the four measurements can be carried out and presented.[5] The last two measurements—individual autonomy and interunit independence—could be best arrived at, however, only after drawing an informalogram chart, like the one appearing in Figure 7.4 on page 360.

These four structural measurements can give us a clear picture of the structure of any organization at a particular point in time. Table 3.2 provides the expected results of these measurements for each of the three basic managerial structures presented at the beginning of this chapter.

Thus we see, for example, that we can expect a functional managerial structure to come up with a low informal activity, a high formal–informal coverage (both scores indicate a high degree of formalization, i.e. of formal clarity) as well as an independent individual autonomy and a dependent interunit independence (both scores indicate a high degree of centralization).

3.3.4 Examples of the Use of the Informalogram[6]

In Table 3.2 the question is, what are the highs and lows, quantitatively, for the measurement of the degree of formal clarity (informal activity and formal–informal coverage) and what are the quantitative ranges for dependent and

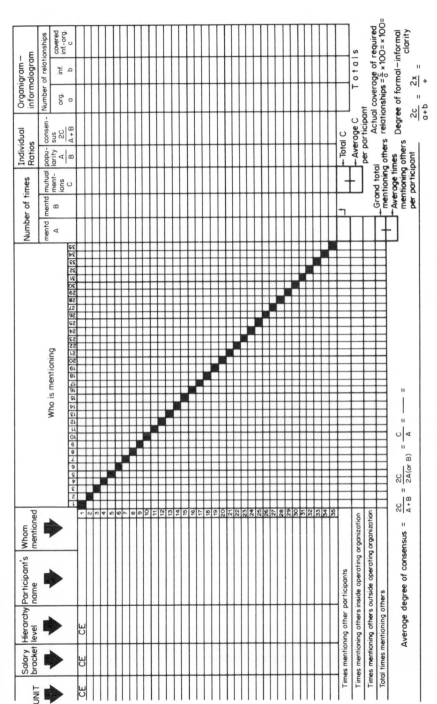

Figure 3.11 Informalogram summary table

Table 3.2 The relation between structural measurements and managerial structures

| | Structural measurements | | | |
| | Degree of formal clarity | | Degree of autonomy | |
Managerial structures	A Informal activity	B Formal– informal coverage	C Individual autonomy	D Interunit independence
Entrepreneurial	High	Low	Dependent	Highly dependent
Functional	Low	High	Independent	Dependent
Decentralized	Low	High	Very independent	Independent
Anarchic	High	Low	Completely independent	Highly independent
Multistructure	Different in relation to different main units of the managerial structure			

independent measurement of degree of autonomy (individual autonomy and interunit independence). The answers to these questions can only be arrived at empirically.

The empirical methodology for establishing the ranges of the four structural measurements is simultaneously to study an organization through action research and, sociometrically, by means of the informalogram. This enables one to establish the managerial structure on the basis of the clinical action research while, at the same time, structure is measured sociometrically by the informalogram, calculating the scores for each of the four structural measurements.

The scores of the four structural measurements for each of the managerial structures are a function of the number of participants in the study. More specifically, the scores of the first measurements for a managerial structure would depend on the size of the studied group (i.e. the total number of participants in the study), while the scores of the fourth measurement, interunit independence, are dependent on the average number of participants per unit. This means that, in order to arrive at useful dynamic dimensions for each of the four structural measurements, it would be necessary to study, sociometrically and through action research, a large number of organizations, so as to cover different ranges of numbers of participants in the studies.

Nevertheless, it seems that the sociometric and action research of 18 organizations provides us with a reasonable approximation of the ranges in each measurement. Figures 3.12 to 3.15 summarize the results of the four structural measures of the informalogram for each of the 18 organizations studied. Figures 3.12 to 3.15 present the comparisons between those results and the results of the action research carried out separately within each of the organizations. Each figure deals

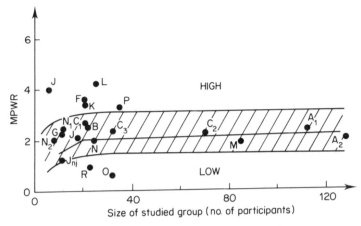

Figure 3.12   Informal activity

with the results of both structural research methodologies regarding one out of the four structural measures included in the informalogram. In each figure all 18 organizations were first plotted on the graph according to their informalogram scores on the particular structural measure discussed. The action research findings for these organizations were then checked, and the organizations were divided into those which scored high on the particular structural measure and those which scored low on that measure (according to the action research findings only). In the case of the two autonomy measures, organizations were divided between independent and dependent ones according to the action research findings. The curves appearing on each of the four graphs in Figures 3.12 to 3.15 are, in fact, the dividing lines between the high-scoring and the low-scoring organizations, or the dependent and the independent organizations, as determined by the

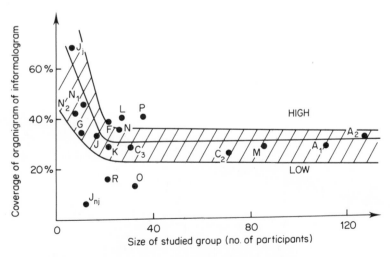

Figure 3.13   Formal–informal coverage

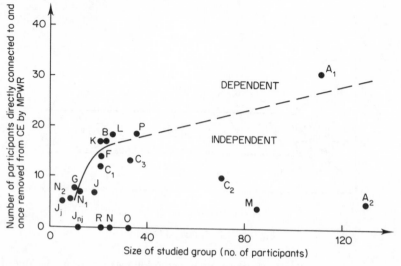

Figure 3.14 Individual autonomy

action research. Few organizations scored a result on the informalogram which was contrary to the results of the action research, e.g. a high score in informal activity as measured by the informalogram and a low classification on the same measure according to the results of the action research. These cases were dealt with one by one and checked for a possible reason for the contradiction.

If such cases repeat themselves, the particular measure in the informalogram must be looked into and corrected. In this fashion the measure of formal/informal coverage was revised and adjusted to the measure of informal activity. For several years, maladjustments were found between these two measures. It turned out that

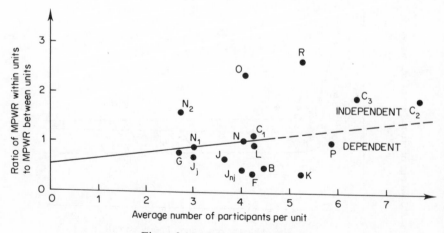

Figure 3.15 Interunit independence

only under clearly defined conditions of informal activity is the formal/informal coverage consistent with the formal activity.[7]

The research regarding the validity of the informalogram as a tool for measuring managerial structure has, as mentioned, been limited to 18 organizations. Any additional organizations that will be studied in the future using both the informalogram and the action research techniques will contribute to the validation of the informalogram.

Let us look into the actual process by which the managerial structure of an organization can be diagnosed with the aid of the already existing curves. We calculate the scores of the particular organization on each one of the four structural measures of the informalogram (on an informalogram summary table as per Figure 3.11). We check their location on the graphs (Figures 3.12 to 3.15) in comparison to that on the curve. We can now determine the diagnostic results for that organization, i.e. whether it is high/low and dependent/independent on each one of the four measures. We then turn to Table 3.2 and compare the diagnostic results for our organization with the data in the table, to determine its managerial structure. If, for example, the results show that the organization under study scores low on informal activity and high on formal/informal coverage, that it is independent on the measure of individual autonomy and dependent according to the measures of interunit independence, we can easily determine, with the aid of Table 3.2, that this organization is run in a functional structure.

Sometimes the overall combination of results more or less fits into one of the basic structures, but the result on one of the measures contradicts that which is expected according to this structure. In such cases one must return to the full data collected in the action research to find whether the actual state of affairs existing in the organization can explain the contradiction. Table 3.3 provides such an analysis for 18 organizations discussed in this section. It shows the diagnostic results of each one of these organizations on the four structural measurements, and it seeks to explain possible contradictions that arise between the combinations of the four results and the data in Figure 3.11, on the basis of the reality in the field, as reflected in the action research.

All in all, the informalogram is a good tool for measuring organizational structures. On the basis of the research in 18 organizations on which it was tested,[8] this tool seems to make possible the determination of the managerial structure within which the organization functions, by a method which is both simple and rapid. The informalogram is the only tool known to us that makes possible the determination of any managerial structure. It was not possible before to conclude from the use of any existing tools that, for example, the managerial structure of an organization is entrepreneurial or anarchic,[9]

3.4 SUMMARY

Chapter 3 discusses basic issues concerning managerial structure. The organization, as its SDM expands, must alter its structure to be able to cope effectively with its environment, and thus to ensure its survival.

Table 3.3   Summary of informalogram structural measuremer

Details about studied organization

			Code	A_1	A_2	B	C	D	E	F
			Year	1957	1959	1968	1969	1961	1966	19(
			Country	USA	USA	Israel	Israel	Israel	Israel	Isra
			Industry	+	+	+	+			
	Type of organiz-ation	Ser-vice	Profit							+
			Non-profit					+	+	
Structural measurement			Participants	111	127	22	21	682	863	21
Measuring formalization			Informal activity[a]	2.4	2.0	2.5	2.7	0.8	0.65	3.5
			Formal–informal coverage[b]	28%	31%	NA	NA	NA	NA	38%
Measuring autonomy			Individual autonomy[c]	71% 31	95% 5	18% 17	38% 12	98% 10	99% 4	28% 14
			Interunit independence[d]	NA	NA	0.50	1.15	4.65	39.14	0.4

Notes:
NA = not available.
[a] Measured by means of average MPWR per participant.
[b] Measured by means of coverage of organigram formal relationships by informalogram MPWR.

When an organization is founded, and throughout its first years, while it is struggling to establish itself, it can be run by one form of management only—the entrepreneurial structure. The informal and centralized nature of this structure gives it the necessary flexibility and enables it to cope adequately with the new, unpredictable environmental demands.

As the organization grows and its DMP expands, it can no longer be controlled on an informal basis. The SDM is reflected in the number of managers of the organization. As the managers become more numerous, the head of the organization can no longer run his business in his typical entrepreneurial fashion. He can no longer rely on his memory regarding the growing number of environmental issues to be dealt with by the large number of managers, all responsible directly to him. Therefore, as an organization reaches the size of about 100 managers, it must alter its managerial structure to a formalized structure. The only structure which is formal but still centralized is the functional structure. Within it, roles may

organizations studied by action research

ils about studied organization

	J	K	L	M	O	P	C₂	N	R	C₃
9	1971	1972	1972	1971	1969	1972	1975	1979	1979	1980
ce	Japan	Israel	Israel	UK	Israel	Israel	Israel	Israel	Israel	Israel
						+	+			+
	+	+	+							
				+	+			+	+	
	18	21	25	84	32	35	69	24	21	32
	2.1	3.4	4.2	1.9	0.6	3.3	2.2	2.0	1.05	2.4
	31%	29%	40%	23%	13%	40%	25%	36%	17.5%	33%
	55%	14%	32%	94%	97%	45%	82%	96%	95%	62.5%
	7	17	18	4	0	18	10	0	0	12
	0.68	0.38	0.93	6.90	2.33	1.00	1.85	1.00	2.7	1.92

pper line: percentage of those participants not in direct contact with or once removed from CE, through PWR.
wer line: number of participants in direct contact with and once removed from CE through MPWR.
easured by means of the ratio between MPWR within units to MPWR between units.

be precisely defined and procedures formalized so as not to burden the memory of the managers within and without the focal organization.

The functional structure is suitable for organizations in which the number of managers ranges from about 100 to about 1000. Beyond this range the formal, centralized structure again becomes inadequate. Procedures hamper the effectiveness and efficiency of the system. The growing number of hierarchical levels slows down procedures and sabotages the ability of the organization to respond to its external demands. The various negative aspects of a bureaucracy increasingly disturb the smooth operation of the organization. A new form of structure is now necessary to cope with the growing SDM. The solution is to decentralize the structure.

The functional structure can be decentralized according to product or service lines or according to area. Whereas the autonomy of the direct subordinates of the chief executive officer within a functional structure is limited to one week only, these managers within a decentralized structure are completely autonomous for longer periods of time. The decentralized periods may be one month, three months, six months, or one year, depending on the size of the organization.

The transfer from one structure to another requires managerial time and a certain rigidity in the implementation of the new structure. The period of formalization can last from several months to a few years. During this process, it is difficult for the organization to continue growing. It has to retain more or less the same SDM in order to formalize the new structure. Only when it has been established can the organization continue to grow. In order to enable growth to take place, there should be a period of stability in the rigidity of the structure. It should become less formalized.

The number of managers within an organization is only a crude indicator of its SDM. It is very important, though, to assess this factor more accurately, in order to determine the appropriate managerial structure needed for an organization at a particular point in time. The SDM is affected by the quantities of the organizational number of employees, total financial assets, sales turnover, etc., and also by the complexities of the items handled—different types of employees, the variety of the capital structure, the product/service diversity, etc. It has been established that the managerial structure is primarily related to three main aspects of organizational strategy: the level of the technology, the product/service lines diversity, and the geographical dispersal.

When an organization is created, it usually has one product/service line and operates in just one area. As long as its level of technology is relatively low, it can be managed in an entrepreneurial structure. This structure ceases to be suitable when the level of the technology is high. A one-product, one-area organization, operating at an advanced level of technology, should be managed preferably in a functional structure. When the organization diversifies into two or more distinctly different product/service lines, the suitable managerial structure would be a decentralized product/service line one. When, however, the organization moves to one or more additional areas in which the DMP conditions are significantly different from one another, a decentralized area structure is preferable.

Organizations operating in different business areas grow and expand at different rates (chapter 2). Therefore an organization in a business area with a slow rate of DMP expansion operates for longer in the same managerial structure than an organization in a business area with a faster rate of DMP expansion. The rapidly expanding organizations, operating in fields such as electronics and aeronautics, may thus face only short periods of stability and formalization, in order to keep up with the pace of development and growth in their field. They must cope, therefore, with the difficulties arising from the frequent organizational changes and the replacement of managers in key positions.

The three basic structures presented in this chapter may be categorized along two parameters: the degree of autonomy of the subordinates of the CE, and the degree of formal clarity, i.e. the extent to which the intermanagerial relationships and the procedures by which the work is organized are defined and made clear. The entrepreneurial structure is basically an informal and centralized structure, in which the CE's subordinates are autonomous up to one day only. The functional structure is formally centralized, permitting the CE's subordinates autonomy up to one week. The product/service line and area structures are formally decentralized, within which the CE's subordinates are autonomous for at least one month.

A fourth structure is possible from the combination of the two parameters of autonomy and formal clarity. It is referred to as the anarchic structure. It occurs in centralized structures during changes from one CE to another, or transfers from one structure to another. If, however, it lasts too long, it could lead to chaos and/or stagnation. There are organizations which are run continuously in an anarchic structure. Their main characteristic is a short lifespan.

The structure within which an organization operates is a measurable factor. The informalogram is a research tool developed to measure it. It establishes the managerial structure by comparing the informal with the formal relationship structure. The former is operationally defined as composed of the mutually perceived working relationships (MPWR). The formal relationship structure is based on a detailed organigram (organizational chart), or only on the divisions of managers into formal units.

The degree of autonomy is then calculated on the basis of two indices, both measured in terms of the MPWR: the extent of the CE's penetration into the management structure, and the degree of independence of subordinate units from each other and from the CE's unit. The degree of formal clarity is also established on the basis of two indices: the amount of informal activity and the degree of overlap between the informal and the formal relationship structures.

The use of the informalogram in 18 organizations over the past 25 years and the comparison of its results with those of clinical research indicate the effectiveness of this research tool. The technique of the informalogram is a simple one. Both the effectiveness and the simplicity of this research tool make it a very attractive one for all organizational research and consultancy purposes.

Three organizational examples illustrate the specific managerial structures in which they operate, and demonstrate their need to move to other structures, because their SDM has outgrown their existing structures. These are the main points to be learned from the three examples.

The Army Logistics Organization

A military ordnance organization, operating within a formally centralized structure, finds itself unable to perform its duties properly as part of an army which has developed both in scope and technologically. It is evident that this organization must be able to operate within a more decentralized structure, so that it will be able to render its services to the fighting forces during war effectively.

The Devon Corporation

This is a growing organization which struggled over a period of 15 years (from 1957 to 1972) to suit its managerial structure to its SDM. During the preceding

30 years it had been growing in a spectacular way—in terms of its product lines, integrating back from consumer products to the intermediary and basic raw materials, as well as in its technological/scientific context. All this growth had been performed in an entrepreneurial structure. However, in spite of the efforts of its entrepreneurial manager-owner to change its structure and adapt it to the SDM, he could not change himself. During two periods between 1957 and 1972, it seemed that it would be possible to grant the organization a suitable structure, but each time the entrepreneur brought back the structure to his own style.

ITT

This large conglomerate corporation had seemed to be the prototype of international success. It had two of the three characteristics which make a multinational, namely a wide geographical dispersal and a supracultural attitude on the part of its steering management (chapter 6 deals in detail with multinationals with these aspects).

ITT has been managed, however, by Harold Geneen, as president and chairman, in a one-month decentralized structure. This structure is unsuitable for a post-Second World War SDM, which encompasses operations in such diverse countries as, for example, Chile, Israel, South Africa, the UK, and the USA. Unless it adopts a multistructure (a federated structure as described in chapter 5) it is predicted that it will face ever-growing problems threatening its Total Organizational System.

NOTES

1 When we use the term 'organizational *size*' in this book, we mean those quantitative and qualitative elements of the organization which have an effect on its *managerial structure*. These concepts are explored in more depth in chapter 4.
2 Joan Woodward (1958) used her own classification of the level of technology, classifying organizations according to what she called the 'production system', into one of three categories: unit (and small batch) production, mass (and large batch) production, or process (automated) production. John Stopford (1968) distinguished between product/service lines by using the American Standard Industrial Classification (SIC). He identified the different product/service lines on the basis of the two-digit classification of SIC, the maximum possible number of such lines being 100 (from 00 to 99). The one-digit SIC classification divides the occupations of organizations into 10 areas (from 0 to 9). A more detailed division than that used by Stopford for his multinational corporation research (described in an organizational example at the end of Chapter 6) could be a three-digit SIC classification with a maximum possible number of 1000 product/service lines (from 000 to 999). Stopford distinguished between geographical areas by identifying them along country borders. Consequently, the maximum possible number of areas in which a multinational corporation in Stopford's research could operate, in manufacturing and/or in marketing, is equal to the number of countries in the world.
3 Stopford (1968) found that establishing what we refer to in this book as the SDM, could be done on the basis of the organizational product/service line diversity and the geographical diversity only, without using the third measure of technological level. This was correct in his research of multinational corporations, in which the

product/service line diversity and geographical diversity are prevalent. This is not necessarily so in other cases. The great majority of organizations in Joan Woodward's research (1958) of the South Essex industry (organizational example at the end of Chapter 4) had only one product/service line in a SIC two-digit classification (see above, note 2), and of course they were all in one country—Britain.

Stopford (1968) devised simple measurements for both the product/service diversity and the geographical diversity, as follows:

$$\text{Degree of product/service diversity} = \frac{\text{Sales turnover of all product/service lines except for the country with the largest sales turnover}}{\text{Total sales turnover}}$$

$$\text{Degree of geographical diversity} = \frac{\text{Sales turnover in all countries, except for the country with the largest sales turnover}}{\text{Total sales turnover}}$$

4 This hypothesis has been generally supported by the findings in the studies reported later in this chapter. It is described in detail in Weinshall's first study (Weinshall, 1960, Appendix B, pp. 9–12).
5 A detailed description of all the stages in calculating the four measurements, from the individual response to the informalogram question, can be obtained from the authors.
6 This subsection is based on various sources, but primarily on Weinshall (1973). The details of the additional informalogram and action research studies since 1973 were drawn from the four organizational research reports listed in Table 3.4. (We are unable to disclose the names of the organizations.)

Table 3.4 Organizational research reports used as basis of study

Year	Type of organization	Study performed and research report prepared under auspices of	Principal researchers
1975	Manufacturers of chemicals	Weinshall-Raveh Ltd	T. D. Weinshall
1979	Military operational services	Weinshall-Raveh Ltd	T. D. Weinshall and Y.-A. Raveh
1980	Semi-governmental organization (helping to absorb new immigrants by forming them into R&D teams)	Israel Institute of Business Research Faculty of Management. The Leon Recanati School of Business Administration, Tel Aviv University	T. D. Weinshall and Y.-A. Raveh
1980	The top management of an average sized chemical conglomerate (about ten different product lines)	Weinshall-Raveh Ltd	T. D. Weinshall and Y.-A. Raveh

7   The two limits around the dividing line of the informal activity chart (see Figure 3.12) indicate that only in those organizations where the average numbers of MPWR per participant are somewhat higher or somewhat lower than those of the dividing line, will the informal/formal coverage (see Figure 3.13) indicate the degree of formalization and behave according to the rule that 'the higher the degree of formalization, the lower the informality, and vice versa'. Thus, only the organizations which are within the two areas around the dividing lines (curves) in Figures 3.12 and 3.13 behave according to this rule (Weinshall, 1960). The reasons why organizations beyond these limits behave contrary to the rule are:

(a)   When the informal activity is much higher, all the formally required relationships may be covered by MPWR, i.e. the informal/formal coverage would be higher.

(b)   When the informal activity is much lower, the fact that the MPWR are not covering the formally required relationships is not indicative of the degree of formalization, but rather the degree of formalization is so high that the informal activity is brought down to a minimum.

On the whole, the informal/formal coverage measurement is the least important of the four measurements of the informalogram. The fact, therefore, that some of the studied organizations do not have it, is not crucial for establishing their managerial structure.

The original research, in which the relationship between informal activity and degree of formalization was found, was carried out in the organization marked A in Figures 3.12 to 3.15 (A_1 for the 1957 study and A_2 for the 1959 study).

8   We have had the chance to use the informalogram in scores of other organizations over the years, but without accompanying thorough action research studies. The informalogram was used either as part of other research studies, e.g. in the Israeli and French organizations of the Heller and Wilpert (1981) studies, or in organizational studies carried out by students of the authors in Britain, France, and Israel. We have included in the charts of the four measurements only those organizations in which we ourselves have carried out both the informalogram and the action research.

9   Authors of some of the best-known organizational studies, whose contributions to managerial and organizational theory have been considerable, have based their diagnosis of managerial structures on the organizational charts of managerial relationships. Such organizational charts could, at best, be considered as approximations of formal managerial structures. However, organizations with informal structures, like the entrepreneurial and anarchic structures, usually do not have organizational charts. If they do, they are insignificant and irrelevant to their structures, because they are, in fact, ignored by the members of the informal structure. This is why many researchers have not studied informally structured organizations, or have removed them from their studied samples. Examples are studies by the Ann Arbor social psychologists (e.g. Katz and Kahn, 1966), by Joan Woodward (1965), by Alfred Chandler (1962) mentor of the structure and strategy group, and by Ray Vernon's (1971) multinational corporations group; also by John Stopford (1968), who is a product of these two latter HBS groups.

SELECTED BIBLIOGRAPHICAL SOURCES

Chandler, A. D., Jr., 1962. *Strategy and Structure*, MIT Press, Cambridge Mass.

Heller, F. A., and Wilpert, B. with others, 1981. *Competence and Power in Managerial Decision Making, A Study of Senior Levels of Organization in Eight Countries*, Wiley, Chichester.

Katz, D. and Kahn, R. L., 1966. *The Social Psychology of Organizations*, Wiley, New York.

Stopford, J., 1968. 'Growth and organizational change in the multinational firm', unpublished doctoral dissertation, Harvard University.

Vernon, R., 1971. *Sovereignty at Bay: The Multinational Spread of U.S. Enterprises*, Longman, London.

Weinshall, T. D., 1960. 'The effects of management changes on the organizational relationships and attitudes', unpublished doctoral dissertation, Harvard University.

Weinshall, T. D., 1973. 'The informalogram as an indicator of managerial structure', The Leon Recanati Graduate School of Business Administration, Tel Aviv University, working paper number 167/73.

Woodward, J., 1958. *Management and Technology*, HMSO, London.

Woodward, J., 1965. *Industrial Organizational Theory and Practice*, Oxford University Press.

Chapter 4

Fundamentals of TOS Dynamics

The awareness that organizations are developing, changing, growing, and ageing systems, not completely unlike the human beings comprising them, has matured ever since the 1960s. As in the case of many other things, once this awareness was there, the ideas about *how* organizations develop, change, grow, and age took several different directions.[1] Let us consider several of these views of the dynamics of organizations which evolved to become what we nowadays refer to as 'contingency systems'.[2] We shall follow the development of some of the different schools of research and thoughts about contingency systems, according to the chronological appearance of their first publications, with our own approach appearing at the end.[3]

The one who may well be considered as the first of the contingency pioneers is Chester Barnard. He is more versatile than all his followers in the 1950s and 1960s whom we shall presently cite. He concerned himself with all the systems of what we refer to in this book as the Total Organizational System. Conceptualizations and principles which he developed were based on his own managerial experience rather than on research.[4]

A later contributor to organizational contingency theory was Herbert Simon, whose first book was a well-presented interpretation of, though somewhat divergent from Barnard's.[5] However, as time went on, Simon developed more and more into a 'modelistic' interpreter of contingency systems. He could therefore be considered as the pioneer of the 'modelistic' approach to organizational contingency theory.[6]

Before moving to the main trends which appeared during the 1960s, let us mention another school of research and thought, from which the first publication also appeared, like Chester Barnard's, around 1940. This is what we presently refer to as the Human Relations School. The main contributors to this school were the Hawthorne Research group led by Elton Mayo and Fritz Roethlisberger.[7] Most of the work in organizational behaviour since 1940 can be traced back to the findings of this group. There were, however, two additional groups, who followed the Hawthorne group in contributing to the Human Relations School. The first could be referred to as the Ann Arbor Michigan group, and the second as the Tavistock Institute London group.[8]

Before describing our own Total Organizational System (TOS), let us survey the main original contributors to contingency theory in the 1950s and 1960s, according to the dates of their first publications.

Joan Woodward's (1958) research in the South Essex Industry was carried out in the early 1950s. It is described in our organizational example at the end of this chapter. Her main contribution was in finding out the connection between technology and organization.[9]

Tom Burns, (1961) like Woodward, is a sociologist and consequently looked at the Total Organization. He studied the electronics industry in his native Scotland in the late 1950s. His main contribution lies in relating periods of activity, on the one hand, and absence in the rate of activity with growth, on the other hand. He related the presence or absence of innovations to the managerial structures in which the organization was run at every stage. In growth and innovation he found that managements functioned in what he called an 'organismic' structure, while in bureaucracies and in periods of stagnation, organizations were run in a so-called 'mechanistic' structure.[10]

Alfred Chandler (1962) is a business historian. His original research was a historical analysis of the organizational development of four large US corporations which Chandler considered to be the pioneers of a decentralized managerial structure; namely Du Pont, General Motors, Sears, Roebuck & Company, and Standard Oil of New Jersey (which eventually became EXXON). He found in his research that as the organizations grew quantitatively and qualitatively, they changed their structures and their chief executives, until all four of them reached what he considered to be decentralization.[11]

Derek Pugh (1963) led a group of researchers working at the time at the University of Aston, Birmingham, England, who came to be known as the Aston group. They achieved the nearest thing to a systematic study of a large number of organizations as total systems. The basis for Pugh's conclusions was a random sample of 46 organizations in 1963–1964. Their research methodology has been duplicated many times since then in various countries. One of their main findings is that the degree of formalization is independent of the degree of centralization or decentralization.[12] Many of the Aston findings confirm the hypotheses of the TOS described in the following paragraphs.

As the above four contingency research trends developed, their findings predominantly supported the TOS hypothesis. We shall refer to some of these findings in the following section.

The first publications related to contingency theory of the contributors, described in the preceding paragraph, appeared within five years of each other (1958–1963). Interestingly enough, three of these writers are British: Woodward, Burns, and Pugh.

Our own Total Organizational System, which likewise drew directly on Chester Barnard and the Hawthorne research, started from the doctoral research performed by the first author within the same period of time (1959–1960).[13] The TOS includes the main systems which affect the contingency of the organization over time. In the present chapter we shall discuss the main aspects of the dynamics of the TOS, namely the movement of the organization from one contingency point to another. This is the first of three chapters to explore the dynamics of the TOS over time. This and the following chapters are based on the description, information, and analysis of the six principal systems presented in chapters 1–3, as illustrated in Table 4.1. Chapters 1–3 have barely touched upon the two principal components of the management main system. Chapters 4–6 deal with more detailed aspects of the managerial characteristics and structure systems. Chapters 5 and 6 focus mainly on the principal systems shown in Table 4.2.

The present chapter deals with the contingency relations between the two main systems—the decision-making and the management systems—including four of the factors which accompany the growth of organizations and the dynamics of the relation between decision-making and management systems. The first factor (subsection 4.1.1) is concerned with the number of managers, which increases from one stage of growth to another (i.e. from one contingency position to another). The second factor (subsection 4.1.2) represents the continuous expansion in the organizational strategy which creates increased competition and draws pressures from the immediate and wider environments.

The third factor (subsection 4.1.3) deals with two organizational characteristics which impose constraints on the TOS, mainly on its managerial structure: the degree of involvement of customers in the TOS, and the national culture of the organization. Thus, for example, if the customers of a travel agency are involved in the organizational decision making, or the organization is operating in a country in which the environmental socio-cultural system is very informal, one could expect to operate in an informally centralized structure in order to cope with the constraints.

The fourth factor, managerial attitudes (subsection 4.1.4), is like a thermometer of organizational life and survival, and constitutes a sort of a cybernetics feedback factor.

Section 4.2 describes the dynamics of the TOS, as the organization moves from

Table 4.1 Six principal systems presented in chapters 1–3

Chapter	Section	Principal organizational system	Main organizational system
1	Whole chapter	Immediate environment	
2	2.2	Wider environment	Decision-making system
	2.1, 2.3	Organizational strategy	
3	3.2	Scope of decision making	
	3.1, 3.3	Managerial structure	Management system
	3.2	Managerial characteristics	

Table 4.2 Principal systems presented in chapters 5—6

Chapter	Section	Subjects discussed	Relating to principal systems
5	5.1	Managerial leadership and followership characteristics	
	5.2	The major effect of managerial characteristics and inter-organizational mobility	Managerial characteristics
	5.3	The constraints of managerial behaviour in the hierarchy, when adapting managerial structure to SDM	
	5.4	The 'multistructure'—a federated rather than a uniform structure	Managerial structure
			Different principal systems
6	6.1	Wider environment in which business and other types of organizations operate	Wider environment
	6.2	What are multinational corporations?	All six principal systems
	6.3	Universal consequences of the inevitable development of multinationals	Immediate and wider environments, organizational strategy, and SDM

one structure to another. The contingency conditions in moving from an entrepreneurial to a functional structure, from functional to product line structure, and from product line to multistructure, are described.

4.1 FACTORS IN ORGANIZATIONAL DYNAMICS

Each analysis of the movement of organizations from one TOS stage to another (i.e. from entrepreneurial to functional, to product/service line structure, and to multistructure) is divided into *structural* reasons and *contextual* reasons.

4.1.1 Increase in the Number of Managers

On the whole, the larger the size of the organization in terms of its SDM, the larger the number of managers necessary in it. Managerial role and responsibility call for continued cooperation with the integral decision-making factors, i.e. the human factors without whose cooperation the organization cannot survive. Thus a foreman is a manager because he ensures the continued cooperation of a group of workers; a salesman is a manager because of his customers' cooperation with the organization. Similarly, a buyer ensures the cooperation of his suppliers and a person in charge of contacts with government makes sure that the government intervention is not detrimental to the organization. According to the same definitions, the reason the chief executive is a manager is that he ensures the continued cooperation with the organization of those managers who report to him, and because without his leadership of the whole organization, it cannot survive.[14]

Thus, theoretically, if we divide the total organizational SDM by the average share of SDM expected from every manager, we should arrive at the number of managers necessary to take care of the total SDM. This theoretical calculation is dependent, however, on two conditions which are rarely realized:

(a) The managerial behaviour must be in line with the required needs of the SDM, whether the managerial characteristics are in line with the managerial structure or not. Otherwise additional managers would have to be hired in order to account for the disparities between the SDM and the managerial structure. Such additional managers usually serve in staff functions fulfilling liaison and coordinating roles, which would have been redundant had the structure fitted the SDM.

(b) The managers perform optimally, i.e. the average SDM per manager is such that by multiplying it by the number of managers we arrive at the total organizational SDM. This is an unrealistic assumption because managers with characteristics unsuitable to the managerial structure perform their roles with less motivation, efficiency, effectiveness, and satisfaction than would managers with characteristics suitable to the managerial structure. We can assume that, as a result of the TOS dynamics, the number of managers with characteristics unsuitable to their roles is larger than the number of those with suitable characteristics. Furthermore, even those managers who possess the necessary characteristics do not always operate at the same optimal rate of performance, effectiveness, and efficiency. There are those who claim that managers always try to do less than they could do.[15]

Had we been able to assure the two above-mentioned conditions, management structure adapted to SDM, and an average optimal SDM per manager, we could have measured the SDM by the number of managers in the organization. These two conditions rarely occur, and therefore we cannot assume their existence.

The only situation in which the two optimum conditions may occur is one in which the management operates in an entrepreneurial structure, i.e. in an informally centralized structure, at the initial stage of creating and launching an organization. At this stage the great majority, if not all, the employees are managers, because every employee, perhaps with a few exceptions, may have a direct bearing on the survival of the organization. The entrepreneur and his chief employees do not try to run the organization at this stage, when the organization is vulnerable, in a formalized structure of any kind. One cannot plan in advance a division of labour, or a timetable, when one deals with all the unknowns in the creation and launching of a new organization.

During the first period of organizational life, when everyone involved feels that his or her contribution is crucial for the organization's survival, every employee would endeavour to do his best. This is what makes all, or almost all, the employees managers at this stage.

Thus, we see that during this initial period of the organization the two conditions, which we have to assume in order to use the number of managers as a yardstick for SDM, are indeed fulfilled. The managers operate in the managerial structure which is right for the SDM at that stage, and every one of them undertakes an appropriate share of that SDM. Therefore, during the first period of the organization the number of managers, defined as those who are concerned with the cooperation of other members of the organization, may be considered as proportional to the SDM. Such other members may embrace other managers, workers, customers, suppliers, shareholders, etc.

We could likewise accept the statement that, as the organizations are growing in terms of their SDM, and their structures become advanced, the number of their managers will grow roughly proportionally. Thus, the number of managers, defined by their TOS role, in a specific organization will usually grow when the SDM and managerial structure move from an entrepreneurial to a functional stage, and again from a functional to a product/service line stage and, finally, from there to a multistructure.

However, when we consider the TOS dynamics, we do *not* regard the increase in the number of managers as a *contextual* (SDM)[16] reason for moving from one TOS stage to another. We rather consider the *structural* implications of the increase in number of managers as a reason for moving from stage to stage.

4.1.2 Expansion in Organizational Strategy

We have already seen in chapter 2 that the organizational strategy[17] is expanding over time, or else the stagnation and eventual contraction in organizational strategy would lead to organizational collapse. This happens again and again except in rare cases of small, personal service organizations with a select clientele.[18] It is only in conditions of emergency and war, when governments intervene in the management of business and other types of organizations, that organizations can survive without growth in their organizational strategies, i.e. in their technologies, product/service lines, and geographical dispersal.[19]

The principal divisions of the system of decision making, in the midst of which we find the organizational strategy, is presented in Figure 2.5. The three organizational strategy questions guiding managements in their operations are: How? What? and Where? This is indeed the historical order in which organizations started the major expansion of their strategies. First came the raising of the technological level, which started with the Industrial Revolution at the beginning of the nineteenth century. For over one hundred years most organizations remained with one-product line strategies, trying to survive the competition with each other by raising their technologies as much as they could.

The multi-product/service line organizations, or 'conglomerates', started to appear on a significant scale following the First World War. These organizations may have been imitating the Japanese zaibatsu which preceded them, or perhaps ITT, which was one of the first Western organizations to adopt a conglomerate organizational strategy. The Far Eastern trading companies, including Western-based companies like the British Jardine-Mathesson, were probably the business pioneers of product/service diversification, while the Roman Catholic Church, described in Chapter 7, was the first non-nation state to introduce and practise it. Possibly, the beginning of multi-product/service line organizations lay in the concentration of power in the hands of some so-called industrial families; this was the case of the Japanese ziabatsu and that of the Behn brothers, the founders of ITT; or, the beginning could have been in somebody looking for a 'not putting all the eggs in one basket' policy. However, whatever prompted a diversified product/service line policy, once it was successfully started by some organizations, many others had to follow suit. The reason for this is that once your competitor has a wide line of products/services, he has a better chance of competing for the customer against other organizations. How *wide* a line of product/services? There are differences of opinion as to this, and there are those who say that the diversification cannot spill over and away from the same area of industrial specialization—metals, textiles, etc.[20]

There is also a difference of opinion as to the desirability of diversifying vertically, so as to become one's own supplier and/or one's own customer. The organizational example of the Devon Corporation which appears at the end of Chapter 3, presents, among others, the main problem of vertical integration, namely the inability to balance completely the input–output ratios between the various levels of vertical flow. This, in turn, means that for the remaining surpluses, which are not transferred to following levels, one has to compete with one's own suppliers and/or customers. In another organizational example, that of Henry Ford I (appearing at the end of chapter 5), we see that he had almost a mania for self-sufficiency. This contrasted with General Motors, which has had since its beginning the organizational strategy of avoiding vertical integration and favouring a horizontal diversification.[21]

The main thrust of moving to other countries has occurred in the years following the Second World War. As in the case of product/service diversification, where one occasionally finds organizations which had diversified before the First World War, so it is with geographical dispersal as well. There was a considerable number of organizations which were geographically spread before the Second World War. Among them were some of the famous British trading companies, oil companies, and others. However, the organizational implications of such a geographical dispersal before the Second World War were of secondary importance; what was important was the absorption of new technologies and the diversification of the product/service line. Until the Second World War, moving to other countries usually meant moving within the boundaries of the same empire, or colonial system. In such international operations, organizations regarded their geographical dispersal as expanding their operations within the same political system and as imposing on the organization additional transportation and communication problems. After the Second World War, the geographical dispersal meant a cross-cultural, multinational dispersal. We shall discuss the difference between international and multinational organizations in more detail in chapter 6.

These three factors (technological-scientific level, product/service diversification, and geographical dispersal) or organizational strategy, which constitute the three aspects of the organizational SDM, will be referred to as the 'contextual reasons' for moving from one managerial structure to another. However, there are two additional factors affecting the whole organizational dynamics: types of organizations classified by the degree of customer involvement and those classified by the national cultures of their land of origin.

4.1.3   Different Types of Organizations

4.1.3.1   The Degree of Customer Involvement

The TOS has enabled us to develop a meaningful organizational classification. Customer involvement represents an awareness that different types of organizations may have different scopes of decision making which would entail different types of management, because something in the culture of different types of organizations affects the SDM differently; but what is this 'something'? It could only be connected with the human factors of decision making, which affect various types of organizations differently. Customer involvement is a factor that cuts across all organizations and, at the same time, has a substantial effect on several decisive aspects of organizational behaviour.[22]

Figure 4.1 presents a hierarchy of eight types of organizations according to the degree of the involvement of customers in their decision-making processes, along with examples of the various types. At one end there are organizations with no involvement of customers in them. At the other end, there are organizations in which the customers are involved as suppliers, are being processed as the 'raw material', and are physically and mentally involved in the services rendered to them.

It is evident that the examples on the right-hand side of the pyramid of Figure 4.1 cover a wide variety of organizations. These types of organizations include organizations all the way from family and religious organizations, through educational, health, and governmental organizations, ending with business organizations in all walks of life—agriculture, banking, commerce, industry, insurance, transportation, and various personal service organizations. Thus, for example, this classification helps us in analysing the effect of type of decision making and management in industrial organizations. The following discussion is taken from a book about industrial management.[23]

Industrial organizations will usually fall into one of the five upper levels of the hierarchy presented in Figure 4.1. Figure 4.2 presents the 'hierarchy of service' pyramid of manufacturing organizations, while Table 4.3 specifies the anticipated requirements of production managers in these five different types of manufacturing organizations.

102

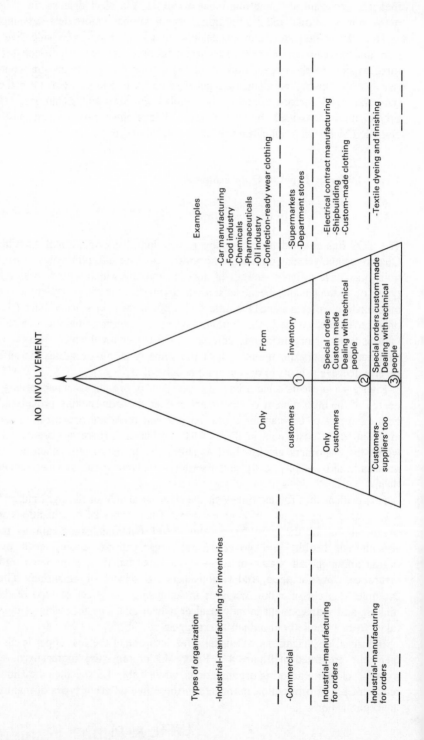

103

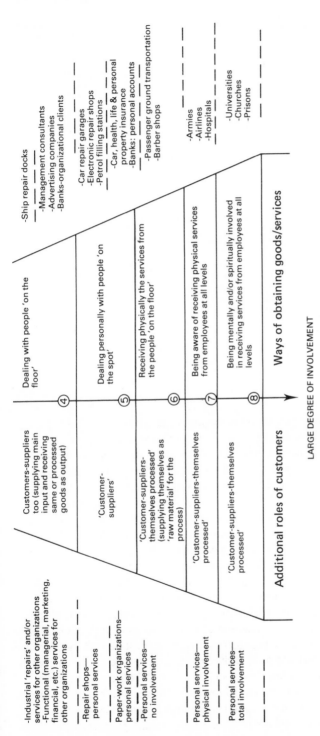

Figure 4.1 The involvement of customers in the decision making

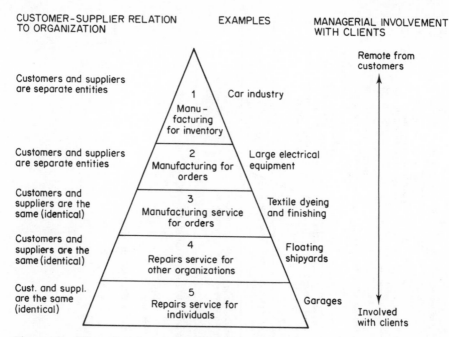

Figure 4.2 'Hierarchy of service' pyramid of manufacturing organizations: from least to most involved customers

Generally speaking, one can say that the more the type of business organization requires the production managers to be in contact with managers in another function, the less knowledgeable they can afford to be in the intricacies of that function. Thus, the more service oriented the organization is, the more involved the production managers are with the financial function, and the less knowledgeable they have to be in financial matters. The absence of a better knowledge of financial matters was probably one of the principal reasons for the crisis in Rolls-Royce (the organizational example appears at the end of chapter 1), which operated in the two highest levels of the hierarchy of service. Likewise, the more service oriented the organization, the less are the production managers likely to be involved formally with the marketing department, since they have more direct contact with clients and, therefore, the more knowledgeable they should be in marketing. In this case, the production managers assume a partial direct responsibility for the continued cooperation of the customers with the organization. In these circumstances, the production managers must be well aware of the dynamics of the total organization and the crucial importance of the customers' cooperation with the organization for the survival of the whole organization.

The complete customer involvement hierarchy presented in Figure 4.1 seems to have several characteristics which make it meaningful for a TOS analysis. Thus, the more involved the customers are in the decision-making process (i.e. the lower

Table 4.3 The effects of degree of customer involvement on the role of manufacturing managers

Requirement of production managers	Level in the hierarchy of service				
	1 Manufacturing for inventory (cust. and suppl. are separate entities)	2 Manufacturing for orders (cust. and suppl. are separate entities)	3 Manufacturing for orders (cust. and suppl. are the same)	4 Repairs for organizations (cust. and suppl. are the same)	5 Repairs for individuals (cust. and suppl. are the same)
Involvement with clients	None	May know client's name	Know client's name and may have met him	Client has his managers visit from time to time	Client is waiting inside the organization. Knows personally production managers
Contact with financial function	Almost none	Only a little	Not much	Much	Very much
Contact with marketing function	Much	Very much	Not much[a]	Only a little[a]	Almost none[a]
Contact with purchasing function	Very much	Much	Not much[b]	Only a little[b]	Almost none[b]
Know-how about human beings	About the operating organization (workers and other managerial functions)			About the total organization (the effects of FDM, e.g. customers, suppliers, government, banks, etc.)	
Know-how about financial matters	Very much required			Required to a lesser extent	
Know-how about marketing	Required to a lesser extent		Very much required		

Notes:
[a] In these types of organization the marketing function is limited because one does not usually cater for customers.
[b] In these types of organization the main object of manufacturing is provided by the customer-supplier.

the organization appears in the pyramid of Figure 4.1):

—the more informal the managerial relationships,
—the more flexible the hierarchy,
—the larger the number of hierarchy levels,
—the more the customers are committed to the same suppliers,
—the less ethical advertising is considered to be, and
—the less the growth of the organization is dependent on the performance of its management.

This is not the only organizational classification which focuses on the organization's clients and on the service rendered to them. We found, however, only three classifications with which customer involvement could be compared:[24] Etzioni's 'means of obtaining compliance', Parsons's 'social needs orientation', and Blau and Scott's 'prime beneficiary'.[25] The relation of the eight classifications of our customer involvement to those of Etzioni, Parsons, and Blau and Scott are presented in Table 4.4. This table appears almost exactly as it was first presented.[26]

Figure 4.3 presents the role of managerial attitudes in the TOS, which we shall discuss in subsection 4.1.4. On the TOS arrow chart we present all the significant links among the six principal systems, including three additional links, in broken lines, two of which, appearing on the right-hand side of the chart, we have not discussed in the previous three chapters.

The first additional link, appearing in Figure 4.3 as a broken line, is between the organizational strategy and the MS (managerial structure). This is the degree of customer involvement which we have just discussed. The choice of product/ service range, the *what* in the organizational strategy, establishes the type of organization in terms of customer involvement. This, in turn, as we have just seen, has an effect on the MS, regarding the degree of informality and flexibility on managerial relationships and on the number of hierarchic levels.

There is, however, another effect on the MS which stems from the organizational strategy. This is the decision about *where* the organization is operating, in which wider environments. It is not concerned with cultural aspects of the organization itself, i.e. the degree of customer involvement, but rather with the socio-cultural effects of the wider environment, which affect similarly all the organizations operating in the same wider environment. We shall discuss these socio-cultural effects on the MS in chapter 6, section 6.1.

4.1.3.2 Classifying Organizations by National Cultures

The relation between culture and management is quite strong. Indeed, organizational scientists have been asking themselves whether this relation between culture and management leads to national cultures converging upon each other or diverging from each other. There is no doubt that the spread of organizations, along with the shortening of distance between countries as a result of the development of high-speed transportation and communication, led to cross-country cultural fertilization. We likewise witness an emergence of what we could

Table 4.4 Comparing the TOS customer involvement classification with other organizational system classifications

The TOS organizational classification according to customer involvement in decision making	Similarity to other organizational system classifications:		
	Etzioni's 'means of obtaining compliance'	Parsons's 'social needs orientation'	Blau and Scott's 'prime beneficiary'
1. 'Customers'—for inventory			
2. 'Customers'—custom-made manufacturing			
3. 'Customer-suppliers'—custom-made manufacturing	2. Utilitarian organizations	1. Economic production oriented organizations	2. Business concerns
4. 'Customer-suppliers'—institutional repairs or servicing			
5. 'Customer-suppliers'—personal or servicing			
6. 'Customer-supplier-raw material'—no involvement		2. Political goals oriented organizations	1. Mutual benefit associations
7. 'Customer-supplier-raw material'—physical involvement	1. Coercive organizations	3. Integrative organizations	3. Service organizations
8. 'Customer-supplier-raw material'—total involvement	3. Normative organizations	4. Pattern-maintenance organizations	4. Commonwealth organizations

108

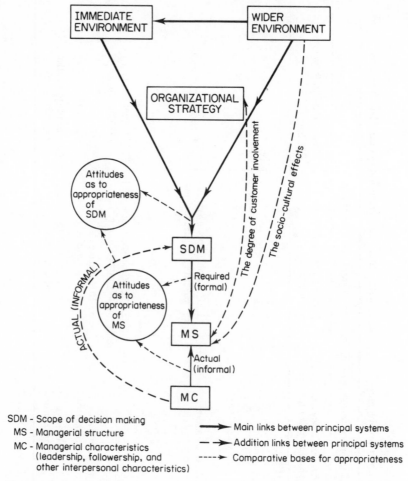

Figure 4.3   Attitudes as to the appropriateness of the scope of decision making
and the managerial structure in the TOS

refer to as aspects of a multinational culture; i.e. similar managerial behaviour
manifested by people from different countries who find themselves operating in
the same multinational corporations.[27]

Nevertheless, even though national cultures change at least to the degree that
enables multinational corporations to operate in almost any country of the world,
those national cultures still impose some decisive constraints upon organizational
behaviour. We shall presently mention some of these aspects of national culture
which have an effect upon the dynamics of the TOS.

Table 4.5 presents the results of a comparison between Britain, France, and
Germany, regarding top management control in industrial organizations. This
research is described in an organizational example at the end of this chapter.

Table 4.5 Effects of national culture on managerial structure: Comparisons between Britain, France, and Germany regarding top managerial control

Control variable	National culture		
	Britain	France	Germany
1. Control as a consequence of planning	1, 2 low	1, 2 low	3 high
2. Control as a motivation	1, 2 high	1, 2 high	3 low
3. Control as police	1 low	2, 3 high	2, 3 high
4. Finance oriented control	1 high	2, 3 medium	2, 3 medium
5. Production oriented control	1 low	2, 3 high	2, 3 high
6. Marketing oriented control	1, 2, 3 medium	1, 2, 3 medium	1, 2, 3 medium
7. Control evenly distributed through the organization	1 yes	2, 3 no	2, 3 no
8. Degree of control detail	1 overall	2 detailed	3 very detailed
9. Control orientation	1 future	2, 3 past	2, 3 past
10. Qualitative or quantitative control	1 some quantitative	2, 3 quantitative	2, 3 quantitative
11. Frequency of control	1 month	2, 3 week	2, 3 week
12. Centrally prepared control	1 low	2, 3 high	2, 3 high
13. Degree of systematization and standardization	1, 2 high	3 low	1, 2 high
Average ranking order for 13 control variables	1.2	2.3	2.5

Source: Horovitz (1980, p. 103).
Note: High and low are only meant to be relative terms. More appropriate terms would be 'higher' and 'lower'. The figures 1, 2, and 3 appearing above the 'high', 'medium', 'low' indications, etc., are the ranking orders of the three countries for every control variable.

Jacques Horovitz, who conducted this research, selected the organizations which he studied in these three countries from the same types of industry, so that he accounted for SDM (Scope of Decision Making), thus reducing to the possible minimal any contextual differences between the samples of organizations in Britain, France, and Germany.

From the 13 control variables in Table 4.5, only 'marketing oriented control' did not produce any differences between the three countries; we shall therefore omit this variable from the following analysis. The three countries are not only arranged in Table 4.5 in alphabetical order, but this also happens to be the order in which, on the whole, managerial control practices spread. When the control variable is 1, it means that the control is:

(1)   not a consequence of planning,
(2)   motivating,
(3)   not serving as police,
(4–5) finance, but not production, oriented,
(7)   evenly distributed throughout the organization,
(8)   an overall rather than detailed control,
(9)   oriented towards future,
(10) qualitative,
(11) performed every month (rather than every week),
(12) not prepared centrally, and
(13) systematic and standardized.

The average ranking order in Britain is 1.2, very close to a perfect 1. The average ranking orders for France and Germany are, respectively, 2.3 and 2.5. We see that France and Germany are not only far removed from Britain, but they are likewise quite close to each other in their top management control practices. This can be shown also in terms of the number of control variables in which the results of each pair of two countries are similar to each other. The distribution of control variables among pairs of countries is from the highest to the lowest number of times, as follows (see Table 4.5):

—France and Germany have eight cases of similarity (control variables 3, 4, 5, 7, 9, 10, 11, 12).
—Britain and France have two cases of similarity (control variables 1 and 2).
—Britain and Germany have one case of similarity (control variable 13).
—There was only one case in which the change from country to country was gradual (moving from an overall to a detailed and to a very detailed control, in variable 8).
—And, finally, there was one case in which the degree of control was equal in all three countries (control variable 6: 'marketing oriented control').

These results, relating to top management control in Britain, France, and Germany, are consistent with the findings relating to structural change factors in the same three countries appearing in Table 4.6. These are four different measurements which indicate, on the whole, the degree of democratization, the involve-

Table 4.6 Comparisons of structural change between Britain, France, and Germany

Factors	National culture		
Structural change factor	Britain	France	Germany
1. Social mobility factor	1 high	2 medium	3 low
2. Interorganizational mobility of chief executives	3 low	2 medium	1 high
3. Acceptance of interorganizational managerial mobility	1, 2 high	1, 2 high	3 medium
4. Role in learning process	1 positive	2, 3 negative	2, 3 negative
Average ranking order for four structural change factors	1.6	2.0	2.2

ment of people with one another, and the absence of social stratification, when moving from 1 to 3.[28] The fact that the trend in interorganizational mobility of chief executives (structural change factor 2) is reversed when compared to the trends in the three other factors, could be explained by the relative stability in Britain in the institutions of government and army since the time of the French Revolution. In the other two countries the political turmoil meant that people did not serve for prolonged periods of time in either government or army, and in the Church things were not too steady either. This state of affairs over the last two hundred years was even more pronounced in Germany than in France. Therefore, the habit of serving during one's whole lifetime in the Church or government or army was stronger in Britain than in France, and in France than in Germany. The stronger these habits were, the stronger the anti-interorganizational mobility feelings.[29] Otherwise the results of structural change factors 1, 3 and 4 in Table 4.6 are in line with other research findings, which indicate that social stratification in Britain is relatively smaller than in the continental countries in Western Europe.[30] Thus, for example, communication studies have shown that interpersonal communication in Britain has been much more oral, i.e. person to person and by the telephone or intercom, than in France. In France the communication is much more in writing, following Max Weber's bureaucratic model.[31]

The consequence of our discussion in this section is the broken line on the right-hand side of Figure 4.3, which indicates the effects of the socio-cultural environment on the MS. This link is similar to the dotted line indicating the effects of the degree of customer involvement on the MS which was discussed in the previous section. Thus we see that, when classifying organizations, we should indicate both their degree of customer involvement *and* their national culture, i.e. the socio-culture of the country which affects them most. This latter classification does not apply to multinational corporations as a whole (discussed in chapter 6), but it definitely applies to their national subsidiaries, though to a lesser degree than it would apply to national corporations.

4.1.4 Managerial Attitudes—the Organizational Cybernetics Feedback Indicator

The three basic ingredients constituting an organization are its managerial attitudes, its operations, and the relationship among its personnel.[32] The managerial attitudes act as a regulator among the principal systems of the TOS and are referred to as the organizational cybernetics feedback indicator, using the terminology first introduced by Norbert Wiener in his concept of cybernetics.[33]

Figure 4.3 presents the regulating role of managerial attitudes as a feedback indicator destined to maintain the balance among the principal systems of the TOS. We see that it is through the attitudes that management can be made aware of the balance between the following four pairs of principal systems:

4.1.4.1 *The Three Decision-making Systems of Organization Strategy and Immediate and Wider Environments, on the one hand, and the Fourth System of the SDM on the other hand*

It has been previously mentioned in this chapter, when discussing the expansion in organizational strategy, that unless the strategy is adapted to the competition in the immediate environment directed by the pressures of the wider environment, the whole main system of decision making would collapse. An imbalance in this decision-making main system is revealed by the attitudes of the people of the organization, primarily those expressed by the managers.

This first pair-balance is the only one for which the feedback of attitudes from human factors other than management should be sought, because the collapse of the organization could occur from the pull-out of any human factor such as workers, customers, shareholders, etc. Usually management itself is least likely to abandon an organization early in its downward progress, more likely that it would be the last to abandon the drowning ship. It is about the continued cooperation of other integral factors that the management has to worry. This is why managerial attitudes are cardinal in this pair-balance. However, it is most important to seek the attitudes of the other human factors, such as workers, customers, shareholders, government, etc., as well. Managements actually do it all the time, by way of listening to the workers and their representatives, following the sales figures and carrying out occasional market research studies, watching the standing of the shares on the Stock Exchange and discussing matters with the board of directors, keeping in touch with government officials, legislators, etc.

4.1.4.2 *The SDM and Managerial Structure (MS) Pair*

Chapter 3 was primarily devoted to the balance between the SDM and the MS. A serious imbalance between the SDM and the MS is probably the major threat to organizational survival. The other threat is a serious imbalance within the triangle of organizational strategy and the immediate and wider environments, discussed in connection with the balance of the first pair. The cardinal problem in keeping the balance between the SDM and the MS is in the inevitable growth of the SDM, which in turn requires a change in the MS every few years. The length of life of the MS depends on the type of activities of the organization. Organizations which have larger rates of SDM growth will have to change their MS more often than those which grow at a slower rate.

4.1.4.3   The MS and the Managerial Characteristics (MC) Pair

We shall discuss the relation between the MS and the MC in more detail in chapter 5. We have, however, already explained that the MS is the function of a few managers who are in key positions. The manifest managerial behaviour does not necessarily follow the MC. Managers have to conform in most cases to the behaviour required of them. However, whenever managers can revert to a behaviour conforming to their respective MC, they will do so. Managers finding themselves in key positions would therefore relate to their superiors, peers, subordinates, and other managers through the hierarchy in a behaviour which fits their inherent MC.

4.1.4.4   The MC and the SDM Pair

The MC have a decisive effect not only on the MS, but also on the SDM. The MC of the managers in key positions direct the SDM according to their personalities. This may be contrary to the required formal scope (see Figure 4.3), resulting from the triangle of the organizational strategy, the immediate and the wider environments. Thus, for example, an entrepreneur with entrepreneurial aides in key positions will make the organization grow continuously in terms of SDM, even when such growth is contrary to the decision-making triangle, and could lead to organizational collapse.

It is only on the basis of the managerial attitudes that the management itself can establish whether the degree of imbalance within each of the four pairs requires a significant change in one or both of the two parties of the pair. However, a drastic change in one or more of the principal systems actually comes about as a result of the managerial attitudes comparing two pairs, rather than only on the basis of a comparison within *one* pair.

There are two reasons for this double checking. First, it is essential to ensure that the introduction of changes in order to balance one pair of principal systems should not cause a more serious imbalance in another part of the TOS. Management must therefore watch closely the decision-making main system, the wider and immediate environments, organizational strategy and SDM principal systems, as well as the management main system, namely the MC and the MS systems. Only in this way can management ensure that the changes would balance the whole TOS.

The second reason for this double checking is that management can actually introduce substantial changes only in two principal systems—the *organizational strategy* (the *context* of the TOS) and the managerial characteristics which direct the *structure* of the TOS. The other four principal systems are either a function of the organizational strategy and of the MC, or are influenced by factors beyond the control of the management of one organization.

Each of the sets of managerial attitudes compares two of the above described pairs, the so-called 'double-checking' sets; they appear in Figure 4.3 in circles, and are as follows.

4.1.4.5 *Attitudes Relating to Appropriateness of the SDM*

The managers compare the formal, required, scope of decision making created as a result of the organizational strategy and the competition from other organizations in the immediate environment, directed by the pressures from the wider environment, with the informal, actual, SDM which is governed by the MC. We see that this attitudinal check between the balances of two pairs of principal systems, the MC–SDM pair and a pair resulting from the combined outcome of the decision-making triangle of organizational strategy and the immediate and wider environments, on the one hand, and the SDM, on the other hand, is a check for establishing the appropriateness of the SDM.

4.1.4.6 *Attitudes Relating to Appropriateness of the MS*

This second attitudinal check concerns the MS. As in the first attitudinal check, it compares the required formal pressures on the MS with the actual informal ones. The formal pressures on the MS come from the SDM, which would comply with the requirements of the triangle of wider environment, immediate environment, and organizational strategy. The informal pressures on the MS are the consequences of the MC of managers in key positions.

This attitudinal check simultaneously encompasses the two additional links to the MS (in broken lines on the right-hand side of Figure 4.3), i.e. the effects of the degree of customer involvement and of the socio-cultural environmental system on the MS. These two links were discussed in 4.1.3.

Thus we see that while the first attitudinal check governs the appropriateness of the SDM, the second check governs that of the MS. The final question to be answered concerning factors in organizational dynamics is how management can establish the managerial attitudes which will enable it to govern the organization. First, however, let us consider the validity of the attitudes of managers to what is occurring in the TOS. Even when attitudes are what the people really feel and think, they are neither 'objective' nor 'absolute'. This is to say that an 'objective' evaluation of any occurrence does not exist in the organization, and different people may have quite different perceptions, and attitudes, regarding the same 'fact'.[34]

Neither are there any 'absolute' attitudes. Attitudes have an arbitrary nature. Positive or negative attitudes are, for every individual, matters of degree in assessing the present situation. The things with which managers compare the present situation depend on the experience and knowledge each manager has had in every aspect towards which he or she expresses an attitude. Thus, for example, we find that managers with longer service are less critical in their attitudes than those with shorter service.[35]

Therefore managerial attitudes are neither 'objective' nor 'absolute'. It is likewise quite difficult to ascertain attitudes as they are really perceived by the managers and other members of the organization. The reason lies in the fact that managers are usually unwilling to tell each other what they really feel and think about what goes on in the organization.

Yet, in order to carry out the managerial attitudes analysis according to Figure 4.3, we should interpret the feelings and thoughts of managers as accurately as possible. Because it is so important for management to obtain the true feelings, opinions, thoughts, and attitudes of organizational members, we devote much of chapter 7 to this problem. That chapter—'Helping Organizations'—deals with ways and means by which managements may be helped in dealing with the dynamics of their TOS.

4.2 REASONS FOR MOVING FROM ONE STRUCTURE TO ANOTHER

Three movements from one managerial structure to another will be discussed in this section: from an entrepreneurial to a functional structure, from a functional to a product/service line structure, and from a product/service line structure to a multistructure. These four managerial structures are the chief ones in which present-day organizations function and which will probably be with us in the twenty-first century too. The reasons why other known managerial structures are not viable in present-day organizations will be explained in the following subsections, as well as in chapter 5.[36]

This section attempts to explain the conditions in which organizations move from one structure to another, both in order to help people understand the organizational dynamics in which they find themselves[37] and to help the managements to recognize when they have to introduce drastic changes in their organizations. Organizations and the people in them are not robots. The year 1984 will not produce the world which George Orwell predicted for us in 1949,[38] and it is our belief that such prophecies of doom will not come true in the foreseeable future, in the world of our children and grandchildren. We are, of course, moving into a world which will have to be more regulated and coordinated, mainly because there will be less and less employment available even for the world's industrialized inhabitants, and more and more leisure for them. This, in turn, will mean that soon every job will serve as employment for two and, eventually, for three and more people. This would entail not only a certain degree of centralized government regulation, but would also necessitate drastic changes in our present-day education, family, religious, and economic systems, as well as in other aspects of our contemporary way of life.[39]

A larger degree of centralized government of some aspects of our lives neither means the regimentation of human beings nor the automatic regulation of the dynamics of their organizations. Therefore, management should know at what point to consider possible changes in the organizational strategy and managerial changes in key positions; in short, when to consider what type of major TOS changes will have to be introduced. However, these are just signals pointing to the necessity for introducing such changes. The exact nature of the changes, their immediate necessity, and how they are to be introduced, are problems with which management has to be helped.

We concluded a previous passage concerning managerial attitudes by saying that in order to find out what the relevant managerial attitudes are, management needs outside help. The last chapter of this book is, therefore, devoted to the important issue of helping organizations to adapt to the TOS dynamics.

There are two types of signals at each of the three points of moving from one structure to another. They are the *structural reasons* and the *contextual reasons* for moving from structure to structure.

As we have already pointed out, the inevitable expansion of organizations brings with it structural and contextual changes, which in turn make it necessary to move to new managerial structures. The contextual reasons are more obvious than the structural reasons, and therefore constitute the 'signals' for moving from one structure to another stemming from growth in the SDM.

Figure 4.4 will serve as an illustrative conceptual scheme when we discuss the movement from one structure to another in each of the three following subsections. This is a *schematic* chart and serves as an indication of the stages through which organizations might move. There is no organization known to us which actually moved exactly according to the Figure 4.4 progression from structure to structure. Managements would be well advised to heed the signals of this schematic progression. However, whenever they consider moving from one stage of the scope of decision making (SDM) to another they should seek the help of outsiders before making the changes they contemplate. The role of outside consultants is to help the management to look at themselves and consider how both the SDM and the managerial structure should and could be changed; chapter 7 deals with this in more detail.

Figure 4.4 includes only the *contextual*, i.e. the SDM, reasons, for moving from one structure to another. It does *not* include the *structural* reasons. In Figure 3.1 of chapter 3 we indicated the number of managers, on the same axis which in Figure 4.4 measures the SDM by means of technological/scientific level, product/service line diversification and geographical (area) dispersal. Subsequently, we learned that the number of managers defined in terms of the TOS correlates with the SDM as long as the requisite MS for it is an entrepreneurial enterprise. Speculating that the average number of managers defined in terms of the TOS, when moving from a functional to a product/service line structure, is 1000, and when moving from a product/service line structure to a multistructure, is 10 000, is meaningless, useless, and misleading. The reasons for the number of managers not being a good structural measurement for moving from structure to

117

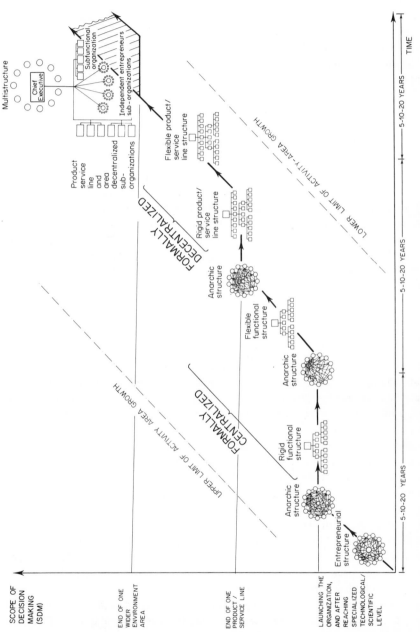

Figure 4.4   A schematic progression of the four basic managerial structures and the multistructure as the scope of decision making increases over time

structure was discussed in the previous section. Another explanation for the inappropriateness of the number of managers serving as an indicator for moving from structure to structure, lies mainly in the additional effects on the MS which the degree of customer involvement and the socio-cultural environmental system have (see two additional links in broken lines in Figure 4.3).

The structural reasons for moving from one MS to another originate in the increase in the number of managers, but are not directly related to this number. Both the structural and the contextual reasons for moving from one MS to another are described in the following three subsections.

4.2.1 From an Entrepreneurial to a Functional Structure

The entrepreneurial managerial structure is dominated by the entrepreneur, even though the managers constitute a majority of all the employees in an informally centralized structure.[40] This is the only structure in which organizations can be created. Therefore, as long as the organization in its infancy suffers from growing pains, the management has to stick to the entrepreneurial structure, otherwise the organization would perish before being able to become a viable entity. Furthermore, the organization should stick to its entrepreneurial structure so long as it has not yet matured, even if the structural and/or contextual reasons seem to make it imperative to move to a functional structure.

4.2.1.1 Structural Reason

The structural reason for moving from an entrepreneurial to a functional structure lies in the increase in the number of managers to the extent that a manager can no longer be personally acquainted with the majority of the other managers. Thus, when a manager receives an assignment from the entrepreneur, he may overlook some managers whom he should include in his implementation team for the assigned task, simply because he is not aware of their existence. The entrepreneur, however, is sure to know them and may even turn to one of these other managers and give him the same assignment. Consequently, two or more groups of managers may be engaged and working in the same assignment without knowing each other.

Such duplication in resources and efforts is inefficient, ineffective, and wasteful. Moreover, it inevitably leads to other dysfunctions. Once the managers in one team discover the existence of another team, working on the same assignment, the motivation, satisfaction, and commitment to the assignment on the part of managers in both teams drops dramatically even when one tries, subsequently, to make them collaborate on the same assignment. The conflict among members of the two groups would make such meaningful cooperation quite difficult to achieve. It is enough to remember that one or more managers from each team may subsequently be found to be superfluous for the efficient and effective operation of a unified team. Indeed, had the managers known each other well throughout the organization, the team which would have been selected would probably have included only the most suitable managers for the specific assignment.

The ability of managers in an organization to know each other well[41] depends on their capability to remember and know other people, and in as much detail as possible. The variance in this proficiency among different people is quite large,[42] and is connected to other aspects of managerial structure and communication than the one in which we are at present interested, namely the top managers through which an entrepreneurial structure can function adequately.

If such a knowledge of other managers does not exist in this informally centralized structure, the MS will not be able adequately to perform the decision making process. The less the knowledge of other managers in the entrepreneurial structure, the more communication and interpersonal problems arise. One of the symptoms of such a situation is that the managers come back to the entrepreneur, asking him to straighten things out. Alternatively, they may try to evade the entrepreneur by burying the assignment. Whichever alternative a manager pursues, it creates tensions and conflict between the entrepreneur and his managers. On the other hand, there exist clashes, jealousies, and conflicts among the managers, who try to survive this competition among themselves. It is in this situation that the managers seem to discern that the entrepreneur has his favourites, whom he drops from time to time in favour of other favourites of the day.[43] Likewise, the entrepreneurial aides may sometimes feel, under these conditions, that the entrepreneur delegates the same assignment to different people who do not know each other. They suspect him of doing it in order to keep them on their toes.

We may derive an approximate upper limit for the number of managers within which our entrepreneurial structure may still be expected to operate adequately. Based upon our experience with entrepreneurial structures, we establish, as a 'rule of thumb', the upper limit of managers in an entrepreneurial structure as roughly 100, or ± 100, i.e. up to 500 managers.[44]

4.2.1.2 Contextual Reasons

One of the characteristics of an entrepreneur is that he is constantly assigning and re-assigning new tasks to his managers. These managers are consequently assigning and re-assigning new tasks to other managers.[45] Therefore, people who were employed on the basis of their professional and technical skills find themselves being moved from one assignment to another. In the best case, the role to which they were originally assigned on the basis of their professional or technical skills serves as a sort of base. They are assigned additional tasks for which their professional skills qualify them. In the worst case, the tasks assigned are unrelated to their skills.

Following are two examples of such mal-utilization of professional or technical skills. A highly technically skilled operator of a numerically controlled (NC) machine tool[46] is being approached by his entrepreneurial chief executive, who instructs him to help in the installation of a new equipment NC machine tool in

120

another part of the enterprise. The entrepreneur does this because he remembers how helpful the operator was during the installation of the NC machine and that he is one of three employees who can operate the NC machine tool. However, the other two operators happen to be absent that day, the entrepreneur being unaware of it. Thus our operator is the only employee who can operate the machine that day. If another manager, not his immediate supervisor, had asked him to give a hand to another job, the operator would have told him he cannot absent himself from the only NC machine in the plant. He is, however, in awe of the entrepreneur and, assuming that the entrepreneur knows what he does, he helps with the installation of the new equipment for the rest of the day. The NC machine tool remains idle for several precious hours.

The second example is of a very specialized physicist who works in the R&D laboratory. He has already been exposed to what he considers a lack of understanding of the importance of what he does for the organization, having been asked to do other things which seemed to him to be beneath his dignity and competence. It is now mid-December, and the accounting department is under heavy pressure to close the books at the end of the financial year. One of the key persons in the accounting department, responsible for performing calculations which are relatively complicated, suddenly has a heart attack and is hospitalized. The entrepreneur comes personally to speak to the physicist in the laboratory rather than calling him on the intercom. He remembers the physicist's reluctance to leave his laboratory for other jobs and considers him a 'touchy fellow'. The entrepreneur explains to him the importance and urgency of quickly replacing the sick accountant, saying, 'The calculations to be performed there are complicated, and you are the only one who can do them.' The physicist protests; an argument follows, resulting in the resignation and departure from the organization of the physicist.[47]

In other words, the organization may have reached a technological level at which its survival depends on the proper utilization of its equipment and of its scientific staff. In such a case the entrepreneur who moves key position technical and professional personnel from job to job, giving them additional and different assignments, may undermine the survival of the organization. In such an event, this is the time for changing the managerial structure from an entrepreneurial to a functional one.

Thus we see that both the structural and the contextual reasons for organizations to move from an entrepreneurial to a functional structure are related to the way in which entrepreneurs deal with the managers. All the managers in an organization are approachable by the entrepreneur, and he assigns and re-assigns managers without formalizing exactly what, how, where, when, and with whom they have to carry out the assignments. Consequently, each manager, and not only the entrepreneur, should know the other managers very well; this is the structural reason why the organization may have to move to a functional structure when reaching ± 100 managers. Furthermore, when its technology is more advanced in terms of equipment and scientific personnel, it can no longer support the idleness of expensive equipment and the improper utilization of highly qualified professional and scientific staff. This is the contextual reason. However, even enterprises which right from the beginning are in a technologically advanced area, through the use of automatic equipment and of highly skilled technical, professional, and scientific personnel, *have* to go through an entrepreneurial structure. For as long as the organization is not safely launched, it has to stick to the entrepreneurial structure, at whatever financial or human cost. Otherwise it would not survive.

4.2.2 From a Functional to a Product Line Structure

The organization run in a functional structure may be perceived as one with up to ± 100 managers[48] and its operators on an advanced technological level, i.e. it has expensive equipment and a highly qualified professional and scientific staff. Let us now see why this functional, formally centralized, structure has to be changed eventually.

4.2.2.1 Structural Reasons

The increase in the number of managers as well as the growth of the SDM, whether it is accompanied by a significant increase in the number of managers (e.g. raising the technological/scientific level, may mean a larger SDM with a reduced number of managers) or not, leads to an increase in the number of managerial levels in the structural hierarchy. An expansion in the SDM, whether or not accompanied by a significant increase in the number of managers, may also mean a flattening of the hierarchical pyramid. This flattening, however, is quite limited. The number of subordinates in levels divided according to areas, product/service lines, or customer groupings is theoretically limitless.[49] There are, however, practical, structural limitations to the number of peer units. In such divisions, one will rarely find more than 50 subordinates to one superior. However, even when subordinates are divided according to such groupings, the superior cannot manage, say, 20 subordinate units in a decentralized structure for a period of 12 months. When the period of decentralization is reduced to one or two months, then the number of subordinate units may be increased to, say, 50 units in order that the decentralization is not undermined. The reasons for these limitations on the number of units in levels divided according to areas, product/service lines, or customer groupings will be explained in subsection 4.2.3, when discussing the structural reasons for having to move from a decentralized to a multistructure organization.

The levels into which the units are divided functionally, such as engineering, finance, manufacturing, marketing, personnel, and procurement, are limited to a maximum of ten functional heads per level[50]. This is so simply because the number of possible managerial functions is limited. To the above mentioned six functions we might perhaps add research and development as a separate entity from engineering and, in larger organizations, legal and public relations functions.

When an organization grows in its SDM and in the number of managers, the number of levels in its hierarchy has to increase as well. As we have seen, an increase in the number of managers in one level of hierarchy may, to a small degree, flatten the hierarchical pyramid.[51] The functional levels with not more than ten functional units appear approximately every second level in the hierarchy.[52] However, even in the levels divided into product lines or areas, in between the functional levels, the number of subordinate units to every superior does not usually exceed 50, as we have seen. This means that a significant increase in the overall number of managers entails an increase in the number of hierarchy levels.

With every addition of a hierarchy level, communication and decision making become more cumbersome and ineffective in the functional structure. The reason for this is that, in formally centralized functional structures, managers avoid making major decisions without the authorization of their immediate superiors, even though they have the authority. Let us consider an example. The CE (chief executive) and the heads of engineering, manufacturing, and marketing discuss in their weekly meeting the urgent need for the development of a new major product. In order to realize this objective they appoint a task force of three managers: Mr A, a development engineer, Mr B, a marketing engineer, and Mr C, the head of a manufacturing department. Messrs A, B, and C are in the third level below the heads of their respective functional hierarchies of engineering, marketing, and manufacturing and in the fourth level below the CE. The CE convenes the three and tells them that they are appointed as a task team whose coordinator will be Mr A, and that they should report directly to him when they terminate their work by a specified date. He furthermore indicates to the three that although they continue to operate in their roles in their respective hierarchies, in this important task they should report solely to him. Nevertheless, when the three get close to a joint conclusion about the new major product, each of them informally, clandestinely, and independently of the other two, contacts his immediate formal superior, saying to him something like: 'Although I need not contact you I thought you might be interested to know that we are approaching the following conclusion.' The immediate superior asks for a delay of a few days before the task team announces the final decision. He then turns to his own immediate superior, saying to him, 'You may be interested to know that Mr A informed me that they are approaching the following conclusion. What do you think about it?' The answer would probably be: 'Why don't you stall Mr A for another few days while I think about it', and off he goes to his own boss, the head of engineering. Something like this happens with Mr B in marketing, and Mr C in manufacturing. Thus, the intention of the CE to let the three work independently of the hierarchy failed. By why?

The answer is the norm of 'no bypassing'. This is the norm which has maintained both organizational hierarchy and social stratification since organizations and societies began. Over the generations we have been teaching our offspring compliance to this norm. This we do by preventing our children from bypassing their mother or father, telling them, 'Don't ask me, after your father has already forbidden you', or, 'You heard your mother say no, so why do you come to me?' Again and again—do not bypass!

The only national culture in which the norm against bypassing the organizational hierarchy does not seem to exist is the Japanese. However, even in Japanese organizations, there is another type of 'no-bypassing'. It is 'no-bypassing' in the opposite direction—when the decision-making process flows mainly from bottom to top, rather than mainly from top to bottom.[53]

Let us sum up our discussion of the structural reasons for moving from a functional to a decentralized structure. The increase in the number of hierarchy levels, along with the no-bypassing norm, makes the decision making in a functional structure more and more cumbersome. In order to facilitate better communication and, especially, better responsibility and commitment, it is necessary to bring the final level of responsibility to a lower level in the hierarchy. This is possible by making the subordinates of the CE, rather than the CE himself, the final point of authority, who decide by arbitration in case of conflict among the functions.[54]

4.2.2.2 Contextual Reasons

When the organization has moved into two or more product/service lines, it can no longer effectively and efficiently be governed in a functional structure. The specialization advantage of the functional structure cannot be well accomplished when the decision-making processes of two or more different product/service lines are contained within one functional structure. Let us consider again the instance of ITT (organizational example in chapter 3), which is a conglomerate of product/service lines which are completely different from one another, including various types of industrial lines ranging from electronics to food products, and insurance, hotels, car rentals. It would be inconceivable to run all these product/service lines in one functional structure, which puts the burden on the CE to make the final decisions in *all* cases when the functional heads cannot agree. It is likewise evident that people who are specialists in, say, the manufacturing of electric wire and cables are not necessarily specialists in marketing insurance, or hotels, or car rentals.

It is clear that when an organization expands to a two or more product/service line strategy, it should move to a decentralized product/service line structure, and benefit from its advantage of accountability. We have already seen in chapter 3 that the CE in a decentralized structure can hold his subordinates fully responsible for the period of their autonomy. They are given all the functions they need for running their autonomous operations for a period of one, or two, or three, or six, or twelve months. This means that, at the end of each autonomy period, the success of a subordinate is his own and nobody can take it away from him. Likewise, if a product/line fails, its head cannot blame anybody else for his own shortcomings.

There are, of course, different levels for identifying and distinguishing between different product/service lines. We have discussed in section 3.2 chapter 3 the way to establish the product/service line diversity, using the American Standard Industrial Classification (SIC) of organizational activities. Thus, for example, a two-digit classification was used for establishing the product/service diversity of the organization which was included in the research described in the organizational example of Multinational Corporations, appearing at the end of chapter 6. In this way an organization which has, say, three product/service lines in the two-digit SIC, may have up to 30 product/service lines in the three-digit; it would be most unlikely, however, that in every one of its two-digit SIC three product/service lines, the organization would operate in all its ten possible product/service lines of its three-digit SIC.

There is a simpler way of using the SIC, in order to decide whether the product/service lines in an organization differ sufficiently to merit a decentralized structure. As long as all the FDM (human factors of decision making) are the same for the different product/service lines of the organization, the management should run the organization in a functional structure. Once different product/service lines have distinctively different populations in one or more of the FDM, the time for considering a product/service structure has arrived. Thus, for example, comparing two of ITT's service lines which exist in many countries. Avis Rent-a-Car and Sheraton Hotels, we find for each of them completely different populations in almost every FDM. The only FDM in which they partially draw upon the same population is the customers; however, there are countries in which the Sheraton Hotels' customers are mainly tourists and visiting businessmen, while the Avis customers, surprisingly enough, are mainly local citizens and local firms. The employees in Sheraton and Avis are drawn from different populations; so are the main suppliers of both service lines. The physical facilities of hotels are depreciated over a period of several decades, while rental cars are depreciated over three years, or even less. Therefore, the shareholders in Avis have a much faster rate of return, while in Sheraton they are long-range investors.

In most organizations, however, the first sign of a contextual difference between two product/service lines which merits a product/service line structure appears in the customer FDM. Once two products have completely different customer populations, one should consider a product/service line structure. This often happens in electronic product firms. Once they have fairly large, clearly differentiated customer populations for their industrial products, military products, hospital products, etc., they start moving to a product/service line structure.

4.2.3 From a Product Line Structure to Multistructure

Let us now describe the federated managerial multistructure which is discussed in more detail in the section 5.4 of chapter 5. For the purpose of our present discussion it is enough to say that a multistructure is a federation of different basic managerial structures, such as entrepreneurial, functional, and area or product line structures decentralized for different periods of autonomy. Every manager, and group of managers, belongs to one precise part of the multistructure. Thus, if Philips of Eindhoven or ITT had been operating in a multistructure, a television factory in Germany belonging to either of them (like Schaub-Lorenz of ITT) would be part of Germany in the area structure, or of the radio and television group in the product/service line structure, or of the manufacturing group in the functional structure.[55]

Let us now consider the structural and contextual reasons why managements have to move from a product/service line structure to a multistructure.

4.2.3.1 Structural Reasons

We compared in the previous subsection the number of up to 10 peer units in a functional hierarchy level, with the possible numbers of peer units in levels according to areas, or product/service lines, or customer groupings. Although, theoretically, there is no limit to the number of units subordinate to one superior when divided according to such groupings, organizations would and should restrict themselves in the number of units reporting to one boss, since it is necessary to maintain decentralization of the subordinate units. Even in a decentralized structure the CE has to control the performance of his subordinate units every one, two, three, six, or twelve months, allocating to them their strategies and resources for the following period. In order to control, plan, and allocate every such period of time, the CE needs a group of people to help him with these functions. The control of the subordinate units by way of analysing their statements at the end of every such period is expected to be done as quickly and thoroughly as possible. In order to achieve such a task within, say, two weeks, the control of every subordinate unit requires, say, a team of three qualified people. If the CE has ten such subordinate units, he requires a staff of 30 qualified people in order to have the analysis of his ten units on his desk within two weeks of receiving their periodical reports.

The big problem is what does one do with these 30 people for the rest of the period. Obviously, they could be engaged in planning the operations of the organization—primarily the financial planning, and the allocation of resources to the subordinate units for the following period. However, the longer the decentralized period the larger the problem of keeping the CE's team busy in operations concerning activities in the following period of decentralization. A CE who decentralizes his ten subordinate units for a period of 12 months, and has the same team of 30 to help him with financial planning and control, will not be able to keep all the members of this team fully occupied in long-range duties. It is unlikely that he will keep more than, say, 20 of his team busy in financial planning for the following one-year period. He would not want to have 10 members of his team having nothing to do for the remaining 50 weeks of the year, because they would start interfering with the subordinate units *during* the year and undermining his decentralized structure. Such a CE would probably have to reduce the number of his subordinate units to five or six in order to maintain the decentralized structure.

With organizations in which the decentralization period is, as at ITT, only for four or eight weeks (see example following chapter 3), the problem is considerably diminished. However, when the autonomy period of his subordinate units is reduced to, say, eight weeks, the CE would want to receive the analysed statements from his team within one week of their submission by the subordinate units. This may increase the number of team specialists per subordinate unit from, say, three to five bringing the size of the CE's team for 10 subordinate units to 50 specialists. For seven out of every eight weeks these 50 specialists will have to be occupied in financial planning and allocation for future eight-week periods. We can imagine that this work load could be found in such an organization for 50 specialists, but not for many more if they are to be prevented from interfering with the subordinate units during the periods they are supposed to be fully autonomous. This means that the number of subordinate units in decentralized structures for longer periods of autonomy should be smaller than in organizations with shorter periods of autonomy. As a rule of thumb we could say that when the autonomy period is six or twelve months, the number of subordinate units should not exceed ten. With autonomy periods of up to three months, the number of subordinate units should probably not exceed twenty.

Thus, when the number of product/service lines of the organization exceeds 20, their heads can no longer be effectively and efficiently run by one superior. This is when the organization should consider moving from a unified product/service structure to a multistructure.

4.2.3.2 Contextual Reasons

The ultimate chapter in the book is devoted to multinationals. We contend that one of the three survival conditions for a multinational corporation is to be organized as a multistructure. The three survival conditions are in the following three characteristics of a multinational corporation:

(a) SDM—operating in two or more countries distinctly different from one another in their wider environments, and especially in their national cultures.
(b) MS—A multistructure.
(c) Managerial attitudes—the management operates in every country more or less within the constraints of the country, but does not extend national culture constraints of one country to other countries.

An expansion of the multinationality of the organization expands the multistructure. In other words, it is possible to maintain an area structure, formally decentralized by regions only within one country, or among countries with similar wider environments, including similar national cultures. This is why we have not stressed area structures in this chapter and have skipped the area structure in Figure 4.4, which is the illustration of all the three movements from one structure to another (entrepreneurial to functional; functional to product line; product line to multistructure).

Contextually, organizations operating in two or more countries should operate in multistructures because of their differing wider environments, their differing national cultures, and the degree of formalization and autonomy practised in each country. Thus, for example, there are countries where without bribery an organization cannot survive. There are also countries in which exist extreme race discrimination, even near-slavery conditions. Adhering to egalitarian organizational principles in such countries will exclude the organization from operating in them. Therefore, an organization cannot impose a formal structure, whether functional or decentralized in an area or product line structure, on its operations in such countries.

An excellent example of the consequences of running a formal structure in different national cultures is found in the operations of ITT in three different countries. The most famous of the three is probably ITT's involvement in Chile. For reasons obvious to multinational interests, which we shall discuss in chapter 6. ITT wanted Allende's removal from power and was involved in his overthrow. It is doubtful, however, if this involvement would have come to the public's attention had it not been for the periodical routine reports which ITT requires all its subsidiaries to submit. It was in those reports that the expenses involved in the supposedly clandestine activities in Chile were discovered.

Likewise, the charges against ITT of being involved in illegal financial contributions to the Republican Party in Nixon's election campaigns could not have been substantiated had it not been for the same periodical reports. Such amounts of money were recorded by the woman lobbyist of ITT and included in these reports.

Another example of ITT's formal procedures being unsuitable for the wider environment of a country is found in their classified telephone directory and hotel operations in Israel. An organizational example following chapter 6 describes some aspects of Israel's TOS. The informally centralized system of the Israeli economy during the third quarter of the twentieth century led to inconsistencies in laws and governmental regulations, as well as to various bypasses around efforts to contain the pressures for raising wages and salaries. The higher the person in the managerial hierarchy, the more his remuneration was realized in non-taxable expenses rather than in income. The ITT headquarters in Brussels was perplexed by the reports from their Israeli subsidiaries explaining that major parts of expenses on motor cars, books, rents, housekeeping, telephones, etc., were disguised forms of remuneration to the employees. Following a thorough report of a special team sent to Tel Aviv from Brussels, which explained the complexities and the often changing basis for remuneration in connection with Golden Pages (the classified telephone directory company), ITT got rid of this company by selling it locally. ITT also got rid of its Tel Aviv Sheraton Hotel during the same period. It was only a few years later, in the mid-1970s, when drastic changes in the taxation of remuneration to employees in Israel were introduced, that Sheraton returned to Israel, constructing a new hotel in Tel Aviv.

4.3 SUMMARY

This chapter presents primarily a conceptual framework for the dynamics of the TOS. Section 4.1 discusses four factors in the organizational dynamics: the increasing number of managers, the expansion in organizational strategy, the degree of customer involvement in the decision-making process, and the managerial attitudes, which serve as the organizational cybernetics feedback regulator.

Section 4.2 explains the structural and contextual reasons why it is necessary for the organization to change its managerial structure every so often. We have followed the movements of the organization, first from the entrepreneurial to the functional structure, then from the functional to the product line structure, and, finally, from the product line structure to the multistructure type of organization.

All these movements are schematically described in Figure 4.4. The following are some special points to notice in this chart.

The organization progresses between the upper and lower limits of its field of activity. An organization could be a leader, near the upper limit, dragging behind it other organizations which follow the innovations in the field of activity; or it could be a follower, near the lower limit, lagging behind other organizations.

There are stabilization and growth periods in the progression of organizations. Stabilization is the period of formalization of a new structure, when the structure is rigidly imposed. The growth period requires relaxation of, and a flexibility in, the formalization of the structure.

Each such progression period lasts for several years. In quickly growing fields of activity, these periods could be as short as two or three years. In slowly growing fields of activity, they may be 20 years and more.

During the transfers from an entrepreneurial to a rigidly formalized functional structure, from a rigid to a flexible functional structure, and from a functional to a decentralized product line structure, the management goes through periods of informally decentralized structure. The reason for this is that the length of actual or perceived managerial control by the CE over his subordinates is a maximum of one day in an entrepreneurial structure and one week in a functional structure. When the CE is changed so that the structure is changed, the new CE will not be able promptly to grasp the managerial control reins. It will be at least a few weeks before he can be considered to be in the saddle, i.e. in control. During this period the managers, who are structured and accustomed to work frequently through the CE, try to carry out their roles by finding out for themselves what to do, when, and with whom. The new CE should not let the management continue to coast for too long. In decentralized structures, when the heads of units under the chief CE are accustomed to operating independently of him and of each other, the change of CE does not cause such an anarchic period.

The reader should be reminded that Figure 4.4 is a *schematic* progression of organizations over time. No organization actually follows the exact path described in Figure 4.4. Organizations behave over time according to the fundamentals of TOS dynamics, on the basis of which Figure 4.4 was drawn. Even when they diverge for different reasons and in different ways and directions from the progression described in Figure 4.4, they continue to pursue over time the fundamentals of the TOS dynamics described schematically in this chapter and illustrated in this figure.

The four organizational examples chosen to illustrate the fundamentals of the TOS dynamics stretch over a wide area of organizational activity; the second and fourth examples are of industrial organizations, the first example deals with a large commercial, retailing organization, while the third example describes the family organization. However, all four examples include the main aspects of the TOS dynamics.

British Chain Stores (BCS)[56]

This example is based upon systematic statistical research carried out by the second author and based upon various contingency models of organizational behaviour. The main findings of this research show a relationship between a series of performance criteria of 30 chain stores of a British retailing chain, and various indicators of the relationships among the managers of these stores. Among others, it showed that high morale is evident when the unit head makes his subordinates feel good and useful whenever he can. Such high morale would tend to produce a positive trend in people to do well in the future, especially for their unit head. These findings were shown to be valid regardless of organizational size and the extent of environmental turbulence within which these organizations operated.

British, French and German Industry (BFGI)[57]

The BFGI example is based upon the research of Jacques Horovitz in the mid-1970s, who studied top management control practices in samples composed of similar industrial organizations in the three countries. The research showed that, compared with control in French and German organizations, the control in the British organizations was significantly *less* as a result of centrally prepared planning. The control in British organizations is, however, significantly *more* motivating and finance oriented, overall rather than detailed, oriented towards future, qualitative, systematic and standardized. In addition, the managerial control in Britain was found to be evenly distributed throughout the organization, by means of monthly reports. The French were somewhat closer to the British organizations than the Germans. The difference between the French and the German organizations was much less significant than that between both of these groups and the British organizations.

Family Organizations

Comparing the TOS dynamics in families with that in business corporations, one can discern many analogies between the two types of organizations. The main difference, however, between the two seems to be that families have established a clear-cut SDM, and contextual signals for changing the structure,

130

while business managements still have to learn how to establish and react to their SDM signals. One such signal for decentralizing the family in Western society has been marriage, when the husband and wife leave their parents' homes. On the other hand, when a business corporation goes into a completely new and different product line, quite often it does not serve for it as a signal for decentralization. This example covers different types of family organizations, from the very strict, rigid and centralized ones in patriarchical societies, to the present day *laissez-faire*, flexible and permissive families, exemplified by American society.

South Essex Industry (SEI)

Joan Woodward's well-known research carried out in the mid 1950s was the first to establish independent variables for management structure. Thus, she was the pioneer in showing how to measure the SDM. The variable that correlated with structural measurements was found to be technology in the SEI research.

NOTES

1   This is very much like the cases of different inventors and innovators in various parts of the world coming up with similar inventions or innovations evolving from a breakthrough discovery, without being aware of each other or knowing of each other's innovations. For example, the first author first used the Communicogram as a research tool in 1959 in the USA. It records one's communications with others', and serves as a measurement for interpersonal communication in management. I did not realize that Tom Burns had used a similar technique in Britain, and that he had published his findings five years earlier (Burns, 1954). When Robert Dubin in going over my paper (Weinshall, 1966) drew my attention to Tom Burns's article, I discovered that Burns and I got the idea from the same discovery by Sune Carlson (1951) about the reciprocity of perceptions of interactions; the discovery of Carlson, the early findings of Burns, and my own later findings are part of the basis of a recent book on managerial communication (Weinshall, 1979).
2   'Contingency' is one of those terms which has assumed all kinds of meanings. Basically it means 'on condition' and 'conditional on'. Our own understanding of a contingency system is that it is not only the whole system which is in continuous change, and that change in various parts of the system would induce change in others. It also may refer to changes in the rules and principles interconnecting the various parts of the system.
3   For a variety of reasons we do not consider that the contributions of such people as Henri Fayol, Mary-Ann Follett, Lillian Gilbreth, and others writing in the first three decades of the twentieth century, pertain to organizational contingency theory and therefore we do not refer to them in the text.
4   Barnard was really the first to make us aware of a great many aspects of the TOS. The most famous aspects of his contribution to organizational theory include the centrality of management to the whole organizational life, the need to secure the cooperation of the organization of human factors other than those of the employees, specifically of the customers, and recognition of the different types of structures and managers that one encounters in organizations.
5   Simon's *Administrative Behavior* (1947) already has in it the seeds of the rational approach to managerial decision making. Yet, one could identify the bulk of that

book as originating from Barnard's teachings. The first author of the present book remembers that, when he was fully exposed to Barnard's writings for the first time in 1958–1959, he asked his teacher in general management at the Harvard Business School, the late Richard Merriam, why nobody had re-edited and rewritten *The Functions of the Executive*. Merriam's answer was that there was no one qualified to do it. On the one hand, he said, someone is required who could thoroughly understand the vast richness of Barnard's contributions. On the other hand, a person who could absorb the whole of Barnard, and rewrite and edit him in a more comprehensible way, would be like Herbert Simon himself. Such a person would have something of himself to add to Barnard, and consequently he would not be a true interpreter of him.

6 A 'modelistic' approach to management and organization is an effort to explain the relations between different parts of the organizational system by way of mathematical relations. The contingency system, on the other hand, means that the rules of the game are changing when one moves from one contingency situation to another, i.e. all the rules of behaviour are correct, even when contradicting one another, each set of rules being effective within certain contingency limits. Consequently, one cannot hope to contain the contingency development of organizations over time within an algorithmic set of modelistic rules and relations. However, within lower levels of a total organizational system, a modelistic approach to decision making and management is possible as, for instance, in inventory planning and control. But the ramifications of using such a model may be dysfunctional effects in other parts of the TOS. We have mentioned the limitations of a modelistic approach earlier in the book. Let us now give an example of what we mean by a lower and a higher level of abstraction.

The first major contribution of Simon and the 'modelistic' school was in *Organizations* (March and Simon, 1958) which offers a comprehensive summary of all the major findings in the various domains of organizational behaviour at the time, arranged in a logical, orderly way in the 212 pages of the book. If one tries to bring together all the small algorithmic relations scattered over the whole book—related to lower levels of abstraction such as group identification, perceived prestige, interaction, and goals—one discovers the futility of such an effort. These small algorithmic relations just do not fit into one another, and one discovers many contradictions between the rules in one limited, low-level system and another. The main followers of Herbert Simon have been his collaborator on *Organizations*, James March, and, subsequently, Richard Cyert (Cyert and March, 1963).

7 The conceptual framework of Elton Mayo (1933) and the research methodology and revealing findings of Fritz Roethlisberger and his collaborators (Roethlisberger and Dickson, 1939) served as stepping stones and inspiration for a large number of researchers in the Harvard Business School. Some of these collaborated with Mayo and Roethlisberger in the Hawthorne experiments. Among them were George Lombard (1955) and John D. Glover and Ralph Hower (1952).

Others followed in their footsteps (Zaleznik, Christensen, and Roethlisberger, 1958; Lawrence and Lorsch, 1967).

8 The work of the Ann Arbor group may be traced to Kurt Lewin (1953), and has included such people as Jack French (Coch and French, 1948), Daniel Katz and Robert Kahn (1966), and McGregor (1960). The Bethel Mayne Laboratories and the Group Dynamics (e.g. Lippit *et al.*, 1958) have been early developments of this group. Organizational Development (OD) is a more recent development of such things as Training (T) Groups, Sensitivity Training and other variations of group dynamics which have evolved between the 1950s and the 1970s. The second group, that of the London Tavistock Institute, started with Fred Emery and Eric Trist (1960) who were interested in 'Socio-Technical Systems', i.e. the relationships between people and the equipment they operate. The Tavistock group included

132

such names as Eric Miller and A. K. Rice (1967) and Frank Heller, as well as Elliott Jacques, a psychiatrist who together with Wilfred Brown (1960), the chief executive of the Glacier Metal Works, conducted studies for 15 years (1948–1963) in that one organization (Jacques, 1951; 1956; 1961). Among more recent followers of Trist and Emery in the Socio-Technical Systems are people such as the American, Louis Davis, and the Englishman, Albert Cherns. The common denominator of the Ann Arbor and the Tavistock groups is that they usually (but not always) research at a socio-psychological level of the group, rather than on the total organization. Some of them have, from both groups, moved to such things as the 'quality of working life' (Davis *et al.*, 1975) and 'industrial democracy' (Heller, 1971).

9 Joan Woodward's first modest publication (1958) was followed by a book describing in more detail her findings and relating them to theory (1965).

10 In our terminology, the 'organismic' is the more informal and flexible structure, while the 'mechanistic' is the formal and more rigid structure (Burns and Stalker, 1961).

11 The notion of 'decentralization' is perceived differently by various researchers. Thus, for example, one French organizational scientist told one of the present authors in the mid-1960s that many French organizations were 'decentralized'. As we felt at the time that only a few organizations, at most, were decentralized in France, the reaction to this declaration was surprise and unbelief. It eventually turned out that what he meant was that many French organizations are geographically dispersed, but very strongly managerially centralized in Paris! Thus what Chandler meant when he diagnosed the structure of his four organizations to be 'decentralized' (1962) was not what we would refer to as decentralized structures. Our organizational example of Sears, Roebuck & Company, at the end of the chapter 5, studied at the end of the 1940s, shows that, according to our definition of centralization and decentralization, Sears was run in a functional, formally centralized structure. Chandler only meant, in our opinion, that the Sears headquarters delegated to the department store managers all decisions in the areas of marketing and manpower. This was in itself quite unusual in the 1920s, when the Sears top management did it. However, it did not give the store managers the full autonomy for one, three, six, or twelve months, which would have meant managerial decentralization.

Chandler has been followed by several Harvard Business School scholars. Chandler himself was at MIT when he wrote his *Strategy and Structure*, in 1962, but later he joined some of his followers at the HBS. Let us mention a few of those who modelled their research according to him. Chronologically they were, amongst others: John Stopford (1968; Stopford and Wells, 1972), to whom we shall presently refer; David Channon (1973) who studied the British scene; Dyas and Thanheiser (1976) who studied the strategy and structure of German and French business organizations; and Richard Rumelt (1974) who found that economic performance mainly affected the way in which the organization structures new business ventures in relation to ongoing activities, rather than by the absolute amount of diversification. We have singled out John Stopford for discussion. He simultaneously belongs to two schools of research at the HBS; his contribution to contingency theory is especially important. John Stopford's research on 170 US-based multinational corporations, with manufacturing facilities in at least six countries, is described in an organizational example at the end of chapter 6. While following Chandler's conceptual framework, Stopford was one of the group researching multinational corporations led by Raymond Vernon (1971).

12 The first article by Pugh describing the research appeared in 1963. About 15 years later the Aston researchers, by now dispersed throughout several British universities, brought together the major projects carried out by themselves, and several replications of their most replicated research performed in various countries

all over the world (Pugh and Hickson, 1976; Pugh and Hinning, 1976; Pugh and Payne, 1977). The Aston group found that many of Weber's dicta on bureaucracy (1947) do relate to what actually happens in organizations. Their measurements of bureaucracy (e.g. 'Formalization', 'Specialization', and 'Standardization') are very Weberian. However, for Weber there was only one bureaucracy: the formally centralized one. Max Weber (1864–1920) could not be aware of decentralized structures, as he died just before their first appearance in the 1920s (Chandler, 1962). The Aston group, on the other hand, found that formal structures may be either centralized or decentralized, as the contingencies may be. This was somewhat contrary to John Child's (1972) conclusion, based on a replication of an Aston study.

13 The doctoral research (Weinshall, 1960) is described in our organizational example, the Devon Corporation, at the end of chapter 3.

14 Cases of organizations which could survive without any managers reporting to their chief executives are quite rare. There are two such cases which happened in our native Israel. The first is the case of Mr Abraham Silberg, the newly appointed head of the Registration and Census Department of the Ministry of the Interior, who continued to come daily to his office in spite of being ostracized for two years by his employees. This case study has been occasionally taught since it actually happened, in 1960, in order to illustrate Chester Barnard's dictum '. . . in all formal organizations selection is made simultaneously by two authorities, the formal and the informal. That which is made by formal authority we may call appointment (or dismissal), that by the informal authority we may call acceptance (or rejection).' (from 'The Nature of Leadership".)

The second case is a more recent one, from the late 1970s. As in Silberberg's case, it happened in an Israeli ministry, the Ministry of Immigrant Absorption, and the ostracizing of a newly appointed departmental head had a mixed ethnic and political background. This case study is being prepared, but it will be some time before it can be released.

15 We do not know the origin of the saying that 'a good manager is the one who makes others work', but we could refer the reader to C. N. Parkinson (1957). According to Parkinson's Law every manager aims to have more people working for him, so as to make himself more important and have himself promoted!

16 We are indebted to Derek Pugh who right from the beginning (1963) used the term *context*, as distinguished from *structure*, for implying what we have meant by SDM (scope of decision making). Although we use throughout our book the SDM term, which implies the managerial consequences of the organizational context, we take the liberty of using Derek Pugh's term whenever we feel that the text merits it. Incidentally, the term SDM is also not ours, but that of Robert Dubin, who suggested it to us (instead of 'scope of decision-making process', which we used until 1976). We take this opportunity of acknowledging the helpful remarks of Robert Dubin about the first drafts of this book.

17 We use the term 'organizational strategy' instead of the common term 'business strategy' for two reasons. The TOS deals with *all* kinds of organizations including, for example, families—of which we present an example (at the end of chapter 4). Therefore, in order to avoid the impression that only business organizations are dealt with, we decided to call it 'organizational' rather than 'business' strategy. The second reason is that 'business strategy' insinuates that organizations should be run in a 'business' fashion, i.e. that the primary aim of a business organization is profit. We present two organizational examples which demonstrate that when management is not aware of its responsibility to ensure the continued cooperation of *all* human decision-making factors, it may undermine the very survival of the organization for which it is primarily responsible. The case of Israeli Cinemas (organizational example at the end of chapter 2) portrays a situation in which giving one of the

human factors, in this case the customers, an additional piece of the cake, which it neither wanted nor demanded at that particular time, could have brought all the cinemas in Israel to a standstill; all this because management ignored the oncoming pressures from other factors.

The second example, that of the Swissair organization (at the end of chapter 1), is specifically concerned with profitability. The Swissair management was told by the board of directors to ensure that dividends would be paid to its shareholders annually. We can see that had the management pursued such a policy of allocating earnings for the payment of dividends every year, without ever resisting such a policy, Swissair could not have lasted for long.

18   Thus, for example, while most grocery shops vanish whenever supermarkets appear, there may always remain an odd delicatessen shop which refuses to expand, and yet is continuously sustained by a select clientele.

19   Conditions of war and emergency introduce, even in the most democratic, *laissez-faire* countries, substantial governmental intervention. This central direction of the whole economy removes the competitive pressures among organizations which are the main reason for the expansion in their strategies. There exist, however, internal organizational pressures for innovation in industrial organizations during wartime.

20   One of the many books which discusses the organizational implications of over-diversification is Brooke and Van Beusekom's (1978) discussion of international corporate planning.

21   The best known horizontal diversification of General Motors is probably in the manufacturing of refrigerators under the trademark of 'Coldspot'. The most famous book about General Motors is Alfred Sloan's *My Life with General Motors* (1963).

22   The first time that the degree of customer involvement occurred to the first author as a factor which has a tremendous effect on organizational behaviour was in one of the first five of six annual Tel Aviv University Chief Executive Seminars held at Safed in the Galilee, (the first author was instrumental in their administration in 1965, 1967, 1968, 1969, 1970, and 1972). The academic responsibility for the first five Safed seminars was in the hands of the late John D. Glover, and most of the professors teaching with him in these seminars (four a year) were from among the distinguished faculty of the Harvard Business School, as he himself was.

It was one of these ten HBS professors (Jack Glover, Ray Goldberg, Tim Healy, Warren Law, Stan Miller, Dick Rosenbloom, Walt Salmon, Ray Vernon, George Von Peterffy, and Abe Zaleznik) who, in one of his classes, gave the example that led to our thinking about customer involvement as a basis for organizational typology. He compared a barber's shop with a dyeing and finishing textile enterprise. He said that a barber would not advertise, or go out into the street to get his customers; they come to him in order that he may cut their hair, and they are attached to him. (In later years a student of mine produced a seminar paper based on an extensive study of the relationship between customers and their barbers, including the loyalty and continued attachment of customers to barbers, even after they move to other neighbourhoods.) He then said that a similar relationship exists between the customers and the manufacturing organization, the case study of which was discussed by the seminar's participants. Here, too, the customer and supplier are one and the same, as he brings in his woven stuff and gets it back dyed and finished.

23   The book is *Managing Industrial Organizations* (Twiss and Weinshall, 1980). This passage is taken from the chapter on 'Manufacturing and managers' and includes a section on 'the effect of type of business on production managers' (pp. 219–220).

24   The three taxonomies were chosen from 'Several ways to classify organizations' presented by Kast and Rosenzweig (1970, pp. 503–504).

25   Based on the following sources: Etzioni, 1961; Parsons, 1960; and Blau and Scott, 1962.

26 The first comparison of the customer involvement taxonomy with other taxonomies appeared in Weinshall, 1976, pp. 83–85.

27 We refer the reader to a book, entitled *Culture and Management*, in which several of the main research findings and various aspects of the relation between culture and management are discussed (Weinshall, 1977). Four of the readings in this book are especially relevant to our discussion:

Ross Webber's 'Convergence or divergence?', which appeared originally as Webber (1970), introduces these two concepts with reference to the effects of the level of technology and innovation on the culture of the land. Thus, the condition of 'divergence' denotes a situation in which cultural values and norms persist in spite of the spread of technology and innovation. 'Convergence', on the other hand, implies that cultures are being brought closer to one another, as a result of similarities in technology, innovation, and standard of living (Weinshall, 1977, pp. 39–55).

Howard Perlmutter's 'Emerging East–West ventures: The transideological enterprise', which appeared originally as Perlmutter (1969), deals with how the differences between the Western and Eastern bloc countries will evolve when business corporations are moving across national boundaries with ever-growing ease. Perlmutter conceptualizes four relations between the cultures of different countries—'divergence', 'submergence', 'convergence', and 'emergence'. The latter, 'emergence', relates to the culture which will eventually be created by multinational corporations in the countries in which they operate (Weinshall, 1977, pp. 140–162).

Weinshall's own work on multinational corporations (1977, pp. 383–432) and multinational managers (1977, pp. 163–214) will be referred to later in this book and, especially, in chapter 6 about the multinationals.

28 The material in Table 4.6 is drawn from four different sources, as shown in Table 4.7 on page 136.

29 For a more detailed discussion about attitudes regarding the anti-mobility value, as they differ from country to country, see Weinshall (1977, pp. 188–191).

30 The world of *Little Lord Fauntleroy* (Burnett, 1886) is nowadays a complete fiction, quite removed from reality.

31 For a more detailed discussion of national culture differences in communication see Weinshall (1979, pp. 233–278).

32 As per George Homans, who established that the organization is made up of the actions, interactions, and sentiments of its people (Homans, 1959).

33 Norbert Wiener (1894–1964) was the pioneer of *Cybernetics* (Wiener, 1948), which was popularized by him in *The Human Use of Human Beings* (Wiener, 1950).

According to Wiener, cybernetics is the science of communication and control. The control is performed through communication, both for the transfer of information and for purposes of command (instruction) of a person over a machine and over a fellow person. *Cybernetics* defines the principals as directing systems of various sorts (mechanical, biological, social, economic, and other systems) in an abstract and mathematical way. Two other scientists, C. E. Shannon and W. Weaver (1964), developed mathematically the theory of communication and information. The simultaneous development of 'operations research' and 'system analysis' helped Wiener to legitimize cybernetics. He also used 'games theory' and 'decision theory' which had been previously developed, respectively, by Von Neuman and Abraham Wald. Wiener likewise emphasized the dominant role of data processing and feedback in an effective and reliable control system. According to Shannon and Weaver, a typical 'information system', the function of which is only the transfer of signals (rather than their interpretation), includes the following parts: (a) the source of information; (b) an encoding system turning the raw message into a set of signals; (c) the channel through which the signals are transmitted; (d) a decoding system for reprocessing the signals into a message; (e) a target.

Table 4.7   Sources for Table 4.6

Structural change factor	Britain	France	Germany	Source
1. Social mobility factor (educational inequalities measured by an inequality ratio—'non manual worker sons of non manual workers', divided by 'non manual worker sons of manual workers')	(less than 250) high	(250– 290) medium	(300– 499) low	Bendix and Lipset, 1966, pp. 582–601; in Weinshall, 1977, p. 177
2. Interorganizational mobility of chief executives (% of chief executives who were employed in three organizations or more, previous to their present ones)	(19%) low	(28%) medium	(40%) high	De-Bettignies and Evans, 1977; in Weinshall, 1977, p. 288
3. Attitudes to inter-organizational managerial mobility (% of those who backed decision to fire a chief executive whose leadership did not suit the organization any more; average between the responses of INSEAD participants at the beginnings of the 1969/1970 and of the 1970/1971 classes)	(9.5%) high	(8.5%) high	(5.5%) medium	Weinshall; in Weinshall, 1977, pp. 196–197
4. Role in learning process (averages of ranking orders with participants from other countries', 'contributing to the learning of others', and 'benefiting or receiving from learning process' among the responses of INSEAD participants of the class of 1965/1966)	(1.7) high	(6.0) low	(6.5) low	Weinshall; in Weinshall, 1977, p. 194

The control and navigation system deals with the feedback, receipt, and analysis of the information. This is an open system which the *input* enters, and the *output* leaves. One example which is often given for a control and navigation system operated by a feedback mechanism is a heating system with a thermostat, as in a house boiler for heating water. The system is operated by fuel-energy which creates heat, part of which raises the temperature of the thermostat; when it reaches a certain level, the thermostat causes the shutting off of the system. When the physical environment, including the thermostat, cools off, the thermostat will once again activate the system, thus starting a new cycle.

The cybernetic system in our case is the TOS, and the feedback mechanism is the managerial attitudes.

34 Just consider the absence of a unanimous fact, and the different attitudes towards one and the same occurrence, in the following example, used to impress upon our students in classrooms the concept and understanding of perceptions.

We ask our students to have a sheet of paper ready and to write on it their impressions of what they are going to see. We take a breakable ashtray (one of those made of plastic, used in public places) full of cigarette butts, and with vigour we throw it on the floor, smashing it to pieces and scattering the contents. Thereupon the students record their perceptions of what has happened. Here are some of the things they write: 'The professor wastes our time with stupidities.' 'The teacher gets away with damaging university property.' 'The poor janitors, they will have to clean up the mess.' 'The professor lost his mind.' Etc.

35 One example of attitudes which are not absolute, and how length of service affects them, is the expression of the degree of satisfaction among the managers of the Devon Corporation. The percentages in Table 4.8 give the distribution of responses to the question, 'All things considered, how satisfied are you working for Devon Corporation?' (Weinshall, 1960, p. 104.)

A possible explanation for the higher satisfaction among old-timers, and the relation of this phenomenon to managerial turnover, is given as follows (Weinshall, 1960, pp. 113–115):

When a person enters a company, he might, for example, have chosen it from among, say, five employment alternatives. Until he joined the company he would have had five images of himself being employed. Once he joined the company, one of the images was destroyed and he retained only four images. Thus during the first period he is disappointed that reality did not correspond with his image (not realizing that the other four images would not necessarily correspond with reality either).

In due course, however, the other four alternatives become less and less realistic (both in his image and in the practicability of being employed there), and the discrepancy between his present employment and the image he had of it disappears. He 'gets used' to the place, which means also that he forgets the image and compares it not to experiences in other places, but to previous

Table 4.8 Degree of satisfaction among managers working for the Devon Corporation

| | Old-timers (more than 7 years) | Newcomers | | |
		A (5–7 years)	B (2–5 years)	C (less than 2 years)
Number of respondents	37	9	37	25
Very satisfied	54%	45%	30%	24%
Satisfied	46%	55%	48%	52%
Dissatisfied	—	—	19%	20%
Very dissatisfied	—	—	3%	4%

138

experiences he had in the same place. With time he 'gets used' to many attributes of the company and the community, including such things as social benefits (pensions, etc.) and the whole social setting, on top of his business status. By now the chances are small that any perceived alternatives he might still entertain would be more satisfying than his present employment.

The fact that people tend to leave the organization early in their service rather than later probably derives from the same reason. Those whose disappointment and dissatisfaction are so strong that they decide to quit do it within the period when the 'images' of the alternatives are still 'realistic'. This in turn intensifies the situation of 'the longer the service, the higher the satisfaction', as the majority of those who left would have probably expressed negative attitudes had they prolonged their sojurn in the company.

36 The reasons why an area-decentralized structure cannot operate in the post Second World War era will be explained in subsection 4.2.3. Why the matrix structure is not a practicable structure at all will be explained in subsection 5.3.3 of the next chapter.

37 The dynamics of the TOS may be compared to our planet turning on its axis and rotating around the sun, as part of the solar system. Human beings are not aware that all these movements take place, and it seems to us that 'as things have been, they remain'. The same is true about our feelings regarding the organizations within which we function. While a lot of movement occurs within the dynamics of the TOS, to those who are within the turbulence it seems that, basically, things are as usual. This is why a man like Henry Ford I could not understand why he, the man who pioneered successfully the first mass-production line, should change his organization. Related to this phenomenon are the underlying assumptions of *The Peter Principle* (Peter, 1969) which states that once a person is in a position of competence, he will always be competent in it. This is not so, because every few years the requirements of any specific role may change at least in terms of the MC.

38 *Nineteen Eighty-Four* was George Orwell's (1903–1950) last book, written in 1949 when he was already gravely ill with tuberculosis. It is a book of despair, depicting a situation which could have evolved from the totalitarianism which was predominant in the fascist regimes before the Second World War, the spread of Soviet Communism after the war, and central government control, even in Western democracies, during and immediately after the Second World War. It describes the complete destruction of the creative and moral personality by the almighty state bureaucracy. Orwell's second most famous book, *Animal Farm* (1945), was also written in the gloomy days at the end of the war. The period between the publication of Orwell's two famous books was marked by enormous economic aid for the reconstruction of the economies of the powers who lost the war.

39 A more detailed description of the dynamics of technology and employment is presented elsewhere (Twiss and Weinshall, 1980, pp. 175–190). In chapter 6 we will point out that countries will cede to multinationals a lot of power and many of their present-day roles. This will coincide with the major effects of the introduction of the electronic chip which, it is predicted, will be felt at the beginning of the twenty-first century. Therefore, while many present-day rules of behaviour among nations in peace and war, e.g. international relations, will vanish as the multinationals assume more world power, the nations will assume more and more roles in the area of economic regulation, welfare, recreation, and education.

40 This is because of the nature of the entrepreneurial structure in which a large number of the employees are directly approachable by the entrepreneur. Indeed, when the entrepreneurial structure suits the SDM, the great majority of the employees are involved in making sure the organization will survive.

41 The sort of things that 'chums' ('buddies' in the USA, or 'copains' in France) know

of each other, and/or the sort of things that a foreman knows of those workers who
have been with him for, say, ten years and more.

42 There are those who are incapable of remembering more than a few faces and
names, and they often fail to connect those few faces with their names. On the
other hand, there are those who have the facility of remembering thousands of
people, and know many details about them and their families. One person who had
such a phenomenal memory for people was the late Moshe Sharett (1894–1965),
the second prime minister of Israel (1954–1955).

43 Although an entrepreneur seems to encourage his subordinates to reveal
entrepreneurial capabilities of their own (e.g. 'Why do I always have to be the
source of all the ideas over here? Why can't you come up with some good ideas of
your own?'), he actually resents anybody who tries to introduce anything not
originated by himself. These entrepreneurial aides should have a certain degree of
initiative in carrying out directives without receiving from him detailed instructions
as to how to do them. Their initiative should not, however, go much beyond this
degree of being able to implement and realize his assignments. Therefore, beware
any entrepreneurial aide who falls into the trap of an entrepreneur who seemingly
encourages his subordinates to volunteer big ideas. Such an entrepreneurial aide
will generally not last long with the entrepreneur.

Several of the cases of the 'orderly genius', or 'favourite of the day', were such
entrepreneurial aides who volunteered big ideas and then, because they did it, fell
out of the entrepreneur's graces. Other 'favourites of the day' are eager-beaver
entrepreneurial aides, who want to prove themselves to be better than others. As
long as they can stand the strain of working quite closely with the entrepreneur,
they may last as his favourites. However, the moment that the entrepreneur realizes
that the person is not the superman he expects him to be, out he goes.

44 We have already mentioned in note 42 that memory varies considerably from
person to person. Therefore, the averages of different levels of remembering people
given in Table 4.9 should be considered only as possible hypothesis. They are
based on our own experience and not on any research; they are, at best, only
averages of quite widely spread distributions.

The latter type of memorized knowledge of people is the ability to identify how
one came to know the person. When one sees somebody with a familiar face in a
public place or vehicle without being able to remember who this individual is, one
tries to imagine him dressed in different uniforms. One imagines him in a police-
man's, or in a barber's, or in a waiter's, or in a driver's until, hopefully, one realizes
why this face is familiar. This is 'connecting a face with a place'.

45 Let us remember that an entrepreneurial management operates in an *informally*

Table 4.9 Memories for people: average and range

Type of things one remembers of others	Number of people remembered	
	Average	Range
Basic knowledge of people as mentioned in note 44	±100	up to 500
Their names and a few details about the people	±1000	500–5000
Connecting a face with a place	±10 000	5000–50 000

centralized structure which is characterized by lack of formal definitions of who is doing what, and when. Furthermore, assignments are based to a large extent on an *ad hoc*, piecemeal basis.

46 Numerically controlled (NC) machine tools have been in existence since about 1958. Conventional machine tools have a number of mechanical functions which are performed manually by an operator, namely starting, changing speed, changing feed rate, moving table to a specified dimension, changing cutting tool, opening/shutting off coolant cycle, reversing direction of revolution, and stopping machine.

In automatic machines these are operated by a program installed in the NC machine tool, instructing it what and how many to manufacture. The NC machine has three principal elements: the machine; the 'inter-phase' which serves as 'handle-turner' using servo-motors and hydraulic or electrical servo-systems; and the 'control system'—the program—which can read, decipher, memorize, calculate, and examine.

47 Even if the physicist had agreed to perform the task of an accountant for a few weeks, this would have been at a substantial financial cost and loss to the organization.

48 Whenever we mention managers in this book, we refer to those who are defined as employees who are responsible for the continued cooperation of one or more other members of the organization. Under these conditions the ± 100 managers constitute the majority of the employees in the organization. If any reader is bothered by what may seem limitations of 'span of control', he need not worry. The 'scientific management' approach to span of control is mostly associated with Lindall Urwick (1956). In a contingency theory like the TOS there is no place for a static notion like the span of control. This is discussed in more detail further on in the following sections. It is also one of the main highlights of the Sears, Roebuck & Company organizational example at the end of chapter 5.

49 This is probably the main reason why ITT top management divided the world into two parts, each of which comprises about 30 product/service lines. This halves the number of product/service lines reporting simultaneously to the same chief executive at US headquarters. The ITT CE travels to and fro between Brussels and New York; he used to convene the heads of product/service lines in each place every four weeks; in 1981 it was every eight weeks. Some of these product/service lines on both sides of the globe, like the Sheraton hotels, have more than 100 subsidiary units; this means that, by dividing the world into two, the number of subsidiary units to every product/service line brings them within a range of manageable decentralized control every one or two months.

50 The functions of the organization are something like functions of the organs of a human or animal body. There are only so many functions for an organization to perform: manufacturing, marketing, securing capital, etc. Similarly, there are only so many functions that a living human being or animal needs: walking, transporting, seeing, hearing, smelling, eating, etc. For all these functions human beings and animals have legs, hands, eyes, ears, noses, mouths, teeth, etc.

With both organizations and living beings, the more complex they are, the more functions are necessary, and the more refined they should be. In small organizations several functions are performed by the same manager, thus selling and purchasing are usually in the hands of one manager in smaller organizations. Similarly, the less developed the animal, the less advanced his organs.

51 Thus, in an example of 'multiple levels of grouping in a multinational firm', presented by Henry Mintzberg (1979, p. 120), we find the levels of hierarchy in the organization chart shown here in Table 4.10.

52 What we refer to as 'functions', Mintzberg calls 'business functions'. What he calls 'work functions' is the sort of grouping we find in manufacturing of the unit

Table 4.10   Levels of hierarchy

	Type of grouping
1. President and Corporate secretariat	
2. General Managers of Canada, Tahiti, and Andorra	By area
3. Vice Presidents (subordinates of Canada's General Manager) for Snowblowers, Frostible Remedies, and Charters to Florida	By product
4. Managers (subordinates of Snowblower's VP) of Manufacturing, Engineering, and Marketing	By business function
5. General Foremen (subordinates of Manufacturing Manager) for Fabricating and Assembly	By work function
6. Foremen (subordinates of General Foreman) for Fabrication of Turning, Milling, and Drilling	By work function
7. Workers (subordinates of Foremen)	

production type (see the South Essex Industry organizational example at the end of this chapter). The grouping is indeed functional in nature, as the units are dependent on each other, and nothing complete can be produced without the participation of at least several of the functional departments. The nature of the 'work functions' is different from that of the 'business functions' described in Table 4.10. The 'business functions' are similar in all types of organizations in their having to deal with the continued cooperation of employees, customers (or clients), suppliers, owners, etc. The nature of the 'work functions', on the other hand, depends on the type of organization and will differ from a specific industry to a bank, a government office, etc. Nevertheless, we find in practice that when grouped by 'work function', the maximum number of units reporting to one superior is, as in 'business functions', ten at the most, whatever the type of organization.

53   The Japanese 'ringi' decision-making process is actually hierarchical decision-making upside-down. In all organizations except for the Japanese, the decision is taken by the superior and subsequently, as it is processed through lower hierarchical levels, it is 'made'. In Japanese organization the decision making process goes the other way around, from the lower levels upwards, and only when it reaches the top—the decision is taken by the superior (Drucker, 1954; Yoshino, 1968; Weinshall and Tawara, 1978).

54   The shirking of responsibility by referring it to higher authority is referred to as 'passing the buck'. Passing the buck is a process rather than a single act; an example of it is given in the text. We cannot remember to whom the following statement is attributed; when this leader wanted to stress that he does not shirk responsibility and is capable of taking the necessary decisions, he said: 'The buck stops here.'

55   It so happens that neither ITT nor Philips operate in a multistructure. ITT still operates in a product/service line structure, decentralized in the early 1980s to an eight-week autonomy period. This is described in note 49. Philips has been operating since the Second World War in a sort of a matrix structure. This structure, which we consider, at best, to be a possible transitional structure from a functional or an area or product/service line decentralized structure, to a multistructure, is discussed in more detail in subsection 5.3.3 of chapter 5. This structure of Philips' is briefly described in Weinshall (1973, pp. 166–167).

56   The BCS example is based on the doctoral research of the second author (Raveh, 1976), who included among her research hypotheses and tools some which are directly related to the TOS.

57   Carried out by Jacques Horovitz (1980) it differs from the three examples in the retailing areas (BSC, Marks & Spencer, and Sears): (a) It studies different types of organizations rather than similar sub-organizations within one large organization; (b) the organizations investigated were in different countries, while each of the retailing groups was in one country only (BSC and Marks & Spencer in Britain, and Sears in the USA). This example helps us to explore the socio-cultural effects on the MS, which are of a similar nature to the effects of degree of customer involvement on the MS (these two effects appear as broken lines on the right-hand side of Figure 4.3).

SELECTED BIBLIOGRAPHICAL SOURCES

Bendix, R., and Lipset, P. K., 1966. *Class, Status and Power*, Free Press, New York.

Blau, P. M., and Scott, W. R., 1962. *Formal Organizations: A Comparative Analysis*, Chandler, San Francisco.

Brooke, M. Z., and Van Beusekom, M., 1978. *International Corporate Planning*, Pitman, London.

Brown, W., 1960. *Exploration in Management*, Wiley, New York.

Burnett, F. H., 1886. *Little Lord Fauntleroy*.

Burns, T. 1954. 'The directions of activity and communication in a department executive group', *Human Relations*, VII (I), pp. 74–97.

Burns, T., and Stalker, G., 1961. *The Management of Innovations*, Tavistock, London.

Carlson, S., 1951. *Executive Behavior: A Study of Workload and the Working Methods of Managing Directors*, Strombergs, Stockholm.

Chandler, A. D., Jr, 1962. *Strategy and Structure*, MIT Press, Cambridge, Mass.

Channon, D. F., 1973. *The Strategy and Structure of British Enterprise*, Macmillan, London.

Child, J., 1972. 'Organization structure and strategies of control: replications of the Aston study', *Administrative Science Quarterly*, pp. 163–177.

Coch, L., and French, R. P., 1948. 'Overcoming resistance to change', *Human Relations*, I (4), pp. 511–532.

Cyert, R. M., and March, J. G., 1963. *A Behavioral Theory of the Firm*, Prentice-Hall, Englewood Cliffs, NJ.

Davis, E. L., Cherns, A. B., and Associates (eds), 1975. *The Quality of Working Life*, Free Press, New York.

De-Bettignies, H.-C., and Evans, P. L., 1977. 'The cultural dimension of top executives' careers: a comparative analysis', in T. D. Weinshall (ed.), *Culture and Management*, Penguin, Harmondsworth, Middx.

Drucker, P. F., 1954. *The Practice of Management*, Harper, New York.

Dyas, G. P., and Thanheiser, H. T., 1976. *The Emerging European Enterprise*, Macmillan, London.

Emery, F. E., and Trist, E. L., 1960. 'Socio-technical systems', in C. W. Churchman and M. Verholst (eds), *Management Science Models and Techniques*, vol. 2, Pergamon Press, Oxford, pp. 83–93.

Etzioni, A., 1961. *A Comparative Analysis of Complex Organizations*, Free Press of Glencoe, New York.

Glover, J. D., and Hower, R. M., 1952. *The Administrator*, Irwin, Homewood, Ill.

Heller, F. A., 1971. *Managerial Decision Making*, Tavistock, London.

Homans, G. C., 1951. *The Human Group*, Routledge & Kegan Paul, London.

Horovitz, J. H., 1980. *Top Management Control in Europe*, Macmillan, London.

Jacques, E., 1951. *The Changing Culture of a Factory*, Tavistock, London.

Jacques, E., 1956. *Measurement of Responsibility*, Tavistock, London.

Jacques, E., 1961. *Equitable Payment*, Heinemann, London.

Kast, F. E., and Rosenzweig, J. E., 1970. *Organization and Management: A Systems Approach*, McGraw-Hill, New York.

Katz, D., and Kahn, R. L., 1966. *The Social Psychology of Organizations*, Wiley, New York.

Lawrence, P. R., and Lorsch, J. W., 1967. *Organization and Environment*, Division of Research, Graduate School of Business Administration, Harvard University, Boston, Mass.

Lewin, K., 1953. *A Dynamic Theory of Personality*, McGraw-Hill, New York.

Lippit, R., Watson, and Westley, B., 1958. *The Dynamics of Planned Change*, Harcourt, Brace & World, New York.

Lombard, G. F. F., 1955. *Behavior in a Selling Group*, Division of Research, Graduate School of Business Administration, Harvard University, Boston, Mass.

March, J. G., and Simon, H. A., 1958. *Organizations*, Wiley, New York. Used with permission.

Mayo, E., 1933. *The Human Problems of an Industrial Civilization*, Macmillan, New York.

McGregor, D., 1960. *The Human Side of the Enterprise*, McGraw-Hill, New York.

Miller, E., and Rice, A. K., 1967. *Systems of Organization*, Tavistock, London.

Mintzberg, H., 1979. *Structuring of Organizations: A Synthesis of Research*, Prentice-Hall, Englewood Cliffs, NJ.

Orwell, G., 1945. *Animal Farm: A Fairy Story*, Secker & Warburg, London.

Orwell, G., 1949. *Nineteen Eighty-Four*, Secker & Warburg, London.

Parkinson, C. N., 1957. *Parkinson's Law and Other Studies in Administration*, Houghton Mifflin, Boston, Mass.

Parsons, T., 1960. *The Structure and Process of Modern Societies*, Free Press of Glencoe, New York.

Perlmutter, H. V., 1969. 'Emerging East–West ventures: the transideological enterprise', *Columbia Journal of World Business*, IV (5).

Peter, L. J., 1969. *The Peter Principle*, Souvenir Press, London.

Pugh, D. S., 1963. 'A conceptual scheme for organizational analysis', *Administrative Science Quarterly*, **8**, 289–315.

Pugh, D. S., and Hickson, D. J. (eds), 1976. *Organizational Structure in its Context: The Aston Programme I*, Saxon House, Aldershot, Hants.

Pugh, D. S., and Hinning, C. R., 1976. *Organizational Structure: Extensions and Replications—The Aston Programme II*, Saxon House, Aldershot, Hants.

Pugh, D. S., and Payne, R. L. (eds), 1977. *Organizational Behaviour in its Context: The Aston Programme III*, Saxon House, Aldershot, Hants.

Raveh, Y. A., 1976. 'Managerial behaviour in retailing', unpublished doctoral thesis, University of London, Graduate School of Business Studies.

Roethlisberger, F. J., and Dickson, W. J., 1939. *Management and the Workers*, Harvard University Press, Boston, Mass.

Rumelt, R. P., 1974. *Strategy, Structure and Economic Performance in Large American Industrial Corporations*, Division of Research, Graduate School of Business Administration, Harvard University, Boston, Mass.

Shannon, C. E., and Weaver, W., 1964. *Mathematical Theory of Communication*, University of Illinois Press, Urbana.

Simon, H. A., 1947. *Administrative Behavior*, 2nd edn, Macmillan, New York.

Sloan, A. P., 1963. *My Life at General Motors*, Doubleday, New York.

Stopford, J. M., 1968. 'Growth and organizational change in the multinational firm', unpublished doctoral dissertation, Harvard University. (Published by Arno Press, New York, 1980.)

Stopford, J. M., and Wells, L. T., 1972. *Managing the Multinational Enterprise*, Basic Books, New York.

144

Twiss, B. C., and Weinshall, T. D., 1980. *Managing Industrial Organizations*, Pitman, London.

Urwick, L. F., 1956. The manager's span of control', *Harvard Business Review*, May—June, pp. 39–42.

Vernon, R., 1971. Sovereignty at Bay: The Multinational Spread of U.S. Enterprises, Longman, London.

Webber, R. A., 1970. 'Convergence or divergence?', *Columbia Journal of World Business*, IV (3), May–June.

Weber, M., 1947. *The Theory of Social and Economic Organization*, translated by A. M. Henderson and Talcott Parsons, Oxford University Press.

Weinshall, T. D., 1960. 'The effects of management changes on the organizational relationships and attitudes', unpublished doctoral dissertation, Harvard University.

Weinshall, T. D., 1966. 'The Communicogram: a method for describing the pattern frequency and accuracy of organization and communication', in J. L. Lawrence (ed.), *Operational Research and the Social Sciences*, Tavistock, London.

Weinshall, T. D., 1976. 'The Total Organizational System (TOS) and the interdisciplinary approach in management and organization', in P. Verburg, P. C. A. Malataux, K. T. A. Halbertsma, and J. C. Boers (eds), *Organisatiewetenschap en Praktijk* (Organization Science and Practice), H. G. Stenfert Kroese, B. V. Leiden, Holland, pp. 55–106.

Weinshall, T. D. (ed.), 1977. *Culture and Management*, Modern Management Reading Series, Penguin, Harmondsworth, Middx.

Weinshall, T. D., 1979. *Managerial Communication: Concepts, Approaches and Techniques*, Academic Press, London.

Weinshall, T. D., and Tawara, J., 1978. 'Managerial structure of a nationally mixed organization in Japan', *Journal of Organization and Administration Sciences*, 8 (4), Winter.

Wiener, Norbert, 1948. *Cybernetics or Control and Communication in the Animal and the Machine*, Herman, Paris.

Wiener, N., 1950. *The Human Use of Human Beings, Cybernetics and Society*, Houghton Mifflin, Boston, Mass.

Weinshall, T. D., ed. *Culture and Management*, Penguin, London.

Woodward, J., 1958. *Management and Technology*, HMSO, London.

Woodward, J. 1965. *Industrial Organization: Theory and Practice*, Oxford University Press.

Yoshino, M., 1968. *Japan's Managerial System*, MIT Press, Cambridge, Mass.

Zaleznik, A., Christensen, C. R., and Roethlisberger, F. J., 1958. *The Motivation, Productivity and Satisfaction of Workers*, Division of Research, Graduate School of Business Administration, Harvard University, Boston, Mass.

Chapter 5

Managerial Characteristics and Advanced TOS Dynamics

This chapter is principally devoted to the people who steer the organization—the managers. Organizations are contingency systems. The pressures of the immediate environment (competing organizations) and the wider environment (the employment, money, and consumer markets, and the technological and socio-cultural systems) lead to continuous innovation and expansion in the technology, product/service diversity, and geographical dispersal of organizations. These, in turn, make it necessary to adapt the managerial structure from time to time to this growth in the scope of decision making (SDM). In order to achieve such structural changes, managers with leadership and followership characteristics suitable for the required structure should be found in key positions of the managerial structure. This means that whenever one structure changes to another one, the managerial characteristics of the CE (chief executive) and other key position managers should be suitable for the new managerial structure. We shall expand this topic in the first two sections, about the leadership and followership characteristics, and the interorganizational mobility of managers. The third section is devoted mainly to the reactions of managers to their functioning in hierarchies, to their resulting interpersonal aspirations and motivations, and also to some structural solutions for dealing with complex scopes of decision making. The fourth section is devoted to the multistructure, encompassing different basic structures—entrepreneurial (informally centralized), functional (formally centralized), as well as product/service lines and areas (formally decentralized)—but federated in one structure, directly reporting to one CE.

5.1 LEADERSHIP AND FOLLOWERSHIP CHARACTERISTICS

Let us first consider managerial leadership and followership, and other interpersonal characteristics as they relate to different people in the TOS.

There are two underlying assumptions regarding the dynamics of the TOS.

(a) *The primary objective of managers is to ensure the continued operation and survival of their organization.* Therefore, their organizational strategies are secondary to the achievement of the continued operation and survival of the organization. These strategies include what, how, and where they are to operate, both in manufacturing and marketing: in short, the product/service lines, the scientific and technological means of operation, and the areas to be covered.

The continued organizational operation and survival is a generalized *primary objective* and responsibility of all managers, in whichever organization they are. It should be regarded as their yardstick for evaluating their suitability to the 'managerial class', in which they compare themselves to other managers, in trying to belong to a more stable, less collapsible, and longer lasting organization.

In this the managers are similar to other human groups comprising the organization. The workers try to have better working conditions, including wages, working climate, job security, and peer and superior appreciation, than workers in other organizations. The customers, the 'consumer population', try to have cheaper, better, and more easily obtainable goods than customers of the same products or services in other organizations. Suppliers try to be better and sooner paid than are supplies to other organizations. Shareholders try to have higher dividends in comparison with other shares in their reference group, the Stock Exchange.

The involvement of all the above mentioned human groups, other than managers, may be regarded as opportunistic, in the sense that individuals would stay with the organization only as long as it serves their purpose. The managers, on the other hand, are altruistically involved in the organization because the basis for comparison with others in their reference group is the strength of the organization for continued operation and survival.

(b) *The managerial characteristics (leadership, followership, and other interpersonal characteristics) are part of those personality traits which are acquired during one's first years (up to, say, 6, 4, or even 2 years of age).*[1] The more the managerial characteristics fit the interpersonal roles required, and the more they are in line with the organizational SDM, the more a manager feels fulfilled, i.e. the higher the motivation, satisfaction, and feeling of achievement. Subsection 5.1.1 discusses in more detail the nature and effects of one's managerial characteristics. The other subsections explore additional aspects of the relations between these leadership, followership, and other interpersonal characteristics, the degree of behavioural flexibility, and their effects on the managerial structure.

5.1.1   The Relationships between Managerial Characteristics and Managerial Style

5.1.1.1   *The Conditions in which Managers Behave Differently from their Managerial Characteristics*

Managerial leadership and followership characteristics are part of one's personality. They are manifest in one's interpersonal relationships downwards and upwards in the hierarchy, in conducting one's relationship according to one's own inner will and inclinations. One's managerial style, however, is the nature of the actual and/or perceived relationships of a person with the people surrounding him in the hierarchy: superiors, subordinates, and peers. The aggregated managerial styles of all the managers constitute the informal relationship structure which is, consequently, composed of the actual and/or perceived relationships of the management structure. Examples of the managerial leadership and followership characteristics and their relation to managerial style and structure are part of the organizational examples at the ends of the two previous chapters which dealt with aspects of the manager's role in the dynamics of the managerial structure (chapter 3) and of the TOS as a whole (chapter 4). Readers are especially advised to consider the characteristics and style of the managers of the Devon Corporation and of ITT, organizational examples appearing at the end of chapter 3, as well as the managerial characteristics revealed in the example of British Chain Stores and that of family organizations, both at the end of this (chapter 5). All the four organizational examples following the present chapter are concerned with managerial characteristics and advanced TOS dynamics.

Managerial Characteristics are composed of the traits which govern the way one would relate voluntarily to one's subordinates (leadership characteristics), superiors (followership characteristics), and other people in the organization—peers, farther removed managers, workers, customers, suppliers, owners, bankers, government and union officials, etc. The traits are neither inherited nor acquired during one's lifetime, but are formed in one's personality at a very early age.

In the great majority of cases, people can adapt their interpersonal behaviour to interpersonal role requirements not in line with their own managerial characteristics, but with varying degrees of difficulty. We shall refer to the resulting behaviour as *managerial style*. The differences between one's managerial characteristics and one's managerial style, and the degree of difficulty in bridging the gap between the two, will negatively affect one's motivation, role achievements, and satisfaction. The larger the gap between managerial characteristics and style, and the greater the difficulty in bridging it, the smaller one's motivation, achievement, and satisfaction.

There are, however, on the one hand, rational cultures in which managers are brought up, on the whole, with an ability for a greater degree of flexibility. Thus, in the Japanese zaibatsu example immediately following this chapter, we discuss the ability of the Japanese, and the Germans too, to be at one and the same time rigid and flexible, as well as formal and informal, and oriented towards centralizing as well as decentralizing. This means that for Japanese and German managers it is, on the whole, easier to bridge the gaps between their managerial characteristics and styles; and, consequently, they are more motivated, have more feelings of achievement and satisfaction, than managers in other national cultures with the same gaps between their managerial characteristics and styles.

We also know, and shall discuss in more detail in section 5.4, that CEs of multi-structures, in countries other than Japan and Germany and particularly in the USA, are able to lead their subordinates in a heterogeneous rather than a homogeneous way. That is to say that they control their subordinates through different degrees of formality and different degrees of centralization. This means that in national cultures other than those of Japan and Germany, at least some human beings are brought up in babyhood and very early childhood to have a more flexible interpersonal personality. We can assume that the number of people who are capable of easily and comfortably conducting interpersonal relations other than those conforming with their own specific managerial characteristics is constantly increasing, especially in the industrial democracies of the world.

On the other hand, one encounters occasionally a person who can behave only according to his or her managerial characteristics, and is unable in any circumstances to adapt to another managerial style. It would be useless to try to persuade or even to coerce such a person to behave other than according to his inherent managerial characteristics.[2] Luckily for the world and its different types of organizations, the number of such people is small.

Finally, before specifying the different TOS managerial characteristics and styles, let us consider the connection between the psychological environment of the manager and his ability to conform easily to a style radically different from his managerial characteristics. We consider the psychological environment of people in terms of the level in Maslow's hierarchy of needs at which the environment happens to be at the time. The psychological environment may be, on the whole, that prevailing at the time the managerial characteristics were formed in a person, i.e. when one of the need levels was fulfilled, and so were the need levels below it (see Figure 5.1).[3] Thus, for example, when the belongingness and love levels in Figure 5.1 are fulfilled, then the lower physiological and safety levels are fulfilled also. It is then that people need, or aspire to, esteem and/or social standing, and even more self-fulfilment.[4]

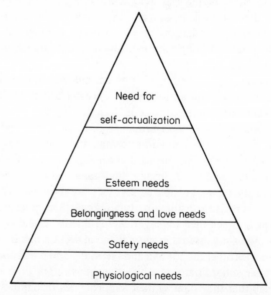

Figure 5.1   The Maslow hierarchy of basic needs

Most of the managers in the industrial countries were born into this level of immediate search for social standing. Managers in one or more countries may discover in times of strife that the psychological environment suddenly drops by one or more levels in Maslow's hierarchy. Thus, when a war breaks out the people in the involved countries may well find themselves with a psychological environment as low as that of searching for physiological and safety needs (see Figure 5.1).

It is when the psychological environment drastically changes that individuals can and do voluntarily change their managerial characteristics. This phenomenon of people naturally, willingly, and even enthusiastically changing their most profound interpersonal characteristics for characteristics which are necessary for surviving major emergency and strife is an enormous asset to the organization in trouble, be it a whole country or a business organization, or large group of people within it. Thus, for example, during wartime, the great majority of the people joining the military forces give up their inbred managerial characteristics, and willingly accept serving in a rigidly disciplined organization. The same goes for all the managers in the organizations in a country at war. The scopes of decision making of manufacturing and distributing organizations in a country at war become very much smaller than their SDM in peacetime; this is primarily true of Western, democratic non-totalitarian countries. The SDM of all these organizations requires functional, formally centralized structures. Thus, for example, an organization with a decentralized product line is, in wartime, directed by the government to manufacture only certain products to be purchased by the military. It is provided with the necessary materials, promised a contract for determining costs, and allocated the minimum of necessary manpower. Such conditions call for a functional structure. Its top managers, who had managerial characteristics suitable for a decentralized structure, will now have to content themselves in functional structure roles.[5] It turns out that people operate even better, managers as well as workers, in times of war than in times of peace.

However, the moment the emergency is over, and the psychological environment moves back to normal, the people revert to their inbred managerial characteristics.[6]

5.1.1.2 Different Types of Managerial Characteristics and Styles in the TOS

Table 5.1 presents ten different types of managers and several of their characteristics. This table is a continuation of, and complimentary to, Figure 4.4, which appears towards the end of chapter 4. Figure 4.4 presents schematically the progression of managerial structures, as the SDM increases over time. Table 5.1 marks the various stages of the TOS, and provides the decriptions of the types of managers, and their managerial characteristics, for every one of the managerial structures, whether at a growth or at a stabilization stage of the progression.

Table 5.1 is self-explanatory. Managerial characteristics of every one of the ten different types of managers are specified. In the text we shall try to bring to life these ten types of managers, by presenting examples of them. However, we should warn readers of the limitations of the types of managers presented in Table 5.1.

Table 5.1 Relation of managerial characteristics to style and structure: ten different types of managers and their characteristics

Role of manager		Names of types of managers and their managerial characteristics	
		(suitable for either growth or stabilization periods)	
In what managerial structure	In what managerial role	Flexible leadership (growth)	Rigid leadership (stabilization)
ENTREPRENEURIAL	ENTREPRENEUR	1. ENTREPRENEUR 1. Imaginative, inventive, etc.[a] 2. Ignores formal hierarchy 3. Assigns ideas, but not detailed instructions 4. Nevertheless expects reporting on progress 5. Does not worry about duplicate assignments to different people[b] 6. Does not bear having partners in big ideas[c] 7. Likes keeping his people on edge 8. Likes to slave drive them 9. Himself works long hours, 7 days a week, etc.[d] 10. Does not know how to relax from work[d] 11. Has 'charisma' (leader attraction for followers) 12. Does not bear being interfered with by any superior boss 13. Manipulates people and sometimes other resources[e] 14. Sometimes believes the experiences he went through explain his achievements[f]	
	ENTREPRENEURIAL AIDES (ALL OTHER MANAGERS)	2. ENTREPRENEUR'S AIDES 1. Have enough initiative to carry out entrepreneur's ideas 2. Ignore formal hierarchy 3. Do not bear receiving and following detailed formal instructions (with whom, how, where, when) 4. Do not have enough imagination and/or risk taking for entrepreneuring big ideas by themselves 5. Hard workers, but not as hard as entrepreneurs 6. Manipulates people and sometimes other resources[e] 7. Needs paternalistic–entrepreneurial guidance	

FUNCTIONAL

FUNCTIONAL HEAD (CE), OR PRODUCT OR AREA HEAD WITH FUNCTIONAL SUBORDINATES

3. FLEXIBLE FUNCTIONAL HEAD
1. Suspicious of people, pessimistic
2. Has enough initiative to encourage and enable coordinated growth (through heads of functions)
3. Respects formal hierarchy
4. Feels he 'loses control' if not centralizing authority
5. Needs somebody to control him every few weeks or months
6. Follows routine procedures
7. Ready to assume responsibility[g]

4. RIGID FUNCTIONAL HEAD
1. Suspicious of people, pessimistic
2. Has enough initiative to introduce new structures
3. Insists (pedantically) upon formal hierarchy
4. Feels he 'loses control' and integrity, if not centralizing authority
5. Needs somebody to control him every few weeks or months
6. A 'possessed' bureaucrat (in following routine procedures)
7. Ready to assume responsibility[g]

HEADS OF FUNCTIONS (AT ALL LEVELS WITH FUNCTIONAL DIVISIONS)

5. FLEXIBLE HEAD OF FUNCTION
1. Has enough initiative to enable coordinated growth with other heads of functions
2. Respects formal hierarchy
3. Needs somebody to supervise and coordinate with him every few days
4. Follows routine procedures
5. Is not ready to assume responsibility[g]

6. RIGID HEAD OF FUNCTION
1. Conservative, reluctant to do things in different ways or new things
2. Insists (pedantically) upon formal hierarchy
3. Dependent upon being supervised and coordinated every few days
4. A 'possessed' bureaucrat (in following routine procedures)
5. Is not ready to assume responsibility[g]

PRODUCT/SERVICE LINE

DECENTRALIZED HEAD (CE), OR ONE WHO HEADS PRODUCT LINE OR AREA SUBORDINATES AT LOWER LEVEL

7. FLEXIBLE DECENTRALIZED HEAD
1. Believes in people, optimistic
2. Has initiative to undertake new ventures for the organization
3. Respects formal hierarchy
4. Does not feel he 'loses control' if does not know for weeks or months what has happened in subordinate units
5. Follows routine procedures
6. Ready to assume responsibility

8. RIGID DECENTRALIZED HEAD
1. Believes in people, optimistic
2. Has enough initiative
3. Insists (pedantically) upon formal hierarchy
4. Does not feel he 'loses control' if does not know for weeks or months what has happened in subordinate units
5. Follows routine procedures
6. Ready to assume responsibility

152

Table 5.1 (*continued*)

Role of manager		Names of types of managers and their managerial characteristics (suitable for either growth or stabilization periods)	
In what managerial structure	In what managerial role	Flexible leadership (growth)	Rigid leadership (stabilization)
MULTISTRUCTURE	MULTISTRUCTURE HEAD (CE)	9. FLEXIBLE MULTISTRUCTURE HEAD 1. Is basically an entrepreneur (above 1), or a flexible functional head (above 3), or a flexible decentralized head (above 7) 2. However, is much more flexible and open, so as to see and treat his entrepreneurs (above 1), entrepreneurial aides (above 2), functional heads (3 and 4), heads or functions (5 and 6), and decentralized heads (7 and 8) according to their managerial characteristics	10. RIGID MULTISTRUCTURE HEAD 1. Is basically a rigid functional head (above 4), or a rigid decentralized head (above 8) 2. However, is much more flexible and open, so as to see and treat his entrepreneurs (above 1), entrepreneurial aides (above 2), functional heads (3 and 4), heads or functions (5 and 6), and decentralized heads (7 and 8) according to their managerial characteristics

Notes to Table 5.1:

[a]He would have a personality mainly influenced by his right-hand side brain hemisphere, the heuristic (synthetical-emotional) side, rather than by his rational left-hand side brain hemisphere. However, he would not have a completely dominant right-side brain hemisphere (see note 2 at end of chapter).

[b]As already mentioned in chapter 4, entrepreneurs are sometimes accused of giving the same assignment to two or more persons, on purpose. They do it, according to their accusers, in order to create competition and jealousy among their subordinates. It is perceived as a sort of 'divide and rule' doctrine. It is similar to the feeling of competing lovers for one beloved. This, in turn, is related to the 'charisma' mentioned as the eleventh characteristic of an entrepreneur, as well as to the tendency of an entrepreneur to prefer a particular aide, changing this favourite from time to time. The latter tendency may be perceived as similar to that of an attractive person transferring his or her favours from one lover to another.

[c]There are entrepreneurs who would say to one or more of their entrepreneurial aides, from time to time, something like this: 'Why is it that I am always the one who comes up with the big ideas; why can't you come up with some big ideas of your own?' This, however, is just a manner of stressing his own importance and centrality in the organization. Actually, if an aide takes the entrepreneur's challenge literally, he may find himself out of a job. The reason for an entrepreneur not liking 'big ideas' coming from his aides, are one or more of the following:

(1) He may interpret it as a criticism by the aide of himself; i.e. that he could not have thought of the idea himself.
(2) He may perceive that the aide is doing something outside his jurisdiction. Since the aide does not have the final authority, as all the power is concentrated in the entrepreneur's hands, the responsibility for the success or failure of the new idea will in any event be borne by the entrepreneur.
(3) He may consider it as a way of evading responsibility because, while the aide is dealing with the new project, he is unable to devote all his time to the assignments received from the entrepreneur.

[d]Even during his after-office time, the entrepreneur is continually aware of his organization and will try to have his aides available for work in the evenings and weekends. However, when he is on a longer vacation and unable to devote time to his organization, he will busy himself with other work, only occasionally being able to divert himself to some purely leisure activity, like reading fiction, music, theatre, cinema, etc. In some national cultures, however, entrepreneurs are more inclined and able to devote time to such leisure activities. In this the French entrepreneurs and other types of managers are quite different from the US counterparts (Eggers, 1977, pp. 138–139; Weinshall, 1977, pp. 172–173).

[e]Certain entrepreneurs and entrepreneurial aides 'manipulate' financial resources as well as certain laws and regulations and even break the law. This is why one would probably find that the percentage of convicted entrepreneurs and entrepreneurial aides is larger than the percentage of other types of convicted managers.

None of the famous business entrepreneurs built his fortune by way of saving his pennies. Just to give one example, the Kennedy and Fitzgerald grandfathers of John F., Robert, and Edward Kennedy were reputed to have made most of their fortunes out of bootlegging (smuggling whisky) to the USA during Prohibition. The same holds true for whisky manufacturing and distribution by Al Capone, the Mafia Capo de Capi, at that time. Kennedy and Fitzgerald are just two examples out of all the successful business entrepreneurs who succeeded in building financial empires within a short while. Many of these made their money during wartime out of profiteering and/or armament smuggling (sometimes to both sides concurrently). These served as models for Rhett Butler in *Gone with the Wind* (Mitchell, 1936).

[f]This is why some entrepreneurs advise younger people to 'climb the ladder, the hard way'. Other entrepreneurs may urge their children to follow the formal education path denied to the father. It seems that both trends stem out of the fact that entrepreneurs are found to have less formal education than other types of managers.

[g]The autonomy of functional heads in a decentralized structure (subordinates to its CE) is for periods of one, two, three, six, or twelve months; they have no partners in their success and nobody for whom to blame their failures. The period of autonomy of their subordinates, the heads of functions, however, is only one week. Thus, it is true for them that 'success has a hundred parents, while failure is an orphan'.

Similarly, for all the behavioural subjects discussed in this book, a list of types of managers with their managerial characteristics cannot be exhaustive either in terms of encompassing all the types of managers, or of including all the characteristics of each of the ten types of managers. In other words, a typology of behavioural characteristics of different types of managers must always be black and white, while in real life behavioural characteristics of managers come in all shades of grey.

We chose, however, to present these specific ten types of managers because they seem to be most important in carrying organizations through the dynamic progression of the TOS. Therefore, we describe the characteristics in managerial and organizational behaviour terminology rather than in psychological or socio-psychological or sociological terminology.[7]

Table 5.1 is divided into four columns. The first two describe the managerial structures and roles which we usually find in the organizations. However, each managerial role, except those in the entrepreneurial structure, actually requires two different types of managers. The types of managers required for the new structure formalization (i.e. stabilization) are different from those by which the organization will be managed in growth. Thus we need more flexible managers in periods of functional structure, product/service line structure, and multistructure growth, as compared with the more rigid managers we need in periods of functional structure, product/service line structure, and multistructure stabilization.

The following are illustrations of the ten different types of managers included in Table 5.1. Some illustrations are taken from organizational examples earlier in the book; others are short descriptions of managers in other organizations.

1 and 2 of Table 5.1: Entrepreneur and Entrepreneurial Aides

Several of our examples are those of entrepreneurial structures.

The Devon Corporation (at the end of chapter 3), an American company, had a CE who headed the organization for almost 40 years. After having brought about remarkable growth, especially in the early 1950s, he found himself in an organization which required a formal managerial style and structure. He introduced to Devon an executive vice president (EVP) who was destined to formalize the organization. This had only short-lived success, between 1958 and 1959. The EVP and the newcomer executives whom he brought in to help him change the structure and decision making were under pressure both from the CE and from his oldtime entrepreneurial aides. Eventually the CE got rid of the EVP and the other newcomers. At a later stage, there was another adaptation of managerial structure to the SDM. This was when the CE, along with his closest aides, moved to Europe in the mid 1960s to entrepreneur Devon's expansion. In doing so, the CE relinquished his entrepreneurial leadership of the company in the USA. This period did not last long either, apparently because of the failing health of Devon's

CE. Nevertheless, he returned to Devon and, with all his oldtime entrepreneurial aides, assumed control and led it, in a style which conformed with his managerial characteristics, until his death in the early 1970s. Devon, which had lost all its survival resilience by then and was dying, was soon afterwards taken over by one of the large petrochemical corporations.

Henry Ford at the end of this chapter 5 is probably the most referred to entrepreneur in management education. The reader is advised to read this organizational example which concentrates upon Ford's managerial personality.

Israel TOS (at the end of chapter 6). This is for the most part an account of decision-making processes in Israel. The focus of this example is the so-called 'Sapir Regime', the entrepreneurial structure in which the whole Israeli economy was run during almost a quarter of a century, from about 1950 to 1975, a major part of its short history as a sovereign state. The entrepreneur, whose name was Pinhas Sapir, started his ascent to the head of this entrepreneurial structure with its enormous SDM in the early 1950s. He successively held the positions of minister of trade and industry, minister of finance, and, finally, chairman of the Jewish Agency.[8] But throughout this quarter of a century, until his death in 1975, he retained this position of *the* Israeli entrepreneur, with thousands of entrepreneurial aides (who included all the heads of business, industrial, and other types of organizations, and of government ministries—ministers as well as directors-general—also trade union leaders, heads of the employers' associations, members of Parliament, etc.) around him. Gradually, all the aspects of the informal culture of an entrepreneurial structure appeared in Israel.

The Mafia (chapter 2). The Mafia crime families are all independent entrepreneurial structures, headed by entrepreneurs who are nicknamed 'capi' (plural of 'capo', or 'head', in Italian) or 'godfathers'. The overall structure of the US Mafia, for example, is peculiar to this sort of SDM. The Mafia is an international operation owning widely diversified product/service lines in many countries. In ordinary circumstances, the US Mafia would be run as a multistructure,[9] but the central governing board of the Mafia, the so-called Council of the Capi (the 'family' heads), is itself run by the Capo de Capi (the US Mafia chief) in an entrepreneurial structure. Entrepreneurs do not usually bear cooperating with each other, and certainly not under the command of another entrepreneur. This puts constraints on the functioning of the Mafia Council, as well as on the territorial and crime service line allocations among the Mafia families in the USA.

Illustration of an entrepreneur One of the most spectacular entrepreneurs of the twentieth century is Admiral Hyman Rickover. He was born in 1900. He came into prominence when the first atomic powered submarine, the *Nautilus*, was launched in 1955. He continued his entrepreneurial activities until the 1980s when, after nearly 65 years, he became the longest serving officer in the US Navy.

Rickover never adhered too much to the formal constraints imposed upon an officer in the US Navy. He did not pay much attention to regulations regarding the state of his uniform (polished shoes, shining buttons, well pressed uniform) and the wearing of an officer's hat, or to saluting his superiors and acknowledging the salute of his subordinates. Indeed, he had all the characteristics of an entrepreneur. Thus, for example, he kept his people on edge, and wanted to get the maximum out of them.[10] Likewise, he did not respect the Navy's formal hierarchy: he made a point of working with whoever he felt was useful for the attainment of his goals, regardless of rank and position. His disregard of formal regulations made him notorious in the Navy and even in the public's eye. Thus, even in 1981, towards his retirement, he was twice accused of severe negligence in not observing safety regulations when commanding experimental manoeuvres.[11]

His entrepreneurial behaviour had two seemingly conflicting effects on his naval career. On the one hand, his promotions through all the naval ranks up to admiral were deliberately delayed by the chiefs of the Navy who resented his 'unfitting' naval officer behaviour.[12] On the other hand, as a result of his achievements, which could not have occurred without his entrepreneurial behaviour, his service was prolonged for over 20 years beyond his official retirement in 1962.

It can be said that if the USA had not had him in its Navy, the Americans would not have had a nuclear submarine in 1955.[13] However, if the Navy had had, say, 20 admirals with managerial characteristics similar to Rickover's, it could not have survived.

4 and 6 of Table 5.1: Rigid Functional Head and Rigid Head of Function

This type of manager is required in periods during which the managerial structure has to be formalized into a functional, formally centralized structure. Let us consider, first of all, one of our organizational examples which illustrates the characteristics of these two types of manager.

The Sears, Roebuck & Company (at the end of this chapter 5) was run as a functional structure. However, while the part with the A-type structured stores (discussed below) was in a flexible growth structure, the part with the B-type structured stores was run as a rigidly stabilized structure. This part consisted of 500 of Sears' 700 stores. They were run as a managerial structure with three levels of hierarchy: general store manager, deputy store managers, departmental managers or 'buyers'. The decision making was formally centralized at both the general store manager level, supervising four to six deputy store managers, and at the level of the latter, each supervising four to six of the 'buyers'. The B stores general store managers, who may be considered the heads of the operational function in this structure, were found to be pessimistic and suspicious. They were not ready to assume responsibility but rather shared it with their subordinates, the deputy store managers. The latter shared their responsibility with their subordinates, the buyers.

Thus we see that the B part of Sears was run in a rigid functional structure, by controlling the level of the heads of functions (i.e. the general store managers level) and its subordinate level in a rigidly formalized manner.

3 and 5 of Table 5.1: Flexible Functional Head and Flexible Head of Function

This type of manager is required whenever the two previous types of managers have already performed their role of introducing a functional structure into the organization. In a variety of situations the heads of functions do not have to be exchanged when the organization is moving from a rigid to a flexible structure. An example of the latter is a research and development function, which would invariably need a flexible functional head, even when the whole management is run under a rigid leadership. The two following organizational examples illustrate these two types of flexible functional heads and flexible heads of functions.

Sears, Roebuck & Company (end of this chapter 5). The part in the Sears organization which consisted of the 200 A stores (out of the total of 700) was organized in a flexible growth structure. Here every general store manager had directly under him 32 departmental managers (buyers), and he managed them in a decentralized structure. The general store managers were found to be optimistic, believing in people. Each of their buyer subordinates was ready to assume responsibility as a consequence of being granted the authority. Thus, we see that the general store managers themselves, who were the operational heads of functions of the A stores, could not have delegated full autonomous responsibility since they were part of a functional structure. But the fact that their subordinates were decentralized and did assume responsibility turned the 200 A-type stores of Sears into a flexible growth structure.

Army Logistics (end of chapter 3). This organization operated in a flexible functional structure. The army ordnance base described was part of the operational function, very much dependent on the other functions in the military and defence organization of the country. Discipline and adherence to military regulations in the armed forces of A were not enforced, however, in an extremely rigid manner. The socio-culture of A was not formal and, consequently, the structure of the various parts of its military forces could be considered as 'flexible' rather than 'rigid'. The various heads of functions of Base Ordnance Depot described in this case study, as well as its functional head, the 770 Base Commander Colonel Ignazio (a disguised name), describe their work, duties, and relationships. This enables us to deduce that the types of managers and their managerial characteristics which are suitable for this organization are those of a flexible functional head and flexible heads of functions. We can likewise gather that the objectives of BOD and its proper functioning (i.e. its SDM) could have been much more successfully achieved if it had been more autonomous, i.e. if the base had been allocated all the resources necessary for operating independently of other parts of the defence and armed forces system for periods of, say, three months.

8 of Table 5.1: Rigid Decentralized Head

In order to integrate several unrelated functional structures into one product/ service line structure, the organization needs a rigid decentralized head. He should insist on the introduction and maintenance of the communication and reporting system, according to the formal requirements and regulations. Thus, if the organization is decentralized for, say, three months, he would insist on receiving all the reports every three months, on the specified date. He would likewise refuse any approaches to him by the product/service line heads during their three-month periods of autonomy. The organizational example for such a CE is ITT.

ITT (chapter 3). Harold Geneen was a typical example of a rigid decentralized head. He used to convene his product/service line heads—who were running their sub-organizations either as rigid or flexible functional heads or as rigid decentralized heads—every four weeks. This kept these sub-organizations more or less on a permanent level of SDM. We can clearly deduce from this example that the ITT structure should have been gradually moved through the three stages so as to accommodate the enormous SDM of the organization, in terms of its widely diversified product/service lines and the vast geographical dispersal. The first step should have been to increase the autonomy period; this, we understand, ITT has done by prolonging it from four to eight weeks. The next stage which would seem desirable is for ITT to move from a rigid to a flexible product/service line structure; we do not know whether those who have taken over from Harold Geneen will indeed be more flexible in managing the eight weeks' decentralized structure. Finally, of course, ITT should find either a rigid or a flexible multi-structure head (9 and 10 in Table 5.1). We witness in this organizational example the problems which ITT had in the 1970s because it was operated as a rigid decentralized structure. Furthermore, not being multistructured, it will have to face what difficulties the 1980s may bring.

7 of Table 5.1: Flexible Decentralized Head

This CE should be more lenient in the enforcement of the *formal* decentralization of the structure. He should neither insist on the punctuality of the reporting, be it every one, two, three, six, or twelve months, nor refuse seeing his subordinates during the periods of autonomy, if they need him. In other words, he should run his staff in a flexible way, so as to enable them to develop. Examples of this type of manager may be found in John Stopford's research.

Multinational Corporations (at the end of chapter 6). Two of the structures which John Stopford found in his research, described in this example, are generally headed by flexible decentralized CEs. The Area Divisions and the World-wide Product Divisions, the managerial structures found among the organizations in Stopford's study, were as follows: 108 organizations had a functional structure, 38 had a decentralized structure, and 24 had what seems to be a multistructure or what may have eventually evolved to a multistructure. Although some of the 38 decentralized corporations were headed by rigid decentralized heads, of whom Harold Geneen was the prototype, we can assume that the majority of these corporations had flexible centralized heads, otherwise they could not have survived in their international operations for long. We may also assume that the 68 organizations with a functional structure were on their way to becoming decentralized structures, or would become multistructures directly.

9 and 10 of Table 5.1: Rigid and Flexible Multistructure Heads

There are three organizational examples in this book which are illustrative of the types of organizations operated as multistructures.

Multinational Corporations (at the end of chapter 6). We have just implied that all the organizations studied by Stopford will eventually become multistructures, in order to survive in a multinational environment. Even the above mentioned 24 organizations in his sample were not all found to be multistructures. Stopford said that he found 18 of these organizations to have mixed structures—i.e. a federation of several structures, which we refer to as a multistructure—while the remaining six organizations had matrix structures. We shall see that a matrix structure, discussed in subsection 5.3.3, could serve, at best, only as an intermediary structure. We consider matrix structures, therefore, in the case of multinational corporations, as the first phase of a multistructure.

Japanese Zaibatsu (at the end of this chapter 5). The Japanese zaibatsu were the first business corporations to introduce a multistructure and to operate it successfully. Zaibatsu are alternately run by a rigid multistructure head and a flexible multistructure head. The Japanese adoption of the multistructure explains the ability of the zaibatsu, and the Japanese economy as a whole, to adapt to the fluctuations in the world economy better than the large business corporations of the Western industrial nations.[14] Thus, in periods of economic stagnation, recession, and depression, the zaibatsu must have been run by rigid multistructure heads, while in periods of economic boom and prosperity they probably had flexible multistructure heads.

The Roman Catholic Church described in the beginning of chapter 7, is run as a multistructure. The Pope supervises the Curia in the Vatican in a functional structure, while the national prelates (e.g. of Poland and Hungary) are his decentralized area subordinates, and the heads of the various orders and associations manage either decentralized service line or entrepreneurial substructures. Our knowledge of the managerial characteristics of some of the popes enables us to point out the following examples of a rigid and a flexible multistructure head.

   Pope Pius XII was elected in 1939. He turned out to be a rigid multistructure head with a type of leadership which was unsuitable for running the RCC during the Second World War.[15]

Pope John XXIII, who was elected immediately after Pius XII's death in 1958, led the RCC as a flexible multistructure head in the greatest growth period which the RCC ever experienced.

5.1.2 Leadership and Followership Characteristics as Part of Personality Traits Acquired at an Early Age

'Managerial style' is the managerial behaviour manifested in organizations. 'Managerial characteristics', on the other hand, are some of those personality traits which are formed in human beings at an early age, usually before one is 6, 4, or even 2 years old. A spontaneous managerial style, i.e. managerial behaviour, free from organizational pressures, would conform quite closely to the dictates of one's leadership and followership characteristics. It would be interesting to speculate how a child of 2 to 6 years could be brought up in order to acquire the managerial characteristics which would make her or him one of the ten types of managers in Table 5.1.

As far as we know, very little clinical research has been undertaken to establish a connection between a child's early upbringing and the type of manager which he will eventually become.[16] There is a tremendous literature on how to raise our children to become brighter,[17] and more creative, but it does not specifically deal with the type of managers the children would become if they were to be raised in this or that fashion.

Generally speaking, the way in which a young child is trained has a decisive effect on his development as a child, a teenager, and a mature person in later years. Thus we can imagine that if we let a child grow up without any direction, guidance, and support (except for providing it with the nourishment it needs in babyhood), the child would develop a personality which would only fit an anarchic (an informally decentralized) structure.[18] On the other hand, if the infant was brought up in a very isolated, regimented, and disciplined fashion, he would probably remain with a rigid formally centralized personality for the rest of his years.

We wonder, however, what are the subtle differences in early childhood upbringing which eventually result in some of the differences between the various types of managers listed in Table 5.1.

5.1.3 To What Degree do Formal (and Informal) Pressures and/or 'Organizational Development' Establish Managerial Behaviour (i.e. Managerial Style)?

Only a small number of the totality of managers in organizations are fortunate in maintaining managerial styles in accordance with their managerial characteristics. Such fortunate managers are mostly found in the higher echelons of management, where the informal activity is relatively higher and the formal clarity relatively smaller when compared to lower levels of the hierarchy. The major cause of assuming managerial styles contrary to managerial characteristics is the formal and informal pressures from the managerial environment. A person may be coerced overtly and/or insidiously into adapting his managerial style to the formal requirements and/or the informal pressures. In such a case the individual's style would not be consistent with his natural or impulsive behaviour, i.e. with a managerial style spontaneously directed by the individual's own personality. An additional cause stems from the efforts of some behavioural scientists, chiefly social psychologists, who claim that changing the managerial behaviour of individuals is both necessary and possible. We shall see that in many cases there is no need for these efforts, because other ways exist to help the organization survive the changes in managerial behaviour required by the dynamics of the TOS. Nor have these efforts by 'change agents' led to the behavioural results claimed by those associated with 'group dynamics' and 'workshops', and more recently 'organizational development'. Consequently, many managers work in managerial styles inconsistent with their managerial characteristics, because they are subjected to formal and informal pressures. In such cases the change is usually temporary, followed by a reversal to the original personality dictated behaviour, whenever possible.

We shall discuss in more detail the limitations, problems, and, sometimes, changes arising from trying to make people behave differently from their managerial characteristics, when we discuss in chapter 7 some cures which have not worked. However, certain aspects of these cures are sometimes necessary, when trying to help an organization for a short time, or where pressures from members of the operating organization for a specific 'magic cure' are such that it is necessary to apply it if only to let the organizational members find out for themselves about its uselessness.

We shall now present examples of two different types of magic cures of recent years. Each of these cures has been tried in different organizations[19] and, on the face of it, succeeded at the time. First we have the idea of Pehr Gyllenhammar, the CE of Volvo who has headed that motor car manufacturing firm since the early 1970s. His experimental plant in Kalmar, Sweden, was one of the many efforts to encourage workers to take over certain managerial decisions concerning their own work. Conveyors, typical of a motor car mass production line,[20] were replaced by 250 computer guided 'carriers', each delivering a frame for a single car. Each team, composed of between 15 and 25 workers, was responsible for a particular step in the car manufacturing. The parts used by the team were supplied by expediters riding bicycles. All this took place in noise-free, well lighted, and airy halls with huge picture windows overlooking the beautiful landscape.

The members of each team were free to organize and divide the labour among themselves, worked at the pace they wished, and took breaks whenever they liked. They had, however, to meet the quality requirements as well as the daily output requirements, i.e. completing their part of the manufacture of a pre-established quantity of cars.

This is a job enrichment solution, which lets the workers decide among themselves, with minimal constraints, by whom, when, and how the job will be done. In a way this adjusts the managerial style to the managerial characteristics, assuming that each team eventually finds its leader and that each leader leads his team according to his own managerial characteristics, without interference from higher levels of management.[21]

There are several problems with these types of 'worker participation in management' solutions.[22] The main one is their irrelevance because they have been developed as a reaction to organizational behaviour problems encountered in unit and mass production.[23] These problems in unit and mass production are completely different from those encountered in the age of electronic chips and industrial robots. The Kalmar plant would not have any human beings in it if manufacture by industrial robots were to spread.

The second example are training methods which have not helped organizations to any large extent (see chapter 7). It presents an approach which, on the one hand, asks one to believe that managerial characteristics may be voluntarily manipulated by the managers themselves and, on the other, that managerial structures and styles which are contrary to general human tendencies in interpersonal relationships would be accepted by the same managers.

This is performed by a variety of so-called OD (organizational development) agencies. For example, we have in front of us an article about the activities of one such agency (for obvious reasons we refrain from identifying it). The article has a noncommittal heading, saying that it presents a typology of managerial styles. The introduction states that the majority of managers tend to operate in one of the styles described in the article. However, from reading the article itself one discovers that what the psychologist-consultants behind this approach are proposing is a *training* method which will help organizations to make their managers shift from one style to another, combine two or more of the styles, and work together with other managers who may have different styles from their own. The latter means creating new and different managerial styles and structures from those which one finds in actual organizations (some of which we described in Table 5.1). This specific approach acknowledges that the roles of subordinates should be complementary to the roles of their superiors.

The main problem of trying to bridge a gap between managerial characteristics and style is that of all such training approaches. Managers who work together in the organization are made to reveal themselves in front of their superiors, subordinates, and peers. We shall see in chapter 7 that this undermines one of the very basic modes of behaviour of managers in hierarchies, namely *not* to disclose all their feelings, thoughts, opinions, and attitudes in their interpersonal relationships.

There are probably two reasons why organizations cling to this last type of magic cure, even if they have been previously disenchanted with another, somewhat different, but essentially similar type of cure. The first is that managers have to acquire and behave in managerial styles different from their managerial characteristics. They find the adaptation to styles which are different from their own characteristics difficult and frustrating in varying degrees. Consequently, they look for help.

The second reason is that there are individuals who have the basic facility to be successful and comfortable in leading various managerial types of subordinates in different styles. We have called them 'multistructure heads'. However, these individuals acquired their tendency to become a rigid or a flexible multistructure head in their very early youth.[24]

Let us now present our last reaction to these two examples. In both cases the managers in the organizations involved express satisfaction, contentment, and, almost, enchantment, with the approach applied. Pehr Gyllenhammar, when speaking or writing about the Kalmar experiment, regards it almost as a panacea for the relationship between management and the workers.[25]

The managers whose reactions to the approach presented in the second example were quoted, had only positively superlative evaluations of this approach and its results in their respective organizations. We may have acquired only a partial evaluation of the consequences in both examples, but in both of them only a few people are quoted as to their feelings regarding the cure and its results. How a CE like Pehr Gyllenhammar perceives his experiment is quite important, but of course, his evaluation is only of the Kalmar situation.[26] Equally important are the evaluations of the managers responsible for training and organizational development in the other example. One has to be aware, however, that any failure in realizing their expectations in applying the cures may mean not only disappointment, but a hurt integrity and personal damage to those involved. In such cases, when the things a person is fully responsible for, and committed to, fail, it is not unusual that he is blind to the symptoms of failure, and clings to minor things in order to convince himself and others that, after all, his expectations came true.

It may well be, of course, that in both examples there would have been a consensus among the large majority of members of the organization, especially the managers, that indeed the cures succeeded at the time. All we are saying is that the process should have been studied by outsiders and not only by those directly involved.

As we said in the beginning of this discussion, elements of the above examples may not only be useful but necessary for organizations. Thus, whenever the managerial structure merits it, the larger the participation of workers in decision making related to them, the better. Then, too, there is a necessity to help managers to be more conscious of their own managerial characteristics, and of the managerial characteristics of others. We strongly believe, however, that this should not be done in a 'mental strip tease' session in which managers with whom they work are involved.

5.1.4 Consequences of the Effect of Managerial Characteristics on Structure—Ways of Studying the Management Main System

The natural inclination of every manager to conduct himself according to his managerial characteristics leads to the accumulated effects of the personalities of all the managers on the managerial structure. This happens especially in the case of the chief executive, who has a better opportunity than the managers in lower levels of the hierarchy to lead the organization according to his wishes. When his subordinate managers do not conform to the way he leads the organization, i.e. their followership characteristics are not in line with his leadership characteristics, he may try to coerce them into behaving accordingly. If this fails, however, he may replace obstinate managers with those who conform to his leadership.

That part of the TOS which we refer to as the management main system represents the relation between the managerial characteristics and the management structure which has to conform to the requirements of the SDM. As we have already mentioned in chapter 4, the balancing element between the managerial structure and the managerial characteristics on the one hand, and the SDM on the other hand, is the managerial attitudes. We referred to the managerial attitudes as 'the organizational cybernetics feedback factor', constituting at one and the same time the consequence of the degrees of balance or imbalance among the TOS systems, and the regulating force which directs the managers to restore the balance among the TOS systems. Managerial attitudes are expressed, of course, directly among the managers themselves. However, this communication of managerial attitudes, although constituting the basis for current decision making, is usually insufficient in helping the organization to introduce the right major changes for remedying the major imbalances among its TOS systems, and securing organizational survival. This is where organizations need outside assistance in helping them to discover their own managerial attitudes.

Of the wide spectrum of studies on managerial attitudes, we shall confine ourselves to two types, one determining the degree of satisfaction with the existing structure, and the other describing attitudes in different cultures. Managerial attitudes should always be studied as part of organizational research, in order to establish whether the leadership and followership characteristics of the managers are in line with the structure dictated by the SDM and with the actual structure. This could be done by a set of standardized questions exploring the attitudes of the managers towards such things as formal organization, freedom and help in doing the job, and, most of all, the degree of satisfaction with various aspects of the work and the organization. Managerial satisfaction should, likewise, be explored through clinical research, i.e. non-directive interviewing.[27]

The importance of finding out how managerial attitudes vary from one cultural environment to another for multinational corporations in different countries is self-evident. Several international studies on managerial attitudes have been carried out since the early 1950s. However, until recently these studies did not necessarily involve specific organizations.[28] Eventually, similar studies were devised for groups of managers in specific organizations, sometimes from different countries with the same multinational corporation.[29] Studies of managerial attitudes in multinational organizations used the same two types of research methodologies as the ones used in other organizations.

The first method involves clinical research both at the top and at the country level, in order to corroborate the multinational behaviour expressed by top management. Interviewees should include not only managers but workers, customers, suppliers, owners, bankers, and trade union and government people.

The second procedure is the so-called group feedback analysis (GFA). The top management of the organization is divided into two levels: all those reporting directly to the chief executive (level 1) and those just below them (level 2). Each group is convened separately for two sessions. The first is a data-collecting session, in which the participants are given a battery of short questionnaires, one after the other. The data from some of these questionnaires are then summarized, and after a short interval the group reconvenes and the participants discuss their own results, which are fed back to them; this discussion is taped and then content-analysed. The questionnaires are almost identical at both levels in order to permit joint comparative analysis. The GFA procedure thus enables us to study managerial attitudes both quantitatively and qualitatively.[30] When utilizing it, the main problem is what kind of questionnaires to use in exploring supranational attitudes; tentative steps have been taken in recent years towards a special methodology for this purpose.[31]

Finally, let us consider what are the main findings which we would like to derive from organizational research of which the study of managerial attitudes is a part. We would like to have the answers to the following important questions.

What is the managerial structure (MS) of the organization? The answer is mainly given by the managerial attitudes to the two parameters of the managerial structure, i.e. the degrees of formalization and autonomy (see Table 5.2). These are expressed either in clinical or in questionnaire research. The MS is likewise established by way of the informalogram.[32]

What are the managerial characteristics of the CE and other key position managers? These are established on the basis of the clinical study, and also deduced from the position of the managers in the informalogram. Additional information about managerial characteristics could be drawn from the results of the communicogram.[33] Finally, managerial characteristics may be discovered through all kinds of psychological tests which are more relevant for potential candidates for managerial positions than for those already in the organization.[34]

Table 5.2   Four basic managerial structures established by the degrees of formalization and autonomy parameters

Degree of autonomy	Degree of formal clarity	
	Informal	Formal
Centralized	Entrepreneurial	Functional structure
Decentralized	Anarchical structure (chaos or stagnation)	Decentralized structure (by product/service line or by area)

What managerial structure does the organization need? The actual managerial structure is dictated by the managerial characteristics of the CE and other key position managers. The required structure is the one in which the organizational SDM can best be managed. We have seen that one can get a good idea of the required structure by analysing the technological level, the product/service diversity, and the geographical dispersal of the organization. This should always be supplemented, however, by analysing the effects on each other of the principal system triangle of organizational strategy, immediately environment, wider environment, which produce the SDM. This analysis can only be done on the basis of clinical organizational research.

The above points and discussion will be dealt with in more detail in chapter 7. We shall focus our discussion there on how organizations may be helped to survive, succeed, and prosper by way of maintaining the balances among their various systems of the TOS.

5.2   INTERORGANIZATIONAL MOBILITY

If organizations have to adapt their managerial structures to their SDM, and if their structures are in the main decided by the managerial characteristics of the CE and other key position managers, it necessarily follows that there should be an interorganizational mobility of these managers. Otherwise, whenever the organization is expanding significantly in terms of its technology, product/service line, and geographical spread, it would not be able to adapt its managerial structure to the growing SDM.

Subsection 5.2.1 shows that people and organizations become accustomed to the interorganizational mobility of their own. Subsection 5.2.2 discusses the managerial interorganizational mobility. Finally, subsection 5.2.3 looks at the implications of having to move managers from one organization to another.

5.2.1   Interorganizational Mobility of Different Human Resources During Stabilization and Expansion of Decision-making Process (DMP)

The different workers, customers, and shareholders comprising the organizational DMP at a specific point in time have a bargaining position *vis-à-vis* the management. There are things which they expect to receive from the organization, while the organization has other things which it expects to get from them. When the organization moves from one managerial structure to another, the management changes its bargaining position towards the various groups, since it now requires different things from them. By the same token, these groups no longer find in the organization the things they expect. This happens especially when the organization moves from periods of expansion to periods of stabilization in its DMP, and vice versa. These shifts in the structural direction of the organization result in substantial turnover among the members of the different human resources of the organization.

Thus, for example, a complete change among the customers and the shareholders of an organization would occur when the organization moves from a flexible managerial structure, facilitating expansion in the SDM, to a stabilization in the SDM, facilitating the transformation from one managerial structure to another. Members of these human resources, like customers and shareholders, used to identify themselves at the beginning of this century with specific organizations and stayed permanently with them. They have changed their attitudes, however, and nowadays customers and shareholders move easily from one organization to another. Table 5.3 presents some of the conditions under which customers and shareholders stay with an organization in growth or in stabilization. These represent very different modes of organizational behaviour from those of shareholders, bankers, customers, suppliers, etc., only about a hundred years ago. In those days every one of these FDM stayed with the organization which, in turn, was loyal to them. Thus if in those days a customer had, say, a Ford car, he would usually exchange it for another Ford car. If Lipton's Tea supplied in those days the royal Court, the Court would not stop buying tea from Lipton's. Likewise, if a shareholder had in those days, say, shares of Shell, he did not sell them in order to buy other shares.

Table 5.3 Different types of customers and shareholders in growth and in stabilization

| *Period of:* | *Factors of decision making* | | |
	Customers	*Shareholders*	*Remarks*
Growth	Ready to pay more, but desiring new, special, innovated products (e.g. new designs of cars, colour televisions).	Expecting the organization to reinvest its earnings, so that the worth of their shares will grow, in preference to receiving dividends.	The company is growing and therefore requires more money from shareholders, as well as from customers for working and investment capital.
Stabilization	Wishing to pay low prices, but ready to buy standard, regular products (e.g. VW, Deux Chevaux, Mini-Minor, black and white televisions).	Expecting the company to pay high dividends.	The company is reorganizing itself to adapt the structure to its SDM, the pace of of which is slow. It can therefore reward its customers in lower prices, and its shareholders in dividends.

Source: Twiss and Weinshall, 1980, p. 29.

168

5.2.2   Interorganizational Managerial Mobility

Unfortunately, employees are often unwilling to move from one organization to another. There have been some changes in employee attitudes towards interorganizational mobility, but relative to the other FDM the shifts have not been impressive.

The need for managers to vacate their posts in order to be replaced by persons of different managerial characteristics is a prerequisite for organizational survival. In an ideal situation, all executive positions in an organization should be held by managers whose characteristics match the requirements of the managerial structure, which is in line with the organizational SDM at the time. For practical purposes, however, it is enough that the CE and several key position managers have adequate managerial characteristics to keep the structure in line with the SDM. Thus, the managerial characteristics of the CE himself are the main key to keeping the organization in line with the dynamics of the TOS. Once a change in top management occurs, a subsequent change in the managerial structure will also occur. Closely following will come the changes in SDM, and along with them, the turnover in the populations of the various human factors: customers, shareholders, etc.

The problem with interorganizational managerial mobility is that managers feel reluctant to exchange organizations. This reluctance stems from a long tradition of being employed in the same organization throughout one's working life, such as governments, armies, and the Church. This has been reinforced by a persistent teaching that one should be loyal to one's organization. This has led to the award of a 'gold watch after 25 years of service' which is disastrous for the survival of many organizations because of the accumulation of 'dead wood'. In most cases, it should have been substituted by a 'gold watch for those who left the organization before 10 years of service'. There is no reason why employees should not relinquish their 'anti-mobility' norm eventually, just as customers, shareholders, and suppliers did, especially during the period between the two world wars.

This, however, would be more difficult now than during the period between the wars. The main difficulties in changing the 'anti-mobility' norm towards the end of the twentieth century stem from the fact that the more industrialized a country becomes, the more scarce employment is. At the risk of ridiculing ourselves as dubious prophets (or 'futurologists', as they have come to be called), we confess to believing that, by the end of the twentieth century, close to 50 per cent of the present total of employees in organizations, using or serving technology, will be redundant. This is the continuation of a long process which caused the reduction in the length of the working week from seven to six days in the nineteenth century, and from six to five days following the Second World War. It seems that the only plausible solution to the evergrowing unemployment in the industrial countries is to ration employment; this can and should be done first by having two employees alternately at work on the same job; while one works, the other is at leisure.[35]

It is more difficult to expect an employee to abandon willingly one position, without having the security of another, more suitable position awaiting him. It is only when employment increases in organizations not related to technology, as the result of the increased leisure, that we may hope for significant progress in making managers move from one organization to another in their search for jobs where their managerial characteristics can best be utilized.

We should stress, however, the progress that has already been made in this area in specific Western countries. There is no doubt in our minds that one of the foremost reasons which contributed to the significant economic, business, and technological advantage which the USA has had over other industrially advanced countries, was the greater acceptance of interorganizational managerial mobility by the Americans. The USA, however, lost the monopoly of this advantage to other European countries, following the Second World War. Table 5.4 presents the percentages of the CEs of the larger business corporations of eleven Western countries (1) who never worked in another organization before, (2) who worked in one or two other organizations before, and (3) who worked in three or more organizations before. It turns out that, at least with regard to the inter-organizational mobility of CEs of large corporations, several other countries have overtaken the USA. Table 5.5 shows the ranking of the countries by the percentages of CEs who worked in one or more other organizations and of CEs who worked in three or more other organizations.

We can see from Table 5.4 that in Germany there were only 10 per cent of CEs who did not work in any other organization before, while in the USA there were 35 per cent. Following Germany, the Scandinavian CEs were the most mobile, followed by France, Italy, and Belgium. The North Western European seafaring

Table 5.4 Mobility of chief executives of large business corporations: Number of other companies worked for before joining present company (% executives)

	Country code										
	B	DK	SF	F	G	GB	I	NL	N	S	USA
No other companies worked for	34	15	30	32	10	46	34	40	21	17	35
1−2 other companies worked for	51	43	45	40	50	35	40	47	44	42	46
3 or more other companies worked for	15	42	25	28	40	19	26	13	35	41	19

Source: De-Bettignies and Evans, 1977, p. 288.
Note: B = Belgium   GB = Great Britain   S = Sweden
           DK = Denmark   I = Italy   SF = Finland
           F = France   N = Norway   USA = United States of America
           G = Germany   NL = Holland

Table 5.5 Ranking order of countries showing interorganizational mobility of CEs

	Ranking order by percentage of CEs who worked in other organizations before	
Country	In 1 or more	In 3 or more
Germany	1	3
Denmark	2	1
Sweden	3	2
Norway	4	4
Finland	5	7
France	6	5
Italy	7, 8	6
Belgium	7, 8	10
United States	9	8, 9
Holland	10	11
Britain	11	8, 9

countries of Holland and Britain happen to be the last on the list. We should remember that the American CEs lead relatively larger organizations than the CEs in all the European countries and this could explain part of the relative drop in interorganizational managerial mobility in the USA. The other point to remember is that the above are indications of the mobility of CEs only, and not of managers at all the other levels. Japan is not included in the above statistics. Japanese conditions are completely different and are often misunderstood by us. As the large Japanese corporations operate in multistructures, they do not need interorganizational managerial mobility in order to survive.[14] We shall discuss this multistructure and its implications for adjusting managerial characteristics to structure by way of intraorganizational rather than interorganizational mobility in section 5.4.

5.2.3 Implications of the Need for Organizations to Exchange Managers in Order to Change their Managerial Structures

The dynamics of the TOS require that the balance between SDM, the managerial structure, and the managerial characteristics will be well maintained. When the SDM grows and moves into new technologies or innovations, new products, and new domains, the managerial structure has to change in order to be able to maintain the new SDM. Usually this can be achieved only if a change of at least the CE and a few key position managers occurs. Consequently, the more acceptance and awareness there is of the necessity for interorganizational mobility, the better for the individual who finds himself within a structure which needs his kind of managerial characteristics. It is likewise better for the organization and drastically improves its chances for survival. Finally, acceptance of interorganizational mobility improves the whole economy which can better absorb new technologies and innovations, strengthening its position *vis-à-vis* other national economies. This is why interorganizational managerial mobility rates are probably the best single indicator of the relative positions of national or regional economies. In this context another indicator of the need for interorganizational managerial mobility is the possible gaps in the availability of necessary types of managers, among different countries. The gap between one country and another as to the availability of managers with the necessary managerial characteristics for a more advanced managerial structure, is about one generation.

Let us assume that in one country the available managerial characteristics are those suitable for roles in entrepreneurial as well as rigid and flexible functional structures. These will not enable the economy and the organization to absorb new technologies, create new product/service lines, and spread to new areas. Such a country needs to have managers with rigid and flexible decentralized heads and, perhaps, also multistructure heads (see Table 5.1).

However, one cannot create such new types of managers overnight, or even in several years. These, as well as the other types of managers, are formed in the personality of individuals and it will take between 20 and 25 years to raise and train new types of managers with the desired characteristics, which is about one generation.

Finally, we would like to point out the role of management consultants who devote their service to helping organizations to find managers for vacant posts. They are nicknamed 'head hunters', but prefer to be called 'executive search consultants'. We feel that this role is very important to the survival of organizations. They may help organizations not only to find suitable managers, but also by relieving them of unsuitable ones; all this is possible, however, only if both the consultant and his client know what has to be done in order to find the most suitable man for the job.

This should be a process in which the consultant tries to find a manager who best fits the survival requirements of the TOS. If possible, this would be an occasion for examining the whole TOS, by way of action research similar to that we describe in chapter 7. The least a consultant should do is examine the principal systems of that part of the organization for which the client seeks a suitable manager: What are its SDM requirements? Who will be the managers he will have around him? Would any SDM and/or managerial structure changes be expected of him?

It is only after having the answers to these and similar questions that the consultant would know what type of manager he is to look for. Unfortunately, there are still many consultants and clients who do not realize that the best help to organizations and executives is to assist them to help themselves: to know what kind of executives they need, and *especially* to realize in what terms to define their needs.[36]

Suitable managers should first of all be chosen for their managerial characteristics: their leadership, followership, and other interpersonal characteristics. The professional skill, education, experience, and other such requirements, important as they are, are only secondary to the managerial characteristics, when searching for the right person to fill the right post.

5.3 HIERARCHICAL PERSONAL CHARACTERISTICS IN COMPLEX SDM

This section deals with several complex organizational situations in which people find themselves, and different ways in which they adapt so as to overcome the difficulties they encounter.

5.3.1 'Unity of Command'—the Reactions of Managers to Hierarchy

Although human beings like a certain degree of freedom and choice in their relationships with other human beings, they need also a certain reassurance as to degree of formal clarity in their relationships (i.e. who is the superior, subordinate, and peer of whom). Human beings belong to several, sometimes too many, organizations such as family, workplace, sports club, trade union, political party, etc. The only thing that keeps them sane in this multitude of organizational roles is that they know, even if only approximately, in each of these activities, who is doing what. This is crucial with regard to their relationships in their work organizations where the task accomplishment requires hierarchies. Ambiguous situations in which it is difficult for a person to distinguish his direct superior from among several people to whom he may be reporting are harmful and often unbearable. Such ambiguous situations are dysfunctional for superiors who are unclear about the degree of authority over their subordinates. Middle- and long-range, sometimes even short-range, planning becomes impossible. Eventually, such a situation in which one subordinate has two or three direct superiors may lead to the subordinate becoming the superior of his bosses.

We would like to cite two examples of such unbearable and, sometimes, dangerous situations.[37] One is quite common in executive-secretarial situations. A compromise has to be worked out between a situation in which every executive has his or her own secretary, and a situation in which every manager has to go through a 'pool' in order to secure necessary secretarial services. The compromise may take the form of a joint secretary for three managers. When problems of priority in the secretary's work arise, the three managers may first try to get together and decide among themselves a procedure which will establish priorities automatically. They soon discover that this is not possible, that they invest too much of their precious time in coordinating the secretary, and that three persons cannot organize jointly even one other person.[38]

The second example is Napoleon Bonaparte's retreat from Russia in 1812. When he saw that the heavy winter prevented him from achieving his goals in

Russia, Napoleon decided to retreat. He knew that his West European enemies would not wait long before attacking France itself, which was in his rear. He therefore decided to hurry back to Paris and organize his defence against his enemies. He could not decide whom out of two of his marshals to appoint as commander of his forces in his place. So he appointed them jointly. The rest is well known; most of the enormous losses inflicted on Napoleon's forces occurred during their retreat from Russia. This, however, was not only the victory of 'General Winter', but rather the defeat of the joint command of the two marshals. They could not lead their forces in an organized way in retreat, which is the most complicated (large SDM) military operation.

5.3.2 Examples of Complex Scopes of Decision Making (SDM)

In chapter 4, a sequence of managerial structures, entrepreneurial, functional, product/service line, and area structures, adapted to the growing SDM, is described. This, of course, is the general direction of events; very few, if any, organizations follow this pattern exactly. They do, however, usually move in the direction described in chapter 4. As we have already pointed out, when the SDM moves from one product/service line into several product/service lines, distinct in their SDM from one another, a managerial structure has to be formally decentralized into a product/service line structure. This is done by delegating to the product/service line units directly subordinate to the CE the authority to deal with all the necessary functions—production, finance, personnel, purchasing, sales, engineering—in order that they be autonomous for the period of decentralization. The delegation of authority means an enlargement of the number of managers dealing with all the functions within the product/service lines and a parallel *reduction* in the number of managers directly subordinated to the CE dealing with the same functions; otherwise there is no decentralization.

There are, however, certain multi-product/service line SDM in which it seems that the total organizational SDM does not enable a straightforward decentralization. These are organizations in which the multi-product/service lines have relatively short lifespans. They are usually organizations requiring science-based personnel, but are not capital intensive, i.e. do not have relatively large investments in equipment. They generally produce reports, with or without accompanying pilot products, rather than consumer or industrial products. Conspicuous examples of this type of organization are management consultants, computer software, and R&D organizations. Such organizations have a large degree of uncertainty when planning their different product/service lines, which are referred to as 'projects'.

The basic difference between this type of organization and other multi-product/service line organizations is to be found in the planning function. The planning in divisions of a product/service line decentralized organization is performed several years in advance. The head of a product/service line division knows that the line has a lifespan of at least several years and he assumes that its activity will not be disbanded within this period of time. Not so with the person appointed as head of a project. In most cases when a specific project is terminated, a new project requiring exactly the same types of human resources is not immediately available.

Let us consider a motor car manufacturing organization as an example of a product/service structure whose product/service lines have relatively long lifespans. When a new division is added to such an organization, say an electric-powered car division, its head is authorized to include in it the functional resources, manpower, engineering, procurement, marketing, finance, etc., which will enable him to run it independently of other parts of the organization for the period of autonomy granted to it, say three months.

Obviously, this sort of longer range planning, as well as the delegation of authority to, and full assumption of responsibility by, the heads of projects is not possible in organizations with complex SDM, such as computer software and R&D organizations.

5.3.3 The 'Matrix Structure' Solution

Complex SDM organizations put pressure on organizational scientists to find a managerial structure solution for them. Being more engineering- and science-minded, their managers turn to engineering schools for help. The result is a matrix structure solution which is an effort to formalize what we have referred to as an entrepreneurial structure. This means that every person may be directly sub-ordinated to two or three different types of authority. For instance, he could be simultaneously a direct subordinate of the project manager, or of the head of the function, and of the person in charge of the geographical region where the activities take place. There are, however, two basic differences between an entrepreneurial structure and such a proposed matrix structure. First, the entrepreneurial organization operates in a very informal structure, rather than in a formal one. That is to say, the entrepreneur, although delegating details for imple-mentation to a line manager, or a functional manager or an area manager, always directly controls and intertwines the work of all three types and their subordinate managers as he sees fit. Secondly, such an entrepreneurial structure is necessary for the first stage of the creation of an organizational DMP, when the SDM con-sists of only one product/service line operating within a limited region. It is unsuit-able for large SDM. The matrix structure, however, is recommended by its developers for a much more advanced and complex SDM.

As matrices have been widely discussed, promoted, and tried in recent years,[39] it is necessary to explain why we feel that this structure does not work and can even cause harm to those organizations which venture to try it.

Figures 5.2 to 5.6 and Table 5.6 not only describe the matrix structure, but present the various basic managerial structures, comparing them with one another and with the matrix organization. The five figures all present structures of organizations which encompass functions, product lines, and countries. However, each chart presents a different structuring of these three elements. Table 5.6 compares the five different structures appearing in the five figures preceding it (the matrix, product line, functional, entrepreneurial, and anarchic structures).

Figure 5.2   This is a highly sophisticated tridimensional matrix organization, more so than the bidimensional project (or product line)—functional matrix. Each operating unit (say, the third operating unit from the top) reports to its country (country B), to its product line (product line 3), and to one function (manufacturing). An example of such an organization used to be Philips of Eindhoven. For example, the general manager of a television factory in France had to report to the head of the French division in the country organization, *and* to the head of the RGT (radio, gramophone, and television) product group, *and* to the TEO (technical, efficiency, and organization) functional division.[40]

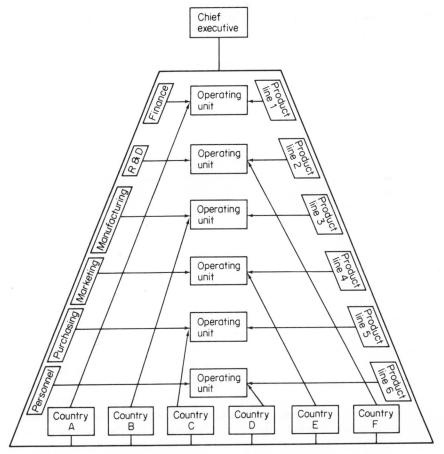

Figure 5.2   Schematic presentation of a tridimensional matrix organization

Figure 5.3 This is an example of a product line structure, in which the third level of hierarchy, whose first level is the CE, is based on a functional division, and the fourth level is divided into countries, reporting directly to Marketing (a thicker line), but to other functions as well. This may be the structure in which the organization embarks upon international operations; sometime later on the organization would probably form an international division as a functional structure; and, finally, it would develop into a multistructure, enabling the organization to turn into a multinational organization (these phases are part of the Multinational Corporations example at the end of chapter 6).

Figure 5.4 The sequence of the managerial structures following Figure 5.3 moves into less and less appropriate structures for an SDM covering different product lines and various countries. Figure 5.4 is an organizational chart of a functional structure. Here both the manufacturing and marketing functions are divided into four product lines. Marketing is further divided into five countries; thus the marketing of each of the four product lines is divided into the five countries in which they are marketed.

Figure 5.5 This is an entrepreneurial structure encompassing the same enormous SDM of the six functions, five countries, and four product lines. Unlike the two previous structures, the *formally* decentralized (Figure 5.3) and centralized (Figure 5.4) structures, the entrepreneurial structure is an *informally* centralized structure.

Figure 5.6 This final structure is an anarchic structure, namely an *informally decentralized* structure. It is, of course, the least suitable for the enormous SDM of six functions, five countries, and four product lines. We shall presently see that this anarchic structure is actually not very different from the matrix organization presented in Figure 5.2.

Let us study carefully the comparative Table 5.6, as it is meant to serve as a summary of the attributes of the four basis structures. In the following discussion we shall only compare the first and the last columns, the matrix, and the anarchic structures. Let us then go down from one row to another in Table 5.6, comparing these two structures.

SDM This row represents the contexts in which the structures are usually used or should be used. In this row only, there is a marked difference between the matrix and the anarchic structures. The matrix is used, as we have already stressed, in the case of a very large SDM, mainly in terms of the technological-scientific level of the organization. The anarchic structure, on the other hand, can usually be found in small organizations with a well-defined, straightforward objective.[41] The organization exists for, and is dedicated to, this one objective, while in other organizations objectives would be changed according to the survival needs of the organization.[42]

177

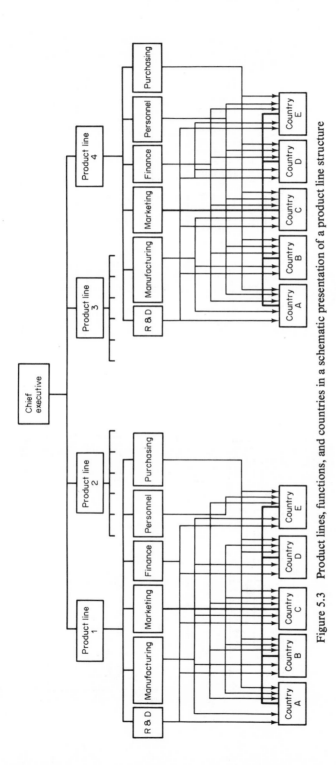

Figure 5.3   Product lines, functions, and countries in a schematic presentation of a product line structure

178

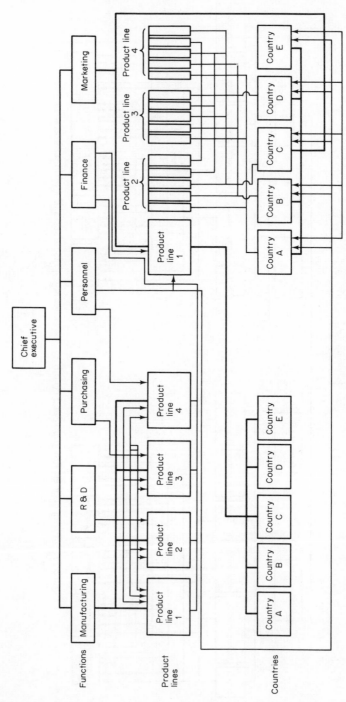

Figure 5.4 Functions, product lines, and countries in a schematic presentation of a functional structure

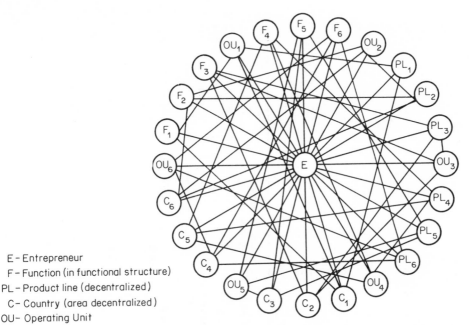

E – Entrepreneur
F – Function (in functional structure)
PL – Product line (decentralized)
C – Country (area decentralized)
OU – Operating Unit

Figure 5.5 Functions, product lines, countries, and operating units in a schematic
presentation of an entrepreneurial structure

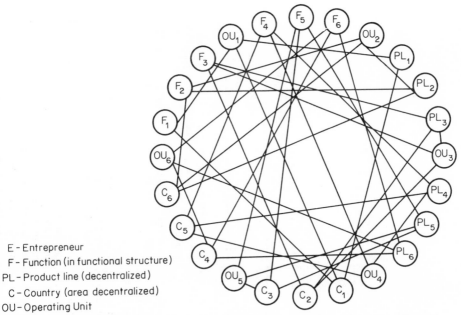

E – Entrepreneur
F – Function (in functional structure)
PL – Product line (decentralized)
C – Country (area decentralized)
OU – Operating Unit

Figure 5.6 Functions, product lines, countries, and operating units in a schematic
presentation of an anarchic structure

Table 5.6 Comparison between 'matrix' and four basic structures

Factor	Matrix structure (Figure 5.2)	Product line (or area) structure (Figure 5.3)	Functional structure (Figure 5.4)	Entrepreneurial structure (Figure 5.5)	Anarchic structure (Figure 5.6)
SDM	Very large (especially in high technology and science-based projects)	Large (advanced technology, diverse product lines or areas)	Medium (advanced technology, usually one product line in one area)	Small	Very small
Expected current changes in basic activities	Frequent (usually every few weeks or months)	Rare (every few to many years)	Rare (every few to many years)	Rare (every few to many years)	Frequent (every few weeks, sometimes months)
Degree of formal clarity	Informal No possibility for advanced clarification of formal relationships	Formal	Formal	Informal	Informal
Degree of autonomy	Decentralized In order to run the matrix, subordinates of CE have to be self-sufficient; consequently the CE cannot centralize the structure as an entrepreneurial CE does	Decentralized	Centralized	Centralized	Decentralized

	Directly to more than one person The same manager reports directly to two or more persons; he may report indirectly to one or more other persons	*Directly to one person only*	*Directly to one person only*	*Directly to more than one person* (usually to the entrepreneur and at least one other person)	*Directly to more than one person* (primarily in times of intense activity)
Reporting					
Responsibility	*Diffused* The responsibility is 'divided', i.e. nobody can be 'pinned down' to the responsibility for any activity	*The direct superior's*	*The direct superior's* (although one person only is formally responsible; 'passing the buck' often occurs because of the limited autonomy—only up to one week)	*The entrepreneur's* (although the entrepreneur's responsibility is overriding, managers are often trying to pass the responsibility on one another's shoulders, because of the confused situation in which their perceived autonomy is only up to one day)	*Diffused* (among all members of the anarchic organization)
Management as perceived by others	*Unclear* Other members of the organization (workers, customers, suppliers, etc.) are even less clear than the managers themselves as to who does what. The management would therefore be regarded as 'disorganized'	*OK* (if the structure is in balance with the SDM; however, if not then management would be usually regarded as 'wasteful')	*OK* (if the structure is in balance with the SDM; otherwise the management may be regarded as 'bureaucratic', 'heavy', 'cumbersome', etc.)	*One man's show* (if the structure is in balance with the SDM; otherwise management will be regarded as 'disorganized')	*Unclear* (outsiders cannot make head or tail of who is responsible for what)

Expected current changes in basic activities The same frequency, of every few weeks, sometimes months, is found in both structures.

Degrees of formal clarity and autonomy The anarchic structure is by definition an informally decentralized structure. The matrix column of Table 5.6 explains why it is also informally decentralized.

Reporting In both structures the people report directly to more than one person. In the anarchic structure this reporting may be dormant. This is because the anarchic structure is either highly active or stagnant. However, when it is intensely active, there would be a lot of reporting by a lot of people.

Responsibility In both structures, the responsibility is diffused, but in different ways and with diverse consequences. In the matrix structure people do not want to assume responsibility, although they are required to share it by the proponents of the matrix. In the anarchic structure, on the other hand, the devotion and commitment to the organizational strategy of the TOS by those who participate in it, is such that the diffusion of responsibility increases, rather than decreases.[43]

Management as perceived by others This is closely related to the reactions of outsiders who happen to observe the activities of, and relationships among, people in both types of structures, and who are confused as to who is responsible for what. They would consider the structures unclear and disorganized.

In conclusion, we see that both structures have similar—almost identical—characteristics. However, the anarchic structure, when used deliberately, is generally applied to very small SDM,[44] while the matrix is applied, most inappropriately, in conditions of very large SDM.

No wonder that matrix, instead of helping organizations to encompass their SDM, is causing confusion, by formalizing an anarchic structure, where even much more advanced structures (namely the functional, product line, and area structures) cannot help. In order to demonstrate the inappropriateness of a matrix structure in situations where it is usually applied, let us recount an anecdote in which the first author, together with other researchers, was involved.

We carried out managerial structure and communication research in a well-known management training centre in the UK in 1971. The data processing, especially of the communications pattern, in this research required a certain amount of computer programming and processing. We turned to one of the largest and most respectable computer software and service organizations in Britain.[45]

It so happened that the head of the organizational behaviour (OB) projects unit was an OB scientist who prided himself on having introduced a matrix structure to this organization. On the one hand, there were project departments, such as the OB projects department, and on the other there were functional departments such as programmers, statisticians, etc.

When we discussed our own requirements with this head of OB projects, he gave us an estimate of the price and length of time of the project. The expected price was a few hundred pounds and the expected time was a few weeks. We had to leave the UK a few months later. The project was not completed by then, and its final cost went up to several thousands of pounds. Likewise, three different programmers consecutively took over the responsibility for this relatively simple project within a period of less than three months.[46]

Before leaving the UK we came to see this OB man again. Expressing amazement that he could continue boasting about the matrix structure, I said to him: 'I used to take my car for repair to a garage back home. The repairs went on and on, and the estimates, of both how long it would take and how much it would cost, grew. You are no better than our garage. You are exactly like a garage.' The man smiled and said: 'Didn't you know that we indeed are like a garage?'

Imagine our surprise several years later when we found in a published book about matrix a description of a claimed success in the same organization, written by the same OB scientist.[47]

There is one more thing we would like to refute, which supporters of matrix often try to demonstrate as a proof that there is no need for 'unity of command' and that matrix can work very well. They claim that the example of parents who jointly raise their children, proves that matrix organizations can work. This problem of dual responsibility is part of our organizational example about the family (chapter 4). More than often when a couple tries to share simultaneously and equally the responsibility for the upbringing of a child, they create difficulties both in the child's upbringing and in the relationship between the couple.[48]

In order to avoid dual responsibility between parents, in the past humankind developed patriarchal or matriarchal societies. In our present-day industrial societies, with their women's-lib, men's-lib, and children's-lib movements, the best in family management is to have a division of functions between mother and father. One, say the mother, would be responsible for providing the economic means, while the other, the father, would be in charge of the children. Such a division of responsibilities could be somewhat modified by, say, the father being occupied in commercial activities several hours a week, two or three evenings, but also managing the household (including the cooking). The mother, on the other hand, could also be doing the purchasing for the house and helping the children with their homework in specific subjects. Every so often the couple could decide to change the division of tasks between them.

This could, perhaps, result in some managerial overlaps, but the same or similar problems are also the fate of a functional structure in which a substantial number of organizations are run. There is, of course, a difference between the managerial structure of a family and that of a business organization. In a family the division of the managerial tasks between the couple and any changes in them have to be agreed by the *two* spouses. In other types of organizations there is *one* head only who does not require the full consensus of all his subordinates regarding the division of tasks among them. This is the inherent problem in a family. However, when organizations are small this problem is of lesser magnitude than when organizations have a very large SDM.

Thus a small cooperative society could be run, after it had been successfully

Table 5.7   Attitudes to matrix among managers from ten countries, and among MBAs and experienced managers from Britain and France

Degree of agreement with the statement that:

'An organizational structure in which certain subordinates have two direct bosses should be avoided at all costs.'

Managers in ten countries

Country	Sample size	% agreeing	Rank
USA	44	50	1
Holland	29	59	2
Sweden	43	67	3
Denmark	36	69	4
Britain	150	76	5
Germany	47	79	6
Switzerland	48	79	6
Italy	24	83	8
France	179	84	9
Belgium	35	89	10

MBAs and experienced managers from GB and France

Country	Group	Sample size	% agreeing	Rank
Britain	MBA students	52	63	1
	Managers	150	76	2
France	MBA students	108	83	3
	Managers	179	84	4

Note: There are three groups of respondents: 635 managers from ten countries, in the left-hand table, and 160 MBA students and 329 managers from Britain and France, in the right-hand table.

launched by an entrepreneur, on a consensus decision-making basis. The larger the SDM of such a cooperative society is, the less it can sustain decision making on a consensus basis.[49]

The attitudes towards matrix may, of course, vary from one country and culture to another and between experienced managers and management students. Table 5.7 presents reactions to matrix in ten countries, and between practising managers and MBA students from two of these countries.[50]

The findings in the ten countries seem to indicate certain groupings among them. The USA (50 per cent against matrix) and Holland (59 per cent) stand alone; then come the Scandinavian countries (average 68 per cent against matrix); GB (76 per cent) along with Germany and Switzerland (79 per cent each), while Italy, France, and Belgium are close to each other at the negative end (83, 84, and 89 per cent respectively). These differences seem to range from the most industrialized country in the world with the largest managerial structure experience to the three smaller Northern countries, which have a wide experience in formally centralized structures; from there to the three largest Western European countries (including Switzerland, which could be considered one of the largest financial countries of the world), whose larger organizations operate in decentralized and multistructured managerial structures. Finally, Italy, France, and Belgium, operating in formally centralized functional structures, have a much more conservative and rigid tradition, since their organizations are more in the formalization and bureaucratization stage than in the SDM growth stage of their functional structures. We have already stressed that in a functional structure many of the managers would have to report to more than one person. However, every manager would generally have one superior whose authority is overriding. As for the comparison between MBA students and managers, we see that there is no significant difference between the two groups in France, but that the British students are less opposed to matrix than the managers. The overall conclusion from the findings in subsection 5.3.3 is that matrix not only fails to help organizations, but that it is regarded with suspicion by many people who have not even experienced it. We shall come back to the inability of the matrix structure to cure the problems arising from the dynamics of the TOS, in chapter 7.

5.3.4 The 'Scientific Slack' (Japanese Solution)

The matrix structure is based on an assumption that the time of the employees should be utilized as fully as possible in the activities leading to the manufacture and marketing of the products and/or services. Hence, when the head of the functional/professional area feels that a person could be better utilized in another project, that person should be transferred.

This uncertainty about time length of commitment to a specific project leads to lack of motivation, dissatisfaction, and frustration among transferred managers; they lack the feeling of full participation in the accomplishment of a project. They have feelings of social unsuitability and malcontent because of having to adapt themselves to a new social and formal environment. The project managers, on the

186

Table 5.8 An example of a computer software organization (Compusowa) creating a hydraulic engineering decentralized project group

Previous one-month periods on which predictions are based	Project numbers simultaneously worked upon	Largest number of people employed simultaneously on projects			
		Programmers	Hydraulic engineers	Statisticians	Operations researchers
January 1982	142, 178, 182, 185, 191, 192, 193, 194, 195	8	2	2	1
February	142, 182, 185, 192, 193, 194, 195, 196, 197	9	3	2	1
March	142, 178, 185, 193, 195, 196, 197	6	1	1	2
April	142, 178, 195, 196, 197, 198, 200	9	1	1	—
May	142, 178, 195, 196, 197, 198, 200	9	1	1	—
June	142, 195, 196, 198, 200, 201, 202, 203, 204	7	3	2	2
July	195, 200, 201, 203, 205, 206, 207, 208, 209, 210	9	3	2	2
August	195, 203, 207, 208, 209, 210, 211, 212, 213	8	3	2	2
September	210, 211, 212, 213, 214, 215, 216, 217	9	2	1	1
October	210, 211, 214, 215, 216, 217, 218	6	2	—	1
November	214, 215, 217, 218	2	1	—	—
December	214, 215, 217, 218, 219, 220, 221, 222	8	2	2	1
Maximum no. of people employed in one month		9	3	2	2
Predicted no. of required employees for 1983		10	3	4	2

other hand, are reluctant to do the best they can, as they never know in advance who in their teams is leaving and who is staying.

Let us, therefore, consider a more efficient structural solution for such a complex SDM which is not based on the maximization of use of time on the different projects. Our solution is to divide all the projects into groups, each consisting of projects which have more or less the same human resources (the same type of employees, the same type of customers, etc.). Each project group will contain enough managers, professionals, and technicians in the different engineering and scientific disciplines to enable the project group to continue to operate on its projects for years, since it has in every engineering and scientific discipline the maximum number of people it requires for the foreseeable future. Consequently, the project group will quite often have a 'slack', in each of its engineering and scientific disciplines, made up of managers who cannot be utilized in any of the current projects within the project group.

For example, let us take a computer software organization in which all the hydraulic engineering projects are put under the jurisdiction of one project group (Table 5.8 and Figure 5.7). We find that, for this project group, the maximum number of technical personnel required at any one time will be, say, ten programmers, three hydraulic engineers, four statisticians, two operations researchers, etc. The management of this project group will include enough people from the various engineering-scientific areas to meet the 'bottleneck' requirements in every area at all times.

This would mean that most of the time some of the people in every engineering-scientific discipline will not be involved in an ongoing project. Their 'slack' time could and should be utilized in updating their knowledge and know-how in their respective fields. This should be done by participation in educational programmes,

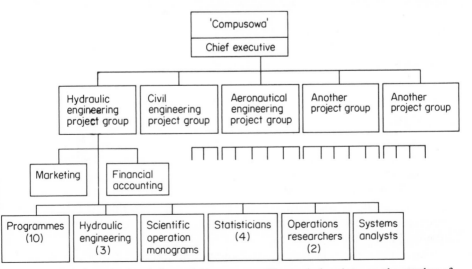

Figure 5.7   Organizational chart of Compusowa. Figures in brackets are the number of personnel (10 programmers, 3 hydraulic engineers, etc.)

sometimes for higher degrees, by reading, by visiting, and by studying related projects, etc. The rate of innovation and accumulated new knowledge in these science-based organizations is larger than in other organizations with less complex SDM. The assumption of time maximization on the specific projects on which the matrix structure is based, therefore, often undermines the survival prospects of the organizations in which it is tried. Such organizations are unable to keep pace with the necessary expansion in the SDM. The scientific slack solution, on the other hand, contributes towards scientifically updating the organization. The main contribution of the scientific slack solution is, however, in structuring the complex SDM into a formally decentralized structure (see Figure 5.3). In the scientific slack structure, people in general scientific areas such as programmers, statisticians, operations researchers, system analysts, and mathematicians specialize in one type of project (e.g. water projects) and, what is more important, operate continuously within the same social and formal group of people. The heads of the project groups assume full responsibility for their divisions, exactly as in all other product/service line structures. They allocate project managers out of the scientific operations management, to the various projects which are active. These project managers can assume only partial, coordinating, responsibility for their projects; they are responsible for their manufacturing. The scientific slack structure is nicknamed 'Japanese' because the large Japanese zaibatsu-type organizations hire their managers and workers on the basis of a 'lifetime employment'. This means that the organization goes through periods when considerable numbers of employees are not engaged in the current operations. These slack periods are used in the Japanese zaibatsu for training and education, exactly as in the scientific slack structure.

5.4   THE MULTISTRUCTURE

The multistructure has already been mentioned in different places in the book, especially in chapter 4. This section, therefore, incorporates some of the things we have already said about this multiple, federated structure.

5.4.1   The Inevitability of Growth in the SDM Leads to the Creation of New Structures

Every time expansion in the SDM has made existing managerial structures obsolete, a new structure has had to come into being. First came the entrepreneurial structure, which has been in existence from ancient times. The functional structure has existed since Jethro suggested it to Moses; it was defined by Max Weber in the nineteenth century as a bureaucratic structure. The product/service line and area structures first appeared in four US corporations after the First World War.

The three basic managerial structures—entrepreneurial, functional, and product/service line or area structures—are *uniform* structures. That is to say, all subordinates of the CE are structured either in an entrepreneurial, or a functional, or a product line or area structure. The three basic structures, together with the anarchic structure, constitute all the four possible combinations in the matrix of degree of formal clarity and degree of autonomy: informally centralized (entrepreneurial), formally centralized (functional), formally decentralized (product/service line or area), and informally decentralized (anarchic). The formally decentralized structure, although managing larger SDM than the other structures, is limited in the SDM that it can handle. Let us now repeat the reasons why the product line and area structure can handle only the limited SDM as described in chapter 4. This limitation is connected with the nature of decentralization. We have already emphasized that the more decentralized the units reporting to the CE, the more resources in finance, manufacturing, marketing, personnel, etc., will be delegated to them, and the smaller the size of the functional units reporting directly to the CE. The decentralized units subordinated to the CE have to be controlled, say, every three months or twelve months by the functional units directly at the disposal of the CE. The periods of decentralization usually terminate at fixed dates. This means that, say, towards the end of March, June, September, and December, the CE's headquarters units have to analyse the decentralized units in terms of their results during the previous autonomous period, and plan for the following period. But what will the people in the CE headquarters units do during the intervals between the concentrated short analysis periods? How will they be occupied? They will not stay idle; they will try to keep themselves busy by controlling the subordinate units, even though not called on to do so. The larger the number of subordinated decentralized units, the larger the number of people who need occupation for their slack intervals. Otherwise, for the lack of having anything else to do, they would interfere with the subordinate units, controlling the state of the functions more frequently than the intended decentralization dictates. The moment that this happens, the autonomy of the decentralized units is lost and the managerial structure reverts to a functional structure. Therefore, in order to maintain the decentralized structure, the number of decentralized units has to be limited. Finally, when the utility of all three structures—entrepreneurial, functional, and decentralized—has been exploited, organizations do not have another basic structure available to grow into.

5.4.2   The Multistructure—a Federated Managerial Structure

This managerial structure may be perceived as if it were composed of different building blocks which may be combined into different kinds of structures. This is done by way of federating in each structure various proportions of different building blocks. Figure 5.8 includes all the possible building blocks: an entrepreneurial structure under the control of the CE, a functional structure headed by the CE, product lines and areas reporting to the CE, and independent entrepreneurs who return to the CE after they have accomplished the launching of their assignments.

The Japanese have been the first to operate their large organizations in multistructures, probably since the First World War. Multistructures first appeared in US corporations and in large organizations in other countries outside Japan only after the Second World War. The Japanese zaibatsu was the first to structure its management in a multistructure form.

190

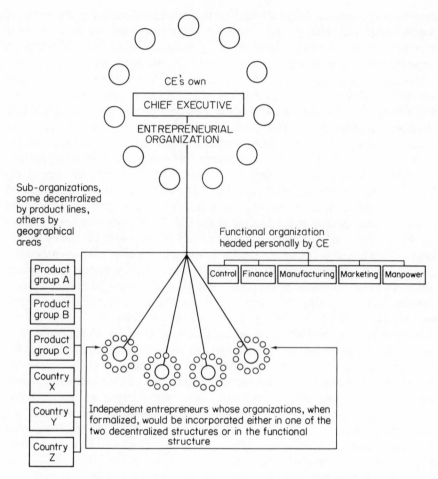

Figure 5.8   The multistructure managerial structure

Among 18 organizations studied in the 1960s and 1970s by both informalogram and clinical action research,[51] one was found to have a multistructure. This was a foreign-owned shipping organization operating in Japan and comprising two distinct parts:[52] one running its shipping lines and the other serving as its shipping agents. It so happened that, while the shipping agency's management was exclusively Japanese, the two top levels of management in the shipping lines were non-Japanese, mostly nationals of the Western country where the owner company was located and to whose headquarters the operations centred in Japan were linked. Analysis of the managerial structures in the two sub-organizations revealed some differences. The non-Japanese sub-organization had a functional structure, partially decentralized in the relationships between the chief executive and the management; a larger degree of decentralization was apparently impossible, due to an insufficient number of managers and other resources. In the

Japanese sub-organization, the clarity of the formal structure and the mutual dependence of individuals and units indicated a functional structure; but the informal activity of the managers did not. In fact, the managerial structure was characterized by Japanese culture-bound behaviour of the so-called 'ringi' decision-making process.[53] In these circumstances it was not surprising to discover through the action research that the chief executive was relating differently to the managers in the two sub-organizations.

Let us consider two other examples of multistructures.[54] The first example is of one of the largest oil companies in the world, the headquarters of which is in the USA. This corporation diversified into a variety of related product lines, one of them being paints. Mr Gaine, one of the corporation's entrepreneurs, was sent to Holland to start an oil manufacturing and marketing operation there. When asked how the headquarters was controlling him, he said that they were not. Although the law required him to report periodically to headquarters, the latter was not reacting to his reports. 'They fulfil all my requests, which have been mainly connected with the investment and working capital which they have provided me with', said Mr Gaine. When asked how much longer the corporation would keep him in Holland, he replied: 'This is not my first assignment of this sort. They expect me to come back to them when I feel that my entrepreneurial, promotional assignment is over, and I am ready for a new one'.

We can learn from this example two aspects of a multistructure. First, we realize that Mr Gaine will exercise his entrepreneurial leadership only as long as it is required by the promotional and SDM needs of the organization. The moment that organization is launched, he will report to the CE at headquarters. The latter will either appoint a functional head to the organization, thus making it a decentralized product line, or decide that it is not large enough to become a product line by itself. In the case of the latter, the CE will probably make one of the factor managers belonging to his functional structure run it, or nominate another formalized manager to head it, who may be part of either the Western Europe area sub-organization, or part of the international paints division.

The second thing to note in this example is that the CE does not interfere with Mr Gaine's operation. He is probably controlling every one of his subordinates as often as necessary. Independent entrepreneurs should not be interfered with at all. The CE would probably be at the disposal of his independent entrepreneurs all the time, but he will only look into what they have done when they are ready.

The second example is that of Weinstock. His main reputation has been in bringing about the mergers of some of the biggest electronics industries in Britain. Had he only done this, he would probably have been known as one of the biggest entrepreneurs of our time. He is not, however, involved only in this type of activity. He is actually at the head of the very largest corporation, connected mainly with electronics, which he helped to bring together. He is apparently running the organization as a multistructure, with all the substructures appearing in Figure 5.8. This means that he has an entrepreneurial organization of his own as well as functional organization product line and area sub-organizations and, finally, independent entrepreneurs like Mr Gaine in our previous example, who launch the organization into new products, technologies, and areas in the world.

In chapter 7 there is a discussion about the Roman Catholic Church, which has operated as a multistructure for longer than any other organization in the world, including the Japanese zaibatsu. It is probably due to the decentralized area substructure that the Church has persevered in countries like Hungary and Poland, in spite of the anti-religious pressures in the political environment. It was through the entrepreneurial substructures of some of the monastic orders and associations of the RCC that the lives of many persecuted people, primarily Jewish children, were saved during the Second World War holocaust.

5.4.3 No Need for Interorganizational Mobility and Other Consequences of the Multistructure

The multistructure has several positive consequences. The managers do not have to move in and out of the organization; this helps in staffing the different federated structures with as many suitable managers as possible, because the long experience with and knowledge of managers enables the organization to explore and determine the roles that each manager can best perform. This, of course, increases satisfaction, raises morale, and improves effectiveness. Furthermore, as a result of intra-organizational managerial mobility, many of the managers can be sent for additional study and training in seminars, executive training institutes, etc., especially during periods between two positions.

Another advantage of the multistructure is the manoeuvrability of the rate of expansion of the organizational SDM. As it has several different substructures, it is possible to expand the SDM rapidly, or to decrease it almost at will from a rapid rate to stabilization or even contraction. This is done by performing simultaneously the formalization of new structures in several of its federated units and reducing the expansion rate; or by keeping existing structures flexible for longer periods of time, enabling the expansion to continue. Uniformly structured organizations, on the other hand, do not have flexibility to adapt themselves to the rates of growth or of contraction in their environments, nor are they able to adapt their managerial structures to their SDM with relative ease.

The most important consequence of the multistructure is that it does not require interorganizational managerial mobility. Whenever one part of the multistructure matures to a point where it can no longer manage the expanding SDM, that part of the multistructure is moved to a more advanced structure and manned with executives with the appropriate managerial characteristics.[55]

However, even in a multistructure there may be difficulties in finding people with suitable managerial characteristics for all the necessary roles. The most difficult staffing problem of all in the multistructure organization is selection of the chief executive.

There are very few people to be found today who can adapt themselves to different leadership styles and to different people. It is exactly such a 'flexible' leader who is needed for the position of chief executive of a multistructure.

Let us consider what the role of a chief executive of a multistructure organization (Figure 5.8) would be *vis-à-vis* his subordinates.

The managers in his immediate vicinity, constituting part of his own entrepreneurial 'entourage', would expect him to interfere with their work at will at any moment. The managers heading the various functions in the functional structure would be controlled by him, usually not more than once a week. The heads of the decentralized product/service divisions and of the decentralized area divisions would report to him on a monthly or, say, a six-monthly basis and in the meantime would be free to run their sub-organizations as they see fit. Finally, the independent entrepreneurs might be free for five or even ten years before the chief executive would want to find out whether their sub-organizations had reached a size necessitating formalization of the managerial structure.[56]

It is interesting to note that the 'span of control' of the chief executive, i.e. the number of people reporting to him directly, varies widely from one substructure to another. In his own entrepreneurial entourage he may have any number of people (100 or more) with whom he is in constant, direct contact. In his functional substructure he has up to ten heads of the functional departments, while in the decentralized substructure he may have several scores of heads of product/service divisions and/or area divisions.

Thus, the chief executive of a multiple structure may have to assume a supervisory position towards his subordinates ranging from every few hours, through every few days and every few months, to every few years.

In these circumstances, his personality traits must include the capacity for flexible leadership in order to be able to establish different interpersonal relationships with different managers.

In spite of the fact that people with such characteristics are rare, no shortage of them has been felt to date, as each multistructure organization needs only one chief executive and the number of such organizations is not very large.

5.5 SUMMARY

Let us briefly summarize the contents of this chapter. Variations in leadership and followership characteristics and the need for a change of managers in order to achieve a change in the managerial structure[57] were discussed in the first section. The second section dealt with the mobility of different human resources when the SDM changes from stabilization to expansion and vice versa; subsequently the need for different rates of managerial interorganizational mobility, in different rates of growth of the SDM, was stressed. Hierarchical personality characteristics in complex SDM was the subject of the third section. The matrix was found to be an unsuitable managerial structure for an organization with successive short-term projects with large SDM, usually science-based projects. Instead, a 'scientific slack' (Japanese approach) solution for large research and development organizations, computer software companies, management consultancies, etc., was proposed. Section 5.4 was devoted to the multistructure, a federation of units with different basic managerial structures, and its advantages.

The organizational examples which directly pertain to managerial characteristics and advanced TOS dynamics are as follows:

Henry Ford

This is the story of Henry Ford I, the entrepreneur of the first motor car mass production line. His leadership characteristics remained the same during all the long period in which he ran the Ford organization. Had Henry Ford not died in the 1940s, the Ford organization could not have survived much longer, because its SDM was much too large for the entrepreneurial structure which he imposed on it.

Japanese zaibatsu

These are the huge Japanese conglomerates, such as Mitsui and Mitsubishi, which have become known throughout the world. Several aspects of their TOS are fundamentally different from those of their large non-Japanese counterparts, the Western multinationals. Their managers are hired straight from the universities, once a year, and are employed for life. The zaibatsu were the first large business corporations to adapt to the multistructure, which has spread beyond Japan since the Second World War. The wide environment of the zaibatsu differs from that of large non-Japanese conglomerates; the zaibatsu cooperate with and are supported by the Japanese government much more than their non-Japanese peers. Finally, the zaibatsu 'ringi' decision-making process is the reverse of the usual method: the decision making flows mainly from bottom to top, rather than the other way around.

Marks & Spencer (M & S)

This British organization is one of three retailing organizations among the examples in this book. British Chain Stores was described at the end of chapter 4, and the example of Sears, Roebuck immediately follows. Two things are especially worth pointing out in this example. First, the removal of various controlling functions in the M & S outlets throughout Britain, increased the autonomy of the personnel in the shops. Secondly, the close relationship which M & S maintains with its suppliers is indicative of its awareness of having to ensure their survival and continued cooperation.

Sears, Roebuck & Company

This was one of the first TOS research projects and one of the best known. Probably the most interesting finding was that if managers are given and are able to assume more responsibility and authority, they will perform better. The research also found that managers have leadership/followership and other interpersonal characteristics which are inherent in them; whenever they can revert to behaviour conforming to these managerial characteristics, they will do so.

NOTES

1   The main pioneering protagonist for the essentially Freudian view of personality was the Italian physician and educator Maria Montessori (1870–1952) who held that personality traits are formed at a very early age. Her views and activities were centred around the motor freedom of the child. Every child develops in his own good time. One does not help him to adapt to his environment, but rather one creates an environment which will enable him to adapt according to his own ability (Standing, 1952). In recent years, more and more child psychologists and early age educators (and students of early age education) have rallied round the Montessori approach. This approach is somewhere on the scale between a strict education based on doctrines imposed by dominant parents, and a completely *laissez-faire* approach to children's upbringing.

The *laissez-faire* approach was advocated earlier in the twentieth century by people like Spock (1955), who dealt with early age, and Dewey (1916), with later school education. They come as close as one may to saying that babies and children should be allowed to follow their heart's or brain's desire.

The new Montessori educators are concerned with very young children only. They reject the imposition of parents' values upon children in that they draw the inevitable conclusions from Jean Piaget's findings of the early 1930s (Piaget, 1966). However, they go farther than that in saying that while children differ from their parents, they likewise differ from one another. We can offer them the means and educational support which would enable them to be brighter (Beck, 1975).

In recent years Dr Spock has changed some of his approach which was believed to have led, among other things, to the appearance of the protest youth of the 1960s. Spock first supported but subsequently retreated from his approach. Unlike Spock, Montessori asserts that in many things parents should give their children support and guidance. They should guide but not coerce them; they should attract their attention to things which may make them brighter.

Although personality traits are formed during babyhood and very early childhood, the raising of children by parents ranges from absolute dictation and control by parents to absolute *laissez-faire*. On the one hand, we have the patriarchal societies in which the father is the absolute ruler of his children's lives while; on the other, we have the 'your children are not your children. . . . They come through you but not from you' approach (Gibran, 1931). The two extremes are described in our example of the Family Organization, in chapter 4.

The following are two examples, from different parts of the world, of educational modes which are continuations of the Spock approach applied to children up to and including teenagers. In the USA there are the followers of Dewey (1961) who advocate an almost free-choice educational system, in which the child is not obliged to follow any study course not to his liking. An amazingly similar approach was found in the past in the kibbutzim in Israel. Here children were protected from competing with each other and from discovering that some are better than others—by *not* having to take any examinations. Those kibbutz children who may have wanted to enter universities, usually following their military service, were encouraged to attend external courses preparing them for high school matriculation examinations. These classes were held, however, in non-kibbutz schools, usually in the evening. The so-called 'children's-lib' movement, popping up in different ways in various countries, is also an offspring of the Spock approach.

The upbringing of children to teenage level should be a compromise between a completely imposed form, as in paramilitary schools, and giving the children free rein. This can be done by offering children and young people a choice of course, to suit their education to their capacity for learning, talents, and desires. This must be done, however, without depriving the children of areas of education and study courses which society as a whole feels are necessary to enable them to cope with their future, whether the children themselves like it or not.

Thus, for example, it is known that in the twenty-first century people will have to accommodate themselves to leisure during at least half of the days of the week. In order to prepare people for this abundance of leisure they should get some feeling for and knowledge of the arts, humanities, and applied behavioural sciences. Children should receive at least some basic education in these areas, whether they choose to or not.

2   The managerial characteristics are part of the traits related to the two hemispheres of the brain which establish the synthetical-emotional or heuristic (right side of the brain) and the analytical-rational (left side of the brain) behaviour of the person (Bogen, 1975; Rossi, 1977). Let us consider examples of people whose right (heuristic) side of the brain or left (rational) side of the brain is dominant to the extent that they can behave *only* within either informal or formal roles.

Military administrators are confronted from time to time with a soldier who cannot be indoctrinated into the army because, no matter how hard they try, he will remain a deviant who will never conform. Such recruits usually have distinct artistic, literary, musical, or other intellectual-spiritual talents. If the military does not allow for the immediate discharge of such a recruit, on grounds of unsuitable personality traits, a troubled personal military history will ensue for him. He will not follow military regulations and restrictions, and will often disobey orders. This will lead to endless charges against him, resulting in one punishment after another. This represents a failure to take into account a dominant heuristic (or emotional) personality, which in turn will lead to an enormous waste of time and money for the military. It is, moreover, painful and wasteful for the soldier himself and may cause him irrevocable mental damage. If the military do not discharge him right away, one can predict that his release from the army will occur either because he is mentally damaged, or because he acts as if he were out of his mind, or because the military considers his behaviour to be so erratic that they decide to discharge him on mental grounds.

At the other extreme, people with a dominant left hemisphere of the brain, i.e. with a predominantly inflexible and rational personality, are encountered in all kinds of organizations. These are the 'square' types who, once they can do something in a certain way, it becomes almost impossible to persuade them to try it another way. These are the rigid, bureaucratic types whom it is very difficult to teach anything new.

3   Figure 5.1, as well as the text concerning the Maslow need hierarchy, is based on Abraham Maslow's famous book outlining his concepts of a need hierarchy on which most of the motivation literature has been based (Maslow, 1954, pp. 80–93).

4   One has to be careful when using Maslow's terminology. Sometimes his concepts are intact but, because of misuse of his terms, the order and ranking of his need levels are confused. In a cross-cultural study of perceptions of managerial needs and skills in samples of managers in the USA and the UK, Frank Heller and Lyman Porter (1977, pp. 327–330) based their questionnaire 'on the theoretical classification of needs by Maslow (1954)'. Their hierarchy is somewhat different from Maslow's; especially misleading are their 'security needs', which correspond in their questionnaire to 'the feeling of security in my management position'. This is quite different from Maslow's 'physiological and safety needs', which their 'security needs' could imply. Therefore, it is not surprising that the results of Heller and Porters' questionnaires created a hierarchy with a somewhat different order from that of Maslow's. Table 5.9 shows their average results, in percentages, for 'subjects indicating maximum importance of needs' (ranked by the order in the USA). These results may be explained in terms of the fulfilled needs in the USA and the UK as follows (the more importance attached to the needs the less fulfilled they are):

Table 5.9   Heller and Porter's results for 'subjects indicating maximum importance of needs

	No. of questions on which average is based	USA %	UK %	'Non-specific items'
Esteem needs	3	18.9	15.4	
(Remuneration needs)	1	22.5	25.6	('The pay for my management position')
Social needs	2	23.8	23.2	
Autonomy needs	4	26.7	34.4	
Security needs	1	30.0	23.2	
(Participation needs)	1	41.2	28.0	('The feeling of being in-the-know in my management position')
Self-realization needs	3	50.5	51.0	

In the USA, the esteem needs are the most fulfilled, closely followed by the remuneration and social needs. From there onwards the unfulfilled needs, going up the hierarchy, are autonomy, security, participation, and self-realization.

In the UK, the two ends of the need hierarchy pyramid are as in the USA; except that the esteem needs are even more fulfilled (15.4 per cent in the UK *v.* 18.9 per cent in the USA), while the self-realization needs are equally unfulfilled. The remuneration needs are less fulfilled in the UK (25.6 per cent) than in the USA (22.5 per cent); even more so the autonomy needs (34.4 per cent in the UK and 26.7 per cent in the USA). On the other hand, the need for participation is much more fulfilled in the UK (28 per cent) than in the USA (41.2 per cent).

5   A case study of such a situation of an industrial organization which is composed of 20 decentralized factories is described in Glover and Hower (1952). The organization, the Dashman Company, found itself in a severe materials shortage in 1940, when Roosevelt's 'lend lease' of military materials to Britain came into effect. It encountered severe managerial problems in trying to centralize the purchasing functions. It could have been predicted with certainty that this, and all other industrial US organizations without functional structures, would have formally to centralize the structures within a year or two. Where would they get all their managers for their new functional structures? Yet, all the entrepreneurial and decentralized managers turned into motivated, proficient, achieving, and satisfied managers for the duration of the war.

6   An instance of the return of military personnel to their previous personalities when the hostilities were over, occurred in the British Army in the Far East. The moment the Japanese Imperial Forces signed the armistice agreement at the end of 1945, the British soldiers in the Far East became discontented with the salary, the food, the lodging, and other army 'comforts'. They went on strike and even revolted.

7   There are some managerial characteristic classifications which can be beneficially used, as they can be established with the aid of validated questionnaires. Such questionnaires facilitate the measurement of characteristics which are related to the managerial characteristics listed in Table 5.1 (Fiedler, 1967; Reddin, 1970; Vroom, 1960). The second author used Reddin's measurements in her doctoral research

(Raveh, 1976), which served as a basis for our organizational example on British Chain Stores, in chapter 4. We recommend such measurements of managerial characteristics for application in cases where the organization is willing to invest in both the selection and the placement of the right positions. Chapter 7 is devoted to showing how the organization can go about, and be helped in, balancing its TOS.

8   An organization which serves Zionist Jews (those interested in Israel) in their various contacts with Israel.

9   The US Mafia is much larger than the Sicilian Mafia, but both are predominantly Sicilian. There are personal connections at the top levels of the two organizations. The Mafia has the main attributes of a multinational corporation (described in more detail in chapter 6), in that it does not carry the constraints of one country into other countries, i.e. it is not loyal to any one country, and has a supranational culture. There is, however, another prerogative in becoming a multinational company, namely to manage the organization in a multistructure.

10 Officers who served under Rickover admired him but said that it was insupportable to work with him, Jimmy Carter, the US president (1976–1980), served three years as a technical officer in a nuclear submarine. When he first arrived for an admission interview at Rickover's office, he proudly told the admiral that he graduated from the Naval Academy in Annapolis in 59th place, out of 820 graduates. Rickover retorted curtly: 'Why not the best?'

11 The two cases had to do with causing a submarine to perform a deep dive in a most dangerous way, which was contrary to safety regulations. He was likewise accused of reacting slowly and inappropriately during the exercises. The first experimental manoeuvres were those of the atomic submarine *Jacksonville* in January 1981, while the second were those of the modern attack submarine *La Gulla* in July 1981.

12 In the Navy he was considered to be a difficult and quarrelsome man, as well as a very talented one. Twice did his superiors refuse to promote him to admiral's rank. It was only after the Senate Joint Armed Forces Committee was specially convened to discuss this matter that it was decided to recommend his promotion, which literally meant that the Navy was ordered to appoint him admiral.

13 The first nuclear submarine, *Nautilus*, was launched in 1955, about three years before the Soviet Union launched its Sputnik, the first satellite ever to have been sent around the earth (with the dog Laika in it). It could well be that if Rickover had not entrepreneured the *Nautilus* in 1955, the Russians could have preceded the Americans in launching a nuclear submarine, too.

14 Peter Drucker said that, during its 300 years of existence, Mitsui always had the right CE for the time. He attributed this to the way that young managers are groomed, coached, and informally evaluated in the Japanese zaibatsu (Drucker, 1971). We have to emphasize that we believe that multistructures started to appear in the zaibatsu only in 1912 (see Yoshino, 1968), and therefore our discussion relates only to about one quarter of Mitsui's history.

15 Pope Pius XII's inability to react properly to some of the atrocities carried out by the Germans during the Second World War elicited much criticism in the literature, theatre, etc. (Friedlander, 1966; Hochhuth, 1964).

16 There are now available biographies and autobiographies of world-famous entrepreneurs like Henry Ford I, as well as of all other types of entrepreneurs, including such contrasting people as Cecil Rhodes, the white colonizer of present-day Malawi, Zambia, and Zimbabwe, and Mafia heads. There are only a few biographies and autobiographies of leaders who had managerial characteristics other than those of a successful entrepreneur.

17 Like Beck's (1975) *How to Raise a Brighter Child—The Case for Early Learning*, which we have already mentioned.

18 An 'anarchic structure' is a structure which organizations have to bear with when

their entrepreneurial or functional CEs change, because of moving somewhere else, dying, or being replaced (see Figure 4.4). This is not a desirable managerial structure and surely should be avoided as much as possible. However, as we have to live with it from time to time, we include it in Figure 5.6.

19 There are several organizations around the world which have become known for trying different types of such behavioural cures. Among them is Volvo, which is described in the following paragraphs. Others are Philips, the electronics manufacturers in Holland, and TRW in the USA. The tendency to try several cures concurrently is like giving a patient different types of medicines simultaneously. If he recovers from his disease, it is impossible to decide which drug cured him and which did not, or, perhaps, which combination of drugs did it. We know that certain types of managers, particularly entrepreneurs, have a tendency to call in simultaneously, or in quick succession, several different kinds of consultants, when the systems of their TOS are in severe imbalance (the entrepreneurial CE of the Devon Corporation, described in the organizational example in chapter 3, often used to employ different consultants).

20 As they were first introduced by Henry Ford I, at the beginning of the twentieth century.

21 The problem with this sort of behavioural cure is that we actually know very little about how it really works. We do not know what kind of leadership informally emerged in these groups, and how the different participants in the groups reacted to this behavioural cure. We do know that in different organizations where all kinds of socially and psychologically motivated experiments were done, the managers, along with the CE, who were committed to the experiments, did not allow any outside organizational behaviourists to study the process and consequences. These organizations include Glacier in which, for 15 years, the CE, Wilfred Brown (1960), and the main researcher, Elliott Jacques (e.g. 1961), introduced a variety of changes in managerial methods; only towards the end of this long process was somebody allowed to study it.

22 A more detailed description of the way in which we perceive the different types of participation of workers and of managers in the managerial process is presented in Twiss and Weinshall, 1980, pp. 157–166. The following types of participation are discussed there: group dynamics (pp. 158–160), industrial democracy (pp. 160–165), group technology (pp. 165–166) and continued cooperation (p. 166). The Volvo experiment at Kalmar is of the group technology type but evolves from the ideologies and concepts of all the above types of participation, except for that of continued cooperation. The participation of continued cooperation is *not* the participation of workers in management; it is that sort of cooperation between the organization and the workers (as well as of all the other FDM) without which the organization cannot survive.

23 In this, and in our previous writings, we have preferred Joan Woodward's general classification of technologies (Woodward, 1958; 1965) to those of others. The organizational example in chapter 4 describes her South Essex Industry research, and includes a comparison between her production system classification and another more detailed one.

24 One might think that it would be ideal to be able to bring up all children to acquire managerial characteristics which would enable them to conform easily to various kinds of followership and leadership conditions. This is not the case. If all managers had rigid or flexible multistructure characteristics, they would not feel fully motivated, satisfied, and proficient in any other role than at the head of a multi-structured organization. Somehow, the raising of young children seems to create in the world a variety of managers who are suitable in their characteristics and qualities for the roles that are available in management structures; organizations have to

be helped in order to have the right person in the right job. If too many parents deliberately tried to raise their children to make them into a particular type of manager, we would have too many managers of the chosen types and a shortage of managers of other types. Naturalists do not want us to disturb the ecological balance among the species; we should be equally careful that the balances among different types of managers is not disturbed by raising all or most of the young children in a similar fashion.

25 This Gyllenhammar did in his book (1977), and in talking about the Kalmar plant on different occasions (e.g. *Harvard Business School Bulletin*, 1975). He is only one of many with the same approach whose research projects and writings appear under different labels, the oldest of which is 'socio-technical systems' (Pasmore and Sherwood, 1978). Socio-technical systems started with the work, in the Tavistock Institute, of Fred Emery and Eric Trist (1965), and continued with the work of Herbst (1977), Gyllenhammar's neighbour in Norway. Another more recent label for this same area is 'quality of working life', with the US–UK team of Lou Davis and Albert Cherns (1975). Those researching under this label have not all stuck closely to the concept of socio-technical systems, like Bob Dubin, who introduced his *The World of Work* (1959) by saying that it 'is devoted to what people do while they are working, and the reasons for their behaviour'. He subsequently continued to explore and write about the wider aspects of the lives of employees in and out of work (e.g. Dubin, 1973). Even Albert Cherns digressed from his and Lou Davis's mission of quality of working life when he advocated reducing the working life-time as there is going to be less and less employment available (in an address during a Conference on the Quality of Working Life in Toronto, Canada, in August 1981). This is exactly the point we made concerning Gyllenhammar's approach. Even if this were a reasonable cure for bridging the gap in managerial characteristics, it is irrelevant, because soon there will be almost no workers inside our motor car plants. A more elaborate discussion of the quickly diminishing amounts of employment as a result of advancing technology is included in Twiss and Weinshall (1980, pp. 177–190).

26 In many such instances those responsible and directly involved are reluctant to enable outsiders to study the process; this makes one somewhat dubious about what goes on. We gave an example of one such case in note 21 above.

27 In an early work by the first author (Weinshall, 1960), examples of a standardized questionnaire (Appendix A, pp. 3–6) and the analysis of the responses are presented (pp. 100–110, and Appendix A, pp. 3–6). The same source quotes numerous attitudes from non-directive interviews (pp. 37–66). This is the same main source on which the Devon Corporation organizational example in chapter 3 is based.

28 Two of the best-known projects of this type were carried out by Mason Haire and his team (Haire *et al.*, 1966) and Bass and his team (Barret and Bass, 1970). Haire applied elaborate attitude questionnaires to samples from a variety of countries. He then carried out a cluster analysis on the responses and lumped together the countries in which the managerial attitudes were similar. Bass devised concrete business administration situations played by groups of managers in each country. The responses of the participants to the situations serve as a basis for his analysis of differences in managerial attitudes among the countries.

29 Thus, for example, several managerial attitude studies were carried out on IBM employees. David Sirota's study (Sirota and Greenwood, 1977, pp. 261–276) was designed in a similar way to Mason Haire's studies mentioned in note 28. Geert Hofstede (1979), on the other hand, was interested in culture-bound attitudes among IBM personnel in different countries.

30 The GFA methodology was developed by Dr Frank Heller, who has already used it for the completion of two studies of managerial decision making in the USA and UK (Heller, 1971). Heller likewise conducted GFA research on managerial decision

making in France, Holland, Germany, Israel, Spain, Sweden, and the USA (Heller and Wilpert, 1981).

31 This is done in the attitude study part of the Multinational Business Education project, conducted on students of INSEAD (the European Institute for Business Administration at Fontainbleau, France) since 1966. It includes questionnaires exploring attitudes to projective short stories about cultural values affecting managerial behaviour. The first value to be explored was attitudes towards interorganizational managerial turnover (Weinshall, 1977, pp. 183–200). Other values, explored in the late 1970s were attitudes to bribery, confidentiality and punctuality, discussed in the following chapter (pp. 249–251). Another example is Geert Hofstede (1979), who used specially designed value scales for his above mentioned study (note 29).

32 A method for establishing the managerial structure on the basis of the actual managerial relationship structure is the MPWR (Mutually Perceived Working Relationships), in response to the question: Who are the persons with whom you generally work most closely? These MPWR are likewise compared with the formal managerial relationships. The informalogram is described in detail in section 3.33 of Chapter 3 (pp. 78–85).

33 A technique for describing, analysing, and feeding back oral interactions for therapeutic and corrective purposes devised by Weinshall (1979).

34 An increasing number of organizations are nowadays requiring their management candidates to go through all kinds of psychological tests. It is interesting that many of these organizations claim that they get the best results, as corroborated by subsequent managerial style and performance, from graphological tests. We are more aware of the managerial characteristics of those with whom we have worked in the organization.

35 This extremely important problem of our age is beyond the scope of this book. We refer the reader, however, to a discussion of the relation between technology and employment, in which some concrete solutions to the problems connected with their implementation are presented (Twiss and Weinshall, 1980, pp. 175–190).

36 We have in front of us an article entitled 'How Volkswagen found Mr. Right—Capturing a General Motors Man Isn't Easy, Admits the Headhunter' (it is by Robert Irwin, automotive editor of the *Detroit News*; unfortunately, we have not noted on the cutting either the date or the name of the newspaper). This is the story of how Gerrard R. Roch, an executive search man, was asked by Toni Schmucker, Volkswagen CE, to find a top operations executive to establish VW's manufacturing activities in the USA. Roch found James W. McLernon, who was employed by GM. Although Mr McLernon is referred to as 'Mr Right' (for the job) the article does not tell us if the crucial questions about his future role were asked and answered. We know, however, that a decisive factor in the choice of McLernon was the fact of 27 years' achievement with GM. We are likewise told that Mr Roch gave Mr Schmucker a list of three candidates, all top executives of large US car manufacturers, to choose from. On the other hand, it turns out that while Mr McLernon is going to head the US manufacturing of VW, there is already a successful head of VW marketing in the USA, Mr Stuart Perkins, born in the UK. It is not clear whether the two functions, manufacturing and marketing, are meant to be fused into one organization.

37 We leave a third example for the Notes, as it concerns our own academic world. There were times when research students, such as doctoral candidates working on their dissertations, had a committee of several distinguished professors supervising them. These professors could exert any amount of pressure and demands on the candidate. They did this independently of one another, even though one of them was always a formal supervisor of the candidate.

Thus, for example, at the Harvard Business School the doctoral student used to work closely with every member of his committee. There was no defence of the thesis ritual at the HBS, so that a doctoral student had to accommodate the suggestions of the members of his committee who then voted on the thesis once the supervisor decided that it was ready for the vote. Until the mid 1950s a committee could consist of as many as five professors who would, more often than not, conduct the academic disagreements and conflicts among themselves on the back of the student, so to say. Subsequently, it was decided that three members are more than enough to manage one doctoral student.

38　The inevitable structural result of this situation is that the secretary turns out to be the actual boss of her or his three formal bosses.

39　Some of the best-known researchers of and writers in organizational behaviour have devoted their time to writing about matrix (Davis and Lawrence, 1978). Henry Mintzberg thought that Galbraith (1973) 'was really the first to explain clearly the role of modern mutual adjustment devices such as task forces and matrix forms in the formal structure' (Mintzberg, 1979, p. 10). Galbraith himself, on the other hand, refers to John Mee (1964) as the first who used the term 'matrix organization' (Galbraith, 1971).

40　This example of Philips of Eindhoven was used by Weinshall in one of his earlier presentations of the multistructure. (The multistructure is described in detail in section 5.4.) At that time it seemed to the author that the structure (or 'triple structure' as it was referred to then) was a form of multistructure (Weinshall, 1973, p. 167). However, even then it was stressed that 'the actual evolution of multistructures has only recently become the object of systematic research'. Now, it is clear that Philips, which had its origins in the way in which the CE led the organization, was a matrix organization at the time, since it had been based on a dual commerce–manufacturing management at the various levels of the hierarchy.

41　As we mention in chapter 4, anarchic structures can be found from time to time in every organization. This occurs when the head of an entrepreneurial or a functional structure suddenly ceases to lead his subordinates because of resignation, dismissal, long illness, or death. Now that the subordinates are independent of their head, they seek other people with whom to continue maintaining their operations. This is how we get an informally decentralized, anarchic structure whenever the leadership of an informally or formally centralized structure changes. However, this lasts only until the new head assumes control of his people.

42　This is probably one of the main reasons why anarchists hate the term 'organization'. They identify an organization as something that is self-perpetuating and exists only for the sake of its own survival. They are quite correct with respect to all the economically and socially productive organizations in the world. With anarchic structures, one can achieve only a one-shot, non-productive result (e.g. murdering a leader, like President Lincoln, or the removal of a leader, like President Nixon).

43　This is only one of the situations in which people could feel a real responsibility for the results of their actions. Probably the only other situation in which such joint responsibility is felt is where parents are bringing up their children. In both cases, however, it is not uncommon that people may split because of deep rifts over their joint responsibilities.

44　An organization run in an anarchic structure (except for one going through this structure for a short period of time) is usually small not only in its SDM, but likewise in the number of people in its operating organization. When one thinks of an anarchic organization, one usually imagines a group of anarchists plotting to assassinate some hated ruler. An anarchic organization may, however, have quite a large followership; this seems to be a more appropriate term than 'membership' for large anarchic organizations because of the nature of these organizations. However, nobody ever knows exactly how large their followership is. Thus, for example, the SDS (Students for a Democratic Society) may have had a following of several hundred thousand.

45 The communications pattern research (called the communicogram) for which the data processing was done by this organization is described in Weinshall (1979).

46 We were told shortly afterwards that all the three programmers had left the organization. We were likewise informed that the employee turnover in this organization took place several times a year, i.e. employee turnover was a few hundred percent.

47 This appeared in Knight (1977). For obvious reasons, we would not like to identify the author of this contribution in Knight's book.

48 The conflict between the parents could end in two disastrous results. It could terminate in loud rows in front of the child; or in both parents resigning from the upbringing of the child (this may end in the child having his own way all along). Both cases may cause severe harm to the relationship between the couple.

49 In Israel the public bus transportation used to be, until the Second World War, in the hands of small cooperative societies. Since then, these cooperatives have grown and merged; in the 1980s, the remaining two huge cooperative societies were considering amalgamating. The decision making and the personal interrelationships within these organizations gradually worsened, as they became larger. If it had not been for the transportation monopolies which they had enjoyed all along, they could not have survived. It was indeed the competition between them in several areas, over which neither has an absolute monopoly, that preceded their desire to merge. In addition, there was the fear that the Israeli Government might establish competitive public transportation. They know very well that becoming a larger cooperative society will aggravate their decision-making and managerial structure problems. However, they also know that their power to prevent the Israeli Government providing competition will enormously grow if they control all public bus transportation, urban as well as intercity, in Israel.

50 Of the five questions from which André Laurent (1978) claims to be providing some assessment of the readiness of managers to function effectively in matrix organizations, only the one presented in Table 5.7 has a direct bearing on matrix. The other questions have to do with conflict centralization, e.g.: (a) superiors' knowledge of what their subordinates do, (b) clarity of managerial structure, by trying to run the organization simultaneously in a decentralized and a centralized structure, (c) informal versus formal structure (bypassing hierarchial levels). The findings arrived at from the responses to these questions seem to indicate that the British tend to be less centralized and conservative, and more realistic and democratic, than the French. These findings are quite similar to those arrived at by Jacques Horovitz in his research in industrial organizations in Britain, France, and Germany (Horovitz, 1980), which served as a basis for our organizational example in chapter 4. Laurent's findings are also indicative of the *naïveté* of MBA students regarding the realities of organizations. The responses to these other four questions do not, however, indicate anything about the respondents' preferences regarding matrix organizations.

51 The informalogram is a research tool for establishing the managerial structure on the basis of a comparison between the informal and the formal relationship structures. Clinical action research is the methodology by which the organization is helped by outsiders to adapt itself to the dynamics of the TOS. Both the informalogram and clinical action research are described in more detail in chapter 7.

52 See Weinshall (1978).

53 The ringi process has been described by Mike Yoshino (1968, pp. 254–255) as follows:

The word ringi consists of two parts—rin, meaning submitting a proposal to one's superior and receiving his approval, and gi, meaning deliberations and decisions. The ringi system has, indeed, all of these features; the lower echelon managerial staff member must follow a certain procedure. He must draft a document known as a ringisho. In this document he must describe the matter to be decided and his recommendation as to what ought to be done. By complex and circuitous paths, the ringisho slowly works its way up to top management. When the president approves the ringisho by affixing his seal, the decision is final. The ringi document is then returned to the original drafter for implementation.

The ringi decision-making process is also mentioned in the Japanese zaibatsu organizational example in this chapter.

54 We should say that the examples 'seem to be multistructures', because neither structure was studied systematically. In the first case the situation was described to us only by the entrepreneurial head of the sub-organization. In the second case, the description came from a British colleague, who did not himself study Sir Arnold Weinstock.

55 The first author discovered a multistructure and first defined its federated structure in the late 1960s, when questioning the phenomenon of Japan in which the large, zaibatsu-type organizations are economically successful in spite of the 'lifetime employment' of their managers. It became clear that their managerial structures had to change over time, adapting to their expanding SDM. This could not happen without interorganizational managerial mobility. The latter mobility could be meaningful only with different types of managers, i.e. those with different managerial characteristics in different parts of the organization, namely in a multistructure. Thus he arrived in a logical way at defining a multistructure and assumed that the Japanese zaibatsu operate in this managerial structure (Weinshall, 1971, p. 16). Only during his first visit to Japan in 1971 could he verify the existence of the multi-structure.

56 There is a so-called 'timespan of discretion' (Jacques, 1961) of the chief executive's subordinates that ranges from a few hours to a few years. Although it is doubtful whether one could ever establish equitable remuneration for managers exclusively on this basis, Jacques's concept of equitable payment correlated with the timespan of discretion undoubtedly applies in principle to the managers subordinated to the chief executive of a multistructure organization, in that the longer the timespan, the higher the remuneration. Thus, the salary scale of these managers will range from high to low as follows:

Independent entrepreneurs
Heads of the independent product/service line or area divisions in the decentralized substructure
Heads of the functions in the functional structure
Entrepreneurs' aides surrounding the chief executive in his own entrepreneurial sub-structure.

57 The assumptions and analyses regarding the managerial characteristics are related to the inborn structure of personality. This has been obvious from the early stages of relating leadership and followership characteristics to personality traits (Stogdill and Shartle, 1955). Thus, for example, the conclusion of Wilfred Brown, the CE who collaborated with Elliott Jacques on the long research programme in his Glacier Metal Company, was an admission of his mistaken assumptions that people could change basically (Brown, 1960); while managerial characteristics do not change, the managerial style is the way in which the managers actually behave in various situations. This is part of their socialization beyond adolescence.

SELECTED BIBLIOGRAPHICAL SOURCES

Barret, G. V., and Bass, B. M., 1970. 'Comparative surveys of managerial attitudes and behaviour' (comparative teaching, training, and research), in *Proceedings of the Comparative Management Workshop*, pp. 179–217.

Beck, J., 1975. *How to Raise a Brighter Child—The Case for Early Learning* (first published by Trident Press, 1967), Pocket Books, New York.

Bogen, J. E., 1975. 'Educational aspects of hemispheric specialization', *UCLA Educator* (17).

Brown, W., 1960. *Exploration in Management*, Wiley, New York.

Davis, L. E., and Cherns, A. B., 1975. *The Quality of Working Life*, Free Press, New York.

Davis, S. M., and Lawrence, P. R., 1977. *Matrix*, Addison-Wesley, Reading, Mass.

Davis, S. M., and Lawrence, P. R., 1978. 'Problems of matrix organization', *Harvard Business Review*, May–June.

De-Bettignies, H.-C., and Evans, P. L., 1977. 'The cultural dimension of top executives' careers: a comparative analysis', in T. D. Weinshall (ed.), *Culture and Management*, Penguin, Harmondsworth, Middx.

Dewey, J., 1916. *Democracy and Education: An Introduction to the Philosophy of Education*, Macmillan, New York.

Drucker, P. F., 1971. 'What we can learn from Japanese management', *Harvard Business Review*, March–April.

Dubin, R., 1959. *The World of Work, Industrial Society and Human Relations*, Prentice-Hall, Englewood Cliffs, NJ.

Dubin, R., 1973. 'Work and nonwork—institutional perspective', in M. D. Dunnette (ed.), *Work and Nonwork in the Year 2000*, Brooks/Cole, Monterey, Ca.

Eggers, E. R., 1977. 'How to do business with a Frenchman', in T. D. Weinshall (ed.), *Culture and Management*, Penguin, Harmondsworth, Middx.

Emery, F. E., and Trist, E. L., 1965. 'The casual texture of organizational environments', *Human Relations*, 18, pp. 21–32.

Fiedler, F. E., 1967. *A Theory of Leadership Effectiveness*, McGraw-Hill, New York.

Friedlander, S. A., 1966. *Pius XII and The Third Reich: A Documentation*, translated from French and German by Charles Fullman, Knopf, New York.

Galbraith, J. R., 1971. 'Matrix organization designs—how to combine functional and project forms', *Business Horizons*, February.

Galbraith, J. R., 1973. *Designing Complex Organizations*, Addison-Wesley, Reading, Mass.

Gibran, K., 1931. *The Prophet*, Knopf, New York.

Glover, J. D., and Hower, R. M., 1952. *The Administrator*, Irwin, Homewood, Ill.

Gyllenhammar, P. G., 1977. *People at Work*, Addison-Wesley, Reading, Mass.

Haire, M., Ghiselli, E. E., and Porter, L. W., 1966. *Managerial Thinking: An International Study*, Wiley, New York.

Harvard Business School Bulletin, 1975. 'Volvo's Gyllenhammar gives Letherbee Lecture', *HBS Bulletin*, January–February, pp. 33–35.

Heller, F. A., 1971. *Managerial Decision Making*, Tavistock, London.

Heller, F. A., and Porter, L. W., 1977. 'Perceptions of managerial needs and skills in two national samples', in T. D. Weinshall (ed.), *Culture and Management*, Penguin, Harmondsworth, Middx.

Heller, F. A., and Wilpert, B., 1981. *Competence and Power in Managerial Decision-making*, Wiley, Chichester.

Herbst, P. G., 1977. *Alternatives in Bureaucracy*, Nijhoff, Leiden, Holland.

Hochhuth, R., 1964. *The Deputy*, translated by Richard and Clara Winston, Grove Press, New York.

Hofstede, G., 1979. *Culture's Consequences*, Sage Publications, Beverly Hills, Calif.

Horovitz, J. H., 1980. *Top Management Control in Europe*, Macmillan, London.

Jacques, E., 1961. *Equitable Payment*, Heinemann, London.

Kessler, I. I., and Levine, M. L. (eds), 1970. *The Community as an Epidemiologic Laboratory: A Case Book of Community Studies*, Johns Hopkins University Press, Baltimore, Md.

Knight, Kenneth (ed.), 1977. *Matrix Management*, Gower Press, London.

Laurent, André, 1978. 'Matrix organizations in Latin culture—a note on the use of comparative research data in management education', Working Paper no. 78–28, European Institute of Advanced Studies in Management, Brussels, June.

Lombard, G. F. F., 1965. *Behavior in a Selling Group—A Case Study of Interpersonal Relations in a Department Store*, Division of Research, Graduate School of Business Administration, Harvard University, Boston, Mass.

Maslow, A., 1954. *Motivation and Personality*, Harper & Row, New York.

Medalie, J. H., *et al.*, 1967. *Proceedings of Tel Hashomer Hospital*, volume 6, Tel Hashomer Hospital, Israel.

Mee, J. F., 1964. 'Ideational items: matrix organization', *Business Horizons*, Summer.

Mintzberg, H., 1979. *Structuring of Organizations: A Synthesis of Research*, Prentice-Hall, Englewood Cliffs, NJ.

Mitchell, M., 1936. *Gone with the Wind*, Macmillan, New York.

Pasmore, W. A., and Sherwood, J. J. (eds), 1978. *Sociotechnical Systems: A Sourcebook*, University Associates, Toronto.

Piaget, J., 1966. *The Moral Judgement of the Child*, translated by Marjorie Gabain, Free Press, New York.

Raveh, Y. A., 1976. 'Managerial behavior in retailing', an unpublished doctoral dissertation, London Graduate School of Business Studies, University of London.

Reddin, W. J., 1970. *Managerial Effectiveness*, McGraw-Hill, New York.

Rossi, E., 1977. 'The cerebral hemispheres in analytical psychology', *Journal of Analytical Psychology*, **22**, pp. 35–51.

Sirota, D., and Greenwood, J. M., 1977. 'Understanding your overseas workforce', T. D. Weinshall (ed.), *Culture and Management*, Penguin, Harmondsworth, Middx.

Spock, B., 1955. *Baby and Child Care*, Bodley Head, London.

Standing, M., 1952. *Montessori, her Life and Work*.

Stogdill, R. M., and Shartle, C. L., 1955. *Methods in the Study of Administrative Leadership*, Bureau of Business Research, Ohio State University, Columbus.

Twiss, B. C., and Weinshall, T. D., 1980. *Managing Industrial Organizations*, Pitman, London.

Vroom, V. H., 1960. *Some Personality Determinants of the Effects of Participation*, Prentice-Hall, Englewood Cliffs, NJ.

Weinshall, T. D., 1960. 'The effects of management changes on the organizational relationships and attitudes', unpublished doctoral dissertation, Harvard University.

Weinshall, T. D., 1971. *Applications of Two Conceptual Schemes in Case Study and General Organizational Research*, Ashridge Management College, Berkhamsted, Herts.

Weinshall, T. D., 1973. 'A study of organizational size and managerial structure', in D. Graves (ed.), *Management Research—A Cross-cultural Perspective*, Elsevier, Amsterdam, pp. 157–183.

Weinshall, T. D., 1977. *Culture and Management*, Penguin, Harmondsworth, Middx.

Weinshall, T. D., 1979. *Managerial Communication: Concepts, Approaches and Techniques*, Academic Press, London.

Weinshall, T. D., and Tawara, J., 1978. 'Managerial structure of a nationally mixed organization in Japan', *Journal of Organization and Administration Sciences*, **8** (4), Winter.

Woodward, J., 1958. *Management and Technology*, HMSO, London.

Woodward, J., 1965. *Industrial Organization: Theory and Practice*, Oxford University Press.

Yoshino, M., 1968. *Japan's Managerial System*, MIT Press, Boston, Mass.

Chapter 6
The Multinationals

In recent years, much has been written about the phenomenon of the multinational corporation. People have tried to describe it, define it, and, on occasions, study it. However, too little has been said about the reasons for its advent, or about its national and international role.[1] Exploring the development of the multinational corporation will improve our understanding of what it is and where it is headed. It will also help to explain how the multinational corporation differs from other types of corporations from which it evolved, to size up some of its major problems, to describe the ways in which it handles these problems, and to contemplate ways of measuring its managerial structure.

Let us start by listing some of the points which will be described and analysed in this chapter:

—Multinational corporations are an inevitable consequence of the evolution of other types of organizations.

—Like any other organization, a multinational organization can be defined and measured by the scope of its decision making (SDM) and by its managerial structure (MS).

—The main difference between the multinational corporation and its national counterparts lies in its supranational approach, i.e. its tendency to disregard national interests.

—In these circumstances the multinational corporation can only be defined in behavioural terms:[2] A multinational organization is one in which all considerations related to its growth processes and its survival are based wholly on the interests of the organization itself, national pressures having no influence except in so far as constraints are imposed on it by the country within which it functions.

—Being a multinational corporation is not an absolute question of black and white, but rather a matter of degree. More and more large corporations are falling within the above definition.

—Finally, it seems that the worldwide role, influence, and power of multinational corporations is increasing, mainly at the expense of the nation states. We believe this is a development for the better in terms of the true interests, desires, and wellbeing of individuals and groups throughout the world. Be that as it may, they are probably the most important features of the second half of the twentieth century; hence the urgency for a conceptual understanding of what they are, as well as for an idea of where they are headed, and at what pace.

The above opening remarks mean that the more an organization is characterized by every one of the following three elements, the more multinational it is:

—*SDM*. The organization is operating in two or more countries with basically different national cultures.[3]
—*MS*. As a consequence, the management is structured in a more elaborate multistructure: greater product line diversity, a higher technological level, and, most importantly, wider geographical dispersal.
—*Managerial attitudes*. As the organization becomes more geographically dispersed, its managers are less inclined to carry the constraints, primarily the national culture constraints, from one country to another.

This chapter, describing the evolution of organizations from entrepreneurials to multinationals, is divided into three sections and a summary. The first discusses the wider environments of organizations. These wider environments usually exist within the confines of countries, sometimes within different parts of one country, while in other cases the wider environment may combine several countries with the same national culture. Therefore, multinationals which operate in different national cultures are confronted with various wider environments.

The second section describes the evolution of organizations spreading geographically, from international to multinational corporations. National and multinational managers are also discussed. The third section is concerned with the merits of multinationals, and their effects on the world and on the future of humanity.

6.1   THE WIDER ENVIRONMENTS IN WHICH ORGANIZATIONS OPERATE

The wider environment of the TOS has already been described in chapter 2, section 2.2, dealing with organizational maintenance, within the five environmental systems: the employment, money, and consumer markets and the technological-scientific and the socio-cultural systems. We saw that the conditions in each of these environmental systems establish the degree of competition in the immediate environment of the TOS. Thus, if the condition of the employment market is, for example, one of unemployment, the competition among organizations for hiring managers and workers would be quite weak. Similarly, if the money and the consumer markets are in conditions of severe shortage, the competition for customers, shareholders, and banks would be quite strong, but the competition for the suppliers would be much weaker. In countries where the technological-scientific system is at a low level, the competition for employees of higher qualifications would be greater in comparison with countries in which the

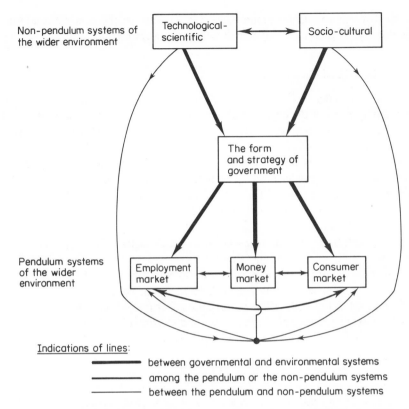

Figure 6.1   The interrelationships between the government and the wider
environment, and among the five environmental systems

technological-scientific system is on a higher level. Finally, the socio-cultural
system affects the competition for all the FDM among organizations in the
immediate environment; thus, for example, working habits such as diligence,
loyalty, accuracy, punctuality, etc., affect the competition for employees among
organizations. In this section we shall concern ourselves mostly with the
differences between governments of the countries because it is the government
which, to a large extent, regulates the conditions in the first three environmental
systems, the employment, money, and consumer market systems, the so-called
pendulum systems. The degree of shortages or abundance, as well as the speed of
moving from one situation to another, in every one of these three systems, is to a
large extent in the hands of the government.

The two other environmental systems, the technological-scientific and the
socio-cultural ones, can be affected by government only to a very limited degree.[4]
Actually, it is the other way round: multinationals affect to a large extent the type
of government that the country has.

Figure 6.1 presents in a schematic way the relations between the government and the five environmental systems, as well as between the pendulum and non-pendulum systems, and among all five systems in every country.

6.1.1 The TOS of Governments

Let us now consider, in Table 6.1, how the governmental regulation of the three pendulum systems of the employment, money, and consumer markets affects the TOS of government itself and of all the other organizations, primarily the business ones, within its jurisdiction.

Table 6.1 is actually part of the text, only it is arranged so that the reader can follow it in two directions: from top to bottom for government (A and C) and for business organizations (B and D), and subsequently from left to right, first for the decision-making main system (from A to B) and then for the management main system (from C to D).

A and C (Table 6.1) The more government regulates the wider environment and takes upon itself chunks of the SDM which used to be part of the SDM of business organizations, the less it is able to structure itself functionally. One should not be confused by the fact that, while it is in the process of taking upon itself the SDM of business organizations, the government is centralizing the whole decision-making process of the country, and it consequently increases its own SDM and has to *decentralize* or even *multistructure* its own decision-making process.[5]

B and D When the SDM of business organizations decreases in times of strife, emergency and war because the government takes control, they have to 'contract' their structures and adapt them to the type of centralized structure in which the government runs the economy, whether entrepreneurial or functional.[6]

From A to B We have already explained how governments affect the wider environment 'pendulum' systems of the employment, money, and consumer markets (see Figure 6.1), and that the more government creates conditions of planned economy, i.e. no competition among organizations for the FDM, the smaller the SDM of business and other types of organizations will be. Thus, for example, in countries with planned economies, as in the socialist states, organizations that on the face of it seem to be as large as similar organizations in *laissez-faire* (non-planned) economies, have actually much smaller SDM.[7]

From C to D Let us now make explicit[8] why it is that when the government runs the economy in a formally centralized way, the organizations in that country should be run in functional structures, and conversely, that in a country whose economy is run by the government in an informally centralized fashion, business organizations have to follow suit and adopt entrepreneurial structures, otherwise they would not last for long.[9]

The best example of an unavoidable formally centralized economy is a country at war.[10] This is when the management does not have to compete for its FDM with other organizations, because the government allocates to every organization its employees, suppliers, and customers, and funds for owners (by a 'cost plus' contract).

Table 6.1 Conceptualization of government intervention in and effects on the TOS main and principal systems of business organizations

Type of organizational systems	GOVERNMENT: the participation and intervention of government in business and the effects on government itself	BUSINESS ORGANIZATIONS: the effects of government on other organizations
THE DECISION-MAKING MAIN SYSTEM: Governmental regulation of the *Wider Environment* Effects on human FDM Consequent effects on SDM	A. The government is participating and/or intervening in more and more aspects of business. By way of the control, regulation, distribution, rationing, etc., of such aspects as investment and working capital, supplies of raw material, power and other services, purchasing power of the customers, wages, and salaries (through taxation and other means), etc., the government is undertaking a larger and larger SDM upon itself.	B. A larger part of the SDM of business organization is taken over by the government, which increasingly regulates the environment and does away with the competition of the business organizations for capital, materials, customer, markets, manpower, etc. This means that, while the SDM of the government grows, that of the business organizations diminishes.
THE MANAGEMENT MAIN SYSTEM: The effect of *SDM* on the: MS The required *MC*	C. Governments have traditionally operated in a functional structure (i.e. a formally centralized or a bureaucratized structure). This structure was suitable to deal with the regular tasks of most governments up till the 1930s. It is suitable for governments who do not undertake more than reasonable regulation of the economy. The moment the government interferes in the above mentioned fashion, it reaches a size (SDM) which could be properly handled only through more advanced forms of managerial structure, i.e. the decentralized structure and the multistructure. Accordingly, some of the government elected and appointed officers in key positions of the functional structure, with formally centralized managerial characteristics, should be replaced by government officers with other managerial characteristics in line with the roles in which they are meant to function.	D. As a result of the above, the seemingly large organizations have smaller and smaller SDMs. Consequently, in order to survive, they have to operate in a simpler and earlier managerial structure, such as the functional and entrepreneurial ones, rather than the decentralized and the multistructured ones. In what type of structure, functional or entrepreneurial, the organizations should be run when government intervention is large, depends on the way in which the centralized governmental control is performed. When the centralized management of the economy is formalized, as in times of war, the structure of all other types of organizations in the economy should be functional. When, unfortunately, the centralized management of the economy is informal, organizations in that country should also be run in informally centralized structures.

Let us analyse what the managerial structure for such an organization should be.[11] Such an organization does not require and cannot afford an entrepreneurial structure, even when its SDM is not large enough for a functional structure. This is because the management has to abide by the formalized framework imposed on it by the government. In such an organization there cannot be any entrepreneurial drives, because these would be against the quotas of FDM imposed on it.[12] In order to follow governmental guide-lines and control, the management should internally follow formalized procedures.

On the other hand, the management cannot be structured in a too advanced formal managerial structure. The sub-organizations, reporting to the CE, cannot be divided according to product lines or areas, because their heads cannot be allowed to have any autonomy in expanding their SDM. In other words, even a minimal formal decentralization for one month, let alone autonomy for three or six or twelve months, cannot be permitted in an organization whose strategy is fully directed, limited, and controlled by government. Consequently, the managerial structure of all business organizations during war-time should be functional.

6.1.2 Various Types of Nation States

The TOS of business organizations operating in a country and the TOS of its government depend primarily on the type of nation state in which the analysis is made at a specific time. What we mean by the *type* of nation state at any specific time is the condition of the five environmental systems at that time. We have already discussed the inevitable changes in the TOS of a nation when moving from peace to war or to another emergency which requires governmental control over all the nation's resources.

Let us now consider the state of government and of the wider environment in eight 'types' of nation states, in normal conditions.[13] Table 6.2 is an effort to analyse schematically some of the major elements of the wider environment of eight nation states. The choice of the countries is not representative of all the nation states of the world; neither is the selection of the areas which we chose for special attention exhaustive. Nevertheless, it is the sort of analysis which corporations moving to other countries should make, and are indeed making, in order to acquaint themselves with the different countries which they have in mind, comparing their advantages or disadvantages for the specific corporation. Indeed, once a corporation is operating in a country, it would want to have a periodical analysis, say once a year, of any changes which have occurred in the wider environment.

Such analyses would be much more detailed than that appearing in Table 6.2. For example, the analysis of the wider environmental systems would include details of various economic indices, while the analysis of the government might and probably would include details about the central personalities in the administration of the country, especially those whose decisions might directly affect the operation of the corporation in the country.[14]

The eight countries analysed are an OPEC country and a non-OPEC country situated in Africa, Asia, or Latin America, as well as France, Israel, Japan, the UK, the USA, and the USSR.[15]

We chose the OPEC and non-OPEC countries, as well as the USSR, because they represent the majority of countries with different types of environments and governments from those of France, Israel, Japan, the UK, and the USA. Thus, we believe that the eight countries analysed in Table 6.2 are representative of the great majority of countries in which multinationals operate, which are almost all the countries of the world.

In each of the eight countries the analysis is focused on twelve aspects of the environment. These aspects are the three 'pendulum systems' of the wider environment, *the employment, money, and consumer markets*, varying from relative shortage to relative abundance; the *technological-scientific* environmental system; four different aspects of the socio-cultural system: *societal structure*, attitudes towards *education*, morality of the *legal* system, and the *political-economic* system; and four aspects of government: *distance of capital from Equator*,[16] *personal (informal) contacts* of citizens with officials, officials receiving *bribes and slush funds*, and the type of *political regime* in which the government runs the country.

The choice of these twelve foci of analysis is our own. They seem to cover the most important aspects of the wider environment of countries in which business corporations may become interested for their operations. The comparative evaluation and rating of each of the eight countries on every one of the twelve foci of analysis, by way of rank ordering from 1 to 8 is, according to our own estimates, based on personal and professional knowledge and experience of these countries.

It is our opinion that averaging the twelve ratings of each country gives a fair idea of its degree of development. For the purpose of establishing the degree of industrial development of the eight countries, we defined the countries with an average ranking order of 2.0–2.5 as developing countries, those with ranking orders of between 4.0 and 4.6 as industrialized countries, and those between 5.6 and 5.9 as highly industrialized countries. Let us analyse in some more detail two of the countries whose 'degree of industrial development' in Table 6.2 does not conform to what seems to be their industrial development image, namely the UK and the USSR.

British industry has been belittled and sneered at for at least the last 20 years.[17] While a few economic indices, as well as isolated socio-cultural phenomena, caused some retreat in traditional British advantage over other industrial countries,[18] the UK has still retained its relative superiority, especially with regard to governmental and socio-cultural factors. We can see from Table 6.2 that Britain is at the top, or nearly so, of every one of the four governmental foci of analysis. This is also true of the UK in the legal and political-economic aspects of its socio-cultural system. Even in its societal structure the UK is less stratified than other Western European countries, of which only France appears in the table.[19]

On the other hand, the USSR, which is perceived to be competing for supremacy with the USA, comes out on the low side of the industrialized

214

Table 6.2　A schematic analysis of the state of governmen[t]

Environmental system	Attention on:	Direction of order ranking from 1 to 7	African, Asian, or Latin-American selected nation states	
			An OPEC country[a]	A non-OPEC country[a]
Employment market	1. Where on scale of unemployment, full employment, & over employment	Shortage ↓ Abundance	1 In shortage (over employment)	8 High in abundance (severe unemployment)
Money market	2. Availability of investment and working capital	Shortage ↓ Abundance	8 In large abundance	1 In severe shortage
Consumer market	3. Purchasing power of customers	Shortage ↓ Abundance	8 In large abundance (but limited by population size & segregated by type of products)	1 In severe shortage (low demand)
Technological scientific system	4. The level and complexity of technology and scientists' expertise	Low level ↓ High level	2 Low	1 Very low
Socio-cultural system	5. Societal structure	Stratified ↓ Non-stratified	1, 2 Elite group and the rest	1, 2 Elite group and the rest
	6. Education	Not-valued ↓ Valued	2 Somewhat valued	1 Not valued
	7. Legal system	Influenced and corrupt ↓ Independent and clean	1, 2 Very influenced	1, 2 Very influenced
	8. Political-economic	Totalitarian ↓ Laissez-faire	2, 3 Centralized	2, 3 Centralized
Government	9. Distance of capital from Equator	Small ↓ Large	(COPEC)[b] 24.40N	(NOPEC)[b] 15.40N
	10. Personal (informal) contacts	More ↓ Less	4, 5 Some	4, 5 Some
	11. Bribery, slush funds	More ↓ Less	1, 2 More	1, 2 More
	12. Regime	Autocratic ↓ Democratic	2, 3 Autocratic	2, 3 Autocratic
Degree of industrial development (Ranking average of 12 rankings)		Developing ↓ Highly industrialized	Total　35.5 Average　3.0 Developing	27.0 2.2 Developing

Note:　The ranking orders of the nation states in every focus of analysis are italicized. Thus, for example, the 5, 6, 7 for no. 6, Education, means that in Israel, USA, and USSR education is highly valued (and that they rank the highest among the seven nation states, following Japan ranking the highest, 8, on education).

nd of the wider environment in selected nation states (1982)

rance	Israel	Japan	UK	USA	USSR
, 7 1 abundance unemploy- ent)	4 Almost balanced (slight un-employment)	2, 3 Balanced (full employ-ment)	6, 7 In abundance (unemploy-ment)	5 In abundance (unemploy-ment)	2, 3 Balanced (full employ-ment)
, 4, 5 alanced	2 In shortage	6, 7 In abundance	3, 4, 5 Balanced	6, 7 In abundance	3, 4, 5 Balanced
, 4, 5 alanced	2 In shortage (especially limited by population size)	7 In abundance (except for specific products)	3, 4, 5 Balanced	3, 4, 5 Balanced	6 Balanced (but limited by type and quality of products)
, 5, 6 igh	4, 5, 6 High	7, 8 Very high	4, 5, 6 High	7, 8 Very high	3 High (but only in specific sciences)
tratified	6, 7, 8 Egalitarian	6, 7, 8 Egalitarian	4 Slightly stratified	5 Mostly egalitarian	6, 7, 8 Egalitarian
, 4 alued	5, 6, 7 Highly valued	8 Extremely valued	3, 4 Valued	5, 6, 7 Highly valued	5, 6, 7 Highly valued
, 5 lean	6, 7, 8 Very clean	6, 7, 8 Very clean	6, 7, 8 Very clean	4, 5 Clean	3 Influenced
ocialist	6 Laissez-faire	5 Mixed	7, 8 Very laissez-faire	7, 8 Very laissez faire	1 Totalitarian
Paris) 8.52N	(Jerusalem) 31.47N	(Tokyo) 35.48N	(London) 51.30N	(Washington) 38.58N	(Moscow) 55.50N
, 7 ess	1, 2 More	1, 2 More	8 Much less	3 Lobbying	6, 7 Less
, 4, 5 ess	3, 4, 5 Less	8 Very much less	6, 7 Much less	6, 7 Much less	3, 4, 5 Less
, 5, 6, 7, 8 Democratic	4, 5, 6, 7, 8 Democratic	4, 5, 6, 7, 8 Democratic	4, 5, 6, 7, 8 Democratic	4, 5, 6, 7, 8 Democratic	1 Very autocratic
7.0 4.7 ndustrialized	53.5 4.5 Industrialized	70.0 5.8 Highly industrialized	69.0 5.7 Highly industrialized	66.5 5.5 Highly industrialized	52.0 4.3 Industrialized

We are thinking of two specific nation states but would not like to identify them by name.
These are the letters by which we identify the capital cities of the two countries whose latitudes are given below.

countries, scoring 4.0 along with Israel. It is needless to point out that none of the foci of analysis in Table 6.2 has directly to do with military might, although several of them have, of course, an effect on the nation's ability to switch from a peacetime to a war economy, and to win a war.[20] What we believe Table 6.2 does indicate is the degree of industrial development, and its potential rate of growth, in peace rather than in wartime.

Let us emphasize once again that the choice of the twelve foci of analysis, as well as the rating of the eight countries on each of them, is our own. We believe that for a quick comparison between the wider environments of nations this is a worthwhile choice of foci of analysis.

6.1.3 Nations and Organizations Operating Within Them, in Democracy and Autocracy

In this last part of the section discussing the wider environments in which organizations operate, the focus is on the relations between nations and the organizations operating in them. We shall first consider different types of organizations which exist in one form or another in the government of every country and in business, as well as in the military.

The regime of a country, whether democratic or autocratic, is the dominant factor in the wider environment. The regime affects to a lesser or greater degree all the other eleven foci of analysis which precede it in Table 6.2. Consequently, whether a nation's regime is democratic or autocratic is probably the most crucial factor for managers who consider operating in that country. We shall see in subsection 6.1.3.2 that both democratic and autocratic regimes have attractions and deterrents for business corporations. A related question for the business corporation is whether the country has a socialist or non-socialist government. There is some confusion as to the use of the term 'socialist' when applied to a regime.[21] On the whole we can say that the more socialist the government, the more centralized (i.e. autocratic) it is.[22] The question whether the government is socialistic or not is in row 8 (political-economic) rather than row 12 (regime) of Table 6.2.

Subsection 6.1.3.3 is a projection into the future of the relations between nations and the organizations operating within them. In this part we distinguish between 'developing', 'industrialized', and 'highly industrialized' countries.

6.1.3.1 Different Types of Organizations from the Point of View of Democracy, Autocracy, and Other Factors

The following comparison between the three types of organizations—business, government, and military—follows the sequence of the comparative factors in Table 6.3. As the choice of the comparative factors and the rating of the three types of organizations according to them was not ours, we decided to leave this table as it originally came into our hands.[23] We shall, however, present our own opinions and emphases in comparing them whether or not these coincide with their original order ratings on each of the comparative factors. We shall follow,

Table 6.3 General and deterministic comparison between business, government, and military organizations in the USA

Comparative factor	Type of organization		
	Business	Government	Military
1. Continuity	Does not outlive man's life	There to stay	There to stay
2. Purpose	Very colourful	More or less fixed	More or less fixed
3. Profit	Limiting factor; validity test	None	None
4. Democracy	Affected by the organization to a large extent	Effect of others limited	Effect of others limited
5. Flexibility	Less rigid and bureaucratic than other two	Rigid and bureaucratic	Rigid and bureaucratic
6. The judicial, legislative, and executive systems	Mixed within each other	Clear-cut division among them	Clear-cut division among them [only in wartime]
7. Advancement of leaders	By appointment, with possible changes	By election	By appointment, with no possible changes
8. Formal and informal organization	[More opportunity for 'job for the man' than in following two types]	'Man for the job' rather than 'job for the man'	[Even more 'man for the job', than in previous type]
9. Stigmas of status	[Less stigmas of status than in the other two]	'Scalar' defined	Uniforms, officer clubs
10. Yardstick of performance	Profitability—goes bankrupt when fails	Never goes bankrupt	Victory in war

Source: Richard Merriam, lectures, 1958/1959.

however, the order of the comparative factors as they were originally presented by Richard Merriam.

Continuity While we agree that government and the military are there to stay,[24] we wonder why Merriam thought that business does not outlive an individual man. The longevity of organizations is discussed and analysed in chapter 7 when examining the longest living organization, the Roman Catholic Church. On the whole, the longevity of business organizations is indeed limited. However, once they get off the ground they generally live somewhat longer than human beings.

Purpose We agree that the purpose of business is very colourful and also that the military purpose is more or less fixed. However, although the purpose of government is more or less fixed and Merriam refers only to the USA, methods may vary from country to country. Furthermore, as we shall see in subsection 6.3.1, the more the multinationals operate in a country, the more they encroach on the authority and power of the nation; consequently, the methods of the government would change accordingly.

Profit We agree that profit is a limiting factor as well as a test of validity for business, and has no role in the government or in the military. Indeed, trying to make the military operate like a business, in an effective and economical way, may undermine its ultimate purpose and eventual success.[25]

Democracy What Merriam meant here is that, in a business organization, the management will decide whether it will be run in a democratic or an autocratic fashion. Government and the military are *a priori* either more democratic or more autocratic depending on the national culture.

Flexibility We interpret 'flexibility' as 'contingency'. That is to say that while business organizations have to adapt their strategics and managerial structures to the environmental conditions, the strategies and structures of government and the military are rigid, i.e. they rarely change and are bureaucratic, formal.

The judicial, legislative, and executive systems The manager of a business alternates between the roles of an executive, a legislator of formal rules of behaviour, and a judge of his subordinates. Merriam had in mind the USA, of course, when he said that there was a clear-cut division among the three systems in government; the USA is probably the only democratic nation in which such a division exists.[26] We are not clear as to Merriam's rating of the military on this comparative factor: that such a division exists only in wartime. To our knowledge, the division among the three systems is not fully maintained in peacetime and even less in wartime. In peacetime an officer can lay down specific rules for the behaviour of his soldiers, put them into execution, and sit in judgement over his soldiers if they do not obey them. This is even more possible in time of war.

Advancement of leaders Here, once more, we gather that Merriam had only the USA in mind, because the *election* of all the three types of government functionaries—judges, legislators, and officials (executives)—is practised only in the USA. In other democracies, only the legislators are elected. As for the other types of organizations, it is generally true that the advancement of leaders in business and the military is performed by appointment, and that in the army it is almost impossible to retract appointments.

Formal and informal organization   It is only in business that there is really an opportunity of a 'job for the man', i.e. taking on a promising person and finding the right managerial position for him. Chapter 5 discusses the problems of the desirability of finding suitable positions for managers. The organizational examples in chapter 5 demonstrate this matter. Thus, in the example describing the Japanese zaibatsu, we see that these business conglomerates are run as a multistructure, a federation of different managerial structures. When persons with specific managerial characteristics are no longer needed in one part of the federated structure, they first go for some additional education and training. Then, when their kind of leadership, followership, and other interpersonal characteristics are required in another part of the multistructure, they are assigned to jobs suitable for them. The Sears, Roebuck example, on the other hand, shows that different kinds of managers create in their jobs the circumstances which fit their managerial characteristics, which is another form of a 'job for the man'.

In government, however, the variety of jobs in terms of the managerial types is much more limited than in business. Government has to look for specific types of managers which fit the available positions. Hence, the requirement of a 'man for the job'.

The variety of jobs in the military is even more limited than in government. In the military, however, the requirements for different types of managers differ drastically for combat units in peace and in wartime.[27]

Stigmas of status   As one moves from business to government, and from there to the military, the stigmas of status become more and more pronounced. This does not mean that business is free of stigmas of status. The ways in which such stigmas are pronounced differ from country to country, from one type of organization to another, and even from organization to organization. There are different manifestations and expressions of stigmas of status in business.

Yardstick of performance   It is interesting to note that while Merriam established bankruptcies as the ultimate indication of failure for business, he does not have a yardstick of failure or of success for government, while for the military he mentions only the ultimate indication of success (victory in war). It is true that it is much more difficult to establish whether a business is really thriving. The fact that a business is doing fine economically is not sufficient. The proper indication of the state of any organization is how well it is surviving. As we have seen throughout the book, especially in chapter 4, the two yardsticks of performance which should be used in business are:[28] (a) To what degree does the organizational strategy enable the business organization to survive in the immediate and wider environments? (b) Does its managerial structure suit the organizational SDM? The same criteria should apply to government and the military but there the combined response to the two questions could be established on the basis of 'the proof of the pudding is in the eating'. The yardstick of performance of government should be sought in the reactions of the public to it. In democratic countries this is expressed by the ballot and, between elections, in letters of complaint or appreciation to the press and directly to the different government branches.

In the military the two questions relating to the strategic adaptability to the immediate and wider environments,[29] and to the suitability of the structure in which it executes its SDM in combat and warfare, are resolved through the outcome of battles and of the war.

We have analysed until now, in Table 6.3, only three types of organizations: business, government, and the military. There are many other types of organizations which could be a combination of either two or all three of the above mentioned types,[30] or organizations which have nothing to do with any of the three types. Let us present two examples, one of each of the two types which do not fall neatly into business or government or the military.

State-owned enterprises (SOE) These are business organizations, dealing with products and/or services, in which the government is the owner, usually the sole owner, of the enterprise. We already know that whenever the same group of people constitutes two or more of the human components of the organization, its decision-making process becomes more cumbersome. Also, the strategies the management chooses in such an organization are not responsive to the conditions prevailing in one or more of the populations comprising the organization. For example, in a manufacturing cooperative society where the owners, managers, and workers are one and the same group of people, the strategy does not necessarily have to respond to either the prevailing pressures of the money market or the conditions in the employment market, or to the specific profitability and employment conditions in similar non-cooperative enterprises.

This means that as long as the enterprise is state-owned, it is 'protected' from pressures from the owners and/or the government, and of the wider environment.[31] It could, indeed, have a preferred and favourite status. However, once it extends its operations to other wider environments controlled by other governments, it will encounter growing difficulties in its competition with other organizations.[32] We will also deal with SOE in the subsection dealing with the encroachment on authority and power of nation states in section 6.3 on the universal implications of multinationals.[33]

Universities This is a non-business type of organization; some universities are owned by government, others are privately owned. They are not, however, owned in the sense that other types of organizations are. Nevertheless, when following Merriam's comparative factors in Table 6.3, we discover that on most factors they are similar to government and the military. Thus (the numbers in parentheses are the numbers of the comparative factors in Table 6.3), (1) they are there to stay; (2) their purpose is more or less fixed; (3) they are non-profit making; (7) the advancement of their leaders is both by election and by appointment; (8) they are more 'man for the job' than 'job for the man'; (9) their 'scalar' status is defined; and (10), until recently, they rarely seemed to go bankrupt.

Only in three out of Merriam's ten comparative factors does university behaviour remind one of business rather than of government and the military: (4) they have a special kind of democracy which resembles neither that of business nor that of the government and the military; (5) they are less rigid and bureaucratic than business; (6) the judicial, legislative, and executive systems are not only intermingled but it is not even quite clear what these systems are in the

university. It is unclear mainly because within each of the two operating managements within the university—the faculty and the administration—the three
systems are mixed. For example, the senior tenured full professor and his
administrative dean may each deal with the *same* issues in the judicial, legislative,
and executive system.

Had we added other comparative factors to those appearing in Table 6.3, we
would have seen that universities do not fall into any of the three types of
organizations, neither are they a sort of combination of two types (like the above
discussed SOE, which are a combination of business and government). Let us, for
example, compare the role of the customer-clients in business, government, and
the military, with their role in universities. Their role in business is cardinal to the
survival of the organization, and consequently they are probably the main FDM
which senior managers take into consideration in their decision making. Their role
in government is less crucial, and in democratic regimes they have an importance
similar to that of business customers and clients only when elections are
approaching; it is only then that management in government would use the cliche
used by business management, 'the customer is always right'. In the military it is
not clear who the customers are; they are probably all the citizens of the country
whose international and, sometimes, national security is threatened; i.e. they
provide the service of maintaining the security of the nation's citizens. However,
those citizens who are drafted and serve in the military, especially in times of war,
are at one and the same time the clients and the employees of the military. They
are the clients because they learn how to fight and defend themselves. They are
the employees, because they are part of the operating organization, officers and
soldiers, alongside the permanent, professional, military personnel who make the
military their career.

A similar role to that of the conscripted citizens is that of graduate research
students in a university. They also are at one and the same time clients and
employees. They aid the faculty in the achievement of the goals of the university
in creating and disseminating knowledge as research and teaching assistants; yet
at the same time they are the clients of the university as students. The analogy
between conscripted citizens and graduate research students continues when we
realize that certain parts of these two populations eventually choose their respective organizations as their careers, and constitute the future faculty of the
universities, on the one hand, and the future regular and permanent commissioned
and noncommissioned officer body of the military, on the other. It is, therefore,
not surprising to find the connection between the military and universities formalized as, for example, in France and the USA.[34] Moreover, it is not surprising
to discover that even when people serve in the military only as conscripted
soldiers, they will sometimes refer to it as their 'school'.[35]

In some ways the relationship between the organization and a certain group of
the clients may be similar when the university is compared with the military. Yet
there is one aspect of the faculty–student relationship in which the university is
unique. In any other type of organization it is the customer-clients who evaluate
the product/service which is provided for them by the management. In the

222

Table 6.4   Types of organizations fitted to degree of customer involvement

Type of organization	Degree of customer involvement	
	Degree	Description
Business	1	From no involvement with people in the operating organization to 'customer-suppliers themselves processed' receiving personal service from employees
SOE	↓ 6	
Government	5	'Customer-suppliers' dealing personally with people on the spot
Military	7	Being aware of receiving physical services from employees at all levels
University	8	Being mentally and/or spiritually involved in receiving services from employees at all levels

Note: 1 = no involvement
8 = highest involvement

university it is the management, of which the faculty constitutes the main part, which evaluates the clients, the students. In most other organizations the managements cannot exclude clients from their products and services;[36] in a university it is the faculty which selects the students to be admitted to a teaching programme or to a specific class,[37] and eventually grades the student and determines who is a worthwhile student and who is not.[38]

Thus, we may conclude that SOE have characteristics in which they resemble either business or government. Universities, on the other hand, though resembling government and, especially, the military in some respects, could not be classified as government, military, or business organizations.[39] These are two types of organizations which do not fall neatly into the business-government-military classification.

We prefer a classification of organizations according to the degree of customer involvement in the decision-making process. Such a classification was presented in chapter 4. Let us fit the types of organizations we have just mentioned to the degree of customer involvement classification (see Figure 4.1): the results are shown in Table 6.4.

6.1.3.2   The Relation Between Nations and Organizations Operating in Them

There is, of course, an affinity between the national culture and the way in which organizations operating within the nation are run. The linkage between the national and organizational cultures is usually seen in the effects of the national culture on the organizational culture. This relationship differs from one country to another and from one type of organization to another.

We have devised Table 6.5 in order to help the reader to follow the differences in the affinity between national and organizational cultures across the various

Table 6.5 Effects of national on organizational culture: 18 degrees of affinity between national and organizational cultures

Type of nation state Degree of industrial development (see Table 6.2)	Type of organization Degree of customer involvement (see Figure 4.1 and Table 6.3) 'Customer-supplier-raw material'—total involvement						General
	'Customer-supplier-raw material'—both physical and spiritual involvement (religious organizations)	'Customer-supplier-raw material'—spiritual involvement (universities)	'Customer-supplier-raw material'—physical involvement (military, airlines)	'Customer-supplier-raw material'—no involvement (public ground transportation)	'Customer-suppliers' manufacturing, repairs or servicing (government civic services)	'Customers'' manufacturing for inventory or custom made (mostly business)	
Developing (an OPEC and a non-OPEC country)	1	2	3	4	5	6	The greater the industrial development of the country, the *less* affinity there is between the national and the organizational culture.
Industrialized (France)	7	8	9	10	11	12	
Highly industrialized (USA)	13	14	15	16	17	18	
General	The *higher* the degree of customer involvement in the organization the *more* affinity there is between the national and the organizational cultures.						

Scale of degrees of affinity between national and organizational culture

				←——— Average ———→				
Extremely large	Very large	Large	Growing →	← Diminishing		Small	Very small	Extremely small
1 2	3 4	5 6	7 8	9 10	11 12	13 14	15 16	17 18

Note: Examples of types of nation states and organizations are given in parentheses.

types of nations and organizations. The grading of the types of nations is according to their degree of industrial development, presented in subsection 6.1.2, on the basis of Table 6.2. Different types of organizations were discussed in 6.1.3.1, on the basis of Table 6.3; however, the classification of organizations according to the degree of customer involvement in them was presented in Figure 4.1.

The numbers appearing in Table 6.5 are derived from the scale of effects of national on organizational culture. The greater the number, the less affinity there is between the national and the organizational culture. The reader should be warned, however, not to interpret the numbers in the table as a quantitative expression of the cultural linkage between different types of nations and different types of organizations operating within them. They are only a set of hypotheses regarding the relative linkage between the two, as one may conclude from the scale at the bottom of the table.

The rank order appearing in Table 6.5 hypothesizes the following two relations:

(a) As the industrial development of the country advances, the affinity between national and organizational culture diminishes.
(b) As the degree of customer involvement in the organization increases, so also the affinity between national and organizational culture increases.

The other hypothesis to be derived from the rank ordering of the 18 degrees of affinity in Table 6.5 is that the effects of national culture on organizational culture are larger than the effects of organizational on national culture.[40] This convergence and divergence may gradually change in the future; this is discussed in more detail in section 6.3.

Let us now analyse religious organizations as one of the examples of the degree of customer involvement in the organization. We have chosen this example because of the general belief that a religious organization could not possibly be affected by the national cultures of the countries in which it operates. This belief stems from the illusion that the religion itself is steadfast and consistent. Therefore it does not change and cannot change from country to country.[41]

It is evident that changes in each of the three major monotheistic religions happened so as to keep religion aligned with the changes occurring in the national cultures. Whenever groups of religious leaders and their followers felt strongly that such necessary changes in their religion were not being instituted, they defected and created another religion or a derivation of the same religion.[42]

Fundamentalists do not budge from the fundamental principles of their religion. It is indeed such groups who either succeed in swaying the national culture their way, like the Shiite fundamentalists in Iran[43] or, alternatively, get into severe, sometimes bloody, conflict with the nation state, as in Egypt and Saudi Arabia.[44] However, as we shall presently see, a twentieth-century fundamentalist regression to the beliefs of the Middle Ages cannot last for long. This does not mean that for relatively short periods of time, nowadays measured in years rather than decades, fundamentalists will not succeed in holding out in countries like Iran. Neither does it mean that the cultures affecting different types of organizations in the various countries will go on being 'national' cultures. Towards the end of the chapter, we describe how multinationals are inducing national cultures to adapt to the economic developmental needs.

The difference between the effects of multinational corporation culture on national culture and the effects of, say, a fundamentalist religious culture on a national culture, is like the difference between a reactionary revolution and a historically progressive evolution. The fundamentalist culture can affect the national culture and decisively influence it only by invading, overpowering, and oppressing the existing culture, both spiritually and physically. The multinational culture, on the other hand, moves in on the waves of technology, industry, standard of living, and quality of life, first raising the degree of industrial development, and along with it affecting the culture of both its own constituent members (employees, customers, suppliers, trade union and government officials, etc.) and, through them, other parts of the nation.

As we move from the religious organizations in Table 6.5, through universities, the military and government, to business, we see that the smaller the degree of customer involvement in the organization, the less affinity there is between the national and organizational cultures. This is apparently because we move from organizational cultures which seem to be more menacing to the national culture, to organizational cultures which seem to be less so.

In summary, *the greater the industrial development of the country, the less affinity there is between the national and the organizational culture.* The general explanation for this is related to the effects of multinational corporations on nations. As the pace of industrial development increases, the indigenous national culture is transformed into a multinational one. Developing nations are obsessed by their indigenous cultures and have an overwhelming effect on the religions operating within them. This is demonstrated by an identification of the religion with the state, usually accompanied by an extreme intolerance towards other religions.

Thus, if we move up the industrial development ladder we find that, in both OPEC and non-OPEC developing countries, there is either an identification between religion and state, and an intolerance of the cultures of other religions, or the tribal indigenous cultures have a large effect on the different religions operating within the area.

In an industrialized country like France, there is a separation between state and religion, yet the nation still preserves the Catholic holidays as its own to the exclusion of the holy days of other religions. Also, the values, opinions, and attitudes of French people in all walks of life are influenced to a large degree by Catholic dogma. However, this Catholic influence does not seem to be too large when France is compared with other predominantly Catholic European countries which are less industrially developed than France.[45]

Highest on the ladder of industrial development is the USA. Clearly, here the affinity between the religious cultures and the nation is the smallest. The same applies to the individual states of the USA, except for Utah where affinity between the state and the Mormon Church is reminiscent of some of the European nations in which Catholicism is dominant.

226

The only exception to the inverse relation between the degree of industrial development and the affinity between national and organizational cultures among the countries included in Table 6.2, is Japan. The reason for this anomaly is not only that Japan is on another cultural plane, but that the enormous speed of industrialization in Japan has exceeded by far the consequent changes in the Japanese national culture.[46]

In the light of recent findings regarding the effects of the climate of a country on its culture, it is not surprising that a nation and the organizations operating within it acquire the same type of culture. Thus, it may well be that there is no necessary causal relationship between national and organizational culture, i.e. that neither national culture affects organizational culture, nor vice versa; it could well be that both of them are affected by the climatic conditions of the country.[47]

On the other hand, we have the case of Israel and the organizations operating within it, described in an organizational example at the end of this chapter. The total organizational system of Israel mainly covers two different periods of time: the British Mandatory period of 1917–1947, and the first decades of the State of Israel from 1948 onwards. The state culture during the British Mandate resembled the national culture of the UK at the time; the organizational behaviour or culture at the time was completely different from the organizational behaviour of both the Israeli government and business and other corporations in Israel during the 35 years which followed. From 1948 onwards the Israeli Government has on the whole run the country in an informally centralized structure. We find that, consequently, organizations operating in Israel have similarly assumed informally centralized structures.

Perhaps this contradiction between the findings relating to the effects of climate on culture, and the two clearly different behavioural patterns in the same country during two successive 30-year periods, stems from two special conditions regarding Israel. First, Israel happens to be in a mild climate. Secondly, until recently, the majority of Israeli Jews were one, two, or three generations away from their European ancestors;[48] thus they could manifest behaviours of both a European country and the country in which they were born and brought up.

6.1.3.3   The Future Development of Developing, Industrial, and Highly Industrialized Countries[49]

The more the world advances, the more difficult it is to predict its progress. This is why the prophecies of doom, on the basis of the increasing rate of technological growth, seemed to us dubious when we discussed the total innovation growth in subsection 2.1.3 of chapter 2.

It likewise becomes increasingly difficult to plan the future of individual organizations and nations. In the mid-twentieth century, the largest US corporations had their long-range planning sights on 30 or even more years ahead; now, towards the close of the century, even 10 years ahead is quite a daring look into the future.[50]

Nevertheless, organizations are moving on according to the dynamics of the

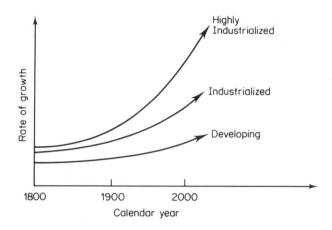

Figure 6.2   Schematic progression of developing, industrialized, and highly industrialized countries

TOS, and such notions as 'zero growth' are not entertained by anybody who is aware of, and sensitive to, organizational developments since the Industrial Revolution. It is relatively easier to engage in technological forecasting for developing and industrialized countries than in prophecies about where the highly industrialized countries will be in, say, 30 years' time. This is because, on the whole, developing countries follow industrialized countries, and industrialized countries are following highly industrialized countries, in both technological innovations and in the socio-cultural changes which accompany them.

All the countries of the world develop, progress, and advance in their technologies and standards of living. This is because since the Industrial Revolution there have been ever-growing pressures for technological and other innovations in organizations. The growth has been an exponential one, looking more or less like the growth curves in Figure 6.2. It may mean that the pattern is not only of a permanent nature, but that the various countries are also drifting farther apart.

The main reason for the above phenomenon is that the differences in the rate of development in the various countries are closely linked to the degree of culture-boundedness or, conversely, to the degree of short-term flexibility and adaptability. This degree of culture-boundedness either holds back or it helps to accelerate the introduction of changes, which eventually will lead to changes in the socio-cultural system.

The reasons for differences in the culture-boundedness and rates of development in different countries are to some extent coincidental, but depend to a large degree on such things as the dominance of tradition, religion, and, especially, the climate, all of which are interrelated.

Another important question with regard to the future of the developing, industrial, and highly industrial countries, is whether there will be an industrial specialization by countries in the future industrialized world; namely whether some countries will manufacture certain groups of products, and others will concentrate on different products. Alternatively one can speculate if, in the future, every industrialized country will wish to manufacture as many products as it can for its own market and for the rest of the world.

Our response to these questions is a qualified affirmative; qualified for two reasons. The first has to do with the groups of products. There will always be groups of products in which there will be country specialization. These include heavy products (expensive to transport); basic living products, e.g. the building industry, part of the food industry and part of the clothing industry; 'national pride' products, e.g. steel; and a basic defence industry. The latter two cannot be universally generalized and will not, in our opinion, last for very much longer as 'national' product lines. The above mentioned include industrial products only, and not services in which there would be much less geographical specialization on the whole.

The second reason relates to the term 'countries'. We do not believe that 'countries' remain the same over long periods of time. 'Countries' in ancient times, in the Middle Ages, in the seventeenth, eighteenth, and nineteenth centuries, and in the twentieth until the Second World War, have been very different from one another. Since the Second World War there have been tremendous pressures, first for the grouping of countries and, subsequently, for the world turning more and more into one large entity. Section 6.3 discusses the universal implications of multinational corporations. The conclusion of that discussion is that the world is slowly moving into a situation in which countries will be stripped of many of their 'national' peculiarities, as we have known them up till now. One of the things which we believe will completely disappear by the first half of the twenty-first century is borders serving as barriers to the flow of goods and services between countries.

One of the things which will expedite this development, in addition to the role of multinationals, is the fact that countries, because of geographical, demographic, and other natural differences, have different inherent types of specialization. Countries may differ from one another in certain natural resources: e.g. minerals, crops, solar and water energy, etc. However, this is particularly evident in the most important of natural resources, the human resource. Some countries like China, India, and Egypt have enormous quantities of people in relation to their fertile geographical areas, and they have low levels of technology and education. The human resources of other countries have a relatively much higher level of education and technological preparedness.

The bottleneck potential of some of these natural resources in the world economy system will force all the countries to ensure the free flow of resources from one area to another. Otherwise, the whole world will be threatened and its economies may be destroyed. The best example of this danger is the oil resource. It is inconceivable that the world will accept for much longer the situation forced upon it since the 1973–1974 oil crisis. In specific services, some are more specialized than others, and there is a flow of services over the borders of present-day countries. The oil-producing countries are drawing upon the services of some of the industrialized and highly industrialized countries. For example, the UK provides the oil countries with teaching services at all levels by receiving large groups of students in the UK and sending British teachers overseas; it provides medical services by sending patients to the UK for treatment and sending medical staffs from the UK; and even in such things as football and other areas of sport.

Let us see what are the main things that countries could do in order to accelerate their rate of industrialization. We shall take as an example the three Latin countries of France, Italy, and Spain.[51] Comparing these countries with other European countries, we find that they are more culture-bound because of a strong socio-cultural and organizational tradition. Consequently, they need a speedier process of opening up. This is an educational process which, in the case of France, would to a large extent mean getting away from the Cartesian approach to problem solving. It would also mean an education which would gradually reduce the social stratification which is strongly in evidence in many of the European countries.

We do not believe that scientific and technological training will achieve anything by itself. In fact, we think that the humanistic and liberal arts education which is implied by what we called 'opening up' is far more important. Education of this kind would enable 'closed' countries to open up to benefits they could derive from other cultures. This would also make countries more attractive for the multinational corporations to operate in; consequently the multinationals, as we shall see later in this chapter, may help the countries to become more industrialized, as well as improving their standards of living.

6.2 MULTINATIONAL CORPORATIONS

Both international and multinational organizations operate in two or more countries. International companies, however, have had one dominant nationality (or two nationalities, in so-called 'joint venture' companies)[52] whose interests have been foremost in the business strategy of the companies concerned. They have usually a formally uniform structure, a functional or product/service line or area structure. Some of these have even maintained entrepreneurial structures for extended periods of time. The national dominance and the uniform structure of international companies were closely linked to the colonial system. The dominant nationality was that of the ruling country. The international company usually operated only within the confines of its specific empire. It therefore encountered the same wider environmental conditions wherever it operated. An international company operating in the colonial system of the British Empire, for example, had the same environmental systems whether in Nigeria, South Africa, India, Hong Kong, or Australia. This enabled such a company to operate in a uniform structure and control effectively its worldwide operations even in a functional structure.

Subsection 6.2.1 includes a more detailed description of the international companies which preceded the multinational corporations, until the Second World War. Subsection 6.2.2 deals with the geopolitical reasons for the creation of multinational corporations, or the turning of international into multinational ones. The essence of subsection 6.2.2 is as follows:

The collapse of the colonial systems and the emergence of distinctly different national entities prevented the international companies from continuing to operate in the manner they had been accustomed to until the Second World War. The new, emerging nation states emphasized their special cultural characteristics, insisting that companies doing business in their countries conform to their cultures and systems. Increasingly, foreign companies are required to abide by the laws of the country, to employ local manpower at the higher levels, to use the language of the country, and to admit local ownership. These pressures, from local public opinion as well as from the legal codes of the different countries, prevented international companies from pursuing the interests of their 'parent country'. They also could not maintain a uniform formal structure in the countries in which they operated, but had to adapt to local custom. International companies had, therefore, to move to another type of organization with different characteristics from those in which they had operated until the Second World War. In order to distinguish between the two basically different types of organizations, we refer to the newly emerging organizations as multinational corporations.

Subsection 6.2.3 specifies and defines what we mean by multinationals in this book. A multinational corporation may be identified by three characteristics: (a) its SDM, the degree of its geographical dispersal; (b) its managerial structure, the extent to which it operates as a multistructure; and (c) its managerial attitudes, the degree to which it abandons the interests of its parent country. A multinational corporation is, therefore, as we have defined it since 1967, an organization operating in different countries, in which all considerations related to its growth processes and its survival are based on the interests of the organization itself, national pressures having no influence except in so far as constraints are imposed on it in each of the countries in which it operates.

Organizations operating in different countries have to abide more and more by such a multinational approach in order to survive. Subsection 6.2.4 focuses on the differences between multinational managers and national managers. We see the distinction between the two in the multinationals' managers being able and willing to live and function in countries and cultures different from their own. However, it is not only that they do not mind being expatriate managers for prolonged periods of time, sometimes all their working lives, but that, if necessary, they should also be able to abandon their national culture in their managerial behaviour.

6.2.1 International Companies Preceded Multinational Corporations until the Second World War

When a corporation competes with other corporations within the borders of its own country, its national loyalty is not at stake; it is, in fact, irrelevant. By contrast, the management of a corporation with a major part of its operations outside its home country is often faced with conflict between national loyalty and its organizational responsibility.

At first, every national corporation turning international tends to subordinate its own interests to those of the nation within which it operates, but as its operations expand its attitude gradually changes. For one thing, it becomes more and more dependent on its foreign operations and, unless it puts its own interests first, its economic existence may be jeopardized. For another, its original national identity becomes blurred as its membership (owners, managers, workers, customers, etc.) is 'diluted' with foreigners. By this process, in fact, the organization acquires both the main characteristics of a multinational corporation, namely a multiple structure and a supranational approach.

Terminology has changed along with the transformation undergone by organizations operating in more than one country. Early international companies always identified themselves with their home countries. Their operations, largely commercial, closely followed the colonial pattern of the country, adhering to the managerial structure and procedures which they found most appropriate at home.[53] Their national identity was even reflected in their names (e.g. US Steel, British Petroleum, etc.); an organization with two 'home countries' to which it was equally committed and loyal used a double name, e.g. Royal Anglo-Dutch Shell, Anglo-American Tobacco Company, etc. By contrast, the more recent term 'multinational' implies that the corporation operates throughout the countries rather than transacts its operations between them.

6.2.2 Geopolitical Reasons for the Creation of Multinational Corporations

Significantly, the advent of the multinational corporation coincided with the demise of the colonial empires. It could well be that, with the loss of its colonial outlets, the international company lost its sense of national affiliation. Moreover, now that some of the industrialized nations, e.g. the Western European countries, are abandoning their independent economic positions, the way is open for the large corporations to move even further in their supranational attitudes.

Another boost to the supranational trend has recently been provided from some unexpected quarters. Certain national trade unions decided to start moving towards amalgamation and the creation of regional, e.g. European, or even world-wide trade unions. In a totally different context Ralph Nader is advocating world-wide customer associations.[54] These developments fit into the conceptual scheme referred to earlier; each human factor in the DMP has its own objective and, *vis-à-vis* the management, would like to get the most out of its participation in the organization. An organization operating in different countries and facing different trade unions and customer populations has the advantage of being able to choose for a specific operation the country where it will encounter the least resistance in this respect. While coordinated action by trade unions, customers, or any other factors would make things much tougher for the multinational corporation, it would strengthen its position *vis-à-vis* the nation, as its dealings with the factors would take place, so to speak, over the heads of the local government. In these circumstances, national groups of other factors, e.g. suppliers or bankers, would have to form a united front against the corporation, and eventually so would the governments.

232

6.2.3 What are Multinational Corporations?

Let us summarize our conception of multinational corporations.

In order to qualify as such, a multinational corporation must operate in several countries, with control of its constituent agencies throughout the world combined in a system comprising some elements of a multiple managerial structure.

This means that we can measure the potential capacity of a given organization for operating as a multinational corporation through its scope of decision making and its managerial structure. However, we can only establish whether it is actually multinational on the basis of its worldwide behaviour.

It has already been pointed out that, as a multinational corporation moves into more and more countries, the more it tends to operate within a so-called multi-structure. This becomes especially necessary if the organization embarks on operations which penetrate deeply into the socio-cultural structure of the nation states. The multinational corporation finds out fairly soon that in order to move into, say, manufacturing operations, and achieve more or less similar results, in two socio-culturally different countries, it has to control its operations in them through essentially different managerial structures. For example, organizations operating today in countries of what used to be the British Empire no longer have to deal within identical political and financial frameworks, but are almost fully exposed to the free interplay of distinct environmental systems. Fortunately, or perhaps inevitably, the multinational corporations started to employ local managers familiar with the effects of culture on management in terms of both attitudes and relationships, which the earlier organizations, staffed almost exclusively with 'home country' managers, had lacked.

One can regard the advent of multiple structures as an inevitable consequence of the dynamics of the effects of growth (see Figure 5.8 in chapter 5).

6.2.4 Multinational and National Managers

There are two main periods in a person's life which may affect his or her future performance as a manager. The first is the forming of one's managerial personality at an early age. We discussed the effects of early upbringing on the future leadership, followership, and other interpersonal characteristics, in chapter 4. Let us now turn to the second period, which is much longer and is one in which one could acquire either national or multinational attributes.

Most of this subsection is the result of a research programme carried out at INSEAD since 1966.[55] The subsection is divided into four parts. We shall first look at several managerial aspects which differ from country to country. Subsequently, we shall discuss the ability to distinguish between culture-bound and universal behaviour, as well as the ability to function in national culture environments different from one's own for prolonged periods of time. Next comes the question of what kind of people would make appropriate multinational managers. Finally, the problem of how to train multinational managers is raised.

6.2.4.1 Cross-cultural Management: Managerial Differences Between Countries

When a group of people from a variety of countries are gathered into the same formal organization, they bring along with them all the differences in communication behaviour, education, social stratification, organizational structures, and languages which we discussed in the previous two chapters. Nobody could better describe the consequences of such a gathering than the author of Genesis in his account of the construction of the Tower of Babel (Babylon):[56]

> Once upon a time all the world spoke a single language and used the same words. As men journeyed in the east, they came upon a plain in the land of Shinar and settled there. They said to one another, 'Come, let us make bricks and bake them hard'; they used bricks for stone and bitumen for mortar. 'Come,' they said, 'let us build ourselves a city and a tower with its top in the heavens, and make a name for ourselves; or we shall be dispersed all over the earth.' Then the Lord came down to see the city and tower which mortal men had built, and he said, 'Here they are, one people with a single language, and now they have started to do this; henceforward nothing they have a mind to do will be beyond their reach. Come, let us go down there and confuse their speech, so that they will not understand what they say to one another.' So the Lord dispersed them from there all over the earth, and they left off building the city. That is why it is called Babel, because the Lord there made a babble of the language of all the world; from that place the Lord scattered men all over the face of the earth.

One has to consider a 'language' in its wider meaning and exchange the type of organization from a construction organization building the Tower of Babel to, say, a military one defending the Western democracies (NATO) or to political ones, preserving the health and culture of the world (WHO and UNESCO), and we are transplanting this passage from about the twenty-eighth century BC to the twentieth century AD.[57]

Five areas in which such national 'language' differences occur are communication, education, social stratification, organization structure, and language itself. These are not the only areas which affect management and in which one would find national differences. Nevertheless, these five seem to be the most predominant in so far as they affect multinational management.

Other areas influenced by cultural values, though sometimes crucial for multinational managers, seem to be of secondary importance when compared with the ones chosen for discussion. One such additional area is that of competition and profits, attitudes to which differ substantially from one culture to another. Attitudes also differ substantially with regard to what one might call business morality. This includes such matters as bribery, which in some countries is regarded as outright corruption, and in others is accepted. The degree of government intervention and the extent to which this is considered tolerable is another factor for multinational managers to take into account.

The national differences discussed concern primarily countries which belong to what is commonly referred to as the 'Western culture'. This excludes completely different types of culture, as, for example, that of Japan which has a totally different 'business ideology'. This may be defined as 'any system of beliefs publicly expressed with the manifest purpose of influencing the sentiments and actions of others'.[58] The term 'business ideology' is used in a recent description of the Japanese managerial systems, in which the personal and cultural background and practices of Japanese management are summarized for a period of over 100 years.[59] Communication, education, social stratification, and organization structures are covered by this study, together with a comprehensive discussion of the historical development of Japan's business ideologies. The study shows that the ways of thinking and the decision-making process are being conducted in Japan in an environment that is in no way derived from Western culture. Hence the following discussion will only be concerned with Western types of behaviour, and the references to Japan are incidental.

Communication The existence of different patterns of communication in different countries has often been suggested, but seldom systematically investigated.[60] For greater precision it has been necessary to develop a new analytical tool—the communication diagram, or communicogram as it is now called. This makes it possible to discern and analyse one of the basic differences in managerial structure among different cultural environments, namely that of communications behaviour. This use of the communicogram became evident by coincidence rather than through testing hypotheses concerning management communication. In 1966 a group of students carried out a communicogram study which was conducted in three organizations, one British and two French; this was done simultaneously with another study exploring the relationships and attitudes of the same managers included in the communicogram study. The chief executives of all three organizations had been promised that they would receive not only the results of their own respective studies, but also a comparison between themselves and the other two organizations. However, analysis of the data by the computer showed that the total number of interactions in the British organization for the 50 participants during two weeks was 2639; but the number of interactions for the 21 and 26 participants of the two French companies was 128 and 215 respectively, too small for analysis.

When the British chief executive was presented with the results of his organization, an apology was made for not being able to provide him with a comparison with the two French organizations, on the grounds that the French managers failed to report their interactions. He replied: 'The reason is quite clear to me, they just do not interact orally.'

He was right. We went back to the individual daily interaction sheets and discovered that on each British sheet there was an average of some 15 interactions per person per day, but only two or three interactions per person per day appeared on the sheets of the managers in the two French organizations. The number of reported interactions with other managers participating in the study was usually about one third of the total recorded interactions; this corresponds with the results of an average of 5.3 per person per day in the British organization and 0.5 and 1.0 interactions in the two French organizations. The reasons why such cultural differences evolved probably have to do with the fact that French organizational culture has been more affected by the development of business organizations which have been influenced by the Church, the army, and governmental organizations, than the other way around; French organizations are relatively more bureaucratized (i.e. formalized), and consequently adhere to more written and less oral communication.

Therefore, while the degree of formalization is an indication of managerial structure, it is also an indication of the cultural effects on management. That is to say, that if two identical organizations had been compared from the point of view of their scope of decision making and of their managerial structure, but with one operating in France and the other in the UK, significantly more oral communication would have been found in the latter. The other finding is that when comparing oral communication in the three Western countries (see Table 6.6)—the USA, the UK, and France—the US and the UK figures are found to be similar (4.7, 5.0, and 5.3 interactions per person per day, respectively), while the French figures (0.5 and 1.0) are significantly lower.

The similarity of Britain to the USA rather than to other European countries with regard to managerial behaviour has already been found by others in connection with managerial attitudes and decision-making processes.[61] The almost identical rate of oral communication in Anglo-Saxon organizations on both sides of the Atlantic Ocean is another indication of the cultural affinity between the USA and Britain.

Israel is represented in Table 6.6 by two types of organizations—military and banking. These two types explain why the daily numbers of interactions per person in Israel (2.6 to 4.4) are smaller than those of the UK and the USA (between 4.7 and 5.3). Had we drawn a formal written or informal oral scale of communication, we would have placed France on the formal end of the scale, the UK somewhere between the middle of the scale and its informal end,[62] and Israel at the very extreme of informality.[63] However, the two types of organizations studied in Israel, military and banking, are typically formal, hence the relatively low oral communication. There have been only a relatively small number of studies which have been devoted to explaining the reasons for national differences in communication patterns. The explanation for such differences is in the cultural variances among the countries.[64]

Education   The suggestion has been made that the availability of higher education in a country determines its economic growth.[65] This theory is hard to verify because of the differences in educational methods between countries. Some of these differences affect managerial style more clearly than the general amount of education available. For instance, the difference between the French approach and that of the USA can best be described by saying that one is dogmatic and the other is pragmatic. The French approach is Cartesian: the most systematic and quantitative assault possible on every problem, while taking into consideration all factors which may influence it. The Americans, on the other hand, are more

Table 6.6 Comparison of self-recorded interaction studies in organizations in four countries[a]

	Industrial plastics[b] USA 1959	Marketing pharmaceutical consumer goods[c] UK 1966	Industrial electronic components[c] France 1966	Industrial aircraft production[c] France 1966	Army ordnance[d] Israel 1969	Education: management development[e] UK 1971	Banking[f] Israel 1976 A	Banking[f] Israel 1976 B
Number of managers:								
approached	50	60	26	21	48	32		
participated	34	50	26	21	41	27		
Length of study (number of days)	10	10	10	10	10	10		
Oral interactions with other participants:								
total reported	1708	2639	128	215	672	1272	788	1049
% mutually perceived	26	14	17		7	38	17	16
daily average per person	5.0	5.3	0.5	1.0	2.6	4.7	3.4	4.4
% of interactions:								
by telephone	22	45	73	29	19	14	25	18.5
face to face	78	55	27	71	81	86	75	81.5
% consensus as to type in mutually perceived interactions	47	35	46	73	50	43	51.5	39

[a]The data concerning the first six studies appearing in this figure are from Weinshall (1979, p. 261). The last two columns present the data from two branches of the same banking organization which were studied simultaneously.
[b]Originally published in Weinshall (1966) on which Weinshall (1979, pp. 211–226) was subsequently based.
[c]Originally published in Weinshall and Vickery (1970), on which Weinshall (1979, pp. 259–265 and 411–415) was subsequently based.
[d]Originally published in Tsirulnitsky and Weinshall (1974), on which Weinshall (1979, pp. 291–307) was subsequently based.
[e]Originally appeared in Weinshall et al. (1971), on which Weinshall (1979, pp. 365–373) was subsequently based.
[f]Originally appeared in Nachmias et al. (1978) and Weinshall and Vickery (1970) on which Weinshall (1979, pp. 411–432) was subsequently based.

interested in the usefulness of the result than in the theoretical side of the method used to approach the problem.

Thus, if the same problem is presented to a French and to an American businessman, the former is liable to discover, say, 20 factors which influence it, think of about 50 alternative solutions, and attempt to find the connection between them. Each alternative would be weighed in the light of the conditioning factors. The American, by contrast, would probably look for the three main factors which influence the problem and take these into consideration. He would then decide on, say, five alternative solutions and evaluate them in the light of these factors. The two different ways of thinking show that there is a basic difference in the social, cultural, and educational values of the two people. Many Americans, for example, envy the French for being highly cultured and broadly educated, but despise them for their supposed inefficiency, disorder, and uncleanliness. It is precisely their tendency to specialize, which is so often incompatible with a broad outlook, which seems to enable the Americans to attack their business problems so efficiently. The French broad outlook, on the other hand, and a knowledge of the culture of the world, while they may confer an ability to see the whole picture, also give rise to a tendency to include more and more factors in the analysis of a problem.

The separation between faculty and students, of which the French universities have been an extreme example, has been made possible by both the teaching methods and the design of the physical facilities. The professor enters the lecture hall by a door other than that used by his students and confronts a crowd of hundreds, usually in a hall originally designed to contain a much smaller number. He delivers his lecture, often read, and repeated from year to year with modifications, without allowing subsequent discussion. The students perceive this way of teaching, in many instances, as the pronouncement of the gospel in whatever field of learning this may be.

The physical design of many French universities prevents the faculty from meeting their students out of class, even by chance. Separate facilities exist for faculty and students, e.g. restaurants, toilets, and, even, lifts and staircases.

While continental European universities prefer a separation of faculty and students similar to the one described in France, British universities advocate a certain degree of cooperation. This is chiefly practised out of the classroom in the so-called 'tutoring' sessions. Members of the faculty, usually junior members, coach the students on the material covered in class, or any additional material. The consequence of this cooperation out of the classroom is that there is also a fair amount of participation inside the classroom.

The third learning method advocates, in principle, cooperation between the faculty and the students both in the classroom and outside. This method originated in the USA, but is spreading quickly elsewhere, especially to countries like Israel where the ties with cultural tradition are not as strong as those in western continental Europe.[66]

The purpose of graduate studies in management and business administration is the academic training of managers for middle and higher management levels in economic and public organizations. The former include industry, agriculture, banking, insurance, transport, tourism, and other services. The public organizations are governmental, military, and municipal ones, other public services, and trade unions. Graduate management studies are not for the training of professional people who might serve public and economic organizations in fields such as engineering, chemistry, law, economics, and others. Their purpose is to train people who might fulfil management functions. The training includes finance, control, production, marketing, research and development, personnel, as well as a synthesis which combines all these and is called 'business policy'.[67] As every one of the managers in charge of each of the above mentioned functions has to be in a permanent relationship with the other functions of the organization, every manager has to receive a thorough and all-round training in them all. In the modern organization, the proportion of professional people is increasing from year to year. There are those who believe that within 20 years the number of professional people in an industrial organization will exceed the number of non-professionals.

The manager, who has to be a professional himself, finds himself in charge of one or more functions, each of which involves know-how at an academic level, and many of his subordinates are also professionals: auditors report to comptrollers, economists to finance managers, market research people to marketing managers, engineers and scientists to the research and development and production managers, sociologists and psychologists to personnel and manpower managers.

This means that the manager in the modern organization has to have a profession before he becomes a manager. In many cases, a man acquires a managerial position by working himself up one of the 'functional channels'. Thus, for example, a man starts as a junior engineer in a certain organization, progresses through the various stages of engineering and production, and becomes manager of the production or research and development division. When he reaches management in this way, he is well acquainted with his function but does not always know how to manage it. This is why we sometimes lose a good engineer and gain a bad manager. In other instances, an old-time engineer (or old-time auditor, economist, and so on) will receive management training through advanced management courses or through a graduate school of management. Nevertheless, he has to make this lengthy practical journey along one of the 'functional channels'. He has to have had previous academic training, meaning a bachelor's degree, to ensure that he has the educational ability to know how to study what is going on in the organization. His bachelor's degree might be in any field.

The case studies included in the learning programme are usually chosen to ensure coverage of various situations that have occurred in recent times in business and other organizations which might employ new managers after their graduation. The length of the 'recent times' depends on the circumstances and especially on the rate of the technological changes which dictate the conditions under which the executive operates. The cases studied today in good graduate business schools generally describe situations which have occurred since the Second World War. Most of the cases occurred during the last ten years, and some only in the last five.

Readings, seminars, reports, business games, and all other teaching material complementary to the case method are usually based on the problems to be encountered in the cases. This is why the material studied is very rarely out of the context of the situations in which the manager might expect to find himself during his career. In addition, it has been suggested that there is a need for fictional cases, based on expectations of future managerial situations. Such opinions are prompted by the increasing rate of change occurring in organizations today. Thus, for example, even the study of business history is carried out in relation to those themes that have a direct bearing on what is happening in present situations and are important for the actual performance of the manager's functions. Such an approach results in a large economy of the students' time. These points are relevant to the training of all managers. However, the participative learning method is of special importance in the training of multinational managers, who will have to operate in different socio-cultural environments.

The possible effects of higher education on multinational management have already been discussed. We should, however, realize that management is composed of, and assisted by, people who do not necessarily have a university education. Let us therefore consider the degree of secondary education in several countries. Table 6.7 shows the percentage of 6–17 and 20–24-year-olds in education in different countries. As all the four countries had obligatory education up to at least age 15 at the time (1973–1974), the difference in the 20–24-year-olds' column amount to much larger differences than the percentages of high school students, i.e. people with secondary education, in these countries.

Table 6.7 therefore explains why many jobs which are held in Western Europe by those with a secondary education are held in the USA by university graduates. In Israel, on the other hand, there is a severe shortage of secondary school graduates. A typical example of the different type of people used for the same type of job in the various countries is to be found in secretarial work. Following the differences appearing in Table 6.7; in Western Europe, secretaries generally have secondary education; in the USA they have at least secondary education and there are many who have had higher education. In Israel, by contrast, all these are exceptions; most secretaries have only finished elementary school.

Table 6.7 Flow of high school education to higher education in four countries

	% of 6–17-year-olds in education (1)	% of 20–24-year-olds in higher education (2)	% in higher education of those with previous education (1) and (2)
Britain	94	20	21
Holland	93	23	25
Israel	82	24	29
USA	85	54	64

Source: UNESCO (1976). The figures for Britain are for 1973, those for Holland, Israel, and the USA for 1974.

240

There exists a connection between the education levels of the population and their standards of living, which in turn are related to the rate of development of the country.

One way to explain the degree of economic development of a country is to relate it to the availability of higher education in that country.[68] A study of the six European Common Market countries in the mid-1970s, as well as Britain, the USA and the USSR, showed that within the Common Market as a whole, and in each of its countries individually, the achievements of the children of lower income classes in obtaining higher education were very low.[69]

Social stratification The differences in learning methods in different countries seem to be related to the degree of social stratification existing in those countries. Israel, which may be considered the least socially stratified country in the world, has democratic and participative learning.[66] The USA is the least socially stratified of the larger Western democracies.

One way to measure social stratification in a country is by considering social mobility in that country. Table 6.8 presents the inequality of opportunities in various countries. The countries can be divided into five groups, moving from those with the lowest to those with the highest inequality ratio. The effects of social stratification on the management of national and multinational companies in the different countries are dramatic. Some of these effects carry through from elementary, secondary, and higher education right to the positions for which people are hired in business organizations. Let us consider the cases of Britain and France.

There is still a correlation between the social class of candidates in both countries and their chances of being admitted into Oxford, Cambridge or the *grandes écoles*. Nevertheless, the admission to these universities is based more and more on achievement than on family background. Similarly, those who graduate in the USA from, say, Harvard, and the graduates of Oxbridge and the *grandes écoles*, are preferred by employers to other university graduates. At this point, however, the similarity between Oxbridge and the *grandes écoles* ends.

In Britain and in the USA the companies seek to employ the top graduates. In

Table 6.8   Educational inequalities

Inequality ratio	Countries
Less than 250	Israel (Haifa), Great Britain, USSR (refugees)
250–299	Australia, Denmark, France, India, USA, Brazil, Sweden, Holland, Japan
300–499	Norway, West Germany, Puerto Rico
500–799	Hungary, Finland, Italy
More than 800	Belgium

Source: Bendix and Lipset (1966).
Note:

$$\text{Inequality ratio} = \frac{\text{(Non-manual worker sons of non-manual workers)}}{\text{(Non-manual worker sons of manual workers)}}$$

France those who recruit for organizations from the *grandes écoles* are themselves graduates of those same *grandes écoles*, and they usually go all out to hire from their own *Alma Mater*. Thus, in a certain organization with a top executive from, say, the Haute École de Commerce, there is a good chance that most of the graduates in the organization are from that school.

Another difference between university graduates in US and British as against French organizations is an extension of this relationship between university and job. In the Anglo-Saxon countries a degree from a 'good' university helps one to get a 'good' job, but from then on performance is more important for progress; in France, on the other hand, performance has much less significance throughout a person's career. Once a person has graduated from a *grande école* he has, in the great majority of cases, made it for life. He could be a complete failure, but usually the graduates of his own school will make sure that his career progresses as if nothing had happened. Thus in France one's chances to succeed throughout life are much more related to one's education than in Britain.

In Britain the custom of many companies of placing only members of the higher social classes in positions like that of directors has been gradually disappearing, while it is still common in France. There are still in existence French companies which would not hire a top executive for the formal position of *directeur*—somewhat parallel to a vice president who is a member of the board of directors—unless he belonged to one of the so-called '200 best families' of France. Strong social stratification is evident in other Western European countries as well. In some of them this social stratification seems to be even more polarized.

In most of these countries such things as the way of addressing people in business organizations, and the times at which people arrive at work and leave it, vary according to their social and organizational positions. Thus, while in the USA people usually address each other by their first name whatever their rank, in Western Europe the form of address usually changes from level to level, and differs between two people at different managerial levels. Again, while it is customary in the USA for everybody to arrive at work at the same time, though higher ranking executives may leave later, in Europe the higher the person in the organization the later he often arrives at and leaves work.

Managerial structures Managerial structures are related to the socio-cultural environment and the emerging educational patterns in the different countries. There is a direct connection between the ability of the organizations to grow, to innovate, and to absorb new technologies and their propensity to change and adapt their managerial structures to the growing need to absorb broader scopes of decision-making. However, every managerial structure requires a different type of manager, and therefore managers have to move from one company to another. Alternatively, they could be transferred from one part to another, if the organization is large enough to contain different types of structures within it.

The socio-cultural environment affects the processes of growth, change, and mobility in several different ways, but primarily in the way that new generations of managers are being educated. The preparation of the new type of leader required for a new type of managerial structure takes at least one generation. Fifty years ago the USA had very few people who could become chief executives of decentralized structures. However, as the educational system became more participative and to some degree permissive, more and more decentralized leaders emerged out of American families and educational institutes.

Taking France again as an example, there are few of what might be called 'decentralized leaders' in the country and, therefore, few decentralized structures. As a result, organizations cannot absorb broader scopes of decision-making than their functional structures permit. This fact hinders developments in more advanced technologies, more diversified product lines, and more international activities.

Another environmental effect on the dynamics and adaptability of managerial structures is the 'anti-mobility value' to which we shall return at some length. This anti-mobility value is a constraint on the interorganizational mobility which is required in order to enable the progression of management from an entrepreneurial structure to a functional one and from there to a decentralized system. The anti-mobility value is quite powerful in European countries. It likewise almost completely freezes any movement of managers between organizations in the large corporations of Japan.

However, the appearance of the so-called multistructure organization has enabled countries with strong anti-mobility values to bypass the necessity of interorganizational mobility. It is interesting to highlight two points regarding the anti-mobility value and the evaluation of large Japanese multistructure organizations. The anti-mobility value was introduced into Japanese business only just before the First World War, in order to stop the enormously high interorganizational mobility which existed at the time and was thought to be contrary to the Japanese aspirations of growth and technological progress.[70] Until now a very strict anti-mobility value has been preserved among large Japanese organizations. However, in the smaller ones, where interorganizational mobility is a condition of their survival through a progression from one managerial structure to another, such mobility does exist.

Countries with cultures permitting the establishment of multistructure organizations are able to bypass the anti-mobility value by means of arranging a systematic managerial mobility, not between one organization and another, but rather within the various parts of the same organization. Such multistructure organizations are in existence in both the USA and Europe. However, they are of special importance for European countries where the anti-mobility value is quite strong. Not all Western European countries have welcomed the appearance of very large business organizations through growth, merger, and acquisition.

Managerial structures can be measured and established by way of the degree of autonomy and the degree of clarity in the relationships between the managers of organizations. However, the degree of clarity is related not only to the managerial structure, but also to the culture in which the organization operates. This culture is determined by the country in which the organization functions and the field—business, political, military, and so on—in which it operates. Therefore, when one is measuring the relationships in order to establish the managerial structure of an organization, one should be aware of different flavours of relationships describing essentially the same types of managerial structure. Thus, an entrepreneurial structure of a French organization may be expected to be more formalized than a similar structure in an American organization; and functional structures in France would be more 'bureaucratic' than the same structures in the USA. One of the reasons for these differences is the relative degree of usage of oral and written communication in the different countries.

Spoken languages   Probably the most formidable obstacle to the spreading of multinational corporations throughout the world is the degree of knowledge of 'international languages' in the various countries. These 'international languages' are tending to become just one language, the English language. Just as French was the international language of the nineteenth century, so English has become that of the twentieth century in business, government, and science. This even applies to Russia, China, and Japan. Indeed, the awareness of the ever-growing dominance of the English language has already impressed many *avant-garde* Japanese who, drawing upon their pragmatism, propagandize for a much more intensive study of English in Japan. US technological superiority has undoubtedly contributed to the emergence of the English language as the future world language.[71]

This international spread and increasing superiority of one language is closely linked with the spread and growing influence of multinational corporations. These, in our opinion, will, by the end of this century, do the planning for, and direct the destiny of mankind rather than the nation states. This is, in our opinion, a positive development, because it would entail better understanding among nations, a safeguard against wars, and a better planning of the world. This is the subject of the following section.

However, before we reach the stage of 'one world, one language', the world will have to pass through a period of better international acquaintance and language competence than we have experienced hitherto. Indeed, until the Second World War, language competence was rare. This has been changing rapidly. Technological advances and cheaper travel enable very large numbers of citizens, chiefly of the industrial countries, to visit other countries, spending weeks and months there and learning the local languages and the ways and customs of their neighbours. Many of the heads of business organizations from the industrial countries in Europe are today fluent in several languages and feel quite at ease in the company of their colleagues from other countries. There has even been a marked change in the attitude of Americans towards learning the customs and languages of the peoples with whom they come in contact, particularly since the sensation caused by the publication of *The Ugly American*.[72] Finally, there is evidence that the economic success of smaller countries goes hand in hand with the population's knowledge of and fluency in other languages. Switzerland and Holland are outstanding examples of smaller countries which have achieved economic success in spite of relatively small populations and other limitations. Switzerland, for example, has very limited natural resources and no outlet to the sea; it is doubtful if it would have achieved such great success in tourism were it not for the excellent service it offers in which knowledge of languages plays a big part. Holland, though suffering from the destruction of the Second World War and the loss of its Far Eastern empire, has re-established its eminence in international commerce and tourism in spite of the fact that in the latter it does not have the spectacular geographical attractions of, for instance, Switzerland. Both countries start the foreign language education of children at a very early age.

English, French, and German were the official languages of INSEAD in Fontainebleau, France, when it was set up in order to promote the economic unification of Europe and to help Europe contest the USA's invasion of her sphere of economic interests.[73] The two dominant languages at INSEAD nowadays are English and French. Instruction is based on the case study method which describes a business situation. Small groups of students study, analyse, and discuss the case. Later these groups meet in a class for final analysis, led by a professor. More than 50 students from more than 20 different countries participate in these studies.[74] The case studies are usually in French or English. The discussion groups or the lectures are not necessarily conducted in the language of the case study; the individual student may use any one of the above three languages. Candidates for the Fontainebleau Institute must therefore be fluent in English and French and by their graduation have at least a fair knowledge of German.

There are very strong indications that the ability to speak more than one language is not an inherent talent, but rather is acquired. Indeed, we all know very talented people, brilliant and genial, who find it extremely difficult to speak a second language fluently; and, on the other hand, many untalented people who are fluent in several languages. It also seems that this facility to pick up languages is acquired by people when they are very young. We would hypothesize that the longer a child is exposed simultaneously to more than one language between the ages of 1 and 10 years, the easier it will be for that person to acquire languages which he is motivated to learn at any subsequent time in his life. For example, the Jews had an ability to learn languages because from infancy they spoke either Yiddish (European and US Jews) or Ladino (Mediterranean and oriental Jews) in addition to at least one other language, that of the country in which they were raised; this, we believe, is the explanation for the language facility of Jews at least until the middle of the twentieth century.[75]

We have discussed in this chapter several cross-national differences bearing on multinational management. These differences in managerial communication, education, social stratification, managerial structure, and spoken languages are interrelated. Generally speaking, the more democratic the culture of the country, the more one may expect to discover in it oral communication, participative learning methodologies, low social stratification, decentralized managerial structures, and languages. Multinational corporations operate in a variety of national cultures (see section 6.1). Each culture has its own peculiarities of organizational and managerial behaviour. Let us now see what is required of those managers who have to function within two or more of the national cultures in which their multinationals operate.

*6.2.4.2   Culture-bound and Universal Organizational Behaviour. What is
Necessary in Order to Function in Different National Culture
Environments?*

Let us distinguish between 'culture-bound behaviour' and 'universal behaviour'.
The latter is a term used to indicate behaviour which is affected to a smaller
degree by the various alien cultures in which a person finds himself, than by his
own. Every person's assumed universal organizational behaviour is composed of
his own experience in organizations, from early childhood and throughout his
organizational life. Thus, for example, a person accustomed to work in formally
centralized organizations will continue to behave as though he were in that type of
organizational culture even after moving to another organization with a different
managerial structure. Until this person has become accustomed to the new
organizational culture, he might find it most disturbing to work, for instance, in an
entrepreneurial organization with its informal relationships which disregard and
bypass the formal prescribed relationships and hierarchy of other managerial
structures. Also, a person employed in a top position of a product line organization must realize that the CE expects his subordinates to assume much more
responsibility and autonomy than the CE of a functional organization expects
from his subordinates.[76]
  We are dealing, however, with national rather than organizational cultures, and
therefore assume that within every national environment there is a culture, i.e. a
mode of behaviour to which the people in that environment are habituated. There
are, of course, things which could and should be considered as *universal
behaviour*, in that they do not change from culture to culture. Thus, for example,
in every country and type of structure everyone expects an organization to have a
president or CE.
  An appropriate example could be the difference in manner of communication in
organizations between, say, France and the USA. Let us imagine two similar
organizations, each headed by an entrepreneur and managed in an entrepreneurial
structure, the chief executive communicating with the managers at various levels
of the management rather than only with those directly below him. This is
'universal behaviour'. However, if we were to consider the communication
behaviour of the two entrepreneurs in terms of the intensity of their oral interactions with their managers, we would discover that the American entrepreneur
interacts widely with managers throughout the organization, whereas the French
entrepreneur's oral interaction is much less frequent. Furthermore, the French
chief executive uses written communication to a greater extent than his American
counterpart. This may lead us to the mistaken impression that the Frenchman is a
bureaucratic leader of a formally centralized functional structure. Actually he
runs an entrepreneurial structure but in a different culture of communication
behaviour.
  Closely related to the differences between the culture and the universal
behaviour are differences in attitudes among managers in different countries. One
of the pioneering studies of managerial thinking found that national

246

characteristics, such as religion, language, and degree of technological development, were prominent in explaining variations in the attitudes of managers in the 14 countries studied.[77]

Another study showed that the national culture affected the relationships as well as the attitudes of the managers, and especially the leadership style.[78]

Findings of yet another comparative study of American and European chief executives showed significant differences in the social status of US and European managers and in their opinions concerning the functional experience necessary for a manager to become a chief executive. On the other hand, and contrary to common belief, there were no differences in interorganizational managerial mobility on the two sides of the Atlantic Ocean, between US and European CEs.[79]

We have selected several cultural values which have significant effects on managerial behaviour and which seem to vary to a large degree from country to country. We have studied up till now variations in four such cultural values among participants at INSEAD's Master of Business Administration (MBA) programme. Let us consider them one by one.

The anti-mobility value   The first study was on the cultural value of 'the longer one serves in an organization, the better'. This value resents firing a person, especially when the organization owes something to him, as was the case with Jim Fairfax in the following case study.

> In the U.S.A. a large enterprise finds itself on the verge of bankruptcy. Its charming, debonair General Manager is liked by all, but no longer has full control over the business. Discipline is non-existent. The personnel take an easy-going attitude towards their work. Morale is good but turnover is going down fast.
>
> The Board of Directors is becoming concerned. It quickly takes the decision to appoint a new General Manager to put things right. A strong, energetic man is chosen: Jim Fairfax.
>
> Fairfax is of an extremely sharp intelligence, has a striking personality, is extraordinarily dynamic and ambitious. Discipline is re-established in a short time. The place buzzes with activity. The new manager is indefatigable, leaves nothing to chance, supervises everything, decides everything and makes his personnel work hard.
>
> Some of the personnel live in continual fear of having misunderstood Fairfax's orders. Others complain bitterly of having no real responsibility or of having no powers to use their own initiative. The psychological climate starts to deteriorate. In fact, it becomes very bad. At the end of a trial period of several months, the Board meets again. Fairfax's successes are noted. Business has improved and become profitable again. The Board also notes the worsening atmosphere within the company which is taking on such proportions that it could, in the long run, cause the complete breakdown of morale amongst the managers.
>
> In these circumstances, the Board was confronted with the problem of what to do about Jim Fairfax. The possibilities open to the members of the

Board were:

(a) Fire him.
(b) Appoint him as Chairman of the Board of Directors.
(c) Leave him in his present position, but appoint one or more deputy managers to help him.
(d) Remove him from his post and appoint him as a consultant to the company.
(e) Other solutions.

You are a member of the Board of Directors and you have to vote for one of the alternatives. Please explain your choice.

Table 6.9 shows the results of the vote by the board of directors, as well as the distribution of responses of a sample of thousands of French managers and American board members, who were asked to indicate how they would have voted had they been members of the board. While 80 per cent of the US directors unhesitatingly voted to fire him, only 2 per cent of the French managers indicated they would have voted in the same way. The responses of the remaining 98 per cent of the French managers were distributed almost equally among the other four alternatives; it was as if the French managers meant to say, 'We do not mind what you do with Jim Fairfax, as long as you do not fire him!'

This same case study was given to several student groups at INSEAD who were requested to indicate how they would have voted, had they been members of the board. Thus we have, for example, the 'firing' responses of the MBA class of 1971, in Table 6.10. Let us consider the attitudes of the 205 participants from 15 countries (with 3 participants and more; out of a total of 220 participants from 15 *beginning of the academic year 1970/1971*, soon after they arrived at INSEAD.

We see that the three large participant groups (France, Britain, and Germany) are quite close to each other in their choice to fire Jim Fairfax, respectively 10, 9,

Table 6.9   Results of French and US voting on whether to fire Jim Fairfax

		Distribution of choices	
		French (managers) %	*American (board members)* %
(a)	Fire Jim Fairfax	2	80
(b)	Appoint him as chairman of the board of directors	28	—
(c)	Leave him in his present position, but appoint one or more deputy managers	22	—
(d)	Remove him from post and appoint him as consultant to the company	26	—
(e)	Other solutions	22	Hardly any were mentioned

Table 6.10   Should Jim Fairfax be fired? Responses of a class of INSEAD MBA students

	Beginning of 1970/1971			Towards end of 1970/1971		
	Firing		No. of partici- pants	Firing		No. of partici- pants
	%	No.		%	No.	
USA	50	2	4	50	2	4
Israel	33	2	6	50	3	6
Britain	9	2	22	39	7	18
Luxembourg	0	0	3	33	1	3
Sweden	0	0	3	33	1	3
Italy	22	2	9	29	2	7
Norway	11	1	9	29	2	8
Germany	8	3	39	21	5	24
Switzerland	0	0	16	20	2	10
Austria	0	0	8	17	1	6
France	10	6	59	12	5	43
Holland	0	0	15	8	1	13
Belgium	0	0	8	0	0	5
Denmark	0	0	4	0	0	4
Totals	9.1	20	220	20.3	35	172

Source: Weinshall (1977, p. 197). This table includes only countries with at least three participants at the beginning and end of the year; arranged by the percentage of the 'firing' at the end of the year.

NB: The totals include also participants from another eleven countries with fewer than three participants at the beginning and end of the year.
   Difference between beginning and end of 1970/1971 is significant at the 0.02 level when treated by the binomial approximation to the normal and at the 0.01 level when tested by the Sigma test for two related samples.
   Difference for Britain between beginning and end of year—significant at better than the 0.03 level.
   Difference for Germany between beginning and end of year—significant at better than the 0.005 level.
   The countries are arranged in this figure by the ranking order of the percentage rate of firing towards the end of 1970/1971 (from 50% of US and Israeli participants to 0% of Belgian and Danish).

and 8 per cent. The participant groups from other countries are smaller in size (from 3 to 16 participants). Only four of them came out with higher percentages than those of the three largest participant groups—USA (50 per cent), Israel (33 per cent), Italy (22 per cent), and Norway (11 per cent). All the remaining countries, including Switzerland (with 16 participants) and Holland (with 15 participants), had *no* participants voting to fire Jim Fairfax.

   Let us consider managers from a country in which interorganizational mobility is not considered a tragedy. Suppose American executives are confronted with a situation like that of Jim Fairfax, but occurring in another country, say in Holland or in Switzerland. If they are not aware of the differences between attitudes towards the anti-mobility value in their own country and in the host country, they will probably encounter a culture shock.

Confidentiality—the personal discretion value. This is one of three values, the attitudes towards which were comparatively studied among the participants of the INSEAD class of 1978.[80] The story used for this purpose can be summarized as follows. An interviewer meets an interviewee whom he had not known before. After an hour or so of pleasant conversation, he asks the interviewee: 'How much money do you make?' Respondents were asked to score their feelings on three seven-point scales as to: the behaviour of the interviewer; his intentions; and how the respondent would feel had he been asked the question. The average responses for the 13 countries, from each of which there were at least four participants, are presented in Table 6.11.

The higher the scores, the more negative the attitudes of the respondents. The attitudes towards the 'interviewer's behaviour' were far more negative (4.4) than those on the other two scales (3.2). They were, in fact, more negative than the mid-scale position of 4.0. It is interesting that in projecting themselves as 'interviewees', the respondents from different countries were closer to each other (the difference between lowest and highest country being 1.6) than on the other two scales: 'interviewer's behaviour' (a 2.6 difference) and 'interviewer's intentions' (a 2.2 difference). The narrower distribution of countries in the 'respondent as interviewer' seems to indicate a certain degree of uniformity in the managerial behaviour of INSEAD participants from all countries. This statement assumes

Table 6.11 Confidentiality—attitudes of INSEAD participants from 13 countries: average scores on three scales in response to a story

Country	Number of participants	Average scores on scales		
		Interviewer's behaviour	Interviewer's intentions	Respondent as interviewee
France	59	3.8	2.9	2.8
UK	29	4.1	2.8	3.2
USA	9	4.9	3.3	3.2
Holland	9	4.2	3.7	3.6
Lebanon	8	3.4	3.4	2.5
Belgium	8	4.0	2.9	3.5
Switzerland	7	4.1	3.0	3.1
Japan	7	5.6	3.4	3.3
Germany	5	3.6	3.6	3.6
Italy	5	3.6	3.6	3.4
Israel	5	3.8	2.0	2.2
Greece	4	6.0	4.2	3.3
Denmark	4	5.5	3.2	3.8
Total & averages	159	4.4	3.2	3.2

that the 'respondent as interviewer' represents the manifest behaviour of the respondents, while the two other scales represent his cultural attitudes.

Arriving on time scale When entering INSEAD in September 1977, the class of 1978 were presented with this story: Several managers have convened an important meeting. Participants have been invited from all over the world. All the participants have arrived in town and they know how to reach the company office by 10:00, the scheduled time for the meeting the next morning. Nevertheless, only a few come on time; the others arrive after the scheduled beginning. Several of the latecomers explain their delay and apologize.

The respondents were requested to score on four scales: their feelings after 10:00 when only a few had arrived; when they would have started the meeting; to estimate how many of the latecomers would apologize upon arrival; and how many of these would give the true reasons for their latecoming. The results of the responses to these four aspects of the punctuality story are presented in Table 6.12.

The higher the scores in the first two scales, the more the respondents are disturbed by the tardiness. The higher the scores in the next two scales, the more the respondents distrust the sincerity of latecomers' apologies.

Table 6.12 Punctuality—attitudes of INSEAD participants from 13 countries: average scores on four scales (two subvalues) in response to a story

| Country | No. of participants | Average scores on scales | | | |
| | | Punctuality | | Belief in sincerity of latecomers | |
		Feelings after 10:00	When starting	Apologizing latecomers	Apologizers tell truth
France	59	4.1	3.8	2.4	3.9
UK	29	4.6	3.9	2.3	3.6
USA	9	4.1	4.7	2.0	3.0
Holland	9	4.1	3.9	2.6	3.8
Lebanon	8	3.3	3.4	2.3	2.4
Belgium	8	3.8	4.7	2.4	2.8
Switzerland	7	3.7	3.0	2.4	3.6
Japan	7	4.9	3.7	1.9	4.1
Germany	5	4.2	3.4	2.0	3.8
Italy	5	3.8	4.4	2.4	3.2
Israel	5	5.8	4.6	1.8	2.3
Greece	4	3.5	3.2	1.8	4.8
Denmark	4	5.0	4.0	3.0	3.3
Total & averages	159	4.2	3.9	2.3	3.4

Actually only the first two scales, 'feelings after 10:00' and 'when starting' are directly concerned with attitudes towards being on time for meetings. The latter two scales, concerning apologizing, express the respondents' beliefs as to the behaviour of latecomers.

The lower the averages on the scales, the less strict are the reactions of the respondents on the first two scales, and the more they believe the apologizers will tell the true reasons for being late. The respondents were on the whole stricter concerning punctuality (4.2 and 3.9) than they were hopeful of receiving apologies from latecomers. Attitudes towards punctuality only (i.e. their 'feelings after 10:00' and 'when starting'), revolved around mid-scale.

Respondents were quite optimistic about 'apologizing latecomers' (2.3 on the average, i.e. they expected that about 75 per cent would apologize), and also that the apologizers would tell the truth (3.4 on the average, i.e. they expected that over 50 per cent of those who would apologize would give the correct reason). The 'apologizing latecomers' result (2.3) is likewise farther from mid-scale (4.0) than any of the other eleven scales in Tables 6.11, 6.12, and 6.13 (regarding the values of confidentiality, punctuality, and bribery).

The largest differences among the countries occurred in the respondents' 'feelings after 10:00 (2.5 points between the lowest and the highest country). The greatest uniformity among the 13 countries occurred with regard to 'apologizing latecomers' (1.2 points between lowest and highest). The remaining two scales were closer to uniformity than to disparity (1.5 in 'when starting' and 1.2 in 'apologizing latecomers'). It therefore seems that the 'feelings after 10:00' scores are the most indicative of the four of the divergence of cultural attitudes towards punctuality among the 13 countries represented.

Bribery value (paying and receiving slush funds) The third story presented to the class of 1978, soon after their arrival at INSEAD in September 1977, was as follows. The CE of a large multinational corporation has just learned from a reliable source that one of his subordinates, Mr R.B., the head of a large subsidiary, has been lavishly entertained (including long and expensive weekends) by his suppliers.

The respondents act as consultants to the CE and are asked to score their feelings on five scales: their recommendation to the CE about what he should do with Mr R.B.; what would the respondents have done had they been in R.B.'s position; where they would draw the line about what constitutes acceptable gifts; and whether they would make a distinction between money which is subsequently transferred back to the organization or to a public cause, and money which is kept by the receiver himself (two scales). In drafting a policy, would they make it flexible so as to allow different conduct in different countries? The results of this study are presented in Table 6.13.

The five scales regarding bribery may be divided into two groups. The first three scales concern *behaviour in dealing with slush funds*; the higher the score on these three scales, the more flexible the respondents are in dealing with slush funds. The next two scales deal with *organizational strategy towards slush funds*;

Table 6.13   Bribery—attitudes of INSEAD participants from 13 countries: average scores on five scales (two subvalues) in response to a story

Country	No. of participants	Behaviour in dealing with slush funds			Organizational strategy towards slush funds	
		CE's reaction	Respondent in R.B.'s place	Acceptable gift	Public cause— OK?	Flexible policy
France	59	4.6	3.1	2.2	2.4	3.8
UK	29	5.2	3.3	1.7	2.5	4.1
USA	9	5.8	3.3	1.6	2.9	4.7
Holland	9	4.9	3.4	1.4	2.3	4.1
Lebanon	8	5.8	4.3	3.0	2.4	3.7
Belgium	8	4.8	2.7	2.4	2.1	4.0
Switzerland	7	3.6	3.1	2.0	2.9	4.0
Japan	7	4.6	3.3	2.3	2.5	3.7
Germany	5	3.6	3.0	1.4	2.0	2.8
Italy	5	5.2	3.8	3.0	2.4	5.0
Israel	5	4.0	2.8	2.0	1.4	3.8
Greece	4	5.8	3.8	3.0	3.2	5.5
Denmark	4	5.0	3.3	2.5	2.5	4.0
Total & averages	159	4.8	3.3	2.2	2.4	4.1

the higher the score on these two scales, the more flexible the respondents are in their organizational attitude towards slush funds. Thus, the higher the scores on the five scales of this story, the more lenient are the attitudes of the respondents. Consequently, the most lenient attitudes were those regarding the CE's handling of Mr R.B. who accepted slush funds (average of 4.8).

The next most lenient scale was the one asking whether the corporation should adopt a flexible policy. The average score on this scale (4.1) came out almost in mid-scale. This is an interesting result. The respondents were specifically asked whether the policy towards slush funds should make distinctions among the different countries in various parts of the world in which the corporation was operating. A natural hypothesis is that an international body of business administration students would feel that if a corporation has to operate in different countries and cultures, with varying constraints, both formal and informal, imposed on it, the corporation should draw up flexible policies on such matters as slush funds. This hypothesis was rejected by the respondents.[81]

It is interesting to note, however, the divergence of opinion on this scale of 'flexible policy' among the 13 countries. The difference between the lowest country (2.8), i.e. the strictest one, and the highest country (5.5), i.e. the most lenient one, is the largest among all 12 scales of attitudes towards confidentiality, punctuality, and bribery (Tables 6.11, 6.12, and 6.13).

Finally in this section on culture-bound and universal organizational behaviour, let us compare the results of six values and subvalues among the 13 countries. Table 6.15 and Figure 6.3 rank the countries according to their attitudes towards each of the values and subvalues listed in Table 6.14.[82]

Table 6.15 gives the numerical values of the rankings, while Figure 6.3 presents the same rankings in graphical form. It is because of the graphical presentation that the countries are arranged in Figure 6.3 from the lowest ranking on the left-hand side to the highest ranking on the right-hand side. However, the 13 countries did not rank in the same order on each of the six values and subvalues. There is some order in the seemingly disorganized graphs of Figure 6.3. Let us analyse the rankings in Table 6.15.

On the whole, the more the attitudes of participants from one country are against interorganizational mobility, the more upset they are by personal indiscretion, disturbed by tardiness, distrustful of the apologies of latecomers, flexible about slush funds, and supportive of a flexible strategy regarding slush funds. The exceptions to the above are those ranking which are encircled in Table 6.15. They are at least three rank orders apart from the average ranking. The number of exceptions ranges from 3 to 5 countries, in every one of the six values and subvalues; with 3 countries in *anti-mobility* and the two sub-values in *bribery*, with 4 countries in *punctuality*, and with 5 countries in *anti-mobility* and in *belief in sincerity of latecomers*. Let us analyse, for example, the exceptions in punctuality. These can be explained, at least partially, by attitudes contrary to the stereotyped behaviour of the respondents' compatriots in their own countries. Thus the Israeli respondents were the most disturbed by tardiness, while in Israel punctuality is rarely observed. On the other hand, while the Swiss are stereotyped as the most punctual nation, their participants were among the respondents from three countries (along with the Lebanese and Greek) who were the least disturbed by tardiness. As for the attitudes towards bribery, we have already mentioned that

Table 6.14   Values and subvalues used in Table 6.15 and Figure 6.3

Results presented in	Values and subvalues	The higher the ranking the larger the
Table 6.10	Interorganizational mobility	Anti-mobility
Table 6.11	Confidentiality	Personal discretion
Table 6.12	Punctuality Belief in sincerity of latecomers	Annoyance at tardiness Distrust of the sincerity of latecomers
Table 6.13	Behaviour in dealing with slush funds Organizational strategy towards slush funds	Flexibility in dealing with slush funds Flexibility in organizational strategy towards slush funds

254

Table 6.15 The ranking of attitudes towards six values and subvalues among new INSEAD participants from 13 countries

| | Ranking order of 13 countries | | | | | | | | | | | | | |
Value or subvalue	1 Israel	2 Germany	3 Lebanon	4 France	5 Switzerland	6 Belgium	7 UK	8 Japan	9 Italy	10 USA	11 Holland	12 Denmark	13 Greece	The higher the ranking, the larger the
1. Interorganizational mobility	2	⑥	—	4	⑪.5	⑪.5	5	—	③	①	11.5	11.5	—	Anti-mobility
2. Confidentiality	1	⑧	2	3	5	6	④	⑪	7	9	10	12	13	Upset by personal indiscretion
3. Punctuality	⑬	4	2	5	⑫	8.5	8.5	10	7	11	⑥	12	②	Disturbed by tardiness
4. Belief in sincerity of latecomers	1	⑥	2	⑩.5	⑧.5	4	7	8.5	⑤	③	12	10.5	13	Distrust latecomers' apologies
5. Behaviour in dealing with slush funds	3	1	⑬	5.5	②	5.5	7.5	7.5	11	9	④	10	12	Flexible about slush funds
6. Organizational strategy towards slush funds	2	1	3.5	5.5	⑩	3.5	9	5.5	11	12	⑦	⑧	13	Flexible slush funds strategy

Note: See note 83 at end of chapter.

255

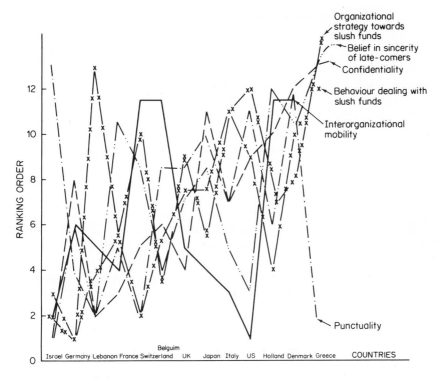

Figure 6.3   Ranking of attitudes listed in Table 6.15

we found a systematic contradiction between the attitudes towards the first four values and subvalues in Table 6.15 and the two subvalues regarding bribery. The respondents of most countries were flexible and positive in their attitudes towards interorganizational mobility, confidentiality, and punctuality, and they were rigid and negative regarding bribery; or they were the other way around—rigid and negative about interorganizational mobility, confidentiality, and punctuality, and flexible and positive regarding bribery. It seems that while the values concerning interorganizational mobility, confidentiality, and punctuality are not necessarily connected with formal organizations, bribery is exclusively related to power and authority positions in organizations.

Therefore, the more experienced managers in business organizations are, the more their attitudes towards bribery will be in line with those towards interorganizational mobility, confidentiality, and punctuality.

The above values are just examples of the many values which affect managerial behaviour in various countries. One does not need much imagination to think of interpersonal difficulties and embarrassing, conflicting, and frustrating situations which arise when managers from one country interact with those from another country without being aware of the differences in their attitudes and values.

6.2.4.3 Multinational Managers—the Ingredients which Make Them

The participants of the INSEAD class of 1966 were asked to evaluate the degree to which they mixed with participants of countries different from their own; their contribution to other participants in the learning process in group and class discussion; and the learning process contributed to them. These three factors of mixing, contributing, and receiving are among the main ingredients making multi-national managers.

The 100 participants in this first research project of the Multinational Business Education research programme were requested to rank the twelve countries represented in the 1966 INSEAD class,[83] and the twelve professional areas (i.e. first university degree areas),[84] regarding the mixing, contributing, and receiving of the participants. Tables 6.16 and 6.17 present the results for the three countries and the three professions with the largest representation in the INSEAD 1966 class. From each of these countries and three professions there was a large enough representation for the 100 respondents to be able to make up their minds how to rank the degree of mixing, contributing, and receiving among the twelve countries and the twelve professions.

Because of the small size of the 1966 INSEAD class (130 students) and number of respondents (100), the findings presented in these tables must be con-sidered tentative rather than conclusive. It is clear that the results may vary con-siderably according to the type of MBA programme we are dealing with. We con-

Table 6.16   Rank orders of mixing, contributing, and receiving for Britain, France, and Germany

| | Detailed rank orders (RO) | | | |
	Mixing	Contributing	Receiving	Average RO
Britain	3	1	1	1.7
France	11	2	5	6.0
Germany	12	4.5	3	6.5

Table 6.17   Rank orders of mixing, contributing, and receiving for engineering, commerce, and economics

| | Detailed rank orders (RO) | | | |
	Mixing	Contributing	Receiving	Average RO
Engineering	2.5	1	1	1.5
Commerce	1	2	12	5.0
Economics	4	3	11	6.0
Average commerce-economics	2.5	2.5	11.5	5.5

sider the INSEAD programme, however, to have been all these years a participative learning process with the emphasis on management rather than on business studies. This is why we believe that the results regarding mixing, contributing, and receiving are indicative of the capacities of the INSEAD graduates to turn into multinational managers.

As the rank orders in the tables are from among 12 countries and 12 professions, 9 countries and 9 professions are omitted from each table. Thus, for example, the German participants were ranked the lowest (12) regarding their mixing with participants from other countries, and the students with first university degrees in Commerce were ranked the lowest (12) regarding receiving (i.e. gaining) from the learning process. On the other hand, the British participants and the Engineering university graduates ranked as both contributing the most to and receiving the most from (1) the learning process. The Commerce graduates were perceived, however, as mixing the most (1) with participants different from themselves.

Let us first consider the results presented in Table 6.16. While the British students were perceived to be very high on all three parameters, the French and German students were perceived as the lowest on mixing, but relatively high on contributing and receiving. On the whole, contributing and receiving are perceived as more closely related to each other than either of them is related to mixing. Generally speaking, when students from one country are perceived to be highly contributing, they are also perceived to be highly receiving, i.e. profiting from the educational process. Mixing is not perceived to be necessarily related to either contributing or receiving.

The findings regarding the mixing, contributing, and receiving of the British, French, and German participants at INSEAD are complementary to those of Jacques Horovitz, whose research is reported in our organizational example on British, French, and German Industry in chapter 4. Horovitz, too, found that the French and Germans are much more similar to each other (in his case, regarding managerial control) than to the British, with the French being somewhat closer to the British than the Germans.

Let us now consider the results presented in Table 6.17. Comparing the engineering with the commerce and economics groups, we see that, as regards mixing, the engineering graduates are between those with commerce degrees and those with economics degrees. The engineering graduates contribute more to the educational process than their colleagues with commerce and economics degrees. As to receiving (profiting from the studies), the engineering graduates rank the highest. Those with degrees in economics and commerce are ranked lowest on receiving. This probably means that the INSEAD studies were perceived to be closely oriented towards commerce and economics, but also to require a high degree of knowledge in quantitative techniques.

These were the perceptions of the 1966 respondents of the relative positions of the three largest national groups (France, Germany, and Britain) and the largest professional groups (commerce, economics, and engineering). When asked 'To what background factors do you think that mixing or not mixing internationally could be attributed at INSEAD?' they ranked the six alternative factors presented to them in the following order:

(1) Mastering the required languages.
(2) Being married to another nationality.
(3) Having parents of two different nationalities.
(4) Social class.
(5) Nationality.
(6) Profession.

Let us consider every one of these background factors separately.

Mastering the required languages   We have already discussed this attribute at length. One has to realize, however, that in this context the emphasis is on the *required* languages, which were at the time French, English, and German.[85] The fact that mastering the *required* languages was chosen as the most important background factor, could simply mean that, without this, the participant at INSEAD could not in any way mix with participants from other countries, or contribute to, and benefit from, the learning process.

Being married to another nationality   One of the reasons for starting this research programme was the fact that, when we first arrived at INSEAD, we discovered that the wives of a large number of the married students[86] were of different nationality from their husbands. We felt that the number of such mixed marriages was so high that it could not be a coincidence, and that such young people may be especially attracted to a school which trains multinational managers and helps bridge the gaps between national cultures.

Having parents of two different nationalities   The problems of children born with mixed ethnic and national parentage are well known. When the nations of the parents are at odds, including being at war with each other, the children often become extreme nationalists of the country of either the father or the mother.[87] However, when the nationalities of the parents are not in conflict, the culture of the grown-up children of such marriages is not very different from the culture of a person marrying a person of another nationality.

Social class   This factor is important to understand, especially for those who are not acquainted with the social structure of Western European countries. We have already referred to social stratification earlier in our discussion. Clearly, the more socially conscious a person feels, the less capable he is of mixing with people perceived to be from social strata different from his own. Also, such socially class-conscious people are handicapped in their participation in the learning process.

Nationality   The differences in national characteristics among the INSEAD participants were another reason for the initiation of this research programme. In order to design the questionnaire from which we derived all these data, we interviewed non-directly about 20 students from a variety of national origins. In comparison with all the other interviewees, the German students mixed less with students from other nationalities.[88]

Profession   We have already seen in Tables 6.16 and 6.17 how nationality and profession affect the perceived degree of mixing, contributing, and receiving of the INSEAD participants of the 1966 class.

We now realize that these two factors of nationality and profession are perceived to be less important as regards mixing, contributing, and receiving than the mastering of required languages, being married to another nationality, being of nationally mixed parentage, and of a particular social class. This could be connected to another finding of this same research project, namely that the more time the participant spent away from his own country—during his school years and to the time he arrived at INSEAD—the more he had acquired multinational attitudes. The mixing, contributing, and receiving at INSEAD are all related in one way or another to the length of stay in different countries, i.e. mastering languages, mixed marriage, and binational parentage. Social class, nationality, and profession, which were perceived to affect the behaviour at INSEAD to a lesser degree, are not related to length of stay abroad.

The above are only some of the ingredients which are required for becoming successful multinational managers.

None of the above factors by itself, not even a profound knowledge of languages, can make a good multinational manager out of somebody who is adequately managing people of his own nationality in a specific managerial style.

There are other requirements of a manager who has all or most of the above mentioned characteristics if he is to be an adequate multinational manager. The main additional prerequisite is an attraction for cross-cultural experiences. This attraction to the cross-cultural life should help the multinational manager and his or her spouse to overcome the enormous difficulties of living in ever-changing environments, with or without children. The feeling of expatriation among multinational managers is probably the most severe problem of multinational corporations. It seems to us that the ability to live and work in countries different from one's own also varies considerably from one nationality to another.[89] The other attribute related to the attraction to cross-cultural life is the holding of certain ideals about people, organizations, countries, and the world. A self-centred manager with personally materialistic values only would not last for long as a multinational manager even if he had all the other necessary attributes. Thus, one needs both cultural curiosity and a sense of humanity in order to be a lasting multinational manager.[90]

Last, but not least, it should be emphasized that not all the managers in multinational corporations are good *multinational* managers. The large majority of managers in multinational corporations are no different from their peers in national corporations. The leadership of multinational corporations, however, has to be dominated by multinational managers. That is to say, the headquarters of a multinational corporation, wherever it is located, should be run by appropriate

260

multinational managers. So also should be the head offices of the multinational corporation in the different countries.[91]

6.2.4.4 How to Develop Multinational Executives

The creation of multinational corporations following the Second World War led to an enormous and inevitable increase in international business, which continues to expand at an ever-growing rate. Mid-1970 calculations showed that multinational corporations accounted for about 15 per cent of the world's production and that US-based multinational corporations alone made up 10 per cent of the world's gross product, while their investments reached 140 billion dollars.[92] Most of the relevant literature deals with values, managerial attitudes, perception, leadership, and personality variables. Only a relatively small number of studies deal with the equally important subject in this area—interpersonal communication.[93] The specific area of multinational managerial development is relatively new and consequently the research which has been carried out in it is even more meagre.

One of these research projects revealed that the majority of the responding US chief executives willingly and enthusiastically supported the enlargement of the international base of the MBA programmes.[94] It is pointed out, however, that many of the respondents remained neutral and passive on this question. The researcher says that chief executives who did not attribute large importance to incorporating an international perspective into graduate programmes suggested that this will not enhance the status of MBAs in their corporations. Such reactions were received from chief executives of both national and multinational corporations. This conclusion is supported by the fact that 40 per cent of the respondents said that none of the MBAs reporting to them were meaningfully involved in international activity. The researcher felt, however, that the most important finding of his research was the large amount of interest expressed by the majority of the chief executives, who put forward concrete suggestions for the inclusion of courses in multinational business activity in MBA programmes.

The question is, of course, whether just adding courses in multinational business activity to MBA programmes of business schools in a country like the USA will contribute additional managers who would be able to operate in foreign countries and, even more importantly, become good multinational managers. Mere addition of courses is by no means enough. Even if we fully accept the previous analysis of what makes people better mixers, contributors, and receivers, in a school like INSEAD, we have to consider what other multinational management researchers say about this problem.

One researcher found that operating with and through foreign nationals is a skill in itself which necessitates an ability to understand and a flexibility over and above those required in conducting local business.[95]

Indeed, when we tested the effects of background factors of the INSEAD participants of the class of 1967 on their multinational integration at INSEAD, we found that they were not very different from what the class of 1966 expected them to be when questioned about mixing, contributing, and receiving.

We have already seen that the students gathered at INSEAD came from a variety of national origins, had gone through different fields of study for their first degree, and had various other different personal characteristics including age, marital status, degree of national complexity, and length of time spent abroad. Had INSEAD let its students structure themselves freely, without any institutional intervention, it is probable that they would have structured themselves along one or more of their personal characteristics. In 1967, the students were divided as follows (the average is calculated by dividing the 144 participants by the number of groups):

National language	12 groups of countries, each including 1 or more countries with similar languages with an average of 12 participants in each.
Profession	9 first university specializations, with an average of 16 participants in each.
Family status	Bachelor and married groups, with an average of 72 participants in each.
National complexity	Mixed marriages and marriages between members of same nationality with an average of 36 participants in each (an average of 72 married participants divided by two).
Age	Young and old groups, with an average of 72 participants in each.
Time abroad	Long and short term abroad groups, with an average of 72 participants in each.

However, the formal structure of INSEAD has been set up so as to counteract the possible effects of the personal characteristics of the participants on their social structure. In other words, the objective has been to mix the students as much as possible. Many other graduate schools of business administration have a similar objective in that they try to mix the students by profession, in order that their different academic backgrounds will continue to stimulate each other, or by age, so that the more experienced will contribute to the less experienced, and vice versa. INSEAD adds one other important mixing factor, namely that of mixing the cultures, nationalities, and languages of its students. This mixing is done through both the learning organization and the living organization of the students. In 1967, they were divided as follows:

Case discussion group	20 groups, with an average of 7 participants in each.
Floor in the residence	15 floors, with an average of 8 participants on each.
Residence	6 residences with an average of 20 in each.
Class at entry	3 classes in the first half of 1966/1967 with an average of 45 in each.
Class at end of year	3 classes in the second half of 1966/1967 with an average of 45 in each.

About 17 per cent of the students did not live in INSEAD residences.
The researchers, therefore, posed two possibly conflicting hypotheses for their

research:

(a) that the personal characteristics of the students affect their social structure;
(b) that the formal structure affects the students' social structure.

The social structure was investigated by means of four sociometric indicators, measuring the perceptions of participants regarding their relationships with other participants: whom they had meals with, met during leisure time, would like to work with, would like to meet socially. The choices of participants in each of these four indicators were matched, and only mutually perceived choices were taken into account. Two sociograms, Figures 6.4 and 6.5, were drawn to demonstrate the network of the closer social relationships between participants. The lines between participants in these two sociograms indicate mutual choices according to more than one indicator. For the purpose of clarity, only those participants appear who had such social relationships among themselves. All the isolates—those participants who had no mutual choices or had them only for one indicator—have been omitted from the sociograms. Figure 6.4 shows the social network superimposed on the geographical map of the different countries. Figure 6.5 shows this network in relation to the accommodation of the INSEAD participants at Fontainebleau.

In both sociograms the types of lines designate the degrees of closeness of social relationships among participants. The closest social relationship is found to be between participants who chose each other on all four indicators for social relationships and is represented in the sociograms by the thick lines. Thus, in Figure 6.4, two thick lines are inside one country, France, while the other three thick lines cross borders between the following pairs of participants: Austrian and Finnish, British and French, French and Lebanese. In Figure 6.5 we see that four thick lines are inside the residences while only one thick line passes outside.

A visual analysis of the sociograms points again to the fact that the school's framework, the residences in this case, affects social relationships among participants more than the background characteristics, i.e. the countries of origin.

Finally, the conclusion of the whole analysis supports hypotheses about the effect of imposed conditions and given conditions on social relationships among participants. There is also a clear indication that the imposed conditions had a larger effect on the social structure than the given conditions. This last finding puts a special emphasis on the importance of international schools such as INSEAD, which, by its formal structure and teaching methods, encourages social relations among participants from different nations and backgrounds.

An analysis of the correlations between the social structure and the personal characteristics of participants on one side, and the formal structure of INSEAD on the other, is presented in Table 6.18. The analysis reveals that the effect of INSEAD's formal structure on the students' social structures is much more dominant than the effects of their personal characteristics.[96]

The most significant factor affecting the social structure was found to be membership of a discussion group. The relationships among members of discussion groups exceeded their randomness by six times. Next in its effect on the social

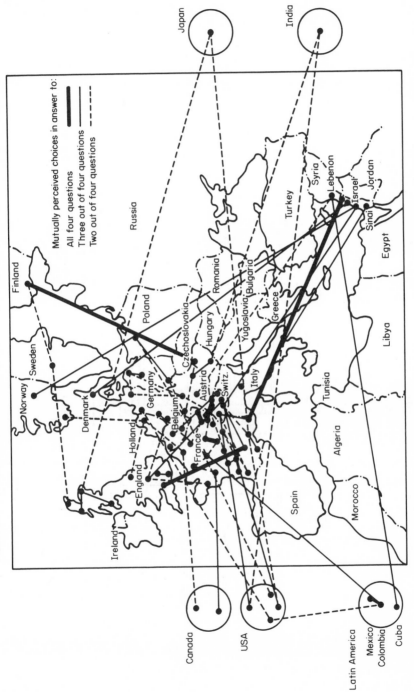

Figure 6.4   The social structure among INSEAD participants in 1967: intercountry sociogram*

* The social structure: mutual relationships between INSEAD participants by countries of origin. The four questions were about choices regarding having meals together, meeting during leisure time, working together in future, meeting socially in future.

264

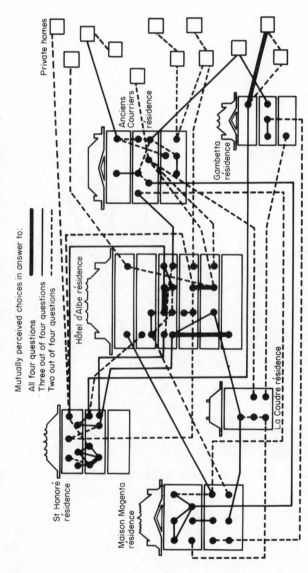

Figure 6.5   Interresidence (dormitory) sociogram of 1967 INSEAD participants*

Mutually perceived choices in answer to:

All four questions
Three out of four questions
Two out of four questions

Private homes

Anciens
Courriers
résidence

Gambetta
résidence

Hôtel d'Albe résidence

St Honoré
résidence

La Coudre résidence

Maison Magenta
résidence

* Mutual relationships between INSEAD participants by distribution of residences and homes in Fontainebleau. The four questions were about choices regarding having meals together, meeting during leisure time, working together in future, and meeting socially in future.

Table 6.18 Summary of effects of independent factors on social structure among INSEAD participants in 1967

Rank order	Factor	Imposed or given conditions	% of mutual choices within own factor group	Approximate average no. of participants in a group	% total mutual choices per participant within own factor group [a]	Relation between % of actual choices within group and % of random choice [b]
1	Discussion group	Imposed	30	7	4.3	×6.1
2	Floor in the residence	Imposed	31	8	3.9	×5.5
3.4	Whole residence group	Imposed	44	20	2.2	×3.1
3.4	National origin group	Given	26	12	2.2	×3.1
5	Professional (first university degree) group	Given	31	16	2.0	×2.9
6	Class at the beginning of the year	Imposed	71	45	1.5	×2.1
7	Class at the time of the research	Imposed	55	45	1.2	×1.7
8	Marital status group	Given	71	72	1.0	×1.4

Notes:

[a] If we take the discussion group as an example for calculation of percentage and total mutual choices per person, the analysis was done in two stages: it was found that 30 per cent of the mutual choices of the participants were among members of the same group. These 30 per cent were divided by 7 (the number of members in each group) which gives the 4.3 per cent of mutual choices per person.

[b] The random being $= \dfrac{100\%}{143 \text{ students in 1967}}$; thus, for example, the last column calculation for the discussion group in the first line is $\dfrac{4.3}{0.7} = 6.1$.

structure is the residence: relationships among students living on the same floor exceeded their randomness by 5.5 times. The next two factors affecting the social structures were their first degree, and the class in which they studied at the beginning of the year. Such a class was usually composed of seven discussion groups. The last two factors appearing in Table 6.18 as having an effect on the social structure were the students' class at the time of the research and their marital status.

All other factors tested were below 1 per cent per participant and very close to the random 0.7 per cent per participant. It can be seen that the factors imposed by INSEAD were predominant in their effect on the social structure both in their number—five factors imposed by INSEAD and only three personal characteristics—and in their variance from random, as follows:

Imposed factors	Membership in a discussion group, 6 times more than random.
	Living on the same floor of residence, 5.5 times more than random.
	Living in the same residence, 3 times more than random.
	Belonging to class at beginning of year, twice more than random.
	Class at time of research, 1.7 times more than random.
Personal factors	Originating from the same national group, 3 times more than random.
	Having obtained the same first university degree, almost 3 times more than random.
	Belonging to the same marital status group, 1.4 times more than random.

Table 6.19 represents the mutual relationships within and among seven country groups. In order to arrive at larger groups, the participants were grouped by countries: three single countries (Switzerland, Britain, and France), two double-country groups (USA and Canada, Austria and Germany), one four-country group (Scandinavia) and one three-country group (Mediterranean).

The chance of having more mutual relationships within a group increases, of course, the larger and more monolithic the group is. This is why the calculation of the degree of mixing is, according to Table 6.19, the difference between the rank order of the total number of participants in the study, and the rank order of mutual relationships per participant out of country group as percentage of total number of mutual relationships per participant (the rank order column on the right of the table minus the rank order column on the left). Consequently, the degree of mixing *relative* to other country groups appearing in the table is: *mixing more:* USA and Canada, as well as Switzerland; *mixing less:* Mediterranean countries; *mixing the least:* Scandinavian countries. These figures of perceived mixing in 1967 are somewhat different from the attitudes expressed in 1966 about the mixing of the British, French, and German participants (see Table 6.16), where the British were perceived to mix much more. This may be due to

Table 6.19 The social structure: mutual relationships inside and between country groups[a] of INSEAD participants in 1967

Country groups	No. of participants — Total in study		Appearing on sociogram[b]			Mutual relationships per participant — Total		Inside country group		Out of country group			Degree of mixing[f]
	Rank order	No.	No.	%	Rank order	Total no.	%	No.	%	No.	%	Rank order	
USA and Canada	1.5	6	6	100	2	4.33	100	0.33	8	4.00	92	1	+0.5
Switzerland	3.5	10	7	70	3	4.60	100	0.80	17	3.80	83	2.5	+1.0
Scandinavian countries[c]	1.5	6	5	85	1	4.00	100	0.67	17	3.33	83	2.5	1.0
Mediterranean countries[d]	3.5	10	7	70	3	4.09	100	0.82	20	3.27	80	4	0.5
Britain	5	16	9	56	5	3.56	100	1.13	31	2.44	69	5	=
German-speaking countries[e]	6	18	13	72	6	4.39	100	1.67	38	2.72	62	6	=
France	7	34	23	68	7	3.47	100	1.82	53	1.65	47	7	=

[a] Only country groups with at least six participants in the study. These include 100 of the 115 who participated in the study.

[b] The numbers of participants appearing on the sociograms (Figures 6.4 and 6.5) are smaller than the total number of participants in the study because the sociograms include only participants with mutual relationships on two, three, and all four indicators (i.e. do not include mutual choices for one indicator only).

[c] 'Scandinavian countries' include participants from Denmark, Norway, Sweden, and Finland.

[d] 'Mediterranean countries' include participants from Israel (5 participants), Italy (3), and Lebanon (2).

[e] 'German-speaking countries' include participants from Austria (4) and Germany (14).

[f] This is the difference between the rank order of the number of participants appearing on the sociograms, and the rank order of the mutual relationships per participant out of country groups as a percentage of the total mutual relationships per person. The rank order of countries as to 'degree of mixing' is therefore as follows: mixing more than relative number of participants merits—USA and Canada, as well as Switzerland; mixing in proportion to their relative number of participants—Britain, German-speaking countries, and France; mixing less than their relative number of participants merits—Mediterranean countries and, even more so, the Scandinavian countries.

differences in the relationships and attitudes towards research tools, and variances between the 1966 and 1967 classes. Such figures mean that an institution like INSEAD has to limit the participation from individual countries, as indeed it does.[97]

The conclusion to be drawn from the above analysis of the social structure of the INSEAD class of 1967 is that INSEAD's formal structure, both the living arrangements and the learning process, has an overwhelming effect on the multinationalization of the INSEAD participants in its MBA programme. This multinationalization was witnessed, of course, only towards the termination of the academic year and does not necessarily mean that these same people will maintain similar behaviour in their professional and social life beyond INSEAD.

We intend to find out more about the managerial behaviour of INSEAD graduates, comparing them to matched MBA peers, graduates of national business and management schools, in the organizations where they are employed. The basic hypothesis we propose is that the managerial behaviour of INSEAD graduates would be 'multinational', while the managerial behaviour of those matched to them would be 'national'. The expectation that INSEAD graduates would manifest multinational managerial behaviour is not, on the whole, based on the multinational training which they receive during their one-year MBA studies at INSEAD. It is rather based primarily on our finding that INSEAD attracts *a priori* graduate students who have the ingredients required for becoming multinational managers. These ingredients include such things as having lived for prolonged periods of time outside their countries before coming to INSEAD, and/or speaking several languages and/or being married to another nationality, and/or having parents of two different nationalities, and/or coming from an unstratified social structure, and/or belonging to a national culture which easily lends itself to multinationalism, and/or having had a first degree university education in a liberal arts and social sciences area.[98]

On the other hand, multinational corporations, as well as other organizations who have people employed in foreign countries (including all the media organizations, foreign offices, etc.), require many more people trained and developed for multinational assignments than those who are available with the above mentioned backgrounds. As we mentioned in the beginning of this section about national and multinational managers, a substantial part of what one needs in order to become a multinational manager could be acquired in management development courses.[99]

A series of studies has been conducted on the preparation of managers for employment outside their countries of origin by way of organizational development (OD) before their departure or during their expatriation.[100] The researchers claim that the conflicts which occur in the relationships between the head office and a multinational's sub-organizations in other countries could be attributed to the differences in their socio-cultural backgrounds.[101] One of the conclusions of their investigations was that it is necessary to develop managers who are to be sent abroad by the parent company *before* they reach the subsidiary company, so as to increase their understanding of, and sensitivity to, local conditions and adapt their managerial style to local expectations.

The same researchers showed in another study that a planned organizational change, including specific changes in managerial behaviour, could contribute to raising the morale in foreign subsidiaries of multinational corporations.[102] According to them, a future manager of foreign subsidiaries should be trained and developed, by the head office, in order to change his managerial behaviour, before he leaves for his foreign assignment. Such head office initiative motivates future managers to change their behaviour once they are abroad. The same authors say that there are several dangers in training the manager in and out of his organization once he is already abroad. The choice of a manager who turns out to be a failure is financially embarrassing to the company which has to incur the costs of transferring him, and psychologically embarrassing to the manager through loss of prestige, dignity, and face. The authors think that the training should be carried out by people who know the conditions in the country of destination and by experts in learning theory, since the main objective is the changing of managerial behaviour, adapting it to the characteristics of the new environment.[103]

On the other hand, it seems that the training of managers who are already involved in multinational management scores impressive results when it is done outside one's own organization. We would agree that bringing managers back from abroad for a training programme at the corporate head office involves dangers to both the person and the organization. Indeed, we believe that the type of training which would help to develop, even partially, a national into a multinational manager could not be achieved with a significant degree of success when carried out at the corporate headquarters, even *before* the manager's departure from his country. Except for informing expatriate managers of specific matters regarding their corporation and their task abroad, the training would better be performed in multinational management programmes run by management schools and centres.[104] We do agree that educating expatriate managers about the countries they go to, in advance of their departure for their assignments, is essential. This, however, is a completely different type of training from the one which helps managers to become more sensitive to culture-bound behaviour.

It seems to us that such a multinational management programme should include as little as possible of international business and commercial matters, and be essentially an organizational behaviour programme. As such, it should include three elements: first, training for interpersonal sensitivity;[105] secondly, learning about different cultural situations, preferably involving managers from one national culture encountering problems in another national culture, and taught by the case method of instruction; thirdly, providing the students with a fair amount of the dynamics of the TOS as it occurs in both national and multinational corporations, and in different countries.[106]

6.3 UNIVERSAL IMPLICATIONS OF MULTINATIONAL CORPORATIONS

We have already established that multinational corporations (MNCs, or multinationals) are concrete and definable. We have also concluded that their advent in the middle of the twentieth century was inevitable and that they are here to stay, encompassing more and more of the industrial and business activities of the world. Now that it is clear that we and our descendants will have to live with this extraordinary phenomenon, let us speculate about its impact on humanity. Are we facing a brighter, better, and safer world, or are we heading for what George Orwell and Anthony Burgess have so vividly projected in *Nineteen Eighty-four*[107] and *A Clockwork Orange*?

The dominant fact is that the MNCs are taking over some of the basic roles traditionally regarded as belonging to the nation states. The implications may be summed up as follows:

—the MNCs constitute barriers to war.
—They move technology, capital, know-how, and more advanced standards of living from the developed to the developing areas of the world, helping bridge existing economic gaps.
—They carry with them the most advanced managerial concepts and techniques.
—They induce less advanced nation states, through their mere presence, to change their cultural environments.

6.3.1 Encroachment on the Authority and Power of the Nation States

Over the years, large corporations have undertaken more and more services for their employees traditionally considered in the Western world as the province of the state.[108] We have also witnessed increasing manifestations of so-called 'public responsibility'. The latter usually starts with the organization contributing to the socio-cultural life of the community within which it operates.[109] The next step is usually a contribution by the organization to some other aspect of life in the country where it operates, not excluding local political activity. The third step consists in the organization allowing, or perhaps even encouraging, its managers to participate in public activities of a variety of types, eventually assuming governmental positions on a dollar-a-year basis (i.e. performing their work voluntarily, without being remunerated).

The degree of public responsibility taken by business corporations depends on two factors: the size of the organization, which includes its scope of decision making, and the socio-cultural system including the political system of the country in which it operates. Thus, small and relatively poor organizations cannot afford such responsibilities where the socio-cultural system is favourable, while even the largest US corporations operating in a country like the USSR are in no position to attempt to undertake them even if they want to.

Obviously, the larger the corporation, the more power and authority it tends to assume.[110] The government does not mind so long as the corporation contributes towards the maintenance of the services which are within its own responsibility. However, the moment it feels that the corporation's actions run counter to its policies, it introduces legislation against it. This becomes problematic when the government is dealing with an MNC. The dependence of countries on MNCs is steadily increasing and governments are becoming less able to discipline them.[111] This is why one could predict, as we have already done, that in the not-too-distant future governments will get together to consider joint action against the manoeuvres of MNCs. This has already happened in specific limited fields like that of currency flow and exchange. Such collaboration between governments may turn out to be the best, albeit unintended, contribution of the MNCs to humanity.

Two points must be obvious from the above discussion. First, MNCs are disliked on the whole by nation states.[112] Secondly, in order to be able to maintain, strengthen, and expand its position within different nation states, the multinational corporation cannot be American, British, French, German, Japanese, etc. The more it is *not* perceived as a corporation of another country, the better its chances are in this or that nation state. We have already discussed this in the previous section.

This is why state-owned enterprises (SOE) *cannot* operate successfully for long in other countries unless they are in monopoly positions like some of the SOE which are in minerals and oil, or when there exist mutual trade agreements between their countries.[113]

6.3.2 Prevention of Wars

The topic of war and peace is as old as history and there is a real question whether wars are altogether unavoidable, considering that 'the imagination of man's heart is evil from his youth' (Genesis 8: 21). It is clear, however, that the more the world advances technologically, the more horror war entails. This goes for localized wars but, of course, it is the prospect of an atomic global war which hangs like the shadow of doom over the human race.

It is here that the MNCs make a significant contribution by preventing armed conflict and perhaps removing its causes, primarily the economic ones. An MNC operating in several countries can ill afford to lose its assets, customer markets, manpower, suppliers, and capital sources, which would be in jeopardy if any of these countries were involved in war among themselves. An outstanding example is Fiat. Whether through licensing or straightforward ownership, the Agnellis, Fiat's manager-owners, have been directly connected with a major part of the car industry in several European countries, e.g. Italy, Spain, France, and the USSR. The involvement of any of these countries on different sides in a war would probably mean a mortal blow to the corporation. There are, indeed, indications that MNCs actively try to prevent the development of situations which might lead to belligerent activities against international business operations resulting in the expulsion of the MNCs from this or that country.[114]

The role of the multinationals in this respect goes far beyond that of a fire brigade. The explorations into *détente* between the USA, on one hand, and China and the USSR, on the other, have been prompted by the MNCs who urged the US Government to open the way for them into these vast potential markets.[115]

6.3.3 Narrowing the Gap Between the Rich and Poor Parts of the World

One of the major problems of the world is the gap between its rich and poor areas. Although the nations have been meeting and seeking solutions, the resulting plans fall short of the needs or are impracticable.[116] In fact, it seems that bringing the poorer nation states closer to the richer ones will be achieved through pressures from the grass roots rather than from the top.

The MNCs, in their search for environments in which they hope to find new and, from their point of view, more suitable supplies of labour, trade unions, customers, suppliers, governments, etc., are also attracted to the poorer countries of the world. Their impact on the economies of these countries produces pressures for higher standards of living and levels of education. In this latter respect, in particular, government efforts have hitherto produced negligible results. For example, African and Asian university graduates returning to their countries often find neither the jobs nor a congenial atmosphere in which they could apply their education productively. Many of them stay in the countries where they were trained, or return to them following frustrating experiences. This situation is being remedied to some extent by the MNCs which provide the employment opportunities while gradually raising the level of the positions staffed with local residents, training them themselves or sending them to appropriate universities.

6.3.4 Using and Spreading Modern and Advanced Managerial Concepts and Technologies

MNCs resort to the most sophisticated concepts and techniques available, both in their current operations and in planning for the future. They are organizations which try to forecast how the environment will develop during the next 10, 20, 30, or even 50 years, and take these forecasts into consideration in their own long-range planning. By contrast, democratic governments limit their 'future' to the period between one election and another which never exceeds ten years. As for totalitarian regimes, although they speak in terms of 'eternity' (Hitler's 1000-year Reich!), their practical lifespan is of approximately the same order as that of their democratic counterparts.[117] Governments often make use of the environmental forecasts and analyses of the MNCs; conversely they may resent and even undermine the MNCs because of their advanced planning activities.[118] As MNCs move from one country to another, they bring with them their accumulated knowledge and know-how, managerial concepts and technologies. This does not mean, of course, that they introduce the most advanced concepts and technologies into every single country. They do, however, go as far as possible.

6.3.5 Inducing Cultures to Adapt to Economic Development Needs

MNCs are what one could refer to as 'change agents'. They are undoubtedly the most powerful cause of the convergence of cultures,[119] as a result of the effects of spreading technology and its attendant factors, such as education, standard of living, etc.

The effect of the MNCs on nation states, in inducing their cultures to adapt to economic developmental needs, may be seen in what has happened in some European countries since the Second World War.

There is no doubt that Marshall Plan aid to Germany contributed enormously to that country's postwar economy. It seems, however, that Germany's achievement is not only in regaining its technological lead over other European countries, but also in adapting its managerial structures to the requirements of the ever-growing scope of decision making. The latter is due to the MNCs rather than to US government aid.

Germany was the country which opened its doors wide to the MNCs, thanks, apparently, to its traditional ability to adapt relatively quickly to new behavioural trends. Take, for example, interorganizational managerial mobility. The stereotype German manager always entered an organization at the lowest level and slowly advanced, in an apprenticeship fashion, up the hierarchy, never moving to another organization. Today, the rate of interorganizational mobility in Germany is higher than in any other European country and the relevant attitudes and norms are rapidly changing (see above Tables 5.4 and 5.5 in pp. 169 and 170).

The effects of the MNCs on the national culture are felt even in France, where behaviour is both more individualistic and more traditional than in Germany. One 'classical' contrast between the two nations is said to be that every German wants to buy what his neighbour has just bought, while every Frenchman wants something different from what his neighbour owns. Organizational behaviour changes may be discerned in France within the boundaries of subsidiaries of MNCs and, although only a few of these changes have spilled over into the environmental socio-cultural system, this is a beginning.

6.3.6 Positive Effects of Negative Characteristics of Multinational Corporations, and the Oil Exception

The multinational seeks the most helpful environment in which to operate: countries in which labour is cheapest, capital is least expensive, customers are the least selective and demanding, etc. The inclination to move multinational operations and capital from one country to another could be disastrous for some countries. However, these same potentially negative consequences provide some of the most important positive possibilities for multinational corporations. The human factor resources which have been menaced by the multinationals—the employees, customers, suppliers, and other factors of decision making of the multinationals in the various countries—have not been slow to react. Thus, for example, trade unions in the same industrial areas in the different countries have been getting together, creating an international trade union composed of over 100 unions of many countries. (See note 54 at the end of this chapter.) This international union is meant to react to those multinationals who may harm the workers in one country by moving their operations to other countries. Another example: the governors of eleven national banks of Western industrialized countries have established a forum for preventing the activities of multinationals from having negative effects on the money markets of these and other countries. They have established ways of counteracting multinationals' sudden transfers of huge amounts of money from one country to another in order to protect economies from being severely damaged by such acts. This collaboration of the governors of the national banks proved effective when the new, potentially large money-movers turned out to be the Arabian oil sheiks.[120] Similar cooperation and coordination may be predicted and may actually develop among the human factor resources in other FDM, such as the customers in different countries. This brings us to the one international human factor whose reaction to the multinationals has not contributed positively to international understanding. This is the factor of the suppliers of oil. Their collaboration in OPEC (Organization of Petroleum Exporting Countries) is similar to the collaboration among trade unions and among the national banks. They, too, wanted to protect themselves against the ill effects of multinationals. The OPEC collaboration, however, has not contributed to building bridges between the nations of the world and improving the relations among their peoples. Unfortunately, it has had exactly the opposite effect because the great majority of OPEC members, organized in OAPEC, belong to the same ethnic, religious, and linguistic bloc. They are sparsely populated and have acquired statehood recently. As in other cases, the gap between the requirements for the smooth operation of a nation, on one side, and the constraints of the cultural and educational reality on the other, has created an extreme nationalistic anachronism. It can be predicted, however, on the basis of the dynamics of the TOS, that this exceptionally nationalistic reaction of the oil suppliers to multinationals will be only a short-lived phenomenon.

Let us elaborate this prediction and explain some of the underlying assumptions and conditions. We have already demonstrated that the appearance and future of multinationals is a result of the dynamics of the TOS which has operated ever since the Industrial Revolution. Consequently, multinationals are inevitable and they are here to stay, growing from strength to strength. However, there are bound to be setbacks to continuous growth.

The states themselves are the main obstacle which multinationals encounter and which interrupt their development and may even reverse it for a time. The more self-centred the states are, the more they will try to reverse the trend, obstructing the multinationals and trying to regain national power.[121] National self-centredness plus political doctrinairism and religious bigotry limit operations by the multinationals to the detriment of the country in which they operate. Nevertheless, even emerging countries in which the opposition to anything foreign and international (the so-called 'Coca-Cola syndrome') is enormous during their initial statehood,[122] often succumb within a few years to the entry of multinationals. Even a politically doctrinaire country like the Soviet Union tries to have the multinational cake and eat it too, by acquiring the technologies and products of the multinationals without allowing them to operate organizationally within the USSR. The danger is that before the multinationals acquire enough power to prevent the states from committing their follies, a nationalistic country like the USSR could overpower and take over the whole free world. As a free world is an underlying condition and assumption of the dynamics of the TOS, it is necessary that the multinationals spread into those countries which could undermine the same free world.

The development of OPEC, and especially OAPEC, is a somewhat different phenomenon from that of the USSR, but not unrelated to it. They represent emerged countries with a predominantly common religion (Islam), language (Arabic), geographical conditions (mostly desert and a hot climate), and a culture unprepared for the acceptance of the TOS and the accompanying managerial structures. OPEC constituted towards the end of the 1970s about four fifths of the world production of oil, while the ten Arab OAPEC countries constituted about four fifths of OPEC, having a dominant influence in the latter's decision-making process.

There are, however, three main reasons why the collaboration between the oil suppliers against the multinational oil corporations does not yield an understanding between the nations of the world and will not last for long. The first is a decision-making process reason, while the other two have to do with the technological-scientific and the political systems of the wider environment.

In order to increase and strengthen their national entities, the Arab countries have first of all to increase their scope of decision making. In order to do so it is necessary to grow simultaneously in all the factors of decision making: management, workers, suppliers, customers, banks, shareholders, etc. Under some conditions an increase of the wider environment helps the constituent countries (as in the case of the EEC, the so-called Common Market) in the growth of their SDM. This, however, has to be accompanied by the adaptation of all the environmental systems to the growth. Thus, in a country like India, in spite of the large population, the circumstances in the systems of the money market, the consumer market, and, especially, the technological-scientific system, lag far behind the potential of the large working and consuming population.

The OAPEC countries do not generally have the population to support the possible growth in the SDM. They could have joined with countries like India, Pakistan, and Bangladesh, and created a basis for combined national development; this, however, they are not inclined to do. They also have constraints on their internal SDM growth, because of religious and other socio-cultural systems. All this explains why they invest their revenues outside their countries.

The second reason has to do with the reaction of the multinational corporations, as well as of the industrialized and highly industrialized countries, to their dependence on OPEC and the escalating price of oil. The search for alternative energy resources is their answer. The present (1982) oil abundance can only be short-lived, unless substantial oil deposits are discovered in industrial and highly industrial countries, other than the Soviet Union. The discovery of large oil resources in the Western world, and in the non-Arab and non-communist countries, too, would change the oil suppliers' collaboration radically and make it similar to those among the governors of the state banks, and among various trade unions.[123]

The third reason is a political one. The intention of the Soviet Union is to take over the oilfields of the Middle East.[124] Neither the multinational corporations nor the Western democracies can allow this to happen. For the latter it would mean the end of the free world. For the multinationals it would mean the end of their existence. In fact, this may eventually lead, probably some time in the first half of the twenty-first century, to the abolition of control by nations over raw materials upon which their survival depends.[125] This does not mean the complete elimination of national sovereignty. There would still be many responsibilities for nations to discharge, including the protection of their peoples against some of the evils of multinationals.[126]

6.4 SUMMARY

This chapter is devoted to the final stage in the dynamics of the TOS, the multinationals. Thus, we have traced throughout the book the development of organizations, from their creation by entrepreneurs, in an entrepreneurial structure, through the various stages of SDM, and have studied managerial structures and characteristics, as well as the attitudes and values of managers. We have seen that this developmental journey is almost as inevitable as the development of a person from infancy through childhood to adulthood. (See the organizational example about family organizations in chapter 4.) There are two main differences between the lives of organizations and those of human beings. The first is that, theoretically at least, the life of an organization could be eternal. The second is that temporary regressions in the dynamics of the growth of organizations are considered to be normal phenomena (e.g. the contraction in the SDM and managerial structure during war and emergency environmental conditions), while among human beings similar regressions are not considered normal.

Had this book been written in the 1930s or 1940s, one could have predicted the emergence of multinationals before their first appearance in the world arena in the 1950s.

We have studied the growth of the international organizations which existed before the Second World War and the subsequent multinationals. The latter have a minimum amount of the following TOS ingredients: (a) their SDM is spread over two or more countries distinctly different from each other in their wider environments, especially in their national cultures; (b) they are managed in a 'multistructure', a federation of two or more of the basic structures—entrepreneurial, function, product/service line, and area; and (c) their managements adopt different degrees of supra-cultural attitudes—but while accepting the constraints of the countries involved, they operate with little special loyalty to the interests of any one country.

Below we present our two main organizational examples for the material included in this chapter.

Israel's TOS

This organizational example describes the TOS of Israel as a whole. This is an example of the wider environments in which multinationals operate. The first part is devoted to the Israeli socio-cultural system. It describes the effects of the cultures in which Jews lived outside Israel in the second half of the nineteenth century (nicknamed the 'ghetto', the 'Bakshish' and the 'naive socialism' cultures) on the emerging socio-cultural structure of Israel. It also discusses the predominant informal managerial structure in which Israeli decision making takes place.

The example demonstrates that the conceptualization of the TOS could be applied in order to describe and analyse the different organizational systems and how the management keeps them together, not only in business corporations, but in a nation which serves as a wider environment for them. The government administration is considered as a TOS which engulfs the whole decision-making process within that country and with other countries.

Also, this example shows clearly what happens when the gap between the SDM and the managerial structure is much too wide. Israel's SDM requires an advanced multistructure for its decision making. However, for almost three decades it has been run in an informal managerial structure, which is suitable for small one-product/service line and simple technology organizations.

Multinational Corporations

This organizational example is based on the late 1960s research of John Stopford on 170 US-based multinational corporations which had operating units in at least six countries. Stopford tried to correlate two changes in managerial structure for every one of his 170 organizations (340 structural changes). The structure in all these situations in Stopford's research was the formal structure, as presented in an organizational chart, rather than the managerial structure, as described and established by us. This was the only way in which he could do it, as his was a historical research based on the data in the archives of the 170 corporations. He compared the changes with the contextual conditions of the organization at the time, i.e. with all possible decision-making variables affecting the managerial structure (e.g. the number of employees, the total sales turnover, the total assets, etc.). He found that the structure was highly correlated with the degree of product/service diversity and the degree of geographical dispersal, measured in simple terms of sales turnover ratios, as well as the technological level of the organization. This research offers two main contributions to the conceptualization and fundamentals of the TOS: first, his discovery that on the whole, organizations move along the same path from one stage of managerial structure to another; secondly, his findings relating to the effects of product diversity, geographical dispersal, and technology on the structure.

NOTES

1 One of the few to deal with the question 'Why multinational corporations and why now?' was Raymond Vernon (1971). He, however, belittles the significance of the phenomenon and, in fact, claims that multinational corporations have been in existence since ancient times. Samuel Pisar similarly maintained (in a panel discussion broadcast over the French radio on 11 February 1973) that the first multinational organization was the Catholic Church and that the first clash between a

nation state and such an organization involved Henry II, King of England, and Thomas à Becket, Archbishop of Canterbury (of *Murder in the Cathedral* fame). In the latter context, although I have myself pointed out the international scope of the decision-making process in some organizations in ancient times (e.g. Egypt under Joseph—Weinshall, 1973d), I beg to differ on definition rather than on fact. The Catholic Church in Thomas à Becket's day was not a multinational organization in the sense that multinational corporations are defined and described in this chapter, although it is certainly so today.

2   Attempts to define multinational corporations without making allowances for their behavioural aspects usually end up in confusion (e.g. Aharoni, 1971). This is so because the underlying analyses fail to explore their evolution and dynamics or to compare their behaviour with that of other types of organizations.

3   The actual number of countries is immaterial (Brooke and Remmers, 1970, p. 2), so long as we are concerned with at least two countries which differ with regard to their basic influence on the scope of the decision-making of the organization. Different researchers have suggested different numbers of countries in which the corporation maintains manufacturing facilities, in order to comply with an 'appropriate' definition of a multinational corporation. Thus John Stopford, following the example of Raymond Vernon's other collaborators in his worldwide research (Vernon, 1971), defines 'multinational corporations with headquarters in the U.S.' as those US corporations which have manufacturing facilities in at least six countries. Seev Hirsch, on the other hand, claims that a multinational corporation could operate even in two countries (Hirsch, 1971). It seems to us that this minimum suffices so long as we accept incorporation of the behavioural characteristics of the multinational corporation in its definition.

The fact of the matter is that Vernon's group adopted the minimum of six because they already had a sufficiently large sample, as it were. Hirsch, on the other hand, studied multinational corporations with headquarters in smaller countries and, had he not chosen a minimum of two, his sample would have been too small. It is strange that writers should try to specify a minimal number without relevance to any pragmatic research considerations or conceptual framework; it sometimes looks like picking a number nobody else has used previously (Aharoni, 1971, p. 35).

4   Probably the most important discovery of Geert Hofstede's renowned cross-cultural research regarding the variables which affect the cultures of different nations, is about the significant effects that the climate of the country has on the behaviour of its people (Hofstede, 1979). He found that there is a significant correlation between the distance of the capital city of the country from the Equator (i.e. its latitude), and the organizational *power distance* among superiors and subordinates. The power distance is the willingness to criticize the superior, as well as the position on a degree of supervision scale (which has very close supervision at its one end, and having a superior who is just an adviser to his subordinates, at the other end).

5   See the organizational example describing the Israeli TOS at the end of this chapter. Israelis were actually managed in an entrepreneurial structure for 25 years. The description of Israel's TOS highlights the problems and dysfunctions of managing an enormous SDM, in a managerial structure which is suitable for creating and launching a completely new organization, or for running a one-product line, low technology, single location organization, like a grocery shop.

6   Just as the government manages the economy in a highly rigid functional structure in a period of war, so also business organizations have to be structured in a formally centralized way in order to accommodate the constraints imposed upon them by government. When the Israeli Government managed the economy for 25 years in an entrepreneurial structure (see above note 5), all the chief executives of business corporations could be considered to have been the entrepreneurial aides of the entrepreneur who ran the Israeli economy in an informally centralized structure.

Every one of these CEs was actually operating his organization as an assignment received from the entrepreneur of the Israeli economy at the time. In order that executives in every organization could contribute to the survival of their organization, they had to have informal access to government officials who had the fate of the economic organizations in their hands because they were able to offer or to withhold resources which they needed for their survival (labour or capital or supply or customer markets). This in turn made it essential for the managers of an organization to operate primarily in informal relationships among themselves.

7   One example of this is the Mafia, described in an organizational example in chapter 2. The SDM of Mafia-owned organizations is much smaller than that of non-Mafia organizations which seem to be identical to them in their product/service diversity, technological level, and geographical dispersal. This is because the Mafia ignores the environmental systems of the employment, money, and consumer markets and the environmental socio-cultural system. This is why it is much easier for the Mafia organizations to ascertain the continued cooperation of the FDM. Consequently, the SDM of the Mafia-owned organizations are much smaller than those of non-Mafia-owned organizations of the same kind and size.

8   We have already referred to it in a general way in the beginning of note 6.

9   The bulk of note 6 is devoted to the inevitable entrepreneurial structures of organizations in an economy which is run by an entrepreneur, who concentrates the SDM of the whole country in an informally centralized structure. Since an entrepreneurial structure is most unsuitable, under any conditions, for running the SDM of a whole country, we shall not discuss such a situation further.

10   We believe that a *laissez-faire* regime is for the good of any country, from the point of view of the liberties of its individual inhabitants as well as their access to advanced products, services, and technologies. This is true not only in socialist states but in any other totalitarian regime as well. Thus the various kinds of fascist regimes like those in Italy and Germany until the Second World War produced the same disadvantages for their citizens as the communist regimes. Only in time of danger to the survival of a country is it necessary and advisable formally to centralize its economy. It is interesting to note that, during such precarious periods for a nation state, some of its genius is manifested in extraordinary inventions and innovations. This may be explained much as we explained the increase in the rate of innovation as a result of the ever-growing intensity of the struggle for survival among organizations in chapter 2 (specifically in subsection 2.1.3, dealing with the total innovation growth). Incidentally, during such periods of perceived danger to a nation state, the employees of industrial, business, and other non-military organizations are found to be trying much more diligently—with greater loyalty, accuracy, and punctuality—to cooperate with the organization than in normal times.

11   As we mentioned in chapter 4, a suitable managerial structure for a given SDM is established in a way similar to artillery range setting, the method in which the guns are set right on target: first try a managerial structure which seem not advanced enough for the SDM, and then try a more advanced structure for the same SDM. If neither of them is suitable, the managerial structure between them is the right one. This is what we do when searching for the right managerial structure for a business organization in a country at war where the decision-making processes are concentrated by the government.

12   The only entrepreneurs which one encounters in such emergency periods are war profiteers, who are illegally trading in rationed commodities, or even in armaments.

13   These are countries with which we are fairly well acquainted and in which the activities and interests of multinational corporations are relatively large.

14   Such a periodical analysis of a country would probably include a survey of the political and economic conditions.

15   We have definite OPEC and non-OPEC countries in mind.

280

16   The distance of the capital city from the Equator is represented to a greater or lesser degree by all the remaining seven systems of the socio-cultural system and of government: the societal structure, education, legal, political-economic, personal contact, personal (informal) contact, bribery–slush funds, and the regime systems. The climatic effects of the distance of the capital city from the Equator are discussed above in note 4.

17   The self-criticism of the British generally, and of British management since the mid-1950s, has replaced the arrogance and conceit which were attributed to them until then. The main reason for this may well have been the aftermath of Britain's phenomenal stand against the Germans in the early 1940s, and the country's difficulties in recuperating its economy and the loss of its empire. By contrast, their foes in the Second World War and the countries overrun by the Germans were generously helped to rebuild their economies by the USA. The effects of the grumbling of the British and the self-assuredness, sometimes the rhetorical boasting, of the European continental countries in the 1950s, 1960s, and 1970s were evident in both the behaviour of the people in these countries and in some of the things which were said about Britain and the countries on the other side of the channel. There has probably been some British self-criticism as a result of the negative declarations about themselves by the British and the positive ones of the French. We can assume that in slashing at themselves the British followed to some degree the stereotype they had created. Likewise, the French may have followed to some degree the stereotyped behaviour attributed to France by such leaders as Charles de Gaulle. Such stereotyped behaviour worked like self-fulfilling prophecies. Thus Herman Kahn of the Hudson Institute, predicted imminent doom for the UK and prosperity for France, which he thought would overtake even Germany (e.g. Kahn and Weiner, 1967). His predictions covered a short enough period for all of us to see that he was completely wrong. (In subsection 6.1.3.3, we point out that the length of time for which forecasting and long-range planning is reasonable, is diminishing from about 30 years in the middle of the twentieth century to about 10 years towards the end of the century.)

18   The British have the advantage over other countries regarding the dynamics of their TOS and this is probably the result of their democratic society. This, we believe, has to do primarily with two geopolitical characteristics of the British Isles. First, there is the distance of London from the Equator, which we have already mentioned in above note 4. London (and the south coast of England) has an advantage over all the other capital cities of Europe in that it has the mildest climate both in summer and winter, the latter because of its nearness to the Gulf Stream, the warm sea current from the Bay of Mexico.

Second, the isolation of the British islanders from their neighbours made them sea-faring and put them in a better position to fight off any invaders. Their spectacular stand against the Germans in the Second World War is one example of this. The interesting thing is that their islands made them more or less unique compared with the other European countries in that they never seriously tried to annex any territory belonging to other European countries. Even their invasion of France in Joan of Arc's time was not a real invasion when compared with the Swedish invasions to the south as far as Turkey in the seventeenth century. The only country in Northern Europe which displayed similar behaviour throughout its history is Norway. The Norwegians, another sea-faring nation, did not even create an 'empire' of conquered colonial countries.

Incidentally, British behaviour, throughout modern history until the 1950s, has been reminiscent of the behaviour of Israelis, who have been a political 'island' since the establishment of the State of Israel (Weinshall, 1968). Both peoples are more democratic than many others. Both demonstrated a large degree of pride, arrogance, and conceit following their stand against the onslaughts of their neighbours in the middle of the twentieth century. People of both nations readily emigrate, unlike those of most of the remaining highly industrialized nations. (This is one of the major problems of multinational corporations which have difficulty in inducing their executives to live in foreign countries.)

As the British are more democratic than many other nations, it is easier for them to adapt themselves and their organizations to the dynamics of the TOS. One of our organizational examples (in chapter 4) compares the managerial behaviour of the British, French, and Germans and clearly shows that the managerial structures in the UK are more suitable for larger organizations than those in France and Germany.

19 This is contrary to common belief. We have already indicated that we suspect people like Herman Kahn (mentioned in note 17) were influenced by the behavioural stereotypes of the British, including their reputation for a socially stratified structure. Cross-cultural comparisons of social stratification, measured by the degree of social mobility, indicate that British society is less stratified than the societies of Australia, Denmark, France, India, the USA, Brazil, Sweden, Holland, Japan and even, to a larger extent, Norway, West Germany, Puerto Rico, Hungary, Finland, Italy, and Belgium (Weinshall, 1977b, p. 177).

20 Let us consider, for example, the employment market in times of peace and war. In peacetime, an abundance of employees, although devastating to the unemployed, has a positive effect on productivity, which is a central aspect of industrialization; or vice versa, the more advanced the industrialization, the higher the unemployment (see Twiss and Weinshall, 1980, pp. 190–195). In wartime, on the other hand, an abundance of employment (i.e. high overemployment), as a result of the recruitment of a large number of people into the armed forces, would harm the economy less than in conditions of shortage in manpower; this is because of the moral pressures on those who do not join the armed forces to help the 'war effort'.

21 'Socialist democracies', or 'popular democracies', are probably among the most ambiguous and misleading terms in the political vocabulary. These are names which the communist countries gave themselves. They have very little to do with what we mean in this book by democracy.

22 The same could be said about moving from the centre right to the extreme right. The more the regime moves to the right, the more autocratic it is. In other words, democracy is the antithesis of extremity and domination in the political and ideological realm. Let us stress that while a fascist regime is always *totalitarian*, a socialist regime could be anywhere between *laissez-faire* and totalitarian. Thus a 'social democratic' regime is generally associated with a *laissez-faire* democracy, while a communist regime on the one hand and a national socialist regime (e.g. the German Nazi regime) on the other, are typical of autocracies.

23 The contents (ideas, language, sequence, etc.) of Table 6.3 are not ours. This insight into the comparison between business, government, and military organizations was presented to the Doctoral Instruction Group (DIG) of the Harvard Business School (HBS) in 1958/1959 by their business policy professor, the late Richard (Dick) Merriam. This is an opportunity for the first writer to pay his tribute to the memory of a wonderful person and great teacher.

Dick Merriam was my teacher both in the DIG and subsequently in a reading seminar in general management, also in 1958/1959. He was the teacher who first led me through the development of knowledge in general management and organization, from the times of its originators, such as Frederick Taylor, Elton Mayo, and Chester Barnard, to the time of our classes respectively, 50, 30, and 20 years later.

He did not write up the vast body of knowledge and wisdom which he transmitted to his students year after year. A mutual friend and admirer of Merriam's once said to me: 'Why should he spend two years on writing a book which will be read at best by several thousand students and then buried by the multitudes of other books and be forgotten?' Instead, he taught during these two years, say, 50 doctoral students who in the course of time will become teachers of tens of thousands of students spreading Dick Merriam's thoughts and insights. I hope that the person whom I quote, who was my teacher but also Dick Merriam's student, was and will be right. This note, in any case, is an acknowledgement of my intellectual debt to Richard Merriam.

It is difficult to ascribe one's thoughts and ideas to their proper origins and sources. We have tried to attribute the sources of the TOS to those upon whom we feel we mostly drew. Our knowledge about the original contributions of these people came mainly from Merriam's classes. It is much easier to discover where one's ideas have gone than whether they were original or derived from others.

Table 6.3 is copied from the notes I took during Dick Merriam's class on two sides of a page headed 'Difference between business and others'. The heading of this table and those of the columns are mine. All the rest is Dick Merriam's including the order of the 'comparative factors'.

There are two ratings in factor 8 (formal and informal organization) and one in factor 9 (stigmas of status) which were missing from the notes taken during Professor Merriam's classes. We have filled the three missing ratings with what we believe he may have said.

24 Nevertheless, we sincerely hope that combat armies in whatever form will disappear from the world arena some time during the first half of the twenty-first century. The reason for our hope is presented in subsection 6.3.2.

25 In an article called 'What the army learned from business', Richard S. Gabriel (1979) (who published, together with Paul L. Savage, a book on *Crisis in Command*) presents a convincing, gloomy description of what has happened to the US Army as a result of incorporating a number of techniques and practices from business. The final sentence of Gabriel's article is: 'For we are now producing an Army that can meet all the "system's norms"; its only problem is that it won't stand the test of combat.'

In the early 1960s, we received from a close friend, who was the minister for the Navy in the UK at the time, his explanation for the abolition of conscription. He spoke about the financial saving to the British Government. We replied that abolishing conscription also means giving up its positive aspects. These include, primarily, military preparedness, but also the following advantages to the young soldiers: training young people to be on their own, yet appreciative of their parents' homes; giving them enough time following their secondary education to ponder on what they want to do in life, whether to go on to higher education and what to study; making them interact and live with people from walks of life other than their own and helping them better to appreciate what their country does for them, i.e. to become more patriotic.

26 In all other democracies (and there are currently fewer than 30 nations in which the regimes are really democratic) Montesquieu's separation into three systems is only partially adhered to. While in the USA the legislative, executive, and judicial systems are independent of each other, in the other democracies the legislative system is supreme. What the legislature passes becomes the law of the land. The legislative and the executive systems are completely and rigidly separated from the judicial system in every democratic nation; but only in the USA are the legislative and the executive systems separated too.

27 During peacetime, the army is run and trained in a formalized fashion. This requires an officer and non-commissioned officer corps which is suitable for a formally

centralized structure. Combat in wartime, however, requires officers and non-commissioned officers who can operate in a much more autonomous fashion. In terms of Gabriel's (1979) article, it is possible to imagine some kind of streamlining of an army for efficiency in peacetime, but any such practices in wartime may drive an army to its defeat. The only way to overcome this structural ambiguity is to try to have men who are suitable to command soldiers in a rigid and formally centralized way, leading the soldiers in peacetime; and men who are suitable to command them in an autonomous way as their leaders in wartime. At the lower levels of command, this is practised by having different commanders at the training bases from those who command at the same levels in the field. The formalized, higher ranking peacetime officers are rarely replaced at the outbreak of hostilities. (The only instance that we know of was the exchange of all the senior officers in command of brigades in the Israeli Defence Army, by the chief of staff, Moshe Dayan, at the outbreak of the 1956 Sinai War.) Because such a thing is not ordinarily done, all armies have problems with their commanding officers at the beginning of a war. Only in due course are they replaced by other officers who prove to be more suitable for combat command. This is probably one of the main reasons for the much quicker rate of promotion during wartime (the other being, of course, the casualties among officers, who have to be replaced).

28 Chester Barnard, in *The Functions of the Executive* (1938), was the first to combine these two yardsticks of performance.

29 In wartime, the immediate environment of the army is found in the enemy armies. The wider environment in wartime is found in the conditions of the terrain, the air, and the sea in which the army is fighting the enemy. In peacetime, the immediate environment is composed of organizations competing for the resources the army needs for its survival; for the financial resources, the competition comes from other government agencies, ministries, or departments; for the human resources the army competes with every organization in the country for its manpower and supplies.

30 At least theoretically one could envisage government-owned business which is engaged in military activities. We do not know whether any mercenary organization clandestinely belongs to a government, or if any terrorist organization sells its services for money. Had there been instances of either or both, we would have witnessed an integrated business-government-military organization.

31 Concerning only the three first environmental systems—the employment, capital, and consumer markets.

32 Now concerning all the five environmental systems—those mentioned and the technological-scientific and the socio-cultural systems as well.

33 A comprehensive list of the literature on state-owned enterprises is presented by Judd (1981).

34 Like the École Polytechnique in France which is an engineering school where all the students are also trained to become officers, and the ROTC (Reserve Officer Training Corps) in certain universities in the USA; these are examples of universities in which the army educates its officers in various academic fields while it trains them as combat officers on their campuses.

35 Thus, the first author considers the British Army, in which he served for four years during the Second World War, to have been his best school, when compared to all the academic schools he has attended. Of course, the military is more a school for life than a school for advancing one's profession and/or intellect.

36 Unless there exists a manifest preference for customer-clients of one kind or another in an organization, the only way to get rid of a certain customer population is to exchange the product/service which they obtain from the organization for another one which will attract another customer population.

37 Both means by which universities and professors discriminate between the

students—i.e. programme entrance requirements and establishment of the course content and level—are similar to the discrimination between customers and clients in other types of organizations. There, too, the discrimination between customers and clients (or workers, or suppliers, or shareholders) is effected by differentiation in the products/services and in the prices required for obtaining them.

38   This is as if the marketing or service people of a business organization would tell the purchasers of, say, a stereo system or an encyclopaedia that they have not utilized them enough, or not in the most appropriate manner, and, therefore, the organization is taking the products away from the customers although they had paid for them. Similarly, a service organization like a public transport company or a philharmonic orchestra could take away season or subscription tickets from those of their customer-clients who have not utilized them enough or did not behave properly when they used the services.

39   We are at present studying the behaviour of university faculties and the ways in which they differ from the behaviour of managers in other types of organizations.

40   This means that the *convergence* of national cultures into a universal culture is far from having reached the stage in which it is larger than the divergence among national cultures. (This subject of national cultural convergence versus divergence is discussed by Ross A. Webber in 'Convergence or divergence?' and Howard V. Perlmutter in 'Emerging East–West ventures: the transideological enterprise', both appearing in Weinshall (1977a).)

41   We present in chapter 7 the dynamics of the Roman Catholic Church (RCC) over time. The short reign of Pope John XXIII (1958–1963) changed some of the values, beliefs, and rites of the RCC so drastically that the transformation could be compared to that from the horse and cart stage to the motor car stage, or from a plane with propellers to a jet-propelled one.

42   This is the way in which the creation of Christianity by a set of Jews could be interpreted. Similarly, Martin Luther protested against Roman Catholicism in the sixteenth century. Other instances of the same phenomenon were the Islamic Shiite separation from the Sunis in the seventh century, and the creation of Hasidic communities in Judaism in the eighteenth century.

43   Fundamentalists exist in different religions. The Irani Khomeinism is only one of several fundamentalisms in Islam. See Gaddafi's puritan Islamic revolution in Libya (Mansfield, 1980, p. 461; Laffin, 1981, pp. 51, 55, and 170–171) and Saudi Arabia's laws of the Koran (Mansfield, 1980, p. 406; Laffin, 1981, pp. 104–105, 121–125, 187–188). Islamic laws, which to Westerners seem both cruelly primitive and highly discriminatory, are practised not only in Libya and Saudi Arabia. The Gulf states have recently adopted laws calling for 'forty lashes for Muslims who drink, sell or manufacture alcohol, amputation of right hand for thieves and of the left leg for second offenders, 100 lashes for unmarried adulterers and public starving to death for their married partners'. Even Sadat's Egypt introduced in the late 1970s laws incurring the death penalty for any Muslim Egyptian guilty of apostasy—'renouncing his religion' (Laffin, 1981, p. 51). Laffin was told of the murder of a Christian priest and of two Muslims he had converted in the early 1970s and no action was taken to find the killers.

Although fundamentalism is strongest in Islam it is not absent from the other two major monotheistic religions. The most extreme fundamentalists among the Jews are probably the Neturei Karta (the Defenders of the Town), a small but quite noisy and violent sect of several hundred in Jerusalem. They still await the Messiah and insist that a Jewish independent state could not and should not have been established before his arrival. Therefore, they do not recognize the State of Israel, but rather have given their oral allegiance to Kings Abdulla and Hussein of Jordan.

Let us cite three examples of fundamentalism in Christianity. The first are sects like the Moonies and the Scientologists, which have been barred from the UK because they cause rifts between and the abandonment of family members—children and parents, wives and husbands, etc. The second is the extreme personality cult, which is not absent from the above two sects, which led to mass murder and suicide in the case of the Jones sect in the Caribbean.

Our third example is that of the Mormons. Although not violent, the Mormons have probably been the most successful fundamentalists in Christianity, having established a fundamentalist state in Utah in the midst of the pluralistic, democratic USA.

44 The assassination of Egyptian President Anwar El Sadat in October 1981 was carried out by a fundamentalist sect, probably linked to Libya. About two years earlier, Saudi Arabia had confronted what turned out to be a fundamentalist revolt in the Great Mosque of the Kaaba in Mecca. This uprising, probably backed by Khomeini of Iran, was quite close to accomplishing a successful *coup d'état* in Saudi Arabia. It is interesting to note that, like Gaddafi's overthrow of King Idress of Libya in 1969, this was also a case of a fundamentalist sect trying to overthrow what they considered to be a corrupt fundamentalist regime. In both cases the existing fundamentalist regime was and is royalist, dependent for its survival on the West and, consequently, supporting the USA and its allies. However, if Saudi Arabia were to fall, and eventually became anti-West, within a very short period of time the survival of the Western democracies would be in jeopardy. If this were to happen before new sources of energy are available, any power in control of Saudi Arabian oil supplies and reserves would have the whole Western world at its mercy.

45 The level of industrial development in predominantly Catholic countries like Ireland, Italy, Poland, and Spain is obviously lower than it is in France. In every one of them the affinity between Church and state is greater than it is in France.

46 The 'zaibatsu' conglomerates encounter ever-growing difficulties the more successful they are, because their organizational cultures remain national instead of becoming multinational.

47 See Hofstede (1979). His main findings are summarized in note 4 above.

48 Let us present ourselves as Israeli examples. The first author is Israeli-born. His parents emigrated with their own parents from Europe to Israel in the twentieth century. The second author is also Israeli-born. Her father has a history identical to that of the first author; her mother, on the other hand, was born in Cairo during a period when her own Israeli-born parents lived abroad. The children of both authors are therefore two to four generations removed from their European ancestors. The majority of Jews in Israel are no longer of European origin. Jews originating from Arab and other Moslem and Middle Eastern countries nowadays constitute the larger part of the Israeli population.

49 We are grateful to Barto Roig-Amat of IESE in Barcelona (the Graduate Business School of the University of Navarra) who included us in 1978 in a Delphi study of the future of developing industrial and highly industrial countries. He thus made us focus our attention and formalize our thoughts on this important matter. Most of this part of the text is based on the document we presented to him then.

50 Even Joseph, when planning the Egyptian wheat supplies for seven fat and seven lean years, was more farsighted than most, if not all, business corporations are today. He could plan for 14 years because his world was much less turbulent than ours.

51 The focus on the three Latin countries is due to one of Barto Roig-Amat's specific questions in his Delphi (see note 49).

52 The best-known European 'joint ventures' are the Anglo-Dutch companies, Shell and Unilever. They were created in the colonial era before the Second World War, when both Britain and Holland had dominant national cultures. The fact that Shell and Unilever are jointly owned has only a limited effect on their operations nowadays. Both companies have turned into multinationals over time. More recent

examples of 'joint ventures' by two dominant nationalities are companies created by Brazilians and Japanese.

53　Some of these organizations applied home procedures to totally irrelevant situations. The story runs that one company sent instructions to its Nigerian branch to the effect that on 1 October electric stoves were to be issued to all offices, and so they were!

54　The 'apostle' of such universal trade unions is the Chemical Workers' Charles Levinson. In fact, there have been several attempts in this direction. Louis Turner (1973) describes these efforts, and analyses problems, successes, and failures. For example, he points out that the International Transport Workers' Federation set a record in dealing with an international industry in its coordination of shipping unions around the world. The most publicized success in achieving international parity of earnings was when Walter Reuther's United Auto Workers got Chrysler to concede equal pay for its US and Canadian employees in 1967. Ralph Nader, the US consumers' spokesman and leader, has recently extended his field of activities to cover the consumers of multinational corporations the world over (Armstrong, 1971).

55　The multinational management education study has been based on a longitudinal cross-national research project at the European Institute of Business Administration (INSEAD), begun in 1966. This has been carried out in the stages shown in Table 6.20. The fourth stage, comparing the managerial behaviour of INSEAD alumni with that of graduates of national management and business schools, is being carried out in the 1980s.

As background, the following is an official description of the school:

> INSEAD was founded in 1958. Its purpose is to prepare future directors and managers for careers in industry, commerce and banking with a particular emphasis on international business. It provides a practical management education designed to bridge the gap between university and business life. Stress is laid on the cultivation of an international approach to business problems and on the effect of European integration on management decisions. Unique of its kind because of its truly international character, INSEAD provides an exceptional meeting place of students from many countries and teachers of different nationalities. Teaching is primarily done by the case method of instruction. Each student analyses the case by himself, then discusses it within a discussion group composed of 7 students and, finally, participates in class discussion with 50 other students, led by a professor.

Table 6.20　Stages of research project at INSEAD

| Stage | Research focus | Started in | When carried out during academic year | | Page numbers in Weinshall (1977a) |
			1 Beginning INSEAD	2 While at INSEAD	
One	Attitudes	1965/1966	+	+	191–195
Two	Relationships	1966/1967		+	200–210
Three	Values	1968/1969	+	+	183–191, 195–200

56 Genesis 11: 1–9, *The New English Bible*, Oxford University Press/Cambridge University Press, 1970.
57 When we first came to Fontainebleau to spend the academic year of 1965/1966 at INSEAD, the NATO headquarters of SHAPE were still in France. The beautiful, historic small town of Fontainebleau had therefore at that time two international organizations operating within it: a military one and an educational one. It struck us right from the very beginning of our acquaintance with members of the two organizations that the atmosphere among the INSEAD people from various countries, students as well as faculty members, was much better than among the NATO people, both non-commissioned ranks and officers. We thought that something must be different in the types of people, the objectives of the organizations, or the way in which they were structured, to account for this.
58 See Sutton (1956).
59 See Yoshino (1968). Yoshino produced the first comprehensive book on the Japanese managerial system. Ouchi (1981) included in his now famous book many of Yoshino's observations. Yoshino does not seem to believe that Japanese managerial culture could be modified and/or integrated into US managerial culture, which is what Ouchi seems to suggest.
60 The rest of subsection 6.2.4.1 is taken mainly from Weinshall (1979, pp. 259–275).
61 Especially by Crozier (1964).
62 Other cross-cultural studies reached similar conclusions. For example, Graves (1972) studied the impact of culture upon managerial attitudes, beliefs, and behaviour in England and France. This he did by comparing the managerial communication findings in two factories of the same multinational corporation, one located in Britain and the other in France. He found that the English have a concept of personal authority (close to our formal structure). Another comparison of the communication culture of two peoples is Russell Egger's (1977) satirical advice to US executives on how to do business with French counterparts.
63 A organizational example in chapter 6 vividly describes the very informal structure of the Israeli TOS.
64 Let us consider two examples. Gardner (1962) showed how participants, located in contradictory cultural situations, may reach conflicting conclusions regarding problems of communication.
   Porter (1972) outlined cultural variables which constitute an impediment to communication. His approach was that the main obstacles occur as a result of misapprehensions in social perception and come about as a result of cultural differences which affect the perception process.
65 See Servan-Schreiber (1967).
66 For an account of the position in Israel see Weinshall (1968). This seems to have changed, and in 1983 there is less cooperation between students and faculty in Israel.
67 There is a basic pedagogical error in the design of the great majority of graduate programmes in management and administration in that they start right away teaching techniques (e.g. statistics, data processing, etc.) and functional courses (e.g. control, finance, marketing, personnel, production, etc.). Before learning the particulars, the students should be introduced to the whole. Only in a few programmes throughout the world is this done. Parts of our present book could serve as an appropriate introduction to the TOS in such graduate programmes (Weinshall, 1976, pp. 86–87).
68 Denison (1967) thinks that this could explain why the USA is leading in the most advanced areas of science and technology.
69 See Poigants and Kohnstamp (1967).
70 For evidence of this statement see Yoshino (1968).
71 Until the Second World War, the French language was considered to be the inter-

national diplomatic language. A language which was acclaimed at the time of its appearance as a world language was Esperanto, created by Ludwik Lazarz Zamenhof (Boulton, 1960). Esperanto first appeared in 1887 as Linvo Internatia (International Language). It was designed by Zamenhof as 'a simple international language, as an easy means for the promotion of relationships and understanding among the nations'. Needless to say, Esperanto failed to fulfil any of the expectations expressed at the time of its inception.

72   *The Ugly American* was written by Lederer and Burdick (1958).

73   This was the notion of some of the founders of INSEAD, later presented by Jean Jacques Servan-Schreiber (1967). This notion is contrary to our own beliefs, expectations, and predictions, because it seems to us that the division of the world into large country blocs is contrary to the trend of the times. We believe that the only visible division in the future will be between parts of the world with different levels of technology and different standards of living. INSEAD, the foundation of which in 1958 coincided with the signing of the Treaty of Rome, was expected by Servan-Schreiber to provide Europe with graduates as weapons to fight what he perceived to be the American economic invasion of Europe. From personal knowledge of INSEAD, we know that both the training and the placement of INSEAD graduates have been all along multinational rather than parochially European.

74   There have been four such sections (class groups) of more than 50 participants each during the last few years, the total number of participants reaching about 250, from about 30 countries.

75   Since the Second World War, Ladino (a corrupt form of Castilian Spanish used by Sephardic Jews) and, especially, Yiddish ('Jewish', which is a mixed jargon of German, Hebrew, and the language of the country, be it French, English, Russian, etc.) have gradually faded from Jewish homes. Thus, the great majority of the young generation of Israelis speak only Hebrew from infancy onwards. They have lost the famous ability to learn languages (which is not an inborn talent, but rather an acquired facility) of their diaspora ancestors.

76   This is illustrated by the famous case study in the pioneering book of our late friends, Jack Glover and Ralph Hower (1952). The year is 1940: Dashman's 20 decentralized manufacturing sub-organizations have made it necessary to centralize the purchasing activities of the company. Mr Post is brought into the decentralized company, because of his rich experience as a purchasing vice president in functional organizations. Although he is not in the same formal culture and even not in a type of business organization identical to the one he has been used to, Mr Post sends instructions to the purchasing managers in the 20 manufacturing sub-organizations, to report to him any purchases over $10 000. He is, of course, completely ignored and undoubtedly seriously baffled and disturbed.

77   Trying to respond to the question whether managerial thinking is similar or different in various countries, Haire *et al.* (1966) conducted comparative research in 14 countries. Their findings indicate that there exists considerable similarity in the attitudes of managers in different countries. However, they found that 25 per cent attitudinal variance could be explained by national differences among the managers. Haire *et al.*, therefore, concluded that national differences clearly and significantly contribute to the differences in managerial attitudes. By arranging the national groups of managers according to their attitudes towards management, they found that groups of nationalities tended to cluster. The countries which were found to be in the same cluster were different from those in other clusters in both their cultures and their technological development. In other words, national affinity in such things as religion and language, on the one hand, and degree of technological development,

on the other, polarizes the managers in their attitudes to management (Haire *et al.*, 1966).

78 Webber (1969) claims that while there are forces which press for the convergence of managerial philosophy and practice in various countries, making it universal, differences in values, beliefs, customs, and cultural traditions affect managerial relationships to a large degree. Webber says that those things which seem to be desirable and important in life within a cultural environment will affect interpersonal relationships and, especially, the leadership style.

79 The US and European CEs, nevertheless, differed in other things, and these variances were attributed by the researchers to different cultural traditions (De Bettignies and Evans, 1977).

80 Tables 6.11, 6.12, and 6.13 present the responses of 159 participants in 13 countries, each of which had at least 4 respondents. All in all there were 188 respondents from 33 countries, but the remaining 29 respondents were from 20 countries in which there were fewer than 4 respondents per country.

81 From the findings reported in another paper, there is reason to believe that a certain degree of idealism, naïvety, and ignorance regarding multinational management among the new arrivals at INSEAD could explain the shifts which occurred in their attitudes towards the three values of confidentiality, punctuality, and bribery. This seems to be especially so with regard to bribery. A class discussion of the bribery story in an executive programme on Managerial Skills in International Business (MSIB) at INSEAD (in August 1978) revealed that experienced managers (two of them happened to be INSEAD MBA alumni, who came back for this programme) are not naïve at all about the realities of such situations.

82 For the purpose of ranking the values and subvalues which were composed of a few scales (i.e. all the values and subvalues except for that of 'interorganizational mobility'), the means of the scores of the scales were calculated for each value and subvalue. Thus, the ranking of the six values and subvalues of the scores of the scales in Table 6.21 were averaged.

Table 6.21   Five values and sub-values which affect managerial behaviour and the tables in which they appear

Value and subvalue	Number	Names	Appearing in table
Confidentiality	3	Interviewer's behaviour; Interviewer's intentions; Respondent as interviewee	6.11
Punctuality	2	Feelings after 10:00; When starting	6.12
Belief in sincerity of latecomers	2	Apologizing latecomers; Apologies tell truth	6.12
Behaviour in dealing with slush funds	3	CE's reaction; Respondent in R.B.'s place; Acceptable gift	6.13
Organizational strategy towards slush funds	2	Public cause—OK?; Flexible policy	6.13

290

83   The twelve countries, each of which had at least three participants in the 1966 class at INSEAD, were: Austria, Belgium, Britain, Denmark, France, Germany, Holland, Israel, Italy, Lebanon, Norway, and Sweden.

84   The twelve professions (i.e. first university degree areas) which the respondents were requested to rank as to their degrees of mixing, contributing, and receiving were: Accounting, Commerce, Economics, Engineering, Languages, Law, Literature, Philosophy and Liberal Arts (both in one area), Political Science ('Government' in the USA), Pure (or 'hard') Sciences, Social Sciences, and 'Without Profession' (INSEAD used to admit up to 5 per cent of participants who had no first university degree, but who had rich managerial experience).

85   During INSEAD's first ten years (i.e. until the late 1960s) the languages used at INSEAD were mostly English and French, and the German language had to be studied by all INSEAD students.

86   There were only male students at INSEAD until 1967. The class of 1968 had two French female students (less than 2 per cent). The female student population at INSEAD has been growing since then, and has reached almost 20 per cent recently.

87   In our own country, Israel, where cross-national (and cross-religious) marriages have occurred ever since the First World War, some of the grown-up children of such marriages have fled the region to avoid the issue. On the other hand, some of these grown-up children have stayed in the Middle East, turning into either Arab or anti-Arab extremists.

88   However, all the interviewees mentioned specifically four or five German students who behaved differently from the majority of Germans. All of those specifically mentioned as internationally mixing received their first university degrees outside Germany, while none of the other German students had done so (Weinshall, 1977a, p. 164).

89   It seems that it is relatively easier for British or Israeli people to emigrate and live away from their country for the rest of their lives, than it is for people from France and the Scandinavian countries. Germans seem to be somewhere between the two extremes of this scale; they could live abroad for longer periods of time than the French or the Swedes, but not permanently like the British or Israelis.

90   Pieter Kuin (1972) concludes his article about multinational management with the following sentence: 'Attitudes of respect for other nations' talents and traditions, of fascination with the variety of other worlds, of readiness to revise one's own prejudices, and of adjustment to local tasks and circumstances—these are the elements of the basic formula for success.'

91   The overall guideline for managing multinational corporations is: 'What is good for our MNC is good for our MNC', not 'What is good for the country is good for the MNC'.

92   See, for example, Schollhammer (1977).

93   See, for example, two managerial communication studies as part of cross-cultural research (Weinshall, 1979, pp. 233–278), one of which serves as the basis for this section.

94   Tarelton (1977) studied the opinions and recommendations of chief executives of US business corporations regarding the course subjects and contents to be included in business administration schools so as to prepare their graduates for employment in multinational corporations.

95   Fayerweather (1960) discusses the influences of values, beliefs, and manifest behaviour in various cultures on the relationships of American managers with people in the cultures with which they come into contact.

96   For the exact method of calculating the figures in Table 6.18, see Weinshall and De Bettignies (1971).

97   In 1971 the limit was 25 per cent of the student body for any particular country. In

recent years, the number of French participants has reached 30 per cent. This might seem a high figure for purposes of integration.

98 Here again, the fact that some people studied the 'hard' sciences and others the 'soft' sciences does not make them different; but the main reason for choosing to study in the one direction or in the other stems from the differences among people. We believe that choice of direction in higher studies has mainly to do with the personality of the student. A person not adept in, and even scared of, human relationships and worried about organizational situations in which he may find himself may prefer to study the 'hard' sciences. Such a person believes that dealing with things like accountancy, chemistry, engineering, mathematics, or physics would act as a protective shield against too much involvement with other human beings. This underlying assumption about the educational and occupational self-selection of human beings is one of the central hypotheses of research we have been conducting into the behaviour of university faculties.

99 That is, once the person has the appropriate managerial characteristics for the role he has to play in the organization; in this, however, there is no difference whether the manager interacts with people of his own country or with people from other countries.

100 Ehud Harari and Yoram Zeira (1974 and 1978), and Zeira and Harari (1975).

101 See Harari and Zeira (1978).

102 See Harari and Zeira (1974).

103 See Harari and Zeira (1974).

104 The first programme in this area was called the MSIB (Managerial Skills in International Business) and was pioneered at INSEAD in Fontainebleau by Henri-Claude De-Bettignies in 1968. He ran this programme annually for the first several years; it lasted two weeks and was taught by four professors.

105 Interpersonal sensitivity is stressed by De Bettignies and Rhinesmith (1970).

106 Whenever one of these three elements was not taught by one of the four teachers on the faculty of the MSIB programme (see above note 104), or when other topics were tried by one or more of its faculty, the MSIB programme ran into problems and failed to achieve its full effect. This happened during the years when learning about cultural situations and providing the students with the dynamics of the TOS in national and multinational corporations were omitted from the curriculum. It also happened when the faculty member concentrated on international business and economics while another teacher gave them an overdose of sensitivity by making them expose their souls in front of each other.

107 *Nineteen Eighty-four* is Orwell's prophetic book on the centralized, formalized, and computerized world he envisioned in 1948. Needless to say, now we have nearly reached 1984, we find that only on the computerization aspect have we fulfilled to some extent Orwell's predictions.

108 The degree of this so-called 'responsibility towards the employees' is closely linked to the socio-cultural system prevailing in the country. Its most extreme manifestation is in Japan, where many organizations provide not only housing and education for their staff, but also schooling and even marriage options for their children (Abegglen, 1958). This lifelong employer–employee relationship is mentioned in our organizational example of the Japanese zaibatsu in chapter 5.

109 See, for example, the comprehensive schooling system, from elementary to university level, established by Philips in Eindhoven; also the Corning Glass Museum in upstate New York. Corning's Glass Museum is not a unique world example of a business organization donating to society a museum in its own field of operation. In the authors' home town, Haifa, Dr Reuben Hecht, the entrepreneur of Dagon (the largest grain silos in Israel), established the only wheat and grain museum in the world.

110   As early as 1963, American firms, some of which were, or subsequently became, multinational corporations, owned the following industries in France: 40 per cent of the petroleum industry, 45 per cent of the rubber industry, 65 per cent of the telecommunications equipment industry, etc. (Servan-Schreiber, 1967, p. 25). According to the same source, the same American organizations held, in 1967, the following shares in Europe's electronics industries: 50 per cent in the semiconductor industry, 80 per cent in the computer industry, and 95 per cent in the integrated circuit industry.

111   A grim example was disclosed by Sampson (1973) of how far a multinational corporation may go in its 'supranational' behaviour; ITT actually manufactured armaments in Germany before and during the Second World War until its installations were destroyed by Allied bombing. All this in spite of ITT being an American corporation.

112   The utmost dislike of an MNC is usually manifested by the nation in which it started and from which it grew to become an international and, subsequently, a multinational corporation. This relationship is somewhat like that between parents and those children who demonstratively prefer, or at least equally accept the company and guidance of, the parents of other children. Indeed, one of the proofs that an international company has turned into a multinational is when it is prosecuted for violation of constraints against it in its country of origin. Thus, it seems that ITT and IBM have more problems in the USA than in other countries in which they function.

113   An extensive bibliography on state-owned enterprises (SOE) was compiled by Judd (1981, pp. 150–164). We cannot agree, however, with the sentence, which we italicize, appearing in the following extract from a statement preceding Ms Judd's article and bibliography: 'US corporations face stiff competition from state-owned enterprises, whose government parentage often gives them undecided advantages over US companies. *Multinational SOEs are particularly worrisome to US executives.*' SOE could operate internationally, but could not become multinational corporations. The reason for this is that they cannot comply with that part of the definition of multinationals which requires them to be supranational, namely they cannot carry the constraints imposed on them in one country to another country. We therefore predict that unless the operations of an SOE in foreign countries are protected by preferential arrangements and agreements, it will not be able to last in those countries for long, mainly because of increased resistance to it as *belonging* to the government of another country.

     Incidentally, even in its own country, the SOE turns out to be less competitive and viable than privately owned enterprises. It is only because, as the above mentioned article puts it, 'the government parentage often gives undecided advantages to the SOE, that other organizations face stiff competition from them'. Indeed, their survival is sometimes decided upon and secured in conditions which would not enable private enterprises to continue functioning.

114   Two such international events can be interpreted in this fashion and given as examples of such active, though clandestine, participation by MNCs: the internal war between Nigeria and Biafra, and the overthrow of the Allende regime in Chile. In the first instance, the operations of BP (British Petroleum) in Nigeria were threatened. At a certain point in the war against Biafra, BP intervened and put pressure on the British Government to supply the Nigerian Government with the armaments which enabled them to overpower the Biafrans.

     ITT was the major factor in persuading the US Government to use the CIA in helping Allende's political opponents to depose him. In this case, ITT did not stop an existing war, as BP had done in Nigeria. ITT's intervention, however, may be looked upon as an attempt to end a regime which would close Chile to multi-nationals.

It is common now to refer to left-wing regimes as 'red nationalists' and 'red imperialists' in much the same way that right-wing regimes have been referred to as 'fascist nationalists' and 'fascist imperialists'. In any case, from the point of view of the multinationals, it does not make a great deal of difference when they are impeded from operating in a country racked by civil war. (See also note 21.)

115 This is indeed one of the dangers facing the survival of the Western democracies centred around the USA, Japan, and Western Europe, including decisions to sell sophisticated armaments or advanced technologies to the communist countries which would increase the power of those countries *vis-à-vis* the Western democracies. If this were to happen before the multinationals have enough power over nation states to prevent wars, it might well endanger and even bring about the downfall of the Western democracies. We do not wish even to try to predict what would happen to the dynamics of the TOS as described in this book if the communist countries were to succeed in taking over the rest of the world before the MNCs could reach a position of power which would enable the whole world to function in *laissez-faire* economies. The most recent example of what we mean occurred when the USA reluctantly slackened its efforts to prevent France and other countries from going along with the construction of a gas pipeline from the USSR to Western Europe. This pipeline is to utilize sophisticated equipment provided by US-based MNCs. Therefore, the cancellation of the pipeline project would have been against their interests. On the other hand, when this pipeline becomes operational, the USSR will control a proportion of the gas supply to Western Europe. This is not as powerful a hold on Western Europe or on Japan, the USA, and the rest of the Western democracies as the Soviet Union would have if it were to succeed in obtaining control over the oil resources of Arabia. Nevertheless, control of the supply end of the gas pipeline could constitute quite a decisive hold on Europe and, through it, on the whole free world.

116 One such plan was put forward by David Horowitz, then Governor of the Bank of Israel, who suggested that every rich nation should devote 1 per cent of its GNP to the poorer areas (Horowitz, 1960). Several years later Robert McNamara, then President of the World Bank, put forward a similar plan around the proposed percentage of 5 per cent. None of these plans ever progressed beyond the academic stage.

117 It is interesting to note that even in ancient days it was common practice for the more tyrannical rulers to speak of their regimes as being there to stay.

118 One such example is of an African country in which one of the largest European corporations was operating on a large scale. On instructions from his headquarters, the local manager prepared periodical reports on the environmental conditions, to be used as bases for long-range planning. As a result, he was charged with espionage; and a neutral organizational scientist had to testify on his behalf to the effect that periodical reports on environmental conditions are part of the managerial technique of modern corporations.

119 The term 'convergence' is included in terminology used by writers on the relationship between culture and management. According to Ross Webber (1970), the divergence and convergence dichotomy consists roughly of some people believing that cultural diversity is there to stay, and others maintaining that the cultures are drawing closer together. Howard Perlmutter (1969) extends the terminology to include four different approaches to predicting the future of the cultures of industrialized countries—divergence, submergence, convergence, and emergence. Emergence is what Perlmutter himself believes to be the outcome of multinational

corporations creating an integrated culture, which would dominate the industrial world, a belief shared by us.

120 At the end of 1974, the 'World Bank estimated that the surplus funds from oil revenues would by 1985 reach the staggering figure of $1.2 trillion ($1,200,000,000,000)' (Sampson, 1975, p. 299).

121 Let us consider examples of two self-centred states—France and Japan. In France, the efforts to curb multinationals were at their peak during de Gaulle's rule in the mid-1960s. Two cases come to mind of de Gaulle's failure to stop the takeover of prestigious French enterprises by multinationals. The first was the takeover of the Bull computer company (named after its Norwegian founder) by General Electric, which subsequently sold it to Honeywell, another US-based multinational. The second case was that of Citroën, the car manufacturer; the French Government tried to prevent the Agnelli brothers, owners of Fiat, from securing an option to take over Citroën; it never materialized, apparently, because Fiat did not care to have a subsidiary in a self-centred country like France.

The second example of national self-centredness is that of Japan. The Japanese are renowned for imposing difficulties on multinationals trying to operate in Japan, including forcing them formally to collaborate with Japanese companies. However, Japanese national self-centredness is most clearly demonstrated in the operation of the zaibatsu, the large conglomerates, outside Japan. The zaibatsu try to retain everything which is Japanese in the management of their subsidiaries abroad. Even when they feel they have to collaborate with local firms, they try to have them operate in Japanese culture. It is interesting to watch the mutual attraction between self-centred nations. When the Japanese collaborate with the Brazilians, another self-centred nation, they form joint ventures, each country believing that its national culture will prevail in them. Joint ventures are an effort to bypass the inevitable need of a multinational *not* to carry over the constraints of one nation to other countries where it operates.

Even in nationally self-centred countries like France and Japan, the trends seem to indicate a move towards the realities of multinationals. Even though Président François Mitterand of France represents a combination of doctrinaire socialism with self-centred nationalism, which could almost have constituted an absolute barrier to the multinational, his government is actually trying to calm the multinationals and attract them to France. The Japanese, too, have become more submissive towards the pressures of multinationals operating in Japan, and towards the various countries in which the zaibatsu operate; they manifest more openness, flexibility, and consideration of the needs and constraints of other nation states.

122 Our own country, Israel, also manifested a 'Coca-Cola syndrome' against any foreign investments at least until the mid-1950s, if not the 1960s.

123 OPEC does not include communist oil-producing countries or certain Western democracies. In the 1970s, two additional Western countries, Mexico and the UK, turned out to be oil-exporting countries. Like the USA, they are not OPEC members. The more the national cultures of oil-exporting countries vary, the less danger there is of a return to nationalism such as Anthony Sampson (1975) described so well.

124 We mentioned Gaddafi's overthrow of King Idress in Libya in 1969 in note 44. Right from the beginning, Gaddafi was instrumental in forcing the oil companies to raise prices, and he simultaneously made contact with the USSR (Sampson, 1975, p. 211). On the other side of the Middle Eastern fields, stretching from Algeria to Iran, the Khomeini fundamentalist revolution succeeded in ousting the oil multinationals, which Dr Mossadegh had attempted to do, but failed, a quarter of a century earlier. Soon afterwards, the funamentalists struck at the richest oil country of them all. The uprising of the Islamic fundamentalists in the holiest centre of Mecca, in November 1979 (Servan-Schreiber, 1980, chapter 12), was a matter of

touch and go, until the Saudi-Arabian authorities finally succeeded in quelling the revolt.

125 It was Karl Marx who said that just as the property of individuals should belong to the states in which they live, so should the natural resources within the boundaries of the states belong to the whole world.

126 For example, the nation states will still have to maintain public order. This would include enforcing law and order and fighting organized crime of the sort spread by the Mafia.

SELECTED BIBLIOGRAPHICAL SOURCES

Abegglen, J., 1958. *The Japanese Factory*, The Free Press, Chicago, Illinois.

Aharoni, Y., 1971. 'On the definition of a multinational corporation', *Quarterly Review of Economics and Business*, II (3).

Armstrong, R., 1971. 'The passion that rules Ralph Nader', *Fortune*, May.

Barnard, C. I., 1938. *The Functions of the Executive*, Harvard University Press, Cambridge, Mass.

Barnet, Richard, and Muller, Ronald, 1975. *Global Reach: The Power of the Multinational Corporations*, Simon & Schuster, New York.

Beissinger, M. R., 1981. 'Soviet factory directors go to business schools', *Wall Street Journal*, 2 November.

Bendiner, Burton B., 1978. 'A labor response to multinational coordination of bargaining goals', *Monthly Labor Review*, July.

Bendix, R., and Lipset, P. K., 1966. *Class, Status and Power*, The Free Press, New York.

Boulton, M., 1960. *Zamenhof: Creator of Esperanto*, Humanities Press, New York.

Brooke, M. Z., and Remmers, H. L., 1970. *The Strategy of the Multinational Enterprise*, Longman, London.

Brooke, M. Z., and Van Beusekom, M., 1978. *International Corporate Planning*, Pitman, London.

Crozier, M., 1964. *The Bureaucratic Phenomenon*, Tavistock, London.

De-Bettignies, H.-C., 1970. 'Leaders across the ocean: comparing American and European chief executives', *European Business* (26), Paris.

De Bettignies, H.-C., 1978. 'Can Europe learn from Japan?', *Chelwood Review*, **4**, pp. 38–46.

De Bettignies, H.-C., 1980. 'Analyse de craintes françaises', *Revue Française de Gestion*, September–October, pp. 16–53, Paris.

De Bettignies, H.-C., and Evans, P. L., 1971. 'Europe looks north at the Scandinavian business elite', *European Business* (31), Paris.

De Bettignies, H.-C., and Evans, P. L., 1977. 'The cultural dimension of top executives' careers: a comparative analysis', in T. D. Weinshall (ed.), *Culture and Management*, Penguin, Harmondsworth, Middx.

De Bettignies, H.-C., and Rhinesmith, S. M., 1970. 'Developing the international executive', *European Business*, January.

Denison, E. D., 1967. *Why Growth Rates Differ*, Brookings Institution, Washington DC.

Eggers, E. R., 1977. 'How to do business with a Frenchman', in Weinshall, T. D. (ed.), *Culture and Management*, Penguin, London.

Fayerweather, J., 1960. *Management of International Operation*, McGraw-Hill, New York.

French, J. R. P., Israel, J., and As, D., 1960. 'An experiment in participation in Norwegian factory', *Human Relations*, **18**, 63–69.

Gabriel, R. A., 1979. 'What the army learned from business', *New York Times*, 15 April.

Gardner, G. H., 1962. 'Cross-cultural communication', *Journal of Social Psychology*, **58**, 241–256.

Glover, J. D., 1970. 'Outline of a system of concepts for environmental analysis and corporate planning, in Barto Roig-Amat (ed.), *La empresa multinacional*, Coleccion IESE, Serie AC–3, Ediciones Universidad de Navarra, Barcelona, pp. 75–106.

Glover, J. D., and Hower, R. M., 1952. *The Administrator*, Irwin, Homewood, Ill.

Graves, D., 1972. 'The impact of culture upon managerial attitudes, beliefs and behavior in England and France', *Journal of Management Studies*, February. Also in T. D. Weinshall (ed.), *Culture and Management*, Penguin, Harmondsworth, Middx, 1977.

Haire, M., Ghiselli, E., and Porter, L., 1963. *Cultural Patterns in the Role of the Manager*, vol. 2, Institute of Industrial Relations, pp. 95–117.

Haire, M., Ghiselli, E., and Porter, L., 1966. *Management Thinking*, Wiley, New York.

Harari, E., and Zeira, Y., 1974. 'Moral problems in non-American multinational corporations in the United States', *Management International*, **14**, 43–53.

Harari, E., and Zeira, Y., 1978. 'Training expatriates for managerial assignments in Japan', *California Management Review*, **20**, 56–62.

Heller, F., 1971. *Managerial Decision-Making—A Study of Leadership Styles in Power Sharing Among Senior Managers*, Tavistock, London.

Hirsch, S., 1971. *The Export Performance of Six Manufacturing Industries: A Comparative study of Denmark, Holland, and Israel*, Praeger, New York.

Hofstede, G., 1979. *Culture's Consequences: International Differences in Work Related Values*, Sage, Beverly Hills, Calif.

Horowitz, D., 1960. 'Statement at the Bank's Annual Discussion, 1960 Annual Meeting's Board of Governors', International Monetary Fund, press release no. 27, Washington DC.

Jacoby, N. H., Nehemkis, P., and Eells, R., 1977. *Bribery and Extortion in World Business*, Macmillan, New York.

Judd, M., 1981. 'Sources on state owned enterprises', *Harvard Business Review*, May–June, pp. 158–164.

Kahn, H., and Weiner, A. J., 1967. *The Year 2000: A Framework for Speculation on the Next 33 Years*, Macmillan, New York.

Kuin, P., 1972. 'The magic of multinational management', *Harvard Business Review*, **50** (November–December), pp. 89–97.

Laffin, J., 1981. *The Dagger of Islam*, Bantam, London.

Lederer, W. J., and Burdick, E., 1958. *The Ugly American*, Gollancz, London.

Mansfield, P., 1980. *The Arabs*, Pelican, Harmondsworth, Middx.

Meltzer, A. H., and Richard, S. F., 1978. 'Why government grows (and grows) in a democracy', *Public Interest* (52), Summer, pp. 111–118.

Nachmias, M., Weinshall, T. D., and Elzion, D., 1978. 'The communicogram as a change agent', presented at the XIXth International Congress of Applied Psychology in Munich, August 1978.

Ouchi, W. G., 1981. *Theory Z—How American Business Can Meet the Japanese Challenge*, Addison-Wesley, Reading, Mass.

Perlmutter, H. V., 1969. 'Emerging East–West ventures: the transideological enterprise', *Columbia Journal of World Business*, **IV** (5). Also in Weinshall (1977a).

Poigants, R., and Kohnstamn, D., 1967. 'A comparative study', in E. D. Denison (ed.), *Why Growth Rates Differ*, Brookings Institution, Washington DC.

Porter, R. E., 1972. 'An overview of intercultural communication', in Samovar and R. E. Porter (eds) *Intercultural Communication*, Wadsworth, Belmont, Calif.

Robinson, R. D., 1976. 'The breach in global reach', *Sloan Management Review*, **17** (2).

Sampson, A., 1973. *The Sovereign State: A Secret History of ITT*, Hodder & Stoughton, London.

Sampson, A., 1975. *The Seven Sisters: The Great Oil Companies and the World They Made*, Hodder & Stoughton, London.

Schollhammer, H., 1977. 'Ethics in an international business context', *MSU Business Topics*, **25**, 54–67.

Servan-Schreiber, J. J., 1967. *Le Defi americain*, Éditions Donoel, Paris.

Servan-Schreiber, J. J., 1980. *Le Defi mondial*, Librairie Artheme Fayard, Paris.

Smith, H., 1976. *The Russians*, Quadrangle, New York.

Sutton, F., 1956. *The American Business Creed*, Harvard University Press, Cambridge, Mass.

Tarelton, J. S., 1977. 'Recommended courses in international business for graduate business students', *California Journal of Business*, **50** (October), 438–447.

Tsirulnitsky, O., and Weinshall, T. D., 1974. 'The quantitative and qualitative measurement of managerial structures—an explanation and description of one field study', *Megamot Behavioural Quarterly* (Hebrew) 20, No. 3, Henrietta Szold Institute, Jerusalem.

Turner, L., 1973. 'Trade unions and the multinational company', in L. Klein (ed.), *Fabian Industrial Essays*, Royal Institute of International Affairs, London.

Twiss, B. C., and Weinshall, T. D., 1980. *Managing Industrial Organizations*, Pitman, London.

UNESCO, 1976. *Statistical Yearbook*, UNESCO, Paris.

Vernon, R., 1971. *Sovereignty at Bay: The Multinational Spread of U.S. Enterprises*, Longman, London.

Vernon, R., 1977. 'Storm over the multinationals: Problems and prospects', *Foreign Affairs*, January.

Webber, R. A., 1969. 'Convergence or divergence?', *Columbia Journal of World Business*, IV (3). Also in Weinshall (1977a).

Weinshall, T. D., 1966. 'The communicogram, a method for describing the pattern, frequency, and accuracy of organization and communication', in *Operational Research and The Social Sciences*, Tavistock, London.

Weinshall, T. D., 1968. 'Organizational behavior in Israel and the West', unpublished manuscript, Tel Aviv University.

Weinshall, T. D., 1973a. 'The informalogram as an indicator of managerial structure', Leon Recanati Graduate School of Business Administration, Tel Aviv University.

Weinshall, T. D., 1973b. 'Overcoming the differences in communication and other cultural characteristics through education of multinational managers, in Michael Brooke and Lee Remmers (eds), *The Multinational Company in Europe: Some Key Problems*, Longman, London, pp. 163–211.

Weinshall, T. D., 1973c. 'A study of organizational size and managerial structure', in Desmond Graves (ed.), *Management Research—A Cross-cultural Perspective*, Elsevier, Amsterdam.

Weinshall, T. D., 1973d. 'The Old Testament as pioneer in the fields of management and organizational behavior', *Organization and Management*, Vol. 18, No. 6 (118) (Hebrew).

Weinshall, T. D., 1976. 'The Total Organizational System (TOS) and the interdisciplinary approach in management and organization', in P. Verburg, P. C. A. Malataux, K. T. A. Halbertsma, and J. C. Boers (eds), *Organisatiewenschap in Praktij (Organization Science and Practice)*, Stenfert Kroese, Leiden, Holland, pp. 55–106.

Weinshall, T. D. (ed.), 1977a. *Culture and Management*, Penguin, Harmondsworth, Middx.

Weinshall, T. D., 1977b. 'Managerial structure of a nationally mixed organization in Japan', *Journal of Organization and Administration Sciences*, **1977**.

Weinshall, T. D., 1978. 'The dynamics of attitudes towards secrecy, punctuality and bribery', mimeographed, London Graduate School of Business Studies.

Weinshall, T. D., 1979. *Managerial Communication—Concepts, Approaches and Techniques*, Academic Press, London.

Weinshall, T. D., and De Bettignies, H.-C., 1971. 'Multinational business education—the social structure study', *Management International Review*, II (4 and 5).

Weinshall, T. D., and Shimshoni, D., 1973. 'A total system research programme for a whole industry', mimeographed working paper no. 144/73, Leon Recanati Graduate School of Business Administration, Tel Aviv University.

Weinshall, T. D., Silver (Shalev), M., and Beal, C., 1971. 'Patterns of communication and organization structure in a management training college' and 'The urbanization structure of a management training college', two mimeographed research reports, Ashridge Management College, Hertfordshire, UK.

Weinshall, T. D., and Vickery, L., 1970. 'Some uses of communication pattern research in analyzing and influencing organizational behaviour', in Roig-Amat, B. (ed.), *La Empresa Multinacional* (The multinational corporation), Coleccion IESE, Serie AC–3, Ediciones Universidad de Navarra, Barcelona.

Yoshino, M., 1968. *Japan's Managerial System*, MIT Press, Cambridge, Mass.

Zeira, Y., and Harari, E., 1975. 'Planned organizational change in multinational corporations', *Advanced Management Journal*, 40, 31–39.

Chapter 7

Helping Organizations (to Adapt to the Dynamics of the TOS)

The discussion on the dynamics of the TOS has revolved around the necessity for maintaining equilibrium among the various subsystems in order to ensure the continued existence of the organization. This aspect of the health of an organization may be compared with the need to maintain equilibrium among the various systems of the human body as a person advances in age. This analogy between the survival of human beings and that of organizations will be followed throughout the present chapter in the discussion of the two main diseases which plague organizations and the disorders which they cause. Three main ailments which endanger the survival of organizations are:

(a) A reluctance to change the managerial structure every few years, because the expansion of the scope of decision making requires a different structure. A basic change in managerial structure can be achieved only if the CE (chief executive) and a number of other key position managers with the new necessary leadership and followership characteristics run the organization. Such a change requires the transfer of those who have run the organization in its present structure to wherever their managerial characteristics are required. If such managerial mobility does not occur with sufficient frequency, the organization may be in trouble.
(b) The tendency of members of the organization to withhold personal feelings from each other creates an accumulation of undisclosed feelings, opinions, and thoughts which weigh upon them and cause anxiety, morale and interpersonal relationship problems.
(c) Last, but not least, the fact that people in organizational hierarchies tell each other only a relatively small part of what they think and feel, means that the executives at the top know very little of the attitudes and ideas of people at the lower hierarchical levels, and vice versa.

Subsequently, consideration will be given to the traditional treatments of these ailments. These treatments, which have had only limited success, may be divided into three main groups:

—Efforts to train managers to change their basic pattern of behaviour.
—Attempts to introduce new drawing-board solutions to managerial structures.
—Recourse to traditional managerial consulting services in which outsiders tell the management what is wrong with the organization and what they should do about it.

Section 7.3 is devoted to ways in which the three ailments caused by the two organizational diseases may be overcome. The Roman Catholic Church (RCC), the oldest organization in existence in the world, illustrates how it has cured its own three ailments. The three cures are:

—Electing an old person as pope, so that the Church has the opportunity to choose a new man every so often to lead the organization. The new pope will adapt the managerial structure to his own leadership characteristics.
—The process of confession helps the members of the Church to relieve themselves of all thoughts and feelings which burden them.
—The two managerial structures of the Church enable it both to run its routine decision making and to bridge the communication gap between the different levels of the hierarchy. The latter is achieved by reducing the six to eight levels of the hierarchy to three levels for the purpose of communication.

As will be seen later, the cures which work in the RCC are, unfortunately, unsuitable for other organizations. There are, however, effective ways to help all other organizations to treat their ailments. Organizations may be helped as follows:

—They should enable their members to relieve their minds (and hearts) through consulting sessions with psychological counsellors.
—From time to time, the things which the managers and other members of the organization say openly should be transcribed. Subsequently, these things should be arranged in logical order and fed back first to the CE and then to managers in lower levels.
—The shaping of a new managerial structure imbued with its leadership and followership characteristics, every few years, may be achieved in one of two ways: either by educating key position managers to change their point of view, so that they come to regard favourably moving from one organization to another; or organizations could be expanded into larger scopes of decision making with several product and service lines operating in different countries. When an organization reaches this scope of decision making, it must be run as a multistructure, i.e. as a federated structure composed of different managerial structures. This, in turn, facilitates managerial mobility within the organization rather than among organizations.

A detailed description of the cures for helping organizations to overcome maladjustments in the TOS, and to contribute towards their survival, concludes this final chapter of the book.

7.1 SICK ORGANIZATIONS

This section first considers the main maladjustments in the TOS which constitute threats to the survival of organizations. Section 7.1.2 makes clear that the use of an analogy between organizations and human beings enables one to understand better why organizations do not usually survive much longer than human beings. Subsequently, the main diseases and the consequent three ailments which plague all organizations are presented. The two main diseases (secrecy diseases) are those of 'anti-mobility' and 'no full disclosure'.

The first ailment, maladaptation to the dynamics of the TOS, is caused by the 'anti-mobility' disease. The second ailment, undisclosed feelings, and the third ailment, the hierarchical communication gap, are caused by the 'no full disclosure' disease.

7.1.1 Causes and Effects of Organizational Sickness and Collapse

The major problem with which individual organizations, as well as the environments in which they operate, are confronted is the organization's need to survive within the dynamics of the TOS. The main threat to survival is the management's failure to maintain the balance among the various principal systems of the TOS. In two particular cases balance is especially difficult to maintain. The first is the balance within the decision making main system, adapting the organizational strategy (the technology, product/service diversity, and geographical dispersal) to the pressures of the immediate and wider environments. The second is the proper balance to be maintained between the two main systems, namely by adapting the managerial structure to the SDM. A schematic presentation of the maladaptations resulting from such failures appears in Figure 7.1. Both difficulties stem from the fact that the managers are unaware of the changing requirements regarding the SDM and the managerial structure which occur as the result of the dynamics of the TOS. The managers think that, basically, things will continue exactly as they have done all along. This situation may be compared to an individual's difficulties in relation to family and community, if he is unaware of changes over time within himself. It may also be compared to a blindfolded person who cannot see those around him, and so he has to face graver difficulties of adaptation than he actually faces within his family and community.

The collapse of an individual organization at the present time is proportionately much greater than the collapse of an organization 100 years ago. Business and industrial organizations were comparatively small in the nineteenth century. The operating organization, i.e. management and the workers, rarely exceeded several hundred people, and the dependent suppliers and customers were likewise limited in number. Nowadays, there are business corporations whose operating organizations alone, i.e. their management and workers, reach hundreds of thousands; their suppliers, advertising agencies, management consultants, and transportation companies may reach many thousands, and their customers run into the millions. A present-day organization may likewise have many dependent

302

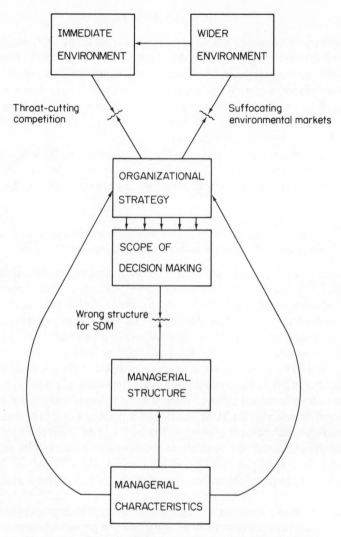

Figure 7.1 Major maladaptations to dynamics of the TOS

shareholders, banks, and other creditors, as well as a variety of individuals, like union and government officials, whose employment is wholly dependent upon it. Thus, when a large business corporation collapses nowadays, the human tragedy and suffering is of enormously larger proportions than those following the collapse of an organization in the nineteenth century. The tragedy involved in the collapse of a large, present-day organization lies in the suffering of all those people directly and indirectly connected with it, i.e. its managers, workers, shareholders, customers, suppliers, and others. An additional tragedy is the chain effect that such a collapse may evoke in other organizations.

Such a chain effect is presented in Figure 7.2 and is like the game children play with dominoes. The collapse of manufacturing organization A may lead to the bankruptcy of transportation organization B. This would bring to a standstill the operations of a marketing organization C which, not able to repay its substantial debts to its bank D, causes the latter's failure. This in turn causes the collapse of insurance company E. The investment company F which owns the insurance company collapses too and drags with it a subsidiary, another manufacturing company G, and so on.

As the number of factors comprising the organizational DMP (decision-making process) grew over the hundred years between the middle of the nineteenth and

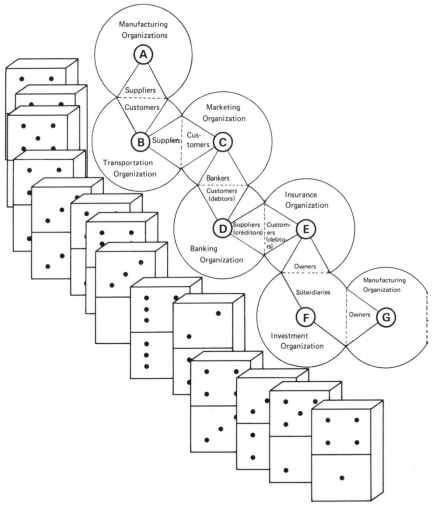

Figure 7.2   Example of a chain effect of collapsing organizations

the middle of the twentieth centuries, so did the dangers of such a chain effect. Prior to the nineteenth century, each organization stood, and sometimes failed, by itself, independently of any other organization. Usually an organization had only one factor in its DMP, the manager-owner; and the manager-owners of different organizations were not usually linked in any way. Nowadays, the chain effect could start with any of the FDM—managers, workers, suppliers, customers, trade unions, government, bankers, or shareholders.

Indeed, the most dramatic example of this chain effect is the US stock market crash of 1929 leading to the big depression in the 1930s. Those who precipitated this disaster, transmitting the collapse from one organization to another, domino fashion, were the shareholders. It is interesting to note that the origin of the 1929 crisis was *not* a financial one, i.e. an abundance or shortage of funds among bankers and shareholders. The main reason was rather an extreme over-accumulation of inventories.[1]

Thus, any severe disease of one or more organizations could easily spread like an epidemic to other organizations. Such an epidemic might be confined to one field of activity, such as one industrial or service field. It could, however, spread to other parts of the economy, affecting a whole country, like the depression resulting from the 1929 crisis. It could even spread beyond the boundaries of one country or region and affect the whole world, as the energy crisis of 1973 eventually did.

When an organization is not large and is not intricately tied in with many other organizations, its collapse should not lead to an epidemic. However, whether large or small, all organizations are constantly sick and quite often in danger of collapse. This last statement needs some elaboration and clarification.

7.1.2 Comparing Human Beings with Organizations

Using terminology usually applied to human beings when discussing the life and death of organizations makes sense on two counts. The obvious one is that organizations are conglomerations of human beings both as individuals and as human groups of various kinds. This conception of organizations as human entities is at the basis of organizational behaviour, be it administrative, economic, financial, marketing, or manufacturing. All other aspects of organizations can only supplement the human behaviour aspect. Indeed, without taking human behaviour into account as part of economic, financial, marketing, and manufacturing explanations, organizations cannot be run at all.

The second reason for using human terminology in connection with organizations is that by drawing analogies between human beings and organizations a better understanding is achieved. Indeed, without such analogies it is impossible to break away from the machine model in which organizations had been regarded until the first third of the twentieth century.[2] The first thing to note when comparing organizations with human beings is that both seem to have a limited lifespan. Human beings die through the biological deterioration of their bodies; however, why should an organization, in which one generation of managers transfers the responsibility for its functioning to another, have a limited lifespan?

This question became pertinent after the so-called 'separation of management from ownership' which began in the nineteenth century, and which has become a universal phenomenon in most medium and large enterprises. In the Western democracies, the ownership of the majority of such enterprises is dispersed among shareholders who are usually not employees of the organization. Even when they are, the size of their ownership is generally small. Therefore, even when managers own shares in the medium and large organizations in which they are employed, it could be considered that management is separated from ownership in these organizations.

In communist countries where almost no private business ownership exists, all organizations are owned by the state. This integration of two factors of decision making—'government' and 'owners'—is only one of several differences between the main system of decision making in communist countries and that in Western democracies. These differences create severe problems for the development of the communist countries and their TOSs, as seen earlier in the book. However, the separation of management from ownership is true to an even larger extent in communist countries than in the Western democracies. Until the separation of management from ownership, whenever a manager-owner passed away, the organization died with him, or at least was in grave danger of doing so. Since the separation of management from ownership, however, one could have hoped that the transfer of responsibility for organizational survival from one generation of managers to another would ensure its life in perpetuity. This hope has not been realized.[3]

Organizations may live longer than human beings, but not much longer. Not many organizations have survived longer than 100 years, only few reached their bicentenary, and only a very few celebrated their 300th anniversary. Only the unique Roman Catholic Church has survived a much longer time.

Human beings believe that being sick is 'not nice'. Sickness imposes on members of the family, or on colleagues who will be overburdened by one's absence from work. Those who do not have any scruples about being sick, whether their sickness is real or imaginary, are considered to be 'malingerers', 'hypochondriacs', or 'les malades imaginaires'. So when somebody does not feel quite well in the morning, he will try to ignore it and go on as if nothing had happened. His situation may, however, deteriorate to the extent that he would feel his sickness quite acutely—high temperature, excessive perspiration, trembling, and being barely able to drag his feet. At this stage or even earlier, one usually consults a doctor.[4]

Organizational sickness occurs among the personnel comprising the organization and they are the first to be aware of it. There is, however, one basic difference between the organizational sickness in which a human being is involved and the medical condition which affects him personally. He does not physically feel the organizational sickness and it does not affect him personally (unless there is not enough money to pay his salary). Consequently, there are no alarms to alert the individual to the organizational sickness, similar to the alarms of physical pain, temperature, perspiration, and other symptoms and bodily sensations of the individual.

In the case of organizational sickness, the individual involved is embarrassed, just as he would be with his own physical problems. In addition, he also faces the blame for any organizational problems within his managerial responsibility. This, of course, would discourage individuals from exposing any symptoms of organizational sickness to their superiors and colleagues.[5]

In consequence, while sick individuals tend to treat their ailments quite early after their discovery, organizations are left to develop their illnesses until it is too late to do anything about them. This is why organizations are constantly sick and quite often in danger of collapse.

7.1.3 Two Secrecy Diseases—'Anti-mobility' and 'No Full Disclosure'

The two diseases which between them cause the larger part of organizational mortality are both related to secrecy. The first disease is the one referred to throughout this book as the 'anti-mobility' value, which is implanted in various degrees of intensity in the cultures of every country in the world.

Closely related to the degree of intensity of 'anti-mobility' is the degree of guarding one's company secrets. The countries in which the 'anti-mobility' norm is the strongest are also the countries where company secrets are guarded most zealously. Conversely, in those countries where interorganizational managerial mobility is tolerated, there is much less secrecy about what is going on in business enterprises.[6]

The second secrecy disease consists in guarding management secrets within the management itself, rather than guarding against outsiders. Managers generally are not completely frank and open with each other.

On the whole, individuals are far from being frank and open with those people with whom they maintain more than casual relationships. In fact, people rarely reveal their thoughts completely, even to those closest to them.[7] This 'no full disclosure' secrecy disease is, however, strongest within management hierarchies. Consider first the 'no full disclosure' outside organizational hierarchies. There are several reasons why people do not disclose to each other everything, even when they are as close as husband and wife or twins. One of the main reasons, especially when people are quite close to and fond of each other, is that they try not to hurt their mates. Other reasons are the behavioural values, norms, and mores with which people grow up from their infancy. When they defy such norms, they may feel compelled to hold back the facts so as not to contravene their upbringing and culture.

Then there are, of course, the personal differences between people, which may in turn affect the degree to which individuals adhere to the two above mentioned social reasons. Consider three reasons for such personal interrelated differences between individuals. The first two reasons are connected with one's personality while the third has to do with the way in which one perceives the roles of others in relation to one's own.

First come the differences between 'extroverts' and 'introverts'. Their personalities differ in the degree of their ability to relate to other people. The second reason is related to the individual's 'inferiority' or, alternatively, 'superiority' complex. One individual may feel that others regard him as 'interesting', 'attractive', 'fascinating', etc., while another individual may feel he is of no significance to the society around him.

The third reason is likewise connected with the way individuals regard themselves in relation to others with whom they interact, but in a sociological rather than a psychological way. This has to do with one's own image within the wider social system and in the social strata. In a very stratified society an individual may just not talk with those he perceives to be below him. In such circumstances he will likewise not dare to talk without invitation to those he perceives to be above him.

The above last two explanations for degrees of openness among people are closely related to the additional dominant reason existing in hierarchical organizations for this phenomenon. The main block to revealing one's thoughts, opinions, attitudes, and other feelings to others in the hierarchical structure lies in the nature of the hierarchy itself. It stems from the fact that a person's future in an organization is dependent on those who are above him and below him in the hierarchy, as well as on those who flank him.

Whenever someone interacts with his hierarchical neighbour, whether superior, subordinate, or peer, he bears in mind, consciously or intuitively, that whatever is said may have a bearing on his future in the organization. This awareness and caution prevails regardless of whether he is ambitious or not. Thus a person's ambition may be to hold on to his job when many others in the organization are losing theirs.

The same caution about what an individual reveals of his feelings regarding what is going on in the organization exists also with regard to all those related to his immediate neighbours. In other words, the circle of those with whom he should be careful when talking about organizational conditions and people, including feelings about himself, is extended to include those who might transmit his feelings to his superiors, subordinates, or peers.

The superior has the power to decide, or at least seriously to affect the decision, whether a person is going to be promoted or demoted (a demotion being also caused by others being promoted in relation to oneself). The superior has likewise a decisive effect on the amount and type of work a person is responsible for, and the different type of assistance available for carrying it out. He will also exercise his power in recommending increases in salary and other remuneration. In short, his superior is the key to an individual's present and future in the organization.

Reporting to the same superior are those who compete with an individual for promotion and for all the other positive things that the superior could offer him. One person's perceived desire to move on or to stay in the same position is irrelevant to the competition among his peers for the favours of the superior. The promotion or relative improvement in the position of one or more of the peers is in effect a demotion and deterioration in the position of the other peers, even though they remain in their respective jobs.

A manager's subordinates are not only helpers and assistants; they likewise undermine and constantly challenge his position. On the whole, subordinates are younger and in command of more up-to-date education and knowledge. They constantly remind their superior of his deficiencies and shortcomings even if not explicitly. Subordinates are also pushing upwards and, at least implicitly, hope that their superior will soon vacate his position.

In consequence, he has to beware of his hierarchical neighbours when he imparts something of his thoughts, opinions, and feelings in the organizational context. He will try to impress a favourable image on his superior. This may be achieved by giving him good news, even when the reality is not so good, and suppressing or minimizing all the bad news, according to what the subordinate perceives as 'good' or 'bad'. For example, when a manager asks a subordinate: 'How are things in your department?', the latter will answer almost invariably: 'Fine', 'OK', or 'Everything is quite in order'. Such an answer probably corresponds with the state of some things in the department; but it may be contrary to the state of other things and is not descriptive of the state of many more things.

The same will happen in an individual's contacts with his peers. He will not want to give his peers any advantage in the struggle for getting on in the organization. This struggle could often be quite severe because of the constraints upon promotion and other ways of improving his lot. After all, the hierarchy has a pyramidal shape and there are only a few positions open at the top compared with the many aspiring candidates. The same restrictions exist in the availability of other means for ameliorating his position—office space, secretarial help, salaries, fringe benefits, etc. So he is constantly competing with his peers for a larger share of the limited cake.

The position vis-à-vis the subordinates is somewhat similar to that of the peers. A manager may feel from the outset at a disadvantage in relation to his subordinates in terms of their education and formal knowledge. Under such conditions the only advantage he has in relation to the subordinates is experience and knowledge of what actually goes on in the organization. If this latter knowledge is acquired by the subordinates, he could well feel defenceless against their challenge.

This means that almost no individual in an organizational hierarchy will reveal his innermost thoughts and feelings to his immediate organizational neighbours. He would tell them most things which he feels would be helpful, or at least not harmful, to himself. He would conceal from them things which may be obstacles to his future in the organization. He would, indeed, twist some of the things that are in his mind and come out with what may be considered as 'lies'.

The question of what is or is not the 'truth' requires some elaboration. There is no absolute truth in organization or, for that matter, in life as a whole. This is closely linked to the non-existence of objective facts in life and in organizations. There are only individual perceptions of what is happening around us. Only when the perceptions of all or most individuals who have witnessed or experienced an event coincide, can one say that this consensus is the truth and a fact.[8]

The only absolute truth that exists is in relation to one's own innermost thoughts and feelings. One can lie to oneself or to others, in revealing one's feelings and thoughts. Alternatively, one can tell the truth, meaning *one's own truth*, which does not necessarily correspond with, and may at times conflict with, the truth as others see the same matter.

With regard to this type of truth, and only to this truth, it may be said that when a manager communicates with his superior, subordinates, and peers, the things he tells them consist of 'the truth', not 'the whole truth', not 'nothing but the truth'. In other words, part of what he tells them is what he really thinks and feels. Another part of his feelings and thoughts he conceals from his listeners. The third part represents things not consistent with, and which are contrary to his innermost feelings and thoughts.

Apparently, no research has tried to establish the proportions among these three components of what people tell each other in organizations.[9] It is therefore a fair assumption that ongoing interpersonal communication is equally divided among the 'truth', 'not the whole truth', and 'not nothing but the truth' *on the average*. Actually the relative weight of each of the three parts, especially the first part (the 'truth') in relation to the subsequent two parts (the 'non-truth'), depends on the degree of balance among the principal systems of the TOS.

Table 7.1 relates the three categories of truth and non-truth in interpersonal communication to five contingency situations of the TOS, as follows:

Contingency position 1 The three principal systems, SDM, managerial structure, and managerial characteristics, are in balance; managerial satisfaction is positive. The relative amount of 'truth', 'not the whole truth', and 'not nothing but the truth' is equally divided.

Contingency position 2 The SDM grew, but the managerial structure and managerial characteristics stayed as they were; managerial satisfaction is negative. The pressures on managers are enormous because the managerial structure is not advanced enough for the SDM. The managers are not able to cope with the SDM. They increase the relative part of non-truth in what they are relating to others, and accordingly decrease the truth in what they say.

Contingency position 3 Although a new managerial structure suitable for the SDM is forced upon the managers, most of them, including the chief executive, remain. The managerial satisfaction of these old-time managers is negative, because they are forced to operate in a structure alien to their managerial characteristics. Therefore the non-truth is still relatively large among them, especially among old-timers and newcomers.

Contingency position 4 Key managers, including the CE, are replaced and new ones, with managerial characteristics suitable to the requirements of the SDM, are brought in. The managerial satisfaction improves, changing from negative to positive, because soon the new managers are going to bring the TOS to contingency position 5. Accordingly there is a reduction in the non-truth.

Contingency position 5 The balance among the subsystems of the TOS is restored, along with the positive managerial satisfaction. The relative amounts of 'truth', 'not the whole truth', and 'not nothing but the truth' are back to average.

The two secrecy diseases discussed, 'anti-mobility' and 'no full disclosure',

310

Table 7.1 Relative 'truth' and 'non-truth' among managers in hierarchies in different contingency positions of TOS subsystems

TOS subsystems		Contingency position					On the average*
		1	2	3	4	5	
SDM		+	+	+	+	+	
Managerial structure		+	−	+	−	+	
Managerial characteristics		+	−	−	+	+	
Managerial satisfaction		Positive	Negative	Negative	Negative Positive	Positive	
Truth	The truth	Average	Much less	Less	Less	Average	$\frac{1}{3}$
	Not the whole truth	Average	More	Much more	More	Average	$\frac{1}{3}$
Non-truth	Not nothing but the truth	Average	Much more	More	Average	Average	$\frac{1}{3}$

* We assume that on the average the total feelings, thoughts, opinions, etc., of a person are equally divided into his or hers telling 'the truth' ($\frac{1}{3}$), 'not the whole truth' ($\frac{1}{3}$), and 'not nothing but the truth' ($\frac{1}{3}$).

cause three ailments which endanger organizational health and consequently lead to fatality among organizations. The anti-mobility disease is linked closely to industrial secrecy. The stronger the anti-mobility norm in a country, the more the industrial organizations keep secrets from each other. 'No full disclosure' is both a personal and an organizational disease. Individuals in organizations do not reveal all their feelings, opinions, and attitudes to each other. The consequences of this to oneself and to one's organizational superior, subordinates, and peers are seen in two severe organizational ailments. One represents maladaptations between the sub-systems of the TOS, while the other represents the weight of accumulated undisclosed feelings.

7.1.4 First Ailment: Maladaptation to the Dynamics of the TOS

There are two types of maladaptation to the dynamics of the TOS which account for the major part of organizational sickness and collapse. They are the inability to adapt to the necessary rate of growth in the SDM and the failure to adapt the managerial structure to the SDM. In both cases it is to a large extent the inability of management to adapt to the changing requirements which causes the maladaptation among the subsystems. There are times, however, when a breakdown within the SDM main system, the first type of maladaptation, occurs in spite of management's adjustment to the dynamics of the TOS. In such cases what happens is an internal maladaptation within one of the principal SDM systems. Thus one must consider such cases in which management is confronted with maladaptation situations beyond its ability to deal with them. These situations may be divided into two groups: insurmountable maladaptation within the immediate environment and cases directly connected with the wider environment.

There are cases in which the immediate environment poses problems for the survival of the organization, and management is unable to cope with them. These problems may appear through any one of the FDM—workers, trade unions, bankers, shareholders, suppliers, customers, and government—or by way of two or more FDM simultaneously. Such problems could originate in one or more organizations in the immediate environment competing with the focal organization for one or more of its FDMs. Consider a simple example. A completely new organization appears in the immediate physical environment of the focal organization which is, say, a large restaurant. The new organization, which appears next to it, is another restaurant which can afford, for various reasons, to offer cheaper and better meals, as well as higher wages and salaries and better working conditions for its employees. The focal organization is simultaneously confronted with two challenges to its survival: losing its customers and its employees. Needless to say, its management should have tried to anticipate such a situation, or to meet the challenge once it appeared. This it could do by improving the conditions for its customers and employees, so that it could continue to operate, either with the same or with different customers and employees. It could, alternatively, move to another line of business, say turn the restaurant into a large delicatessen shop, or move to another part of the city, starting a new restaurant there, or doing both things simultaneously. There are situations, however, in which management is unable to respond quickly enough to such sudden competition, either because it has been caught unawares or for other reasons.

Such pressures from the immediate environment may be prompted by pressures from the wider environment, or be a result of the growth activities of other organizations regardless of changing conditions in the wider environment. The wider environment can exert its pressures on a focal organization either directly or by creating additional pressures through the immediate environment.

Take an industrial organization in which several hundred skilled workers are employed. The environmental employment market has recently moved from unemployment to general full employment with some overemployment in specific skills and trades, including skills which are crucial for the operation of the organization. Some employees may be tempted by the rising salaries and wages offered by neighbouring industrial organizations as the result of full employment. They put pressure on the focal organization to raise their salaries and wages. If the focal organization cannot afford to do so at the time, it will be in serious trouble.

The situation becomes aggravated if the above conditions are reinforced by the appearance of a new industrial plant in the same geographical area, calling for the same crucial types of employees which the focal organization requires for its survival. Now the pressures of the employment market in the wider environment are exercised on the focal organization, both directly and through the new organization appearing in the immediate environment.

In the last analysis, however, the responsibility for the survival of the organization lies with the management, even when the shifts in the immediate and wider environments are abrupt and substantial. For it is the management's responsibility to predict environmental changes, and to have appropriate reserves to meet them in order to adapt the organizational strategy to what, how, and where to operate.

The same is true of the major changes required in the managerial structure to keep it in line with the SDM. Here again, the changes in the independent variable, which is the SDM, to which the managerial structure (the dependent variable) has to be adapted, may be quite abrupt. The above examples portrayed some drastic changes in the SDM, as a result of sharp changes in the immediate and wider environments. There may occur, however, even more drastic changes in the environment which lead to even sharper changes in the SDM. Such SDM changes invariably require immediate drastic changes in the managerial structure.

A particularly traumatic example of such a shake-up in the environment occurred in the USA when the whole financial market collapsed in 1929. Tens of thousands of organizations had to change drastically their SDM in order to survive. This necessitated similar drastic changes in their managerial structures. Such situations arise in countries where there is an abrupt move to an emergency economy, usually when the nation suddenly finds itself at war. The emergency economy means that industrial and other business organizations are stripped of their competitive manoeuvrability regarding employees, customers, suppliers, etc. In other words, the government now assigns to the various organizations quotas of employees (because many former employees are being mobilized), customers (the armed forces being the major one, the others being rationed), and so on. This means that a substantial part of the decision making of individual organizations is done for them by government agencies. This, in turn, results in a substantial decrease in their SDM.

In fact, during wartime the majority of organizations have to operate in stabilized, formally centralized, functional structures in order to accommodate to the SDM with which they are left. On the whole there is no place for growth structures, be they entrepreneurial, functional, decentralized, or multistructured, in times of war. The exceptions are mainly new, innovative, growing ventures working for the war effort. Other exceptions are those working against the war effort, in bypassing the emergency economy by creating black markets and the like. However, here again it is the responsibility of management, first and last, to adapt their structures to the SDM.

As already repeatedly emphasized in this book, without the necessary leadership and followership characteristics in key managerial positions, the managerial structure cannot be changed to what the SDM requires. Interestingly enough, the environmental and moral pressures during times of war and other emergencies, are the only ones to cause voluntary changes in the leadership and followership characteristics of people to take place.[10] It is as if in extreme emergencies the managerial structures change and adapt to the SDM by themselves, because the managers change their leadership and followership characteristics according to the extreme emergency pressures. This means that it is actually easier to adapt managerial structures to the SDM in times of war and strife, when drastic changes occur in SDM and consequently in structure, than it is during other times.

During these 'other times', which constitute the larger part of organizational life, there may be a no less drastic need for adaptation of managerial structure to the SDM, only they do not occur at the next moment for a large number of organizations. Every organization encounters sooner or later the ailment of maladaptation of the managerial structure to the SDM. However, most of the time there are no pressures on managers to change their leadership and followership characteristics. This is why an organizational collapse, resulting from a maladaptation to the dynamics of the TOS ailment, is much more apt to occur during peace than during wartime.[11]

7.1.5 Second Ailment: Undisclosed Feelings

One grave result of the 'no full disclosure' disease is that a large part of an individual's feelings accumulates in his emotional and mental systems. The ever-growing pressure from these undisclosed attitudes, opinions, and thoughts could lead to psychological problems for the individual, as well as interpersonal and morale problems for the organization.

Human beings have an almost innate need to share their thoughts and feelings with others of their kind. This need is present from very early infancy and, in fact, exists to some extent from the moment a baby is born.[12] Without the fulfilment of this need, the mental health of individuals could be harmed. This need for mental health is the equivalent of food and drink for physical health. Indeed, individuals who isolate themselves from their fellow human beings, and talk only to themselves, are considered eccentric. So are people who prefer the company of animals, talking to them rather than to other human beings.[13]

Members of the operating organization, who refrain from telling those who surround them in the hierarchy the whole truth, feel a compelling need to share it with somebody else. However, they have a problem in divulging their feelings about their organizational life to friends who are not part of it. Consider a manager who comes home and wants to tell his wife (or alternatively a female manager wishing to confide in her husband) what went on in the organization—things that he would not tell others inside the organization. Such feelings are on the whole related to other individuals in the organization. They are, nevertheless, usually connected with some concrete functional problem in an area such as manufacturing, accounting, finance, etc. Without first explaining at least the general technical aspects of the problem, one cannot usually plunge into revealing one's feelings about its human and organizational aspects.

For example, a foreman instructs a maintenance worker to perform a certain operation on a machine, but the worker does something else, refusing to carry out his instruction. This may lead to some industrial dispute, involving the union and higher management. The foreman feels that his immediate superior has not backed him in this matter, as he should have. He has not, however, told anybody in the organization. Returning home, he wants to tell his wife about it. He starts telling her what he instructed the worker to do and what the worker did, trying to explain to his wife why the worker was wrong. The foreman finds that he has to go into a technical explanation, which may be difficult for his wife to understand. He discovers it will take him some time to get to the crux of the thing he wants to get off his chest. He is impatient to get through the technical bit as quickly as possible and is irritated that his wife cannot immediately grasp the technical aspects. He gives up. It may even increase his frustration to realize that the only people who would not require any explanation about the technical aspects are those very people to whom he could not and would not disclose his feelings.

The accumulation of unreleased feelings may create serious emotional and mental problems for the individual. The release of the accumulated feelings is not only a cure for mental disturbances and maladies, but likewise a preventive mental health measure to avoid their occurrence.

The effects of the undisclosed feelings may be crucial to the individual, yet they are even more dangerous to the organization. This is for two reasons. First, in the organization one has the accumulated frustration and exasperation of many individuals. The accumulation of the ill effects of this ailment is expressed in the general attitudes towards what is going on in the organization, referred to as morale. Such attitudes are likewise manifested in the interpersonal relationships within the managerial structure, as well as those with other members of the organization, be they workers, customers, suppliers, bankers, and the rest. The other reason for the gravity of these ill effects is the fact that the non-disclosure is both directed towards and concerns the same individuals within one's own organization. The undisclosed feelings weighing upon an individual may negatively affect the atmosphere, the morale, and the relationships within his family. However, the ill effects are much larger within a person's own organization, since this is the source of his undisclosed feelings.

7.1.6 Third Ailment: Hierarchical Communication Gap

The third ailment resulting from failure to disclose fully may be even more serious for organizations than the undisclosed feelings ailment just discussed. It will presently be seen that in consequence of 'no full disclosure' only a very small part of what goes on in the minds of people in the lower echelons of management reaches those at the very top of the hierarchy. Conversely, people at the bottom of the hierarchy do not really know what goes on in the minds of their top managers.

The communication up and down the formal hierarchy usually passes from one level to another, only occasionally bypassing one or more levels. Managers are generally committed to the 'no bypassing' norm, on which people all over the world, except those in Japan, have been brought up. It is different in the entrepreneurial managerial structure, which is very much apart from the organizational chart describing its formal structure; in many entrepreneurial organizations such a chart is not even in existence, even in the minds of their managers. In entrepreneurial organizations, most managers operate in a hierarchy of two levels: the chief executive, i.e. the entrepreneur, and below him all the other managers. However, all other types of structures operate in several levels of hierarchy. The number of these levels is at least three, and may sometimes reach more than twenty managerial echelons.

A hierarchy of, say, five levels is common in medium-sized organizations, structured on functional lines. Consider the extent of the hierarchical communication gap in such organizations. It is assumed, as was done earlier in this chapter, that the people relate to their superiors and subordinates only one third of their true feelings, while the other two thirds constitute the 'non-truth', equally divided between 'not the whole truth' and 'not nothing but the truth'.

Consider first the upward communication in a situation, in which the superior is aware of only one third of the true feelings of his subordinates. His own superior is aware only of a third of what *he* is aware of. Assuming that he is relating to *his* superior only one third of the one third of the truth of his subordinate, the superior's superior will be aware of only one ninth of the truth of the subordinates. In other words, under such conditions, the truth of the lowest level in the hierarchy is exponentially reduced as the communication flows up the hierarchy. The calculation for the amount of low-level truth reaching the top of a five-level hierarchy is therefore:

$$\tfrac{1}{3} \text{ (of true feeling)}^{\text{(number of levels of hierarchy} - 1)} = \left(\frac{1}{3}\right)^4 = \frac{1}{(3 \times 3 \times 3 \times 3)} = \frac{1}{81}$$

This means that under the above specified conditions only a little more than 1 per cent of what the low-level managers in a five-level hierarchy really think and feel reaches their CE. If two more levels of hierarchy are added, there will be seven echelons and six communication gaps. The share of the truth of first level of management reaching the CE drops to little more than 0.1 per cent (3 to the power six makes 1/729).

The same is true when the communication flows downwards rather than upwards. Thus in a hierarchy of five levels under the same assumptions, only somewhat more than 1 per cent of what the CE really thinks and feels is reaching his first line of managers.

It may be a revelation to managers that this communication gap is not peculiar to them and their specific organizations only, but it is a universal sickness. Unlike the undisclosed feelings ailment, of which one often hears complaints such as 'there is nobody I can talk to over here', the communication gap ailment is rarely admitted by managers. Every manager knows, of course, that he is not telling his superior, subordinates, and peers everything on his mind; but this is an indiscretion not to be openly discussed even with people outside the concerned hierarchy.

Not admitting such universal behaviour is especially aggravated in the upper echelons of the hierarchy, often degenerating into hypocrisy. Not many CEs would admit that they are withholding their thoughts and feelings from their subordinates, let alone admit that they know very little of the real thoughts and feelings of their managers in lower levels regarding what is going on in the organization. It is worth stressing that the higher one climbs in the hierarchy the more interpersonal, informal, and oral the communications become.[14] Late in this chapter it will be seen that the relative amount of non-truth drops when one has the opportunity to consider carefully what one communicates to others, as is the case in formal, written communication. Thus, as oral communication grows, there is more concealment in communication with others in the higher echelons. Consequently, a CE is aware of a relatively smaller part of what is in the minds of managers, say, two levels below him, than those same managers in the third hierarchy level know of what the managers in the fifth level, two levels below them, really think and feel.

Another major difference in the relative amount of concealment, and consequently in the severity of the communication gap, is to be found among organizations in different contingency positions, previously presented in Table 7.1 and discussed in the context of no full disclosure. Here again, the more the situation is crucial to the survival of the organization, the higher the rate of concealment among its managers. This is because the greater the disparity between the managerial characteristics of leadership and followership, on the one hand, and the SDM and/or the managerial structure on the other hand, the larger the non-truth in relation to the truth, and consequently the more severe the communication gap ailment.

Consider, for example, a situation in which managers, with leadership and followership characteristics suitable for an entrepreneurial structure, continue operating in the organization, in spite of the fact that its SDM has grown decisively beyond the SDM of an entrepreneurial structure.

At the first stage of imbalance, the organization continues to be run by its CE in an entrepreneurial managerial structure, in which he can approach any of his managers. The SDM pressures on managers are enormous, and their satisfaction drops and their worries about the CE increase. The concealment and, therefore, the communication gap increase considerably.

A second imbalance stage may follow, when a suitable structure for the new SDM is imposed upon the management, without, however, replacing the CE and most of his collaborators who have suitable managerial characteristics for an entrepreneurial structure. This imposed change of structure is usually achieved by planting a few new managers in key positions of the new structure; they come between the CE and the old-time managers, preventing them from operating in an entrepreneurial structure. At this stage the SDM is properly accommodated by the managerial structure, but the majority of the managers, the old-time CE and his collaborators, are dissatisfied, as they are operating contrary to their leadership and followership characteristics. The CE from above and the old-time managers from below feel antagonistic towards the new managers, who are perceived to come between them. Consequently, the concealment and communication gap are considerable in this stage.

Thus, the communication gap is on the whole relatively greater at the top of the hierarchy, where it can be more harmful to the survival of the organization. Furthermore, the more crucial the imbalance among the principal systems of the TOS, the more critical the communication gap ailment.

7.2 THREE CURES WHICH HAVE HELPED ONLY MARGINALLY

The three ailments of sick organization—maladaptation to the dynamics of TOS, undisclosed feelings, and the hierarchical communication gap—are not new discoveries. They have been with organizations for over 100 years. Since the beginning of the twentieth century, they have become increasingly acute, severe, and in many cases terminal.

The main problem has been that these ailments have not been properly diagnosed, although the symptoms have been quite clear. Consequently, the remedies that organizational scientists and consultants have prescribed over the years have turned out, on the whole, to be ineffective. Three such remedies which have been tried since the beginning of this century are presented below. The first remedy to be tried was scientific management 'consulting'. This cure has been tried in organizations since around the turn of the twentieth century. The second remedy, 'changing' managerial characteristics, has been tried in organizations since the early 1950s. The third remedy, 'innovating' managerial structures, first appeared in the early 1960s.

The order of presentation chosen is according to the degree of generalization that the remedy deals with. First comes the remedy of 'changing' managerial characteristics which assumes that individuals and groups can be trained to adapt themselves to different modes of behaviour. Then comes the remedy of 'innovating' managerial structures which tries to encompass the whole managerial structure rather than deal with individuals and groups therein. Finally, there is scientific managerial 'consulting', which is assumed to be a remedy for the SDM as well as the managerial structure of the organization.

The reader may wonder why a possible cure like organizational development, or 'OD' as it has been referred to, has not been included. The basic reason is that the term 'organizational development' has become somewhat ambiguous.

In the concepts and approaches used by those who have lately appeared under the umbrella of OD, there are found amounts of the three remedies just listed. OD, according to its practitioners, contains different proportions of the three cures which have only marginally helped organizations. Unfortunately, mixing them in different cocktails does not seem to increase their effectiveness in curing the three basic ailments. On the other hand, the term 'organizational development', used not in the 'OD' context, could be applied to remedies which could more effectively help organizations. These cures, helping organizations to adapt to the dynamics of the TOS, are described later.

The three cures described below in some detail have only marginally helped organizations. They have persisted in organizations for 30, 20 and 80 years respectively.

7.2.1 'Changing' Managerial Characteristics

There are various classifications of managerial characteristics. In this book, managerial characteristics have been classified according to the leadership and followership characteristics required of the managers in the three upper hierarchical levels of the managerial structures described earlier. These include top managers in the three basic structures, entrepreneurial, functional, and decentralized, and in the multistructure, a federation of basic structures. The different types of such managers are presented in Table 7.2. There are, of course, managers in the upper hierarchical levels of the four structures who do not conform exactly to the description of managers specified in the table. There are also many managers who have the managerial (leadership and followership) characteristics appearing in the table who are employed in lower managerial roles than those specified. Such managers, with the same leadership and followership characteristics, are to be found in organizations with managerial structures different from those appearing in Table 7.2. Such organizations are being run in intermediate managerial structures (see also Table 5.1, in pp. 150, 151, 152).

Table 7.2 shows that the entrepreneurial structure requires two types of managers, an 'entrepreneur' and his 'aides'. The creation of a functional structure requires two new types of managers. The decentralized product/service line and area structures require only one new type of manager, namely a 'decentralized leader' for their CE. Likewise, multistructures require only one new type of manager, that of a 'multistructure leader' for their CE.

The required number of each of these six types of managers varies according to the rate of change in managerial structures, closely linked to the expansion in the organizational SDM in a country or area. In the nineteenth century, the managers were on the whole entrepreneurs and their aides—and only a relatively small number were functional leaders and heads of functions. It may be of interest to estimate the necessary number of managers required in the world whose managerial characteristics are those of CEs of their respective managerial structures. A rough guess in each case appears in the last column of Table 7.2.

A similar estimate is presented of the necessary numbers and types of managers in the world who are subordinates of CEs of entrepreneurial and functional structures, i.e. entrepreneur's aides and heads of functions. Large numbers of these last two types of managers are to be found in the medium and lower hierarchical levels (from the fourth level, downwards) of large functional, decentralized, and multistructured organizations.

The last column of Table 7.2 shows that the estimated required numbers range all the way from hundreds to thousands of 'multistructure CEs leaders'; through tens of thousands to hundreds of thousands of CEs of 'entrepreneurial' and 'decentralized structures', and hundreds of thousands to millions of 'functional CEs'; reaching millions to tens of millions of 'entrepreneur's aides' and 'heads of functions'.

The six different types of managers appearing in Table 7.2 came into existence as countries and organizations advanced in their SDM, requiring in addition to their entrepreneurial managerial structures, first functional, formally centralized structures, then decentralized structures, and, finally, multistructures. The coming into being of new types of managers has been part of the process of socio-cultural change in the wider environments of the countries concerned. Basic changes in education and society have come about with the ever-growing changes in technology, since the Industrial Revolution. This evolution has not only changed the knowledge and know-how of human beings, but also their norms, values, and mores, and has affected, primarily, the way in which they perceive and relate to their fellow human beings. In the wider social structures it has meant that they have become more democratic and aware of what is now referred to as human rights. In the organizational context it has meant that managers have become more participative in their relationships with others in the different hierarchical echelons.

The atmosphere in which children are brought up changes with time, varying from generation to generation. It is primarily dominated by parents and kindergarten teachers; those personality aspects acquired in early childhood are mostly formed by the time one reaches primary school. Interpersonal leadership and followership characteristics are part of this type of personality aspects.[16]

Many of the children who were brought up, say, in New York at the beginning of this century, have grown up to become members of functionally structured operating organizations; i.e. in formally centralized managements. Thus a large number of the above children who had leadership characteristics at all (i.e. future potential managers, rather than workers) could eventually become suitable 'functional leaders' or, in most cases 'heads of functions', performing the roles described in Table 7.2. It usually takes a person, from the age of 5 years onwards, about a quarter of a century to become a practising manager. Thus children born at the turn of the century were ready to run functional structures in the 1920s. In

Table 7.2 Six different types of managers in three upper hierarchical levels of four managerial structures

| Types of managers | Managerial roles in managerial structures | | | | Managerial (leadership and followership) characteristics | Estimated order of magnitude of universally required number of managers[b] |
	Entrepreneurial structure	Functional structure[a]	Product/ service line and area structures[a]	Multistructure		
Entrepreneur	CE			CE's subordinates	Perceives any member of the managerial hierarchy as his immediate superior. His assignments to managers are of a general character, expecting the subordinate to initiate the details himself (including what, with whom, and when to do). Does not accept systematic control of a superior, or a major entrepreneurial initiative among his subordinates.	'0,000 — '00,000
Entrepreneur's aide	CE's subordinates			CE's subordinates and subordinates' subordinates	Has a certain amount of initiative so as to carry out the unspecified details of the entrepreneur's assignments. In so doing, he perceives any other manager as approachable for collaboration in the assignments. He feels that he himself could be approached any day not only by other managers, but by the entrepreneur himself, checking his performance and/or changing his assignments.	'000,000 — '0,000,000

Functional leader	CE	CE's subordinates' subordinates	CE's subordinates and subordinates' subordinates	Generally works through his immediate formal subordinates. Is specific in assigning tasks to them, as to: who does what, how and where, and as to 'if this or that happens—do the following....' Usually controls and directs the performance of his subordinates, at least once a week.	'00,000 — '000,000
Head of function	CE's subordinates	CE's subordinates' subordinates	CE's subordinates and subordinates' subordinates	Expects to receive assignments from his superior in a formalized and routinized way. Has a limited amount of autonomy, not only in the details of carrying out his assignments, but likewise in the length of time he is able to perform independently of the other functions. This degree of autonomy is usually not more than one week. His dependence on other functions makes it necessary for him to rely on his superior's interference, at least once a week.	'000,000 — '0,000,000
Decentralized leader	CE	CE's subordinates		Delegates to his subordinates, who are 'functional leaders', the authority and responsibility for performing independently of each other and of himself. This delegated degree of autonomy is usually established at one month or three months, or six months, or one year, at the most. The delegation of autonomy means that the sub-ordinated functional leader is given full authority for all the functional resources he needs in order to perform independently of other decentralized units, and of the decentralized leader himself, for a period of one, three, six, or twelve months.	'0,000 — '00,000

Table 7.2 *(continued)*

| Types of managers | Managerial roles in managerial structures | | | | Estimated order of magnitude of universally required number of managers[b] |
	Entrepreneurial structure	Functional structure[a]	Product/ service line and area structures[a]	Multistructure	
				Managerial (leadership and followership) characteristics	
Multistructure leader				CE	'00 – '000
				A CE who is capable of controlling directly under himself a federation of different structural units —entrepreneur's aides (under his own entrepreneurial leadership), and/or heads of functions (under his direct functional leadership), and/or functional leaders (who are the leaders of their product/service lines and/or areas), and/or entrepreneurs (granting to them the means and support to operate for several years in complete autonomy). He is different from all the previous five types of managers in that he is not treating and leading his subordinates in a uniform way. He has to be able to control and direct them in different control-yardsticks—entrepreneur's aides, every day; heads of functions, every week; functional leaders, every one, three, six, or twelve months; and entrepreneurs, every, say, five or ten years, or whenever the entrepreneur approaches him, rather than the other way around. In addition to treating his subordinates in different control yardsticks, he has to organize his time well, so as to fit the varying control and directive periods (which require investments of both preparation and direct contact time) into his own timetable.	

Notes:
[a] In *stabilization* periods only. The *growth* functional, product/service line, and area structures have, under their upper level of heads of function (appearing in this table), decentralized leaders.
[b] Including *all* the required managers in all organizations throughout the world (including organizations operating in intermediate managerial structures, e.g. the growth functional and decentralized structures).

the 1920s, US parents started to raise their children in a way that would eventually make them into so-called decentralized leaders—turning them into suitable CEs for decentralized structures a quarter of a century later. After the Second World War, the atmosphere in which some young children were brought up was such that they are the nucleus of potential 'multistructure leaders' until the end of the twentieth century. A similar process has occurred in other countries, except for a lag behind the USA in one or more managerial generation gaps.[17]

In other words the socio-cultural adaptation to technological advancement is generating the new types of managers who are required for the new evolving structures. There may be a certain managerial generation gap in every country; but eventually the supply of new types of managers, like decentralized and multistructure leaders, may catch up with the demand. One should worry not only when organizations, in one country or another, are short of certain types of managers, but likewise when they have an overabundance of managers.

Thus, for example, if a country has an abundance of managers for entrepreneurial and functional structures, but is short of decentralized leaders, its organizations cannot turn their managerial structures to product/service line and area structures. This can become an economic catastrophe and a national tragedy, when the country is ready technologically to move to larger SDM. A country is faced with such a situation when it cannot realize its growth and expansion objectives, or improve its economic lot and standard of living, because its organizations are unable to digest larger SDM for lack of managers required for the more advanced structure.

It may seem that the balance within the TOS system could be permanently maintained, because it contains a sort of *perpetuum mobile* which can prepare adequate numbers of multistructure leaders. These could then fill the roles of all other types of managers by changing their interpersonal behaviour according to the changing TOS needs.

Multistructure leaders have one other unique characteristic which none of the other five types of managers have. They are the only managers whose interpersonal traits to not include followership characteristics. Although entrepreneurs do not like to be subordinate to others, they would accept a subordinated position of 'privileged entrepreneur' in a multistructured organization. That is, they would be controlled every few years, but in return they would not have to worry about raising the basic capital necessary for their ventures because it would be supplied by the multistructure CE. Multistructure leaders, on the other hand, would not voluntarily accept any superior. Although they could lead quite well any type of structure, they would feel uneasy doing it for a long period of time. They would feel uncomfortable directly supervising managers with followership characteristics different from those the uniform structure requires. They would tend to let such subordinate managers operate in the way their followership and leadership characteristics best fit them to do. This in turn means that they would all the time feel the urge to turn the structure into a multistructure.

The short and long of this discussion is that there is a need for all types of managers in the quantities required by the managerial structures of all countries throughout the world. If all managers had multistructure leader characteristics, organizations would have only generals and no lower ranking officers.

Research on personality traits has shown that most people could adapt their behaviour to what is required of them. Only those with an extreme imbalance in favour of either the 'heuristic' or the 'rational' sides of their brains will always behave according to their traits.[18] However, even when people adapt themselves to a certain behavioural pattern their leadership and followership characteristics will not change and they will revert to them whenever possible. Other recent research on individual behaviour indicates that personality is a function of three main factors—parents, adult, and child. The findings of this research seem to show that a substantial number of behavioural characteristics are dependent on what happened to a person in early childhood.[19]

Nevertheless, since the Second World War there has been a school in social psychology whose work revolves around, among other things, the ability to train people voluntarily to change their interpersonal behaviour. Those belonging to this school have maintained, with a wide variety of shades and emphases, that through a proper approach to organizations their members can be helped voluntarily to behave in new and different ways; or, putting it in other words, to assume new roles and change their previous ones. It is possible to obtain both these objectives. The ability to achieve them depends, however, on the individual's previous interpersonal behaviour. If he is confronted with a new situation, in which he could play a role which he has never played before, and if this new role suits his leadership and followership characteristics, he will naturally assume it. A manager will not, however, voluntarily play a new role which is contrary to his managerial characteristics. In some cases, when his brain is either very 'heuristic' or very 'rational', he will not play the new role under any conditions, even involuntarily.

There is another situation in which it is possible to achieve a change in interpersonal behaviour. A person may have performed his roles involuntarily, succumbing to organizational, social, and psychological pressure. In such a case, if one helps remove such pressures he will willingly, sometimes even enthusiastically, change his behaviour to bring it in line with his personality traits.

It must be remembered, however, that in such a case the individual must be put into a different managerial structure position, which requires his type of managerial characteristics. This is the TOS solution for adapting the managerial characteristics to the structure, or vice versa. In this way, however, the individual is not changed. He is rather being helped to get closer to his basic, unchanging personality and the roles which he can best play in conformity with his managerial characteristics.

Incidentally, there is only a limited necessity for training an individual for roles which suit his managerial characteristics. Take, for example, a group of poor businessmen running small, unsuccessful affairs in an Indian village. To help them to become more successful, they do not need training in entrepreneurial role playing since they already are entrepreneurs in their managerial characteristics. They need help not on the managerial side, but rather on the side of the scope of decision making. Indian businessmen could be helped by exchanging their wider environments, namely by helping them to move to other countries in which they would confront less competition from similar types of entrepreneurs. This is indeed a major explanation of the Indian entrepreneurial success in East African countries, and, subsequently, in London and other parts of Britain. The Indian entrepreneurs came to new environments where their managerial characteristics were in short supply.

There are, however, other ways of helping the Indian village entrepreneurs to fare better by utilizing their entrepreneurial characteristics. One effective way is to help them to meet other entrepreneurs, enabling them to talk things over in an atmosphere free of day-to-day pressures. This could result in two advantages. First, it enriches the entrepreneurs' reservoir of ideas about what new ventures they might try and what existing ones should be dropped. Such encounters likewise fertilize the entrepreneurs with new ideas about how and where to operate.[20] The second advantage in such meetings lies in the expansion of their circle of acquaintances, some of whom could be potential collaborators as customers, suppliers, capital providers, or, even, partners.[21]

One cannot change the managerial characteristics of managers who are typical entrepreneurs, or entrepreneur's aides, or functional leaders, or heads of function, or decentralized or multistructure leaders. Nor is it necessary to mould them into whatever they already are.

Management training could therefore be directed towards three main objectives. The first is teaching people about managerial techniques and tools, some of which they may be able to use in the future when the need arises, and which fit in with the managerial structure and characteristics.

A second objective is to cover as many alternative applied organizational situations as possible. This enriches a student's perspective and improves his chances of finding a suitable managerial situation in the future. Such training would also familiarize the student, even if only superficially, with the characteristics of different types of organizations, environments, etc., in a variety of situations.

Last, but not least, good management training should cultivate in the student an awareness of as many as possible situations that organizations may find themselves in. In other words, a manager should know how the main TOS and component systems are related to each other, and what are the various options in each of them. Among others, he should learn to distinguish between different types of managerial interpersonal behaviour and different sets of managerial characteristics. This means that a well-trained manager should eventually be able to diagnose the leadership and followership characteristics of other managers with whom he comes in contact, as well as diagnose his own managerial characteristics.

Those believing in voluntary change claim they can train managers in new roles and that such management training helps achieve a better understanding and diagnosis of the roles played by others, and by oneself. This may well be so, but the question is at what cost does one achieve it, and are there not other ways of helping managers to improve their understanding of their own and their fellow managers' managerial characteristics? In considering these two questions, it will be well to study the social psychology school of thought.

It started in the early 1950s and first went under such names as 'group dynamics' and 'planned change'. Its beginning is associated with training programmes given in Bethel, Maine, while the initial psychological thinking was developed by its founders on the basis of Kurt Lewin's work. Eventually this branched off into T (training) groups, sensitivity training, human workshops, and the like. This sort of training essentially involves a group of people who are encouraged to speak freely in front of each other and analyse each other's behaviour in a forthright and candid way. The group is under the guidance of a 'trainer', who should have prior training in psychology. This enables him to conduct the group members in a process of opening up, reacting to, and analysing each other.

At the beginning, this group training was often performed on managers working together in the same organization. They were either each other's peers or even managers from different hierarchical levels reporting to each other. As we have already discussed the 'no full disclosure' disease, it is not necessary to elaborate upon the negative repercussions of making people tell each other things they would not reveal outside the 'euphoria' of a T-group. The interpersonal tensions and communication gaps, as well as the personal worries created as a result of such a process, overshadowed any possible benefit which could be achieved by these means.

Consequently, some of the founders of this school refrained from including co-managers from one organization in the same training group. Another type of modification of T-groups was what is referred to as 'role playing'. This is an opening up process which is neither full nor personal, followed by a behavioural analysis. In this type of training, group members are assigned roles in a specific situation or problem. For example, a chief executive and his immediate subordinates in a functional structure might be confronted by a certain crisis. The group members play their roles, usually projecting their own behaviour into the role, or sometimes acting out another type of behaviour.

From this school stems a whole new terminology which has been associated with the training. It includes such terms as 'change agents', 'clients', 'action research', and 'organizational development'. These terms may, however, cover more things than just group training, even when used by members of this school. These same terms are sometimes used by organizational scientists not belonging to this school, in a way completely free from the concepts, ideas, and practices just described. For example, 'action research' for members of this school means active participation with the managers in what is going on.[22] But the term 'action research' is often used to denote the results of organizational research which are fed back to the managers and, hopefully, induce them to act.

Finally, it is necessary to return to the two questions posed regarding management training and how it helps people to an awareness of the differences between the managerial characteristics of others and of themselves. The first question is concerned with risks to be borne by group therapy.

The social and interpersonal risks involved have already been mentioned. The aftermath of a thorough opening up is often deep embarrassment felt among those who have disclosed to each other at least a part of their innermost feelings, and have had them openly analysed, sometimes ruthlessly, by other members of the group.[23] As already noted, such a traumatic experience, when involving members of the same organization, could end up in the inability of people to continue working together.

The consequence of such an experience may be even more traumatic, and indeed tragic for some individuals. Persons whose mental state may be in a delicate equilibrium may find it undermined by self-exposure and group criticism. Such occurrences are not, unfortunately, hypothetical at all. Mental breakdowns and even more severe mental consequences, although rare, have occurred. Others have succeeded in concealing the mental scars inflicted on them during the T-groups, sensitivity training, and the like, to which they have been exposed. On the whole, the risks of such a process are too high, when compared with the benefit derived by the majority of participants.

The second question is concerned with other means for increasing the sensitivity to, and awareness of, differences in managerial roles and personalities. One way is a certain use of group training, already mentioned, but without going into an opening up process, but rather through role playing, re-enacting organizational roles. One has, however, to be extremely careful in applying role playing, lest it develop into too much of a 'sensitivity training'.

The chief method for training people to distinguish among different types of interpersonal characteristics is through the analysis of case studies. There are two types of case studies which are most suitable for this purpose. The first are human relations cases, in which one encounters different types of personalities, and sees how they relate to each other, usually in diad (pair) relationships or in groups. The second type are TOS cases. Indeed the development of distinction between, and sensitivity to, the various types of managers which is attained through case studies is unequalled either by way of T-groups or through business games. Group sensitivity training does not give the student the notion of the organization context and the pressures under which people perform their interpersonal roles. Neither intergroup behaviour, nor the effects of a role like that of the CE, are part of T-groups. In business games, on the other hand, especially when the game gets somewhat closer to the organizational reality and behaviour, the participants cannot properly look at themselves, in the heat of the game.[24]

One can think of other ways of training managers, so that their sensitivity to, and awareness of, different types of managerial structure and characteristics can be improved, without exposing them to mental 'group training' of various kinds. Possibly the other major possible method of training, in addition to case studies and business games, is arranging for managers to observe and even participate in managerial structures of organizations other than their own.

This type of training is somewhat like a business game which one observes or participates in. It is, however, a real life situation. It therefore differs from a business game primarily in the dynamics of its various TOS systems which

328

develop as they do, not being bound by a set of relationships according to which the business game model is pre-set. That is to say that decision making in the real life situation is based on a complex combination of inputs and rational, emotional, personal, social, and organizational considerations and feelings. In other words, real life decision making is a mixture of the formal and informal parts of organizational behaviour. The rules of a business game could be based only on the formal aspects of decision making.

The other difference between participation in an organization and in a business game is the degree of commitment and involvement of the manager. It is somewhat like the difference between actors behaving in real life and performing on the stage. In the latter, they sometimes personally identify with their roles, thus making them life-like. As in a business game, there are expressions of likes and dislikes on the stage and other behavioural manifestations among the actors. These are expressed in an informal way, between the lines and in whispered remarks and gestures.

Thus the observation of, or participation in, the functioning of another organization gives the training a flavour of real organizational behaviour by facilitating understanding of different modes of managerial structure and characteristics. The fact that the trainee is not himself a member of the organization reduces his own involvement and enables him to have a more detached appreciation of what is going on. Likewise, the managers of the organization will feel less constrained and more open with such an outsider and unveil to him those aspects of organizational behaviour of which he would not have been aware had he himself been one of the managers.

However, this type of observer or observer-participant role has a serious drawback for management training. The role a management trainee is supposed to perform in such a situation is that of a researcher, rather than a manager. In order to learn systematically from the situation he observes, he has to master the skills of an organizational researcher, e.g. how to listen to people, how to consider contradicting perceptions of the same situation, how to register what he sees and hears, how to analyse it, etc. This means that if it is to be properly done, the trainee must first go through some kind of organizational research training. It also means that during his period in another organization, the person is training not only in management, i.e. in the dynamics of the parts of the TOS, but also in the performance of organizational research. The latter is generally not needed by managers in the execution of their roles. In addition to the unnecessary time and effort invested in becoming an organizational field researcher, there is another fault in this type of training. Some trainees might conclude that they are good at it, and consequently conclude they should devote their life to organizational research or consulting, rather than to organizational practice. This could be a gain for organizational research, but it would certainly be a loss for the organizations who send their managers to be trained in this fashion.[25]

The best way to train managers is by a method combining most of the advantages of the above approaches, avoiding their faults and dangers; that is, to let the managers see how they and the other managers behave in their own organization. This, however, should be done by way of individual feedback. This type of feedback and training is discussed in the next sub-chapter, dealing with ways to help organizations.

7.2.2 'Innovating' Managerial Structures

Ever since the Industrial Revolution, the growing organizational SDM required the formation of new managerial structures so as to encompass these larger and larger SDM. This meant that from time to time new managerial structures had to emerge. The formally centralized (or 'bureaucratic') functional structure first appeared in industrial organizations in the second half of the nineteenth century. The product/service line and the area decentralized structures immediately followed the First World War. The managerial multistructure came next, first appearing in the USA and Western European organizations after the Second World War.

However, since the emergence of the multistructure, organizational SDM seem to continue to grow without any need for a new type of structure. This is because the multistructure is a 'flexible' structure in that it enables changes in the composition of the federated basic structures. One can include all the basic structures—a CE's entrepreneurial structure, a functional structure, a product/service line structure, an area structure, and independent entrepreneurs with their aides—or omit one or more of these basic structures from the multistructure. Likewise, one could have larger or smaller numbers of subordinated product/service units, or of area units, or of independent entrepreneurs. The subordinated product/service and area units may be controlled through different degrees of decentralization, some units every month, others every three months, every six months, and every twelve months. Finally, one could run the functional and decentralized units of the multistructure for prolonged periods of time in concentrated growth, i.e. operating the functional, product/service line, and area structures in a flexible fashion, and increasing their activity in entrepreneurial structure units. Alternatively, the multistructure could go through a prolonged period of stabilization, in which the functional, product/service line, and area structures would be rigidly operated and controlled, and the activities of entrepreneurial structure units very much curtailed (an organigram of the multistructure appears in Figure 5.8 on page 190).

It is evident, therefore, that a multistructure, i.e. a federated managerial structure, may be adapted to a wide range of SDM. In other words, the multistructure may be restructured according to the changing conditions of the immediate and wider environments, and the consequent shifts in the strategy of what, how, and where the organization is to operate.

As seen in the previous chapter, the growth in SDM may develop in different ways. There are what has earlier been referred to as 'complex SDM', which could be absorbed in neither a functional nor a product/service line structure. However, such complex SDM, usually found in science-based organizations, have to be contained within a uniform structure rather than a multistructure.

In the previous chapter the 'matrix' structure was discussed in detail. The conclusion was reached that the ability of organizations to function effectively and efficiently in a matrix structure is quite limited and that the structural solution for complex SDM is a 'scientific slack' (Japanese approach) structure, rather than a 'matrix' one.

A matrix structure is an 'innovation'. The reason for referring to it as an 'innovation' has to do with the difference between an invention which has been implemented and an 'invention' which has ended up, at best, only in the patent office files.[26]

There are three conditions which would make the design of a new managerial structure an innovation. First, it has to fulfil a utility in the TOS; namely it has to respond to a structural problem, raised by new conditions in the SDM. Secondly, it has to be a novel solution, basically different from managerial structures already in use. Last, but not least, it has to be implemented.[27]

It is some time after their introduction that one can establish whether changes in managerial structure, as well as SDM changes in the TOS, have actually been implemented. The introduction of a basic change usually encounters resistance in varying degrees. Only after a while can one establish whether the resistance to the change has been overcome or not. Other changes, usually of a magic cure type, may be enthusiastically welcomed at the beginning, but turn out to be complete failures after a while.

The design of the matrix structure conforms with only one of the above three conditions for an innovation, in that it responds to an SDM need. The SDM problem that the matrix structure is designed to solve is that of a 'complex SDM', which cannot be accommodated within a functional structure and/or a product/service line structure.[28]

The matrix structure does not, however, fulfil the two other specified conditions. It is not a novel structure. It is very similar to Frederick Taylor's 'functional experts' structure'.[29] The matrix structure may be considered as a special case of the general proposition of the functional experts' structure. In Taylor's structure a given subordinate may have several direct superiors, who cannot coordinate his supervision among themselves. In the matrix structure, on the other hand, the number of superiors is usually limited to two (functional and project managers) or three (functional, product/service line, and area managers). Last but not least, the implementation condition is likewise not fulfilled in the case of matrix structures. The previous chapter has already stressed the organizational behaviour rejection of the matrix structure solution, and the reasons for it.

The matrix structure has been derived from the analysis of a complex SDM problem, and a search for a 'logical' solution. Whatever its designers thought at the time of Taylor's functional experts' structure is debatable. It seems, however, that the resemblance did not even occur to them. In fact, it appears as if the matrix structure was designed on a drawing board, which is also reminiscent of Taylor's 'machine model' in scientific management.[30]

7.2.3 Scientific Management 'Consulting'

The oldest and most persistent of the three cures which have only marginally helped organizations is 'consulting'. It originated in the Scientific Management movement, founded and led at the beginning of the twentieth century by Frederick Taylor.[31]

The Scientific Management movement's solutions to organization are often referred to as 'machine models'. Organizations can be considered nowadays only in terms of 'contingency models'. In a machine model there is only one 'right' answer to a specific problem. A contingency model provides different solutions to every problem, the correct solution depending on the configuration of the different systems in the model, i.e. the state of each system itself and in relation to the states of other systems, at a given point in time when the problem has to be solved.

During the first period of scientific management 'consulting', from the beginning of the twentieth century until after the First World War, customers and governments had not yet become integral factors in the decision-making processes of business organizations. The wider environments within which organizations operated in those days were relatively steady, following fixed patterns, and not subject to turbulent and unpredictable effects as they often are nowadays. Until the 1920s, all managerial structures were centralized either in entrepreneurial or in functional structures.

Consequently, a model describing how organizations behaved in those days is relatively simple. This is why the 'machine model' was suitable for explaining organizations in those early early days of scientific management, and is completely unsuitable for present-day organizations. Scientific management 'consulting' had an important contribution to make in the early days. However, since the 1920s in the USA, and since the 1930s in other industrial countries, scientific management could not and has not helped organizations. This is why we put this sort of 'consulting' in inverted commas.

Consider some of the main problems of scientific management 'consulting', and why time after time it fails. It is difficult to estimate how many such consulting projects have been carried out in all kinds of organizations, for over half a century since the 1920s. There must have been at least several hundred thousands of such projects, each lasting a few months and costing on the average several thousand dollars. This means that tens of thousands of man-years have been invested in this type of consulting, and organizations have paid billions of dollars for it.

It is likewise difficult to estimate the rates of success and failure achieved by such 'consulting' projects. There is, however, good reason to believe that the rate of success has probably not exceeded 10 per cent. Thus apparently, at best, only one project in ten has not failed.[32]

One more point needs to be stressed about scientific management 'consulting', before we can proceed to analyse the reasons for its high rate of failure. This is the fact it has persisted for such a long period of time, in spite of the evident inability of conventional consultants to help their clients appreciably. This has been happening for over half a century in all industrial countries. However, it seems to be more prevalent in some, mainly in Western Europe, than in the USA.[33] It may be that the relative excess of use of conventional consultants in Western Europe is related to the relative lack of interorganizational managerial mobility, and in intra-company secrecy, mentioned earlier in this chapter. That is to say that a major part of the real role of conventional consultants in Western Europe is in the transfer of know-how from one organization to another. There may be other reasons why conventional consultants are being called into organizations in spite of their historically poor performance in helping them with their problems. One is that managers want to use consultants in a judicial role, passing on their verdict in cases of unresolved disagreements among managers, and/or to help a certain manager to implement his own solutions, thus enabling him to overcome the resistance of others to them.

Even in these two legitimate and potentially useful roles, conventional consultants have not had much more success than in other areas in helping organizations. The disagreements among the managers do not subside after the consultants' verdict, unless one of the managerial parties to the conflict is removed from the scene. The gamble that the consultant's recommendation would reinforce the manager's ability to implement the change does not usually come off. On the contrary, the resistance to change is sometimes reinforced as a result of a negative reaction to an outsider's 'intervention' and 'lack of comprehension' about what goes on in the organization.

Nevertheless, this phenomenon of turning again and again to conventional consultants for help continues. It is quite amazing, considering the fact that the same managers who have been using conventional consultants in a futile way, would behave in a completely different way towards other human factors in their decision making, in similar situations. The same managers will not return to suppliers who do not respect their delivery and quality commitments. They will not supply customers who are continually late with their payments; and they would not hire employees again with whom they had once had bad experience in areas like attendance, discipline, and productivity.

One possible explanation for this amazing managerial behaviour is that the conventional consultant enables the manager to talk to an outsider about things which he will not mention to insiders. As will be seen in the next section listening to the manager is a very important way to help an organization. The conventional consultant usually does not understand and is not well prepared for this listening role.

There is another possible explanation for managers investing money in conventional consultants, generally without getting any worthwhile return. There are top managers who feel it is a boost to their ego to have a famous conventional consultant around. It seems to them that their status and the standing of their organization is enhanced by their association with well-known consultants. This sort of thing is similar to paying for a computer, or even only for computer services, even though this is not helpful, and may sometimes harm the organization. The top manager will nevertheless be proud of his association with a well-known computer company.

Last but not least are the occasions when managers turn to conventional consultants as a last resort, or even when it is too late for any sort of help. This is very much like a gravely sick human being, who has not been helped by general doctors and specialists, turning for help to an unlikely healer. Such a person will do so, even if he receives information indicating that the specific healer has not helped people even when they were much less sick than himself. A manager whose organization is sinking will turn to conventional consultants and to computers, as a drowning person will clutch a straw.

There are two main reasons for the high rate of failure of scientific management consultants. One has to do with professional integrity, and the other with the consultant's managerial responsibility towards the client organization.

Consider an organization which employs, say, 1000 managers at all levels, the average length of service of whom is, say, 15 years. The organization has problems in its decision-making processes and communication. The CE turns to a firm of management consultants and the latter agree to assign to the organization a team of, say, five persons for the duration of one year. At the end of this year the management consultants present the CE with a report, telling him what they think is wrong with his organization and what in their opinion should be done in order to cure it.

The first reason for the rejection of this sort of 'consulting' is the clear lack of professional integrity. How can a group of outsiders, spending a short period of time in the organization, get acquainted with it to such an extent that they could establish what is wrong and what is right for the organization? Whatever is happening in an organization is interrelated with other things—the technology, the manufacturing process, the people inside the operating organization, people and processes in other parts of the organization (customers, suppliers, unions, government, bankers, etc.), and many more technical and human aspects of the organization. Everything existing today has a history of its own, and explanations as to why things are as they are at present should often be sought in past events and decisions. Without knowing many of these things, including, especially, a thorough knowledge of the individuals in the management and the relationship among them, it is almost impossible to establish what is wrong and what is the best solution to problems involving SDM and managerial structure. Since the problem involves elements of SDM and of managerial structure, reaction to a conventional consulting report would always be that the consultants were not aware of all the facts and overlooked some conditions, etc.

In the present example, as indeed in any other organization, the management might well feel that the five man-years (five consultants spending one year in the organization) are negligible, even for trained, experienced, and bright consultants, when compared with the 15 000 man-years of the organizational management (1000 managers with an average length of service of 15 years). They could have made this calculation before signing the contract with the management consultants. This, however, does occur to them when they subsequently feel that the consultants' report lacks professional integrity.[34]

The other thing that such a report lacks is managerial responsibility. The responsibility for the implementation of the report's recommendations rests with the management, not the consultants. The managers, like all other human beings, do not, on the whole, like major changes, even if they come from within. The resistance to changes recommended by outsiders is therefore even more pronounced when the managers feel that the consultants base their diagnosis on superficial and partial knowledge and draw the prognosis, their recommendations, without having any managerial responsibility for the organization's survival.[35]

The alienation of the clients from the conventional consultants may reach huge dimensions. The willingness of the consultants to analyse and pass judgement on the client may be considered as impudence. Their eagerness to find solutions and recommend action, for which they do not bear any responsibility, may even seem to be immoral.

Only the exceptional conventional consultant can be accused of being cognizant and aware of his shortcomings in professional integrity and managerial responsibility. Many of the famous management consultancy firms attract and employ the best graduates in fields like management, business administration, industrial engineering, social sciences, etc. Indeed, when one compares the average academic standards of such consulting staffs with those of the higher managerial echelons of their clients, invariably the consultants come out on top.[36]

Therefore, the breaches in professional integrity and managerial responsibility are not intentional in the majority of cases. Probably the strongest reason for the failure of conventional consultants is connected with the confusion between the roles of outside consultants and of outside experts, in helping organizations.[37]

Experts are to be found in various areas of organization and management. Areas in which one can find outside expertise are: financial control (accounting, cost accounting, budgeting), production engineering (time and motion study, layouts, planning and control, e.g. PERT (Project Evaluation and Review Technique)—critical path analysis and Gantt—bar-chart planning and control, market research, electronic data processing, and many others.

All these experts do not, however, have a thorough expert knowledge of the organization, its decision-making processes, its managerial structure, and its people. A competent expert, looking at an organization's problem, must realize that the problem does not exist in isolation from other parts of the decision-making process and the managerial structure. Changing a procedure in one area will have its repercussions and affect whatever is happening in other areas. The links between the various component systems of the TOS make it impossible to solve a problem in one area while disregarding its relationship with other parts of the managerial structure.

Experts should therefore offer their expertise in their respective fields, but should not offer to apply their expertise to the particular organization, unless clearly requested to apply a certain expertise to a specific situation. Thus, for example, an expert in planning and control methods could teach managers variations in the use of PERT, but should *not* tell them that PERT, or variations of it, is something which they should or should not use in their organizations. The best he can do is to explain to them under what conditions PERT could contribute to planning and control, and when other techniques would be more appropriate. All this should be done without any reference to their specific organizations. The less the expert knows of what goes on in a specific organization, the less he can interfere explicitly or implicitly in the execution of suggested plans in the organization.

The expertise of the real consultant is in not demonstrating any expertise in functional or other fields of the organization. The consultant should thoroughly understand the dynamics of the TOS. He should be absolutely aware of how an outsider may help an organization. Finally, he should be competent in helping managers and other members of the organization to help themselves. Figure 7.3 presents the different paths by which outsiders may help organizations. On the left-hand side we see that when managers are confronted with an 'Imbalance in TOS' they can be helped by outsiders 'to help themselves'. This can only be done

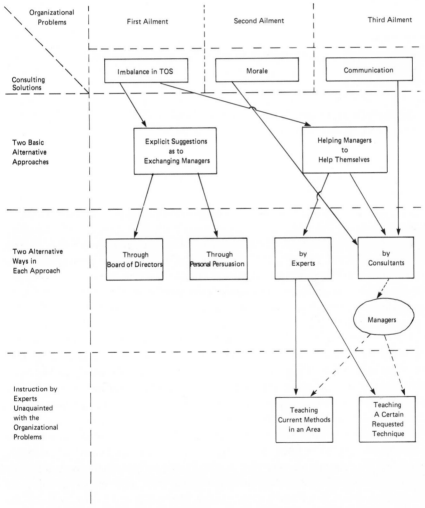

Figure 7.3   Managerial consulting—an algorithmic conceptual scheme

'by experts'. The latter should be 'teaching current methods in an area'. The managers will subsequently choose and apply those methods which are most appropriate for them and for the organization.

The next part of this chapter is devoted to some of the things that outside consultants could do for organizations, working from the inside, and how they should do these things.

7.3 WAYS TO HELP ORGANIZATIONS

Figure 7.3 presents 'consulting solutions' to 'organizational problems'. There are three kinds of organizational problems, which were presented earlier in this chapter:

First ailment: imbalance in the TOS
Second ailment: morale (undisclosed feelings)
Third ailment: communication (hierarchical communication gap)

These three ailments come about as a consequence of the two secrecy diseases—'anti-mobility' and 'no full disclosure'.

The 'imbalance in the TOS' ailment is a result of the anti-mobility disease. There are two solutions for this ailment in Figure 7.3.

Explicit suggestions about exchanging managers A serious imbalance in the TOS, primarily an imbalance between the main systems of decision making and management, can only be corrected by exchanging key position managers. The origins of the more serious imbalances in decision making in management may be often traced to the CE himself.

In such a case, when an outsider is convinced that replacing the CE would enhance the chances of survival of the organization, he can help the organization by explicitly suggesting it. The suggestion may be made to the board of directors, if it is a public corporation with a board. However, even if the organization has a board, there are many cases in which the board has no power over the CE. This happens when the CE has a controlling ownership. Thus, whether he is the chairman of the board or not, the board is, for all practical reasons, subordinated to him rather than the other way around. This may be the case in organizations which are still run by their founders or members of the founder's family. Such organizations are run in an entrepreneurial structure which has outgrown their SDM. In such cases it is impossible to suggest to the board of directors that the entrepreneurial leader should vacate the CE's position.

There are many other cases in which the position of the CE is too strong for the board to be able to replace him, even when he does not have a controlling ownership. An alternative way (see Figure 7.3) is by personally persuading the manager himself. This is a delicate and difficult task as it usually involves the replacement of a CE who has a controlling ownership and is almost invariably emotionally attached to the organization. Nevertheless, it seems that an exchange could be achieved by way of personal persuasion if two change strategies are applied. The CE has to be tempted by a new full-time occupation *outside* the organization. At the same time a replacement whom he can trust should be found and made available. Both things should occur simultaneously and desirably have a certain degree of urgency associated with them. The tempting new occupation for the CE should be seen as an opportunity which may be lost if not taken up soon. The candidate for CE should be available only within a limited period of time, or he will go somewhere else.

Consider an example in which the CE is the founder of the organization, which he is still running although it should have been run in a formalized structure long ago. Obviously, the entrepreneur has to be tempted with a real opportunity to exercise again his creative entrepreneurial abilities, as he did many years ago in his present organization, his 'baby'. However, one must make sure he will be completely absorbed in his new position so that he does not look back to his 'baby' organization; if he does, he will neither get detached from his present organization, nor be able to succeed in his new venture. Once he fails, the chance for trying this strategy again on him is much reduced.

The entrepreneur should not work together with his future replacement, breaking him in, so to say. The chance that an entrepreneur could successfully break in a replacement for himself is almost nil. Before long both managers, the existing entrepreneurial CE and the formal heir apparent, will neither trust nor have any respect for one another. The transfer from one CE to another should therefore be as swift as possible. It should occur while the old CE is plunging into the new venture.

The above mentioned alternatives for replacing managers can be recommended only if 'helping managers to help themselves' (see Figure 7.3) is not feasible. Such a situation will arise if, for example, the above mentioned entrepreneurial CE refuses to be helped by outsiders. In such a case the 'change agent',[38] if sure of the diagnosis, can revert either to turning to the board of directors or to implementing the change by personally persuading the CE himself.

Helping managers to help themselves The first alternative for helping managers to help themselves is through experts (see Figure 7.3). This alternative has already been mentioned. The expert can help managers to help themselves by enriching their knowledge of available techniques in a particular area, leaving it to the manager to decide which method he will apply, if any. Alternatively, the expert could teach the managers a 'certain requested technique', according to the choice of the manager and *not* of the expert.

Both these alternative contributions should be handled in a way which will not be perceived by the client, the manager, as implying the preference of the expert for a specific method for the organization. The expert should not even make any such suggestions or indicate any preferences; i.e. desirably he should be ignorant of the TOS of his client.

The second alternative for helping managers to help themselves (see Figure 7.3) is through consultants.

The algorithmic conceptual scheme of Figure 7.3 indicates that this sort of consultancy helps to cure all the three basic organizational ailments of 'imbalance in the TOS', 'morale', and 'communication'.

338

7.3.1 The Roman Catholic Church Cures

The Catholic Church is unique among all organizations in having survived for almost 2000 years. What can one learn from the Roman Catholic Church (RCC) that would help our organizations to survive and overcome the difficulties they confront every few years? How is it possible to translate these ways in which the RCC overcomes its organizational diseases and ailments, into remedial actions in business and other organizations?

The Catholic Church has survived because it has been able to combat the two most prevalent organizational diseases: ossification of structures and paralysis of communication because of fear. The ways in which the Church has overcome these two diseases are the election of popes of advanced age, confession, and the maintenance of two different managerial structures superimposed on each other. Although these three ways are not adaptable to business, they suggest other means that will perform the same functions.

Selecting elderly popes with short life expectancies provides the Church with frequent opportunities to re-evaluate the adaptability of its managerial structure to the requirements of its decision-making processes. The Church selects a suitable organizational head for its needs at the time, choosing a pope whose leadership characteristics would guarantee the necessary changes in the managerial structure.

Two other special organizational means which contribute towards the survival of the Roman Catholic Church are: (a) conducting its decision-making processes simultaneously in two different communication networks, and (b) requiring catharsis by way of confession. These help the Church to cure the most dangerous organizational disease—the absence of frankness among the organizational members, especially among those formally related to each other.

Members of most organizations accumulate attitudes and feelings which they usually cannot and would not share with others. The Church makes them open up and relieve themselves of all that weighs upon their hearts and minds—by way of confession.

The result of telling others *only part* of what one truly feels is that top management knows only a little of what the feelings and attitudes of people throughout the organization are; and vice versa, the lower echelons know only a little of how top management really feels about what is going on. This restricts the ability of top management to realize what changes are required and how and when to introduce them. This restricted knowledge throughout the organization increases the resistance to change on the part of managers in lower echelons. The maintenance of the Catholic Church's two different networks facilitates the communication of non-routine decision making through an 'express' network consisting of only three levels, thus shortening the distance between top and bottom of the management hierarchy.

There are, however, three reasons why other organizations cannot combat their organizational ailments with the same aids as the Catholic Church.

Managerial characteristics and structure stagnation Old age as a requisite for appointing a CE would not be appropriate for organizations other than the Church as a way of achieving frequent managerial changes. It would also be extremely difficult for the new chief executive who is going to stay in his position for only a few years to reinforce the new managerial structure with people who would cooperate with his leadership characteristics. It is, however, possible for an elderly pope to implement the new managerial structure for which the cardinals chose him, aided by his religious position and authority.

Mental burden of undisclosed feelings The way in which confession is carried out within the ranks of the clergy is unsuitable for the members of business and other organizations. In order to achieve as thorough a catharsis as possible, it should be done before a person who does not constitute a threat for the executive who is to disclose his innermost feelings about what is going on around him in the organization. These accumulated attitudes towards, and opinions about, the management around him are just those things which he has avoided telling to his superiors, subordinates, and peers because he is worried about the effect on his position in the organization. Within the ranks of the clergy, the subordinates do confess to their superiors.

Barriers and distortions in vertical and horizontal communication The Church overcomes blocks to communication by channelling policy and non-routine decisions through a three-level managerial structure (pope–bishops–other priests) rather than through all the levels of the regular managerial structure. An effective utilization of the two simultaneous managerial structures is possible only if two conditions are fulfilled. The first is a very thorough knowledge of all the formal rules which underlie the routine decisions of the organization, without which the lower levels would flood the upper levels with trivial decision making. The other condition is the acceptance by the hierarchy levels between the pope and the bishops, and between the bishops and the lowest level of priests, that they will be 'bypassed' when the three-level policy decision making takes place. In organizations other than the Catholic Church these two conditions cannot generally be achieved, Only in an organization like the Church, in which the members of the operating organization (i.e. the clergy) are indoctrinated in the formal rites from an early age and continue learning these rules for the rest of their lives, can one expect the degree of absorption of the rules required for a selective use of the two managerial structures. As for the other condition, here again it is only a continuous utilization of the two structures that would make people accept the 'bypassing' of decision making in specific cases. The behavioural value against 'bypassing' is very deeply rooted in the cultures of most societies in the world, with the exception of the Japanese culture, which accepts some kind of 'bypassing'.

Thus it is seen that the three cures which help the Roman Catholic Church to overcome the three ailments of maladaptation in the TOS, undisclosed feelings, and a hierarchical communication gap are only suitable under the conditions prevailing in the Church. It is necessary, therefore, to consider ways which could help organizations other than the Catholic Church overcome these same three ailments.

340

7.3.2 Treating the First Ailment—Adapting Management to the TOS

Adaptation of management to the dynamics of the TOS has been extensively dealt with. There are two ways to help organizations to acquire the managerial structure to operate their SDM appropriately for the changing times. The first is to change slowly the cultural value against interorganizational managerial mobility. The speed of such an educational process depends, to a large extent, on the cultural readiness to accept new norms and values. It is not a coincidence that among peoples who abandoned their ancestral cultures in countries like the USA and the Soviet Union norms such as the one against interorganizational mobility were relinquished. Germany, which has a more flexible culture than other Western countries, adapted its managerial culture to American managerial behaviour after the Second World War. It did this more quickly than other European countries into which American business penetrated. Thus, for example, interorganizational mobility among chief executives in Germany has reached a rate double that of other European countries.[39]

The other means for thawing a rigid managerial structure is to achieve intraorganizational mobility, rather than interorganizational mobility. Such intra-organizational mobility is necessary if different types of leadership and followership characteristics are to take over from one another. Such a situation occurs when the growth in SDM in their respective parts outgrows the managerial structures in which they have been run. This happens only in multistructure organizations, whose parts are operated in different managerial structures. When the different parts of a multistructure grow, they will require changes in their respective substructures. These changes may be achieved by shifting managers to those parts which need their managerial characteristics. This is the way in which the large Japanese conglomerates (the zaibatsu) operate. Indeed, it was in these organizations that the multistructure first appeared long before it developed in Western business corporations. The multistructure facilitates the necessary intra-organizational mobility required by the expansion in the SDM *without* the necessity for thawing the rigid interorganizational managerial structure.

The most effective way to help management to adapt to the dynamics of the TOS might be to enable the CE and other managers to regard their reflections in a managerial behaviour mirror, namely letting them see how their managerial behaviour is regarded by the management, as well as by other members of the organization (workers, owners, customers, suppliers, etc.). The manner in which this is achieved, with some examples, is presented further on in this chapter, when discussing the treatment of the third ailment: shortening communication channels.

7.3.3 Treating the Second Ailment—Catharsis

The second ailment is that of undisclosed feelings. The RCC treats it by way of confession within the operating organization, usually by means of the clergy confessing to their immediate superiors in the hierarchy. These may be their superiors in the six-to-eight-level 'regular' structure (i.e. for the purpose of the routine decision process) or their superiors in the three-level non-routine managerial structure. However, the confession process, as practised in the RCC, can achieve only partial relief. In order to help people to release their undisclosed feelings to a larger extent, they should undergo a more comprehensive catharsis.

The cartharsis of members of business and other organizations should be performed by people who are *not* part of the operating organization. That is to say, they should not be within the formal hierarchical structure of the organization. They should not be regarded as subordinates of members of the operating organization or as 'allies' of top management. If they are considered to be part of the managerial environment, they will be regarded as constituting a threat to the members of the organization. There are organizations which have successfully introduced psychological counsellors to help members of the organization 'cleanse' themselves by opening up in front of outsiders. Those organizations which have introduced psychological counsellors during the last 40 years, since the Hawthorne Research at Western Electric, have invariably found that this cleared the atmosphere and raised the morale. The psychological counsellors can be on the payroll of the organization as long as they are regarded as independent of management and can pursue their work according to their discreet professional ethics.

The relieving of the burden of undisclosed feelings, when performed systematically in industry and business, is usually done by persons who are not members of the operating organization.[40] The outsider's ability to help insiders to open up played an important role even in biblical times, thousands of years ago. Thus much of Joseph's reading of dreams was actually part of the catharsis he administered to others.[41]

It is interesting to note that organizations in which some catharsis is performed by insiders have tried to overcome the fear that such insiders constitute a threat to those whom they help to open up. An effort has been made to make such insiders, performing a counselling role, dependent on the employees rather than on top management. Thus, the counsellors serving on the council of the head of the Jesuits (the General of the Society of Jesus) are elected by the congregation of Jesuits rather than appointed by their general. Likewise the shop stewards, who informally play the role of helping workers to open up, are elected by the workers themselves rather than appointed by the unions, whom the shop stewards represent in the organization. This election of counsellors is more than just the democratization of organizational representation and decision making. It gives the people whom they may counsel in the future the feeling that they caused the counsellors to be independent of the hierarchy and, especially, of those who are at the top of the pyramid.[42]

Although a group opening up process positively contributes to organizations, its negative aspects outweigh its utility. It is conducive to a greater awareness of the differences among individuals in terms of their managerial characteristics, and the roles they may play in their interpersonal relationships. However, group therapy is often done in an organizationally unhealthy way which may, in individual cases, cause unhealthy mental reactions (because it undermines the urge of people in the managerial hierarchies *not* to disclose to others related to the same hierarchies all their innermost feelings).

One example of the possible negative consequences of the group treatment of undisclosed feelings is found in the futile efforts of group dynamics social psychologists to introduce such training into kibbutzim in Israel. The kibbutz society is, on the whole, a closed community in which several hundred people interact with each other in work, leisure, mealtimes, and social functions; they also meet other members of the kibbutz at mealtimes and at the bedsides of their children (when in houses of their own, separate from their parents). The degree of undisclosed feelings in such a community is apt to be much larger than among people who just belong to the same organizational hierarchy and interact only during working hours. On the other hand the kibbutz society attracts the attention of behavioural scientists because of its seeming uniqueness.[43]

There is, however, a successful instance of partially overcoming undisclosed feelings by way of a group catharsis rather than in face to face. This method is practised by one of the tribes of India in a community similar in size to a kibbutz. Once a year the members of the tribe convene. They plug their ears tightly, so that they cannot hear anything. Subsequently, members of the tribe who have undisclosed feelings about others will approach them and tell them to their face everything they think and feel about them. Nobody hears what is being said.[44]

From among several behaviourial movements, strongly linked with the need for catharsis, which have been established since the Second World War,[45] one trend merits special attention. This school advocates the application of transactional analysis to psychotherapy. It maintains that behaviour is the product of three types of influence or, to put it another way, there are three different personalities combined in every one of us. The different personalities are manifested in the transactions between individuals. The transactional analysis studies the different parts of each person by way of his relationships and interactions with others.[46]

All the above approaches to helping people to relieve their undisclosed feelings do not specifically deal with people within industrial, business, and similar organizations. They are connected with, or derive their teaching directly from, the foundations which defined counselling and psychotherapy during the Second World War.[47]

The best way to ascertain that the catharsis for members of the operating organization is properly performed as an ongoing process is to put psychological counsellors at their disposal. These counsellors can help the members of the organization to help themselves by way of opening up in *tête-à-tête* sessions. Such sessions should be planned for every member of the operating organization, unless he categorically refuses to go through with them. The psychological counsellors should be available at any time for sessions initiated by organizational members themselves. The frequency of such planned sessions, as well as the consequent necessary number of psychological counsellors for the individual organization, varies according to the number of its members, as well as to the amount of interpersonal concealment at the time.[48]

Another way to accomplish a partial thaw of undisclosed feelings is by way of action research. Action research is described as a treatment for the third ailment, by way of shortening communication channels, in the following subsection.

7.3.4 Treating the Third Ailment—Shortening Communication Channels

The third disorder is the hierarchical communication gap. The RCC cures this ailment by way of applying its decision making through two parallel managerial structures. A hierarchy of up to eight levels is used in the different parts of the RCC's multistructure for its routine decision making. However, a three-level hierarchy is utilized for the RCC's non-routine decision making, both for the new policy and the non-policy decisions. As previously indicated, this solution for overcoming the communication gap can hardly be adapted for organizations other than the RCC. The reasons lie in the resistance to bypassing and the impossibility of making all managers learn all directions for routine decisions.

There are, however, ways to help organizations and their members to overcome their communication gap, by shortening their communication channels in a way different from that of the RCC, i.e. without requiring bypassing or memorizing all the rules. Such a way, which is referred to in this book as action research, 'kills three birds with one stone' in that it helps cure all three ailments: the communication gap and, through it, disturbances in the TOS and, partially, undisclosed feelings. This type of action research is a good basis for achieving objectives other than therapy. It also includes appropriate methodological elements for conducting case research and for carrying out general comparative organizational research.[49] More space is, therefore, devoted to action research than to the other subjects in this chapter.[50]

Action research is essentially composed of the following five stages:

Data collection Collecting data on how the decision making and the managerial structure are regarded by members of the organization.

Release Releasing the data obtained from the interviewees. This stage may be performed concurrently with the following one.

Data analysis and report preparation The collected data are analysed according to several different techniques. The interviews are content-analysed according to different titles pertaining to various elements of the TOS (the immediate and wider environments, the organizational strategy, the managerial structure, and the characteristics of the CE and other key managers). The sociometric data pertaining to interpersonal realtions concern the managerial structure and/or managerial communication. The technique for establishing the managerial structure is the 'informalogram'. The research tool for describing the managerial communication pattern is the 'communicogram'.

Action Research Feedback The content analysis of the interviews, accompanying quantitative information as perceived by members of the organization, and the

344

informalogram results are usually combined in one action research report. The
feedback of the communicogram results is performed personally, i.e. each
manager participating in such action research receives his own results, compared
with the averages of the managerial group, of which he is a member. Therefore,
the communicogram results are usually not part of a combined action research
report. There are, however, cases in which the overall communicogram results are
integrated with the analysis and findings of the other managerial structure tools,
the content analysis and the informalogram.

Counselling Helping managers to help themselves with the action research feedback results. The consultant's role[51] may terminate at the previous stage when it
presents the managers with the action research feedback. However, helping the
managers to help themselves by looking into the organizational mirror, and
finding out about their own managerial behaviour, may be better accomplished by
affording them counselling services as part of the feedback process. The counselling may be voluntary, i.e. counselling services may be offered to the managers
who feel they would like to share their results and interpretations with an outside
counsellor. Counselling may, on the other hand, be made an integral part of the
feedback process, making it necessary for every participating manager to meet
with the consultant who in turn will help him to help himself.

The discussion in this section is divided into the above five action research
stages. The three different types of action research will be discussed separately in
each of the five research stages—first, the information acquired from
organizational members and subsequently content-analysed; secondly, the formal
and informal interpersonal relationship data, subsequently turned into an informalogram; and, thirdly, the perceptions about interpersonal interactions, subsequently data processed into a communicogram.

7.3.4.1 Data Collection

Consider the interviewing process by which information about the SDM and the
managerial structure is acquired. The information acquired in non-directive, open
interviews conducted throughout the organization should occasionally be fed back
to the management. Such interviews may be parts of the counselling process
described previously, or can be performed by outside consultants. In any case,
whether conducting the interviews themselves or using the transcribed interviews
of psychological counsellors, the consultants should be competent in carrying out
this form of consultancy, based on helping the client to help himself. The consultant should collect the data in the following distinctive steps:

Introduction to the organization The consultant should make sure that the CE
of the organization willingly accepts and formally permits this form of consultancy. This permission would probably be granted if the CE is satisfied on two
points: (a) that there is something positive for himself and the organization in it;
(b) that no harm could come to the organization through this consultancy. The
contribution of action research to the organization is manifold; however, the main

contribution is usually found in the managers' opportunity to have a better look at their organization. One of the strict ethical rules, meant to avoid any possible harm to the organization, is that any data collected in the organization will not be used in any form before being released in writing by the CE of the firm. The CE can always refuse to give permission for the release of the final report or specific parts of it, for either internal or external use, because of possible harm, in his opinion, to the organization.

Interviewing the CE   In collecting the data for action research, the first interview should, desirably, be with the CE, to discover how he views the decision-making process and the managerial structure. The interview with the CE should suggest to the consultant what material and data he needs, and give him the first indications on personnel to be interviewed. In addition, the CE should finish the organizational chart reflecting his perception of the formal managerial structure.

The interview with the CE should be conducted in the same pattern as interviews with the other members of the organization. It should be essentially a non-directive interview, in which the interviewee speaks about anything he has on his mind, in his heart, etc. The first part of the interview should be as close as possible to the counselling and psychotherapy type of interview.

The interviewer might pose some general questions that may start the interviewee talking, for instance: 'What are the things that make you satisfied, and what are the things that make you dissatisfied with the organization?' 'What things are most helpful, and what things disturb your work in the organization?' 'How is your work time divided in dealing with problems confronting you?' etc. He can always precede the opening question by saying that the interviewee need not worry about the continuity of his remarks, as the researcher, i.e. the consultant, will take care of the proper arrangement. He should *always* promise the interviewee utmost discretion and tell him that none of his words will be used, even if his name is disguised, before he has a chance to see what the researcher would like to use; and that he can introduce changes, or refuse to be quoted altogether. It is only after the interviewer is positive that the interviewee has opened up as much as possible without posing any specific questions that he can move to the second stage of the interview.

At this stage the interviewer should try to find out whether the interviewee has anything else in mind which is within the framework of the TOS. The researcher, therefore, follows the various main, principal, and component parts of the TOS—management, workers, trade unions, customers, suppliers, owners, government, etc.—exploring whether the interviewee has something more to say about each one of these factors.

The interviewer then tries to find out the interviewee's feelings about the relation between the scope of decision making and the managerial structure in the past, the present, and the future.

When extending the non-directive interview, the interviewer should take great care not to pose leading questions to the interviewee. The second part of the interview should be in the form of putting out feelers, checking whether the interviewee just missed relating some of his feelings and opinions about the various factors of decision making and the managerial structure.

Interviewing managers throughout the organization   The main points concerning the interview have already been convered. It is, however, important to stress that while the CE may worry about revealing his own innermost feelings to other members of the organization and about revealing his organization to outsiders, the other managers generally worry only about being 'uncovered' by their fellow managers, usually by their superiors. This is why the interviewer should stress, before starting the interview, that everything which is said will remain confidential, and should reiterate his obligation to secure the interviewee's consent to use any quotations from the interview before actually doing so.

The number of managers to be interviewed throughout the hierarchy, bears no relation to the total number of managers in the organization. The researcher should try to cover in his interviewing both 'typical' managers and 'special', 'unusual', and 'extraordinary' managers. He should select these managers by following the leads given to him by the CE and, subsequently, by other managers, as he proceeds in his interviewing. However, once the researcher feels that his interviewees are repeating what has already been said and nothing new is added to the accumulated information, he should stop interviewing. Experience shows that the number of interviews may range from roughly 20 to 100; it depends on the organizational SDM, and includes most or all managers in the two upper levels of the hierarchy, just below the CE.

Interviewing other members of the organization   By 'other members of the organization' are meant members other than managers, e.g. workers, customers, suppliers, shareholders, bankers, trade union and government officials. It is sometimes difficult to convince CEs that members of the organization other than the employees should be interviewed. The problem lies in the fact that in spite of the realization of many CE's that customers, suppliers, shareholders, and others constitute part of their organizations, not all of these CEs fully accept the equal importance to the organization of, say, the customers.[52] Another reason for a CE's reluctance to permit the interviewing of, say, his bankers and government officials dealing with the organization is that this may give an impression that the organization is sick.

The importance of including those other members of the organization within any form of organizational research should not be underrated. The opinions of members of the organization other than those of the operating organization in the TOS are eventually fed back to the managers. This makes them aware of the actions, interactions, and sentiments of all the members of the organization, in their own analysis, diagnosis, and prognosis of the TOS.

Collecting quantitative and other written material about the organization   When collecting data for action research the consultant should bear in mind that written material and data about the organization cannot be considered 'objective'. It is, therefore, important to include in it the perceptions of the members of the organization concerning such written material and data. Thus, when a manager presents the researcher with a balance sheet, his comments on the way in which it was prepared, the purpose for which is is made, the reactions of various parties to it, etc., become part of the balance sheet, and should be considered for inclusion in the action research report. When the CE presents his organization chart and accompanies it with remarks on how it 'actually' works, on the characteristics of his various managers, on their personal relationships, it is vital that the consultant jots them all down.[53] Similarly, written correspondence, which is of course part of the decision-making process, is more meaningful when accompanied by perceptions of why a letter was written, how it was written (e.g. in what mood), and how it was received by the addressee.

Collecting data for the informalogram There are three things necessary for establishing the managerial structure by way of an informalogram:

(a) Responses of managers to the request: 'List the names of persons with whom you generally work most closely, regardless of their position in the organization.' The responses to this question might be acquired at the end of the interview or by asking managers to mail their responses in writing to the researcher. The CE and, preferably all the managers in at least the two levels below him should respond to the informalogram question.

(b) A formal grid in which all the managers are divided into vertical formal units (e.g. marketing, manufacturing, headquarters, etc.) and horizontal remuneration (salary plus social security costs and fringe benefits) brackets. It is only with the permission of the CE that the researcher could receive the necessary data about managers' remuneration.[54]

(c) The organizational chart, to be acquired from the CE.

A partial informalogram analysis may be carried out without identifying each participating manager by his remuneration bracket, and without an organizational chart. The only two essential elements for the inclusion of a manager in the informalogram are his response to the question, 'List the names of persons. . .', and his formal unit identification (e.g. marketing).[55]

Collecting data for the communicogram The necessary data for the communicogram are the recollections of the participating managers concerning the oral interactions they have had in their face to face, intercom, telephone, and other oral communication means. Twice a day, before lunch and at the end of the day, they register information concerning the interactions they remember having had during the preceding three to four hours. The information includes the approximate time of interaction, with whom it occurred, who initiated it, who played the main role in it, what type of communication occurred (e.g. information, instruction, advice, etc.), and the respondent's feeling about it (e.g. negative, positive). This data collection should be carried out for several days, usually for two working weeks.[56]

7.3.4.2   Release

Releasing the data from the interviewees is regarded as a separate stage, rather than part of writing the report or the feedback, because of its importance. The emphasis on the release stems from the impact it has on the whole process of action research. By failing to respect professional ethics on this score and not keeping his word to the interviewees, the consultant would blemish his image with possibly disastrous consequences. First of all, it would undermine the therapeutic chances of continued action research in the specific organization, in the forthcoming 'feedback' and 'helping managers to help themselves' stages. Secondly, it might ruin the professional reputation of the consultant, by injuring his chances of carrying out action research elsewhere in future.

This is why the full transcriptions of all interviews should be sent to the interviewees, even if their names will be disguised in the following stage when extracts from their interviews will be fed back to other managers, primarily to the CE. This should be done even when the interviewee said that he does not mind the consultant using any part of his interview in the feedback, or when the consultant forgot to promise discretion to the interviewee during the data collection stage.

One may wonder why employees, who conceal their feelings from others around them in the hierarchy, permit the release of such feelings which they revealed to the consultant. Is it just because he is a discreet outsider? Experience in this sort of consulting shows, however, that 95 per cent of the interviewees release their statements with or without minor alterations.[57] Interviewees are much more outspoken and unworried when quoted by a consultant or researcher than they would be when talking directly with their superiors, subordinates, and peers. The reason for this is that our speech is much quicker than the controlling devices applied by our brains. In other words, the fact that the interviewee has a chance to review his innermost thoughts and feelings, as recorded by the outsider, allows his censorship to clear all or most of it, in 95 per cent of the cases. When he has to answer a query from his superior, such as, 'How are things in your department?', he almost invariably responds: 'Everything is fine.' He instinctively responds in this misleading way so as to avoid revealing things which he cannot control in his spontaneous reply. However, had he a chance to put down in writing the problems in his department, he would feel in most cases that revealing them does not constitute a threat to himself.

During the forthcoming stage of data analysis and report preparation, which is usually carried out simultaneously with the release process, the researcher should respect in detail and totality all the release requests of the interviewees.[58]

7.3.4.3   Data Analysis and Report Preparation

Analysing the interviews and preparing the report   The released interviews are subsequently content-analysed. Quotations and statements from the interviews are arranged by subjects which are found to preoccupy the interviewees. Statements from the members of the organization, sometimes identified only by reference to their departmental position and formal stratum (e.g. 'a senior market-ing manager'), are presented in a written report in which the information gathered in interviews, together with written material collected in the organization, is rearranged. The content analysis is preceded by categorizing all this material into roughly two areas: the SDM and the managerial structure.

The first thing to do in the content-analysis process is to draw up a 'table of contents' of the data collected in the interviews. Schematically the table of con-tents should follow the main and component systems of the TOS, whenever they are found to preoccupy the interviewees:

The scope of decision making

Immediate environment	wider environment:
Management	The employment market
Workers	
Trade unions	The money market
Owners	
Bankers	The consumer supply–demand market
Customers	
Suppliers	The technology (and education) system
Government	The socio-cultural system

The Organizational Strategy
    Present and future policies (and what prompts them) regarding:
    What is the organization in product/service lines?
    How is it producing? (technology)
    Where is it operating? (geographical dispersal)

The managerial structure:	The managerial characteristics:
Formal organization	Personal perceptions of the CE and other key managers
Informal organization	
Relationships	
Attitudes	

The main sections of the table of contents may be divided into subsections, depending on the extent of the material in each section. All the material—interviews and other data—is then divided according to the table of contents. The interviews are divided into quotations, and the quotations and other data pertaining to each topic are gathered together.

The researcher may find that information related to the SDM and to managerial structure is interwoven in the interviews. He should be clear in his mind as to which information belongs to SDM and which to managerial structure.[59]

Once all the material is classified according to the table of contents, the researcher can start writing the action research report. In doing so he should follow two rules:

—The perceptions of members of the organization should be presented by quoting specific persons described by their managerial reference group (old-timers and newcomers, top or middle management, marketing or manufacturing, headquarters or subsidiary, etc.). Their reactions should be made explicit by the use of quotation marks or special print, in order to differentiate them from other parts of the report. The sources of the written material and quantitative data should also be given, as far as they can be established by the researcher, along with any comments that the members of the organization made while presenting the data. They should be quoted verbatim unless, for reasons of disguise or release (i.e. so that the interviewer would feel easy in releasing it), their words have to be slightly changed (but never the contents or actual meaning of what they said).

—The 'non-perceptional' parts of the report should be 'objective facts', i.e. information about which there is consensus among all members of the organization (e.g. the year in which the organization was founded). The researcher should refrain from projecting his own perceptions into the report. The 'objective facts' should be presented in the past tense, because they were found by the researcher when he collected the data, and may have changed since then.

One of the most crucial decisions for the researcher to make when preparing the action research report is what to omit and what to include. He should try, of course, to make sure that the report is representative of the way in which the situation is regarded from within the organization. Decisions about what to include and what to omit introduce the bias of the researcher. Even if the consultant decides to include in the report all the material in his possession, this would not completely remove the subjectiveness of the researcher, because the order in which the material is introduced in it could also be subjective. The researcher's subjective decisions start at a very early stage of the action research process. Two of the most important of these early decisions are whom to interview in the organization and what material to ask for. This is one of the major reasons why it is so important that the consultant should be as uninvolved as possible in the situation, so that he can maintain maximum objectivity.

Analysing the informalogram and incorporating it into the report   The informalogram is a research tool for establishing the managerial structure by way of comparing the informal (actual) with the formal (required) structures. The research technique of the informalogram was discussed in chapter 3. Its results should be incorporated into the action research report, in its managerial structure section, of course.

The results of these structural measurements are fed back either in tabular form, with interpretative comparisons with the results from other organizations, or in the form of an informalogram chart. We will give examples of how this information is presented when discussing the action research feedback.

The data processing of the results of the informalogram, in order to calculate the four structural measurements and to draw an informalogram chart, can usually be done by hand and does require a more sophisticated technique.

Analysing the communicogram results The data processing of the communicogram's daily interaction sheets can usually be done only by electronic data processing. The data processing for a communicogram is about a hundred times more extensive than for an informalogram.[60] The coding of the several thousand interactions[61] is done manually. The coded sheets serve as the input for the computer. The computer program is so designed that its output is in the form of a separate sheet for each of the participating managers. Each sheet includes the personal results of the recipient compared with the average results of the group. The results include such things as:

—The average numbers of daily perceived interactions, face to face, by telephone and intercom, within the managerial group, and with outside people.
—The percentage of reciprocal interactions in which the other party mentioned (in answer to the question 'with whom'), acknowledges the occurrence of the interaction in his own interaction sheet.
—The degree of consensus about what goes on in the mutually perceived interactions; for instance, Who initiated the interaction? Who played the major role in it? What was the type of interaction (information, instruction, advice, etc.)? How did the participants feel about the interaction?

7.3.4.4 Action Research Feedback

It has already been mentioned that the action research report which is fed back to the management includes all the results regarding SDM and managerial structure based on the content analysis, both of additional quantitative and written information concerning SDM and of the informalogram. The communicogram results are fed back separately and personally to each participant.

Action Research Report The first person to receive this report is the CE.[62] He would be urged to distribute it among all the managers, but it is within his discretion whether the feedback should be extended to others. There are several reasons for the CE having this privilege. The first is that, without his permission, such a consulting project as action research cannot be performed. Secondly, the CE is the only manager who cannot be disguised in the report, being unique at his level in the organization. He would naturally attract more comments from other members of the organization than anyone else in the hierarchy. This means that he may feel uneasy if other managers were to read shared opinions about him which he considers to be derogatory. Thirdly, the CE controls future major organizational changes.

In about a quarter of some 20 such projects of which the author is aware, the CE drew the most extreme conclusions when he realized that others considered his particular management dysfunctional. In all the cases where the researchers

352

Table 7.3   Details of managerial action research studies

Organizational details: No., Country Field (Product/service) Year/s	Description of process
1. USA Industrial (Plastics) 1959/1960	Composed of three principal stages—the first stage processing raw materials into a few basic materials; the second stage further processing the basic materials into several different materials which are ready for the final stage; the third and final stage manufacturing end-products for consumer use. Generally, each stage constitutes a separate enterprise and corporation. Although all the three stages operated within this one organization, they were physically divided. The first stage was located far away from the later stages. The latter were located in the same geographical area. The technology in the first two stages is generally more advanced than in the third, and so the number of professional and scientific personnel in the first two stages is larger than in the third stage.
2. Israel Higher education (Teaching/research) 1961–1963	Composed of two main groups in its operating organization—operational personnel and administrative personnel. The products of this organization were people (as in the case of airline companies, hospitals, schools, etc.). The proportion of professional and scientific staff among the total operational personnel was high.
3. Israel Military industrial (Metal) 1965	This organization was essentially a large overhauling plant with supporting manufacture of spare parts. The input consisted of a series of different large vehicles which were overhauled, modified, or re-equipped. Some of the supporting plants were around the central plant, but others were in a radius of some 20 kilometres. The workers and foremen were mostly civilians, but the management was mainly military.
4. Israel Government (Internal revenue) 1965–1967	Composed of three operating divisions. The first and the second rendered services to almost every citizen and organization. These services were of uniform, pre-established characteristics and required continuous contact with the public. Therefore, branches were maintained in towns throughout the country,The third division was itself composed of three different services—one dealing with only part of the public, while the other two dealt with various kinds of businesses. The technology of this organization did not require a large number of professionals.
5. France Industrial (Electronics) 1966	This was an electronics plant, primarily concentrating on television tube manufacturing.

Table 7.3 (*continued*)

Organizational details: No., Country Field (Product/service) Year/s	Description of process
6. France Industrial (Aircraft) 1966	This organization had two parts, one concentrating on research, development, and engineering, the other manufacturing aircraft and air armaments. The organization came into being through a merger of two companies several years prior to the study.
7. UK Marketing (Pharmaceuticals) 1966/1967	This organization was responsible for the marketing of the products of one of the largest British pharmaceutical groups, fully owned by a diversified multinational corporation. Among its other functions it was concerned with product development. It therefore had a relatively large group of university graduates among its management.
8. Israel Industrial (Shoes) 1968	Comparatively simple production processes in the manufacture of consumer products, in which competition was strong. The production processes did not require the employment of many professionals.
9. Israel Industrial (Mining) 1969	Composed of two principal stages. The first stage supplied its output of one type of raw material to the second stage, which further processed them into another type of material. The technology in the second stage was more advanced than in the first stage and therefore the number of professionals in it was larger.
10. Israel Transportation (Shipping agency) 1969	Rendered one service to various types of businesses. The technology of the organization did not require a large number of professionals.
11. Israel Military (Ordnance) 1969	This is a logistical sub-organization providing services to various military units. It has an HQ and several service bases dispersed geographically. Those personnel studied by action research and sociometrically were only from among the HQ management. The HQ numbered at the time about 130 officers and civilians, while the whole operating organization included 1300 people.
12. France Commerce (Export–import) 1969	Supplier of materials, manufactured by other organizations. These semi-manufactured materials belonged to three similar product lines. The technology of the organization did not require a large number of professionals.

Table 7.3 *(continued)*

Organizational details: *No., Country* *Field* *(Product/service)* *Year/s*	*Description of process*
13. UK Management training (Teaching, research, and hotel) 1971	This organization offered adult education in short-term residential courses (lasting from a few days to several weeks). It was therefore composed of three different types of activities and staffs. It consisted, primarily, of teachers in the different areas of its educational field; secondly, it had a research staff, performing research activities beyond the geographical location of the organization, but likewise taking some part in the teaching activities. Both these types of activities had separate and mutual services mainly of a secretarial nature. The third type of activities could be labelled 'hotel and catering', running full services for the students and some of the staff living on the premises.
14. Japan Transportation (Shipping and agency) 1971	This organization was a foreign-owned company operating in Japan. It consisted of two distinct parts: A service transportation organization with a non-Japanese top management group, serving mainly organizations rather than individuals. A service organization, with total Japanese management, serving the first part of the organization and assuming its marketing function. This type of function is identical to that of organization no. 10.
15. Israel Industrial (Precision tools) 1972	Produces, in a relatively advanced metallurgical technology, products for use in other manufacturing enterprises in the metal industry. It produces a variety of products, all in the same product line and serving the same general purpose. This organization had started at the time of the study to produce the materials used for its own manufacture, in other words, it was vertically integrated, one step backwards.
16. Israel Industrial (Precision parts) 1972	This organization was located next to organization no. 15, sharing a few services with it. It was producing only one product at the time of the study, requiring a very high degree of precision and technological know-how. The product was one of many components integrated into a product for institutional use.
17. Israel Industrial (Pharmaceuticals) 1972	This organization had three main production lines, each going through a chemical process and subsequently packaged differently. The organization operated in two different locations in Israel, 30 kilometres apart. The organization likewise provided technical know-how, in the erection and management of similar plants in foreign countries. The industrial field of this organization required the employment of a relatively large number of people with higher university education.

Table 7.3   (*continued*)

Organizational details: *No., Country* *Field* *(Product/service)* *Year/s*	*Description of process*
18. Israel Industrial (Chemicals) 1975	All the 20 production installations of this organization, producing about 60 different products via chemical processes, were located in the same general area. A large number of the products belong to the same product line, marketed to customers in a certain section of the economy. The customers are institutions, as well as individuals.
19A and 19B. Israel Financial services (Banking) 1976	Two branches of one of the largest banking organizations in Israel. The branches are from among the largest in the Tel Aviv area and are subordinated to the Tel Aviv area manager, who in turn is subordinated to the chief executive in the bank's head office, which is also in Tel Aviv. The two branches are similar in the number of employees and in the type of banking services which a commercial bank offers its clients.
20. Israel Military services 1979	This organization provides special services to a certain arm (part) of the armed forces. The organizational head-quarters are attached to the headquarters of that arm, and members of the organization in the field are attached to field units of that arm. The action research covered managers in the headquarters and the field units, both from the organization studied and from the arm it serves (i.e. its customers). Also studied were managers providing the same type of services but in other arms of the armed forces. From among the 43 interviewees, only 24 were included in the sociometric research (the informalogram), all managers in the organizational headquarters. The organization deals with a type of service which requires the employment of a relatively large number of university trained managers.
21. Israel Personal and indus- trial service (A non-profit organization, subsidizing people who start units intended to turn into independent profit-making organizations) 1979	The organization was founded in order both to absorb new immigrants (it is part of a government agency providing financial grants to help new immigrants) and to create out of them the nuclei of industrial organizations (so that they may leave the framework of the organizations studied and cease to receive the initial financial aid). These newly created organizations are such that they require their nuclei to be composed of highly trained scientific people. Consequently, in order to plan and control the new organizations, until they become independent, the organization studied also has to include highly scientifically qualified people. However, it also has to have administratively qualified people, for example for financial planning and control.

356

Table 7.3 (*continued*)

Organizational details: No., Country Field (Product/service) Year/s	Description of process
22. Israel Industrial (Chemicals) 1980	This is a parent organization for about 20 plants producing various products by chemical processes. The plants are located in different parts of the country and there is only small interdependence: the transfer of materials among them. The research, including the informalogram, covered the headquarters of the parent organization, the general managers of the subsidiary organizations, and senior managers from the largest two enterprises (in terms of their relative scope and with regard to their central role in the decision making of the managers in the parent organization studied). From among 3500 employees of the whole group (including the subsidiary industrial enterprises) only 35 managers of the parent organization and 3 representatives of its owners were included in the action research.

felt that the feedback told the CE that he ought to leave the organization and start again in another, this is what actually occurred within a month to two years from the time the CE first read the report. The only feedback reaching the management is composed of statements from the interviews with members of the organization; thus, the researchers never indicate to the CE or anyone else in the organization, in whatever form, what they themselves feel about the situation. Although most of the decisive effects of this sort of action research are to be expected even if the report is fed back to the CE only, it is desirable for as many managers as possible to be recipients of the feedback. There are two reasons for this. First, there is something of a moral, though not a contractual, obligation to show the interviewees the product which their time and candour made possible. Secondly, although the subsequent effects of the feedback would be of a smaller order of magnitude in the case of the other managers, the cumulative effect of the feedback is by no means negligible. In fact, because the CE is usually not aware of 'who said what' in the report, the conclusions which other managers draw may be of great help to him. This is especially so when the CE himself decides that his way of running the organization is the right one, but that various changes in the framework of the managerial structure led by himself should be introduced.

The central role of the CE with regard to receiving the feedback or what really happens throughout the organization is almost self-evident. The Society of Jesus has structured the council of their general (the CE) so as to ensure that the general as well as other line executives will have 'complete knowledge of the truth'.[63]

Table 7.3 gives descriptions of the 22 organizations for which action research included informalogram results (presented in the action research report together with extracts from interviews and other quantitative and written data), and/or communicogram results, fed back separately.

No attempt is made here at an exhaustive comparative analysis of the clinical results in the five countries in which the organizations appearing in Table 7.3 were operating. Several examples, one from each country, of basically different behaviour affecting the SDM as well as the managerial structure will suffice:

USA It was evident throughout the content analysis of the interviews in the US organization that the people were more diplomatic, on the whole, in their references to each other than people in organizations experiencing similar interpersonal strains in other countries.[64] This is a bit superficial, and somewhat disguises the real feeling manifested in their behaviour in actual interpersonal relationships.[65]

Israel The Israeli organizational atmosphere is relatively informal. The way in which the employees at the different levels of hierarchy relate to each other is much more direct and open than one would find in other countries. They usually address each other by their first names rather than by their titles and last names. All this emerged quite clearly from the content analysis of the interviews in the clinical studies of the Israeli organizations.

France The management of one of two French organizations (No. 12) had an entrepreneurial structure. However, its entrepreneur ran the management differently from the entrepreneurs in Israel and the USA. This may be explained as follows:

> Let us imagine two similar organizations, in the U.S. and France, each headed by an entrepreneur and managed in an entrepreneurial structure, the chief executive communicating with the managers at various levels of the management, rather than only with those directly under him. This is a 'universal behavior' proposition. However, if we consider the communication behavior of the two entrepreneurs in terms of the intensity of their oral interactions with their managers, we may fall into a 'culture-bound' trap. We would discover that the American entrepreneur widely interacts with managers throughout the organization, whereas with the French entrepreneur a similar interaction is much less frequent. Moreover, we would discover that the French chief executive uses much more written communication than his American colleagues. This may lead to the mistaken impression that the Frenchman is a bureaucratic leader of a formally centralized functional structure, while a closer look would reveal that he actually runs an entrepreneurial structure, but in a different culture of communication behavior.[66]

Japan The study was carried out in a foreign-owned Japanese shipping organization. The organization consisted of two distinct parts, one running the shipping lines of the company and the other serving as its shipping agent. But while the shipping agency's management was exclusively Japanese, the two top managerial levels running the shipping lines were completely non-Japanese. These non-Japanese were mostly nationals of the Western country where the holding company was located. The link between headquarters and the Japanese subsidiaries was rather weak. The non-Japanese and Japanese structures are so different that it would be misleading to consider them as a unified and uniform structure. The relation between the degrees of informal activity and formal clarity in the non-Japanese part of this organization as in other Western organizations was found constant; the larger the informal activity, the smaller the formalization, i.e. the formal clarity; and vice versa. The same was not true of the Japanese part of the organization in which both the informal activity and the coverage of organigram by informalogram was very high.

UK One effect of the British environmental culture which emerged during the study in this organization was the extreme difficulty of finding out the annual income of managers. Asking people how much money they earn is an impolite thing to do in Britain. The question should have been put to managers participating in executive training programmes, so as to determine at what managerial level they operated and fit them to an appropriate executive programme. The only way in which managers working in different organizations can be compared to each other as to their degrees of managerial responsibility is by assigning them to 'income brackets'. These 'income brackets' are likewise essential for the utilization of the informalogram technique for establishing the managerial structure.[67]

The CE of each of the organizations in which the action research had been primarily based on a wide interviewing process, received an action research report, large parts of which included sociological-type feedback of extracts from the interviews. A sample extract from such a report is presented below, and it includes an example of the type of summary prepared by the consultant at the end of each section of the action research report. This shows how the consultant summarizes his perception of what the members of the organization were saying. The summaries may help the manager to get an overall idea of the contents of the feedback. However, he can always disregard the consultant's interpretation.

In this extract PDG stands for President Director General (the CE—chairman and general manager); Mr M is the PDG; Mr C is the deputy PDG. 'Direction' is top management. The extract is taken from chapter 1 ('The Informal Structure of the Paris Office') which is part of Part C ('The Present Organizational Structure') of this action report.

The PDG, The Head of the Direction

One of the interviewees said:

> Nobody cares what happens to his fellow employees. What is missing is a feeling of unity, a contact between the top management and the personnel. At first I thought there is a lot of contact between Mr M and the people, but it turned out that it is not so at all.

The above does not mean that this or any other interviewee had negative feelings towards the PDG. This opinion only meant that the PDG was seen as part of the 'distance' between the Direction and the others, a feeling which was not without ambivalence when it came to Mr C, as we shall presently see.

Some of the interviewees felt that the PDG should not intermingle with the employees. One of the them put it in this way:

> The most important things is that Mr M should be above all this. He should not interfere in things—so that he will retain his authority. He should understand the problems, but should not do what you are doing, namely hear the problems from the people.

Almost all the feelings expressed towards the PDG could be labelled positive ones. Let us consider some of them:

> I like Mr M very much. He is a little too pedantic.

> I like him very much and have a large respect for him, especially for his ability to create contacts with foreign suppliers.

> Mr M seems to be a very nice person.

> I think that everyone likes Mr M.

> Mr M is a very balanced person and has a lot of understanding. It is this understanding which makes him sometimes accept things he should not have.

The PDG is linked with Mr C in the perceptions of many interviewees, both in personal ties and in his business success. One of the interviewees stated that:

> It is the combination of copper products and Mr C which enabled Mr M to have his business develop quickly and grow quickly.

The personal ties between the two were described by the following interviewee:

> Mr M and Mr C are very different from each other, but they are complementary to each other; they are very necessary to each other.

> *SYNOPSIS 7*: THE MAIN PROBLEMS REGARDING THE INFORMAL STRUCTURE WERE PERCEIVED TO BE THOSE RELATING TO THE DIRECTION. THE DIRECTION WAS REGARDED AS TOO ALOOF FROM THE OTHER EMPLOYEES. THE PDG WAS CONSIDERED QUITE FAVORABLY BY ALL INTERVIEWEES, BUT HE TOO WAS REGARDED AS NOT MINGLING WITH THE EMPLOYEES,

EXCEPT WITH MEMBERS OF THE DIRECTION. SOME
THOUGHT IT WAS GOOD, OTHERS CRITICIZED THIS
'DISTANCE' OF THE PDG.

Action research projects which did not include an informalogram study consisted almost exclusively of passages such as the one quoted. The consequences of
one such action research study, which was carried out in a military logistics unit
of crucial importance, were indicative of the value and potential of such an
exercise.[68]

Another example of the contents of action research feedback is presented in
Figure 7.4. This is an informalogram chart which appeared as part of the action
research report of the French import–export organization appearing as organization no. 12 in Table 7.3. This is also the organization from which the interview
extracts were chosen.

Figure 7.4   Example of action research feedback: informalogram

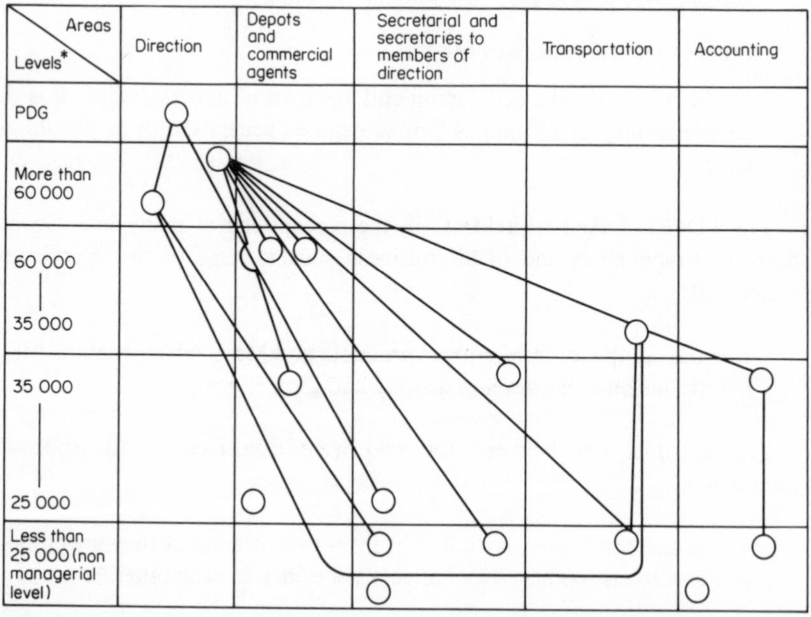

Note: Every circle represents one person; every line between two persons means that they
mentioned each other when requested to mention 'the people with whom you work most
closely, irrespective of their positions in the organization'; circles without connection lines to
others represent 'isolates', i.e. persons who did not have even one mutual choice (these
persons were placed at the bottom left-hand corner of their respective squares).

* Stratified by annual direct financial remuneration (in French francs); the relative level of
every person within a square is not significant of his relative salary or of any other differences
with other persons (the people were positioned within their squares so as to avoid connecting
lines crossing each other).

The communicogram feedback   The self recording and receiving of the interaction reports from the participating managers usually takes a fortnight. The data processed results should be fed back as soon as possible. The communicogram feedback could result in changes which cure imbalances in the TOS, curing the first ailment.

Figure 7.5 presents an example of the personal communicogram output sheet, which every participant receives. Such communication feedback studies have been carried out in different organizations in Britain, France, Holland, Israel, Sweden, and the USA.[69]

The communicogram study was carried out in seven organizations in four countries, much as it was first used in the USA in 1959. The main communicogram results from these seven organizations are presented in Table 7.4. In some of the organizations the communicogram coincided with, or, more often, immediately followed an informalogram study, the results of which were also fed back to the participants. The seven organizations are briefly described in Table 7.3 (they are given the same code number in Tables 7.3 and 7.4).

The total results of communicogram studies, as they appear in Table 7.4, can serve as a basis for different types of research. Consider, for example, how cross-cultural research could benefit from the findings in Table 7.4.[70]

7.3.4.5 Counselling

Recent findings show that the effects of feedback may be increased if the participating managers have counselling services at their disposal.[71] Indeed, in the feedback just described—the action research report, including the results of an informalogram study and communicogram feedback—the occasional counselling offered by the researchers after the actual feedback seems to have improved the degree of helping the managers to help themselves.

The action research report   The main counselling performed until now, following the submission of the action research report to the CE, has been counselling the CE himself. Every CE has a shock on reading the action research report of his organization. It is like seeing one's own image in the mirror for the first time. The degree of shock seems to be related to the degree of preparedness of the CE for this type of consultancy.[72]

The first impact of the report on the CE is likewise affected by how much he feels he is put in a bad light by it. This has to do not only with the actual amount of criticism directed at him, but also with his anticipation of the reaction of others to himself. This, in turn, is affected by his sensitivity towards the feelings of others, the history of relationships with others, and other factors.

The present authors have spent varying amounts of counselling time with a great many CEs. With few exceptions, the first reaction of each CE was: 'What is described in here is not myself'; or, perhaps: 'Some individuals do not know me very well.' The first reaction lasted until he realized that this was how his behaviour was regarded by managers and others.

Figure 7.5 Example of action research feedback: a personal communicogram output sheet

N = 39

	(1)	(2)	(3)	(4)	(5)	(6)	(7)	(8)
TELEPHONE	6	28.97	1	16.13	0	80.00	1	60.00
CONFERENCE	32	71.03	4	19.74	2	80.00	4	73.33
TOTAL	38	100.00	5	18.69	2	80.00	5	70.00

16%
84%

$\frac{1}{2} = 16.7\%$
$\frac{4}{32} = 12.5\%$

$\frac{0}{1} = 0\%$
$\frac{2}{4} = 50\%$

$\frac{1}{1} = 100\%$
$\frac{4}{4} = 100\%$

I am using the telephone less than the average and the conference more than the average.

Any degree of agreement, as is the occurrence of telephone interactions (16.7%), is the same as the average (16.5%) but the agreement as to the occurrence of conference interactions (12.5%) is much lower than average (19.74%).

My degree of consensus as to the feeling after the interaction was lower than the average (80%) in both the telephone and face-to-face interactions.

My degree of consensus as to the type of interaction (information, instruction, etc.) was 100% and higher than the average (60% for the telephone and 73.33% for the conference).

	(1)	(2)	(3)	(4)	(5)	(6)	(7)	(8)
IMPRESSION								
POSITIVE	0	62.62	0	20.90	0	85.71	0	64.29
NEUTRAL	0	6.54	0	7.14	0	0.00	0	100.00
NEGATIVE	38	30.84	5	16.67	2	72.73	5	81.82
		100.00						

$\frac{5}{38} = 13.2\%$

$\frac{2}{5} = 40\%$

$\frac{5}{5} = 100\%$

My feelings after all my interactions were negative while on the average only 30.84% of the interactions aroused negative feelings.

Even on the negative interactions my degree of agreement as to their occurrence (13%) is lower than the average 16.67%.

My degree of consensus as to the feeling following the interaction (40%) is lower than the average (72.73%).

My consensus as to the type of interaction was better than the average, but this is understandable as all my feelings after the interaction were negative.

TYPE	(1)	(2)	(3)	(4)	(5)	(6)	(7)	(8)
A INSTRUCTIONS	17	46.73	3	17.00	2	88.24	3	70.59
B INFORMATION	15	46.73	2	19.00	0	78.95	2	73.68
C ADVICE	6	5.14	0	27.27	0	33.33	0	66.67
D COMPLAINTS	0	0.47	0	0.00	0	0.00	0	0.00
E COMPLIMENTS	0	0.47	0	0.00	0	0.00	0	0.00
F REPRIMANDS	0	0.47	0	100.00	0	100.00	0	0.00
		100.00		100.00				

A Instructions $\frac{17}{35} = 45\%$
B Information $\frac{15}{38} = 39.5\%$
C Advice $\frac{6}{38} = 16\%$
I perceive that I give more advice (11%) than the average (5.14%) and giving less information (39.5%) than the others. My perceived interactions are more or less equal to the average (46.73%).

$A = \frac{3}{17} = 15.7\%$
$B = \frac{2}{15} = 13.3\%$
$C = \frac{0}{6} = 0$
Only on my interactions there is an agreement (15.7%) as to their occurrence more or less equal to the average (11%). The agreement as to the information interaction (13.3%) is lower than average (19%) and not the advice interactions (0%) much lower than average (27.27%).

$A = \frac{2}{3} = 66.7\%$
$B = \frac{0}{2} = 0\%$
$C = 0$
My consensus as to my feelings after this interaction is equal to the average in the instructions (66.7% and 68.24%) but much lower in the information, (0% and 78.95%) where the other party perceived my 'negative' interactions as being 'neutral' or even as 'positive' reactions.

$A = \frac{3}{3} = 100\%$
$B = \frac{2}{2} = 100\%$
The consensus as to the type of my interactions (100%) is higher than the average both in the instructions (70.59%) and the information ones (73.68%).

GENERAL CONCLUSIONS:
The feelings I had as a result of my interactions were all negative and much too pessimistic (columns 1, 2, Table 2). This probably accounts for the fact that my conference interactions are less perceived by the other party as the average (I do not impress the other party enough) (columns 3, 4, Table 1).

Likewise, this is the reason why only in 40% of my agreed interactions ($\frac{2}{5}$) the feeling of the other party following the interaction was as my own feeling

(the average consensus being 80%) (columns 5, 6, Table 2).

On the other hand, I am quite clear as to the type of interaction (instruction, information, advice), once the other party perceives my interactions (100% as compared to an average of 70%) (columns 7, 8, Table 1).

All in all, I should be much more optimistic and I could probably be a proficient line manager and a good 'leader'.

Table 7.4 Comparison of self-recorded interaction studies in seven organizations in four countries

Data studied	Industrial (Plastics) 1[a] USA 1959/1960	Marketing (Pharmaceuticals) 7 UK 1966/1967	Industrial (Electronics) 5 France 1966	Industrial (Aircraft) 6 France 1966	Military (Ordnance) 11 Israel 1969	Management training (Teaching, research, and hotel) 13 UK 1971	Financial services (Banking) 19A Israel 1976	19B Israel 1976
No. of managers								
approached	50	60	26	21	48	32	28	30
participated	34	50	26	21	41	27	20	20
Length of study (no. of days)	10	10	10	10	10	10	12	12
Oral interactions with other participants								
Total reported	1708	2639	128	215	672	1272	398	517
% mutually perceived	26	14	17	21	7	38	17	16
Daily average per person	5.0	5.3	0.5	1.0	2.6	4.7	3.4	4.4
% interactions by telephone	22	45	73	29	19	14	13.5	3.6
Face to face	78	55	27	71	81	86	86.5	97
Consensus as to type in mutually perceived interactions	47	35	46	73	50	43	52	39
Source[b]	Weinshall (1966)	Weinshall and Vickery (1970)			Tzirulnitsky (1969)	Weinshall, Beal, and Silver (1971)	Nachmais, Weinshall, and Etzion (1978)	

Notes:
[a] This is the number under which the organization appears in Table 7.3.
[b] The exact references of these sources could be obtained from the authors, or found in Weinshall (1977, p. 16).

From then on it was just a matter of time before the CE drew his conclusions. In four out of eighteen action research projects, the first author believed that *the* problem of the organization was the CE himself and that *he* was the menace to the organization's survival. This the consultant has to keep to himself, of course, like any other feelings he may have about what is going on in the organization. In all these four cases the CE resigned of his own accord within a period of one month to two years.[73]

In any case, there is no doubt that the more the CEs were helped to help themselves through counselling, the more the feedback helped them. Those who left their organizations seem to have done so with ease, and seem to have learned from the feedback what type of things they should do in the future.

The same seems to apply to those who stayed in the organization.[74] The more they were counselled, the more they seemed to have been helped by the feedback to help themselves to run their organizations in the future. This may be seen in the amount, and especially the magnitude, of changes they introduced, and how these changes succeeded. Table 7.5 presents the results of action research and outside help in 18 organizations. We have already explained the results in the four organizations in row A.

In another eight organizations, major changes in the TOS were introduced by the CEs (row B). In each of these cases the central message in the feedback was the necessity for the introduction of change by the CE.

In the last group of six organizations, no observed major changes were introduced by the CEs (row C). In four of them we felt, when reading the feedback, that no major changes were required in either the organizational strategy (the what, how, and where of the organization) or the managerial structure. In one other organization, an academic institution, the traditional way of doing things and managing them was so strong that, in spite of major maladaptations in the TOS, the existing leadership was sustained for several more years. However, this academic institution has been confronting severe problems in its organizational strategy, which has not been adapted in spite of having changed its CE twice since them.

In another organization, a military ordnance base of the Israeli Defence Army, the writing on the wall, i.e. the serious meaning of the feedback in terms of the management structure, was not correctly interpreted either by its commanding officer (and other officers) or by the action research consultants. It was in this and other similar types of units that grave faults appeared during the first few days of the Yom Kippur War (October 1973).

The communicogram feedback   There is no doubt that the communicogram feedback helps the managers to help themselves much more satisfactorily when it is accompanied by personal counselling. The amount of counselling in communicogram projects has been quite limited until now, but whenever it occurred, it helped.

Counselling was available to participating managers but only if they asked for it. This now seems to be insufficient. It may well be that in this type of feedback,

Table 7.5 Eighteen organizations in which action research and outside help were rendered

Action research results	1 UK		2 France		3 Israel		4 Japan		5 USA		Total
	No. of orgns	Code no.[a]	No. of orgns	Code no.	No. of orgns	Code no.	No. of orgns	Code no.	No. of orgns	Code no.	Total no. of orgns
A CE leaves within two years					3	8, 9, 15			1	1	4
B Major changes in the TOS introduced by CE			1	12	7	3, 4, 10, 16, 17, 20, 21					8
C No observed major changes in the TOS	1	13			4	2, 11, 18, 22	1	14			6
Total	1		1		14		1		1		18

Note:
[a]The code numbers are the same as those in Table 7.3.

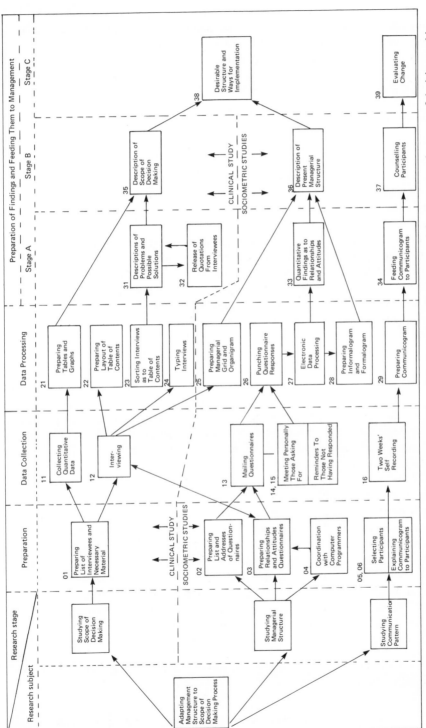

Figure 7.6 Layout of activities sequence in action research on the adaptation of the managerial structure to the scope of decision making

as well as the action research report type, all the participants exposed to the feedback should be prompted to undergo counselling. Moreover, with both types of feedback, the concentrated counselling following the action research should not be undertaken by the consultants who have conducted the research, but rather by other counsellors who have not been involved in it.

7.4 SUMMARY

This chapter opened with a description of the prevalent organizational diseases and ailments. The two main diseases, 'anti-mobility' and 'no full disclosure', create three ailments which endanger an organization's survival: 'maladaptation to the dynamics of the TOS', 'undisclosed feelings' and a 'hierarchical communication gap'. The chapter then proceeded to discuss three of the cures which have been tried on organizations, but which have helped only marginally.

Finally, more appropriate ways of helping organizations were discussed. The cures used by the Roman Catholic Church, although quite effective in helping it to survive for so long, have been found to be inadequate for other organizations. Most of the last part of the chapter was devoted to 'action research' and the way it has helped more than 20 organizations to overcome their three ailments.

The data for the action research are collected by way of open interviews, sociometric (interpersonal relationship and interaction measurements) studies, and other quantitative and written material. The content analysis of the interviews and other written material, along with the results of the informalogram, the sociometric managerial structure study, are subsequently fed back to the CE and other managers. The feedback of the results of the communicogram, the sociometric study of the communication interaction pattern, is performed separately; every participant receives his own results, compared with the group's averages. The whole process of action research is presented in Figure 7.6 as a layout of the sequence of activities.

This sort of action research may be compared with periodical medical check-ups of individuals. Such a medical check-up may reveal some sickness which is subsequently attended to. However, if the check-up is performed after a terminal disease has already affected the patient, it may be to no avail. The same is true in action research, as regards individual organizations. Although the CEs are not as yet sufficiently convinced of the merits of periodical action research, we believe that this will come soon. After all, until after the Second World War it had been unheard of for an executive to take several days off each year in order to undergo a medical check-up, *and* for the organization to pay his salary and full expenses! It is therefore reasonable to believe that many CEs will eventually accept the advisability and necessity of periodical check-ups for their organizations every few years.

NOTES

1 The trauma of the 1929 crash led to drastic developments aimed at avoiding both another crash resulting from an accumulation of inventories, and the chain effect

factor through which it would be transmitted to so many shareholders in US corporations.

Avoiding future accumulation of excessive inventories has been tackled by two new fields of science. The first is that of operations research (OR), which started with inventory control models (Gouderian and Cahen, 1932). The second is that of electronic data processing (EDP); the major managerial use of EDP has been to cut the size of inventories to a minimum, by accelerating the flow of information from storerooms to top management.

Preventing shareholders from panicking under the stress of stock exchange fluctuations has been achieved by regulating and controlling US public corporations. This has been the task of the US government acting through the SEC (Securities and Exchange Commission). The SEC was part of the New Deal of Franklin D. Roosevelt, elected in 1932 to cure the ills of the USA following the 1929 crisis.

2   The main two breakthroughs in understanding organizations were made by Chester Barnard and the Hawthorne Research group (Elton Mayo, Fritz Roethlisberger, and their colleagues). Chester Barnard used his insight into biology in order to translate his own practical understanding of organizations into conceptual relationships which would be meaningful to others (Barnard, 1938). The Hawthorne group drew primarily upon their psychological and sociological training in order to research, discover, and lay the foundations for the way in which we perceive organizations nowadays (Roethlisberger and Dickson, 1939).

3   The types of organizations which perish or are in acute danger of collapse when their CEs pass away were studied in an exhaustive research which produced a book presenting many such case studies (Christensen, 1953).

4   This passage is written in the masculine gender but is, of course, applicable in the feminine too. In fact, the unwillingness to admit fatigue and sickness until they completely overpower a person seems to be even stronger and more common among women than among men. The older of us remembers very vividly that, while serving in the British Army during the Second World War, he was always amazed at the ATS (Auxiliary Training Service) girls' perseverance. They could have gone on for long hours without drink, food, or rest, while their brothers in arms insisted on having their tea breaks several times a day in addition to their scheduled meals. Similarly, he has noticed that women often report to work feeling unwell when men, in a similar condition, would have probably confined themselves to bed. Women have been found to be more task-oriented; Helmich (1974) established among 550 US corporation presidents that female presidents showed relatively less consideration (i.e. concern for people) and more structure (i.e. concern for task achievement) than male presidents.

5   When somebody becomes physically sick, one would not point a blaming finger at him and say, 'You are responsible for having become sick', even though in many cases the person himself is indeed to blame for having contracted the sickness. On the other hand, in most cases individuals are unjustly blamed of being exclusively responsible for causing organizational sickness, when they had nothing to do with its origins.

6   Our own experience with releasing case studies from organizations in different countries is indicative of the secrecy surrounding different aspects of organizations, and of the degree of interorganizational mobility.

The ethics of case writers require them to obtain written permission from an organization before they may use a case for research and/or. This is required even when everything in the case has been disguised, including the names of the organization and the individuals appearing in it.

It is interesting to note that while such permission frequently involves difficulties with the executive who is requested to sign it, the type of obstacles differ from case to case. The executive's reluctance depends to a very large extent on his personality and on the way the case has been written. However, both in our own experience and in the case writing of others, a connection has been observed between the country in which the permission is requested and the areas in which special release problems arise. For example, in the USA one confronts a reluctance to release information concerning individual managers appearing in the case. The same kind of information, even when seemingly embarrassing to the individual concerned, is relatively easily released by French organizations.

The situation changes when one is dealing with facts and perceptions about business processes rather than human processes. One finds extreme difficulty in releasing information about manufacturing, marketing, and finance in French organizations. On the other hand, it is much less problematic to release similar extracts in US cases.

This difference between France and the USA can be understood when one considers that interorganizational managerial mobility is more widespread in the USA than in France. This means that the person who authorizes the release of a case in the USA worries about the effects that personal opinions about managers may have on their employment prospects and careers in other organizations. In France, whatever is said about a person will rarely affect his future career. On the other hand, interorganizational mobility in the USA prevents organizations from keeping too many secrets about their marketing, manufacturing, and finance, while in France, and in other countries where interorganizational mobility is low, organizations may develop a high degree of secrecy in such matters.

7 It is interesting to note that the 'no full disclosure' syndrome may be even more crucial in what are sometimes perceived to be 'open' organizations, like the kibbutzim, in which people live together day in and day out. Whether at work, in the dining hall, in the children's houses, or in public and social meetings, you are together with the same people, usually several hundred. Under such conditions, one can afford to be even less open with one's mates than one could be with people with whom one is only working.

We are similarly aware of the fact that if people find themselves in situations other than at work, their degree of openness with each other tends to decrease. This happens when colleagues with their married mates meet each other socially after working hours. Their rate of 'no full disclosure' could be expected to increase both in the social and the organizational context.

The same would happen, on the whole, when family members join together in business. The interpersonal loyalty among them in business is expected to be greater than if they had not been related. However, the openness could generally be expected to decrease, in relation to the degree of frankness existing among family members who are not also joint members in other organizations. The 'no full disclosure' is a 'fallacy of uniqueness' syndrome, i.e. people do not realize that it is prevalent in other individuals and organizations. Most individuals believe they are unique in not disclosing their own truth to others. The first research in which the terms 'pluralistic ignorance' and 'fictitious norm' (which are synonymous with the 'fallacy of uniqueness' concept) appeared is that of Schank (1932). A more recent description of the fallacy of uniqueness syndrome is by Krech et al. (1962, pp. 248–249).

The antithesis of 'no full disclosure' is that of trust. We have two examples of increasing the trust in and of managers by removing them from the managerial hierarchy. The first is that of the counsellors (or 'godfathers' as Peter Drucker (1971) refers to them) to the new managers in the large Japanese organizations. The godfathers are chosen from among those managers who are told at the age of 45 that they will be retired at 55. They therefore do not perceive the younger managers as a threat to their careers and they can counsel them and sometimes groom them for the highest positions in the organization. The second example is of large Western business organizations in which senior executives are retired to the board of directors whether they have reached retirement age or not. Thus, in organizations like Exxon in the USA (formerly Standard Oil of New Jersey and Esso), and the Coal Board in the UK, one finds sitting on the board people who are at one and the same time knowledgeable about the operating organization and free of the ambitions and interpersonal conflicts which commonly mark those within the managerial hierarchy.

Last but not least, we would like to discuss in this note the so-called internal consultants. It seems to us that their main problem is that they cannot expect to find out 'the whole truth' and, at the same time, inform the CE what he should do about it. It is towards them, perhaps even more than towards other managers, that 'no full disclosure' would be applied. This shortcoming is evident even among those who merely present the point of view of the internal consultant (Kelley, 1979).

8   Let us consider the events of the Japanese play *Rashumon*. There were several witnesses to a man's assault on a young woman. Each has a different story to tell, including, of course, the accused himself. The stories, as told by each of the witnesses, consist of flash-backs. Finally, the assault as it actually happened is shown to the spectators. However, if there are 500 spectators in the theatre, one would probably have 500 different perceptions of the events as they took place.

Even when we deal with such events as the year in which an organization was established, there could occasionally be dissenting perceptions to the majority's recollection as to when it happened. In such a case the event should be described as follows: 'The majority of those interviewed said the organization was founded in 1967; there were, however, a few who felt that it was established in 1956.'

A person's own truth may change over the years. As time plays tricks on his mind, he becomes aware of things he had not perceived before, while other things may be erased from his consciousness. Over time, he may even change his evaluation of things which happened, going from one extreme to another.

9   Research establishing those parts of one's innermost thoughts and feelings which one conveys to others, and those parts which one does not, or conveys to the contrary, would be quite elaborate and of doubtful interest and utility. Such research would require a detailed content analysis of what an individual related in his communication with others, comparing it with a detailed content analysis of what he says when opening up in psychological counselling and psychotherapy. There are several pitfalls in such research. The main one is that one cannot go through an opening up process at the same time as being involved in the communication process inside the organization. When the individual opens up, he may fail to refer to things he had in his mind during his communication with others. He may omit reference to such innermost truth because over time its significance to him is considerably diminished. One could try to help him open up with regard to things he said during the communication process and failed to mention in the subsequent opening up process. There would always be, however, things which he kept to himself at the time ('not the whole truth') and which do not come out in his opening up process. These things can never be recovered.

The other major problem in such research would be to establish the variations in the ratios of 'truth' to 'non-truth' that occur over time in the degree of openness of the same person. First there are the different contingency situations in the adaptation between SDM, managerial structure, and managerial characteristics. Next come the different people with whom the person has communicated in each of these contingency situations. The personalities and the roles of his counterparts, relative to his own, as well as the state of the relationship with each of them at the time, will considerably affect the person's ratio of 'truth' to 'non-truth'.

Finally comes the state of the person's feeling at the time of communication, his fatigue, his stress, his mental involvement in other matters, etc. The ratio of 'truth' to 'non-truth' should, desirably, be found separately for each of these situations. Otherwise mixing them together would hardly provide any explanatory and predictive information.

10   The personality traits of an individual may be seen as part of his 'environmental set' in terms of the surrounding level in Maslow's need hierarchy (Maslow, 1954). Consider a person with specific leadership and followership characteristics who has been brought up in an esteem needs environment. As long as the esteem needs environment persists he may be obliged to maintain interpersonal relationships which are contrary to his managerial characteristics, but he will revert to his leadership and followership characteristics whenever he feels free of situational pressures to behave otherwise. However, if the whole wider environment changes as a result of traumatic events like war, famine, or the like, he will *voluntarily* change his interpersonal behaviour. He will usually tend to do so even when there are no immediate situational pressures on him to do so.

Thus, during times of emergency and war, when the environmental set in terms of a Maslow need hierarchy shifts from esteem to belongingness needs level or, even a safety needs level, the person will usually adapt his personality traits to the new requirements for the surival of the organization. An example of this is found in one of the most famous case studies of the Harvard Business School, namely that of the Dashman Company (Glover and Hower, 1952). The organization operated in a decentralized managerial structure until 1940, when the 'lend lease' preceding the US entry into the Second World War put pressure on the company to formally centralize its structure. Most organizations have to be run in a functional managerial structure during war time, because their SDM are considerably reduced as a result of governmental regulation and direction of their manpower, manufacturing, pricing, distribution, etc. The Dashman case describes a situation of resistance to bringing in a Mr Post as the head of a centralized purchasing function. This is evidently a first step in the process of centralization of all the functions which occurred as the USA became more deeply involved in the war.

The question became one of how the Dashman CE, the heads of the 20 decentralized subsidiaries, and all the other managers would be able to centralize their structure. They had been operating in a decentralized structure for a long period of time, and on the whole had suitable leadership and followership characteristics for it. The answer is that during wartime, when there is a perceived danger to the whole country and its economy, the managers throughout the hundreds of thousands of US organizations adapted their managerial characteristics to those required for running functional structures. This, however, lasted only for the duration of the war and its perceived dangers. The moment that the environment was, in terms of the Maslow need hierarchy, back to the esteem needs level, all the millions of managers reverted to their inherent leadership and followership characteristics.

The same occurs with those who join, voluntarily or by conscription, the armed forces of their country in time of war. The whole multitude of individuals had a variety of tastes in food and clothing, different living habits and standards, and, again, different interpersonal characteristics and preferences, before they joined the armed forces. They became exposed to and, for the most part, accepted the same food, uniforms, habitation, and daily timetable without any need for strict coercive measures. They had to obey and salute people with whom, under so-called peace conditions, they would not have been associated, or in a good many cases would have had as their subordinates rather than their superiors.

However, once the hostilities terminated and the emergency conditions had passed, they reverted to their inherent personalities. Thus, for example, there were mass protests and even mutinies among soldiers of the British Army in the Far East who objected to continuing to live under the same conditions of food, pay, etc., once the Second World War was over.

Another example of the effects of the Maslowian environmental conditions are the shifts in individual and organizational behaviour in Israel during the long confrontation with its Arab neighbours since 1948. There have been marked behavioural differences between periods of relative calm and periods of strife and fighting. In periods of strife the crime rate, in all types of crime, drastically drops, only to return to its previous rate when calm is perceived to be back. Similarly, the rates of absenteeism in industry drop to almost zero when the country finds itself at war. Industrial productivity, in terms of output per man-day, rises under such conditions, sometimes by hundreds of percents.

11 However, many organizations are eliminated by the war conditions themselves.

12 The importance of responding to the need of children, from their very early infancy, to share their feelings and thoughts with their parents or others should by no means be underestimated. It is quite evident that the personality is established to a large extent during the first years of life. Thus, parents can help their child to be brighter in his mature years by enabling him to share his feelings and thoughts with them (Beck, 1975).

13 The exceptional character of people who want to seclude themselves from the world has been a recurrent topic in world literature. Thus, Boccaccio chose the monks isolated in the desert as the topic for one of his more famous (or should I say infamous?!) *Decameron* stories. The best-known example of a story about a man who lived by himself is *Robinson Crusoe*. The usual moral of such stories is that after a while even the most determined isolates cannot live by themselves. One of the monks in the *Decameron* story yields to female temptation, and Robinson Crusoe finds his human companionship in the form of his man Friday.

Children's literature provides us also with many examples of human beings who prefer animal and bird companionship to that of their human brethren. One such idol in children's literature is Dr Doolittle.

14 In comparative organizational research carried out in one US corporation in 1957 and again in 1959, relationships among managers in the different hierarchical levels were studied. The managers were divided into six levels. The actual relationships among the managers were measured by MPWR (mutually perceived working relationships). By definition such a relationship exists between two persons when they mention each other in their independent responses to: 'List the names of the people with whom you generally work most closely, regardless of their position in the organization.' The results of the average MPWR for the managers in every one of the six management levels in each of the two years they were studied, are shown in Table 7.6. Although the rate of informal relationships decreased from 1957 to 1959 in the three higher levels the mutually perceived working (informal) relationships were on the whole larger, the higher the hierarchical level, in both years (Weinshall, 1960).

Table 7.6 MPWR among managers in a US organization

	Management level					
	1 (highest)	2	3	4	5	6 (lowest)
1957	5.4	2.5	2.9	1.7	1.1	0.8
1959	3.4	2.8	2.5	1.6	1.2	0.6

Source: Weinshall (1960, p. 91).

15 This is what happened in our Devon organizational example (see pp. 89–90 and 154–155).

16 One of the best descriptions of the ways by which parents can help in a child's development appears in *How to Raise a Brighter Child* (Beck, 1975).

17 The term 'managerial generation gap' is based on the behaviour of two principal systems of the TOS, comprising the management main system: the managerial structure and the managerial characteristics.

Consider first the managerial characteristics aspects of a managerial generation gap. It takes one generation for a new type of manager to appear, from the time they acquire their leadership and followership characteristics (up to the age of, say 6) until they can lead and be led in their managerial characteristics, say, 20–25 years later. Thus there is a gap of one generation for a country comprising, on the whole, only people with managerial characteristics for, say, entrepreneurial structures. Hence the changing socio-cultural, technological, and educational environment will result in educating children in managerial characteristics suitable for running organizations in functional structures, say, 25 years later.

The managerial generation gap depends on the most advanced structure in which organizations are run in the country, compared with the most advanced structure in which organizations are run in another country with which comparisons are being drawn. Take, for example, the progression of the structures used in this book (from the least to the most advanced structure)—entrepreneurial, functional, decentralized, and multistructure—and consider a country in which there are enough people with managerial characteristics suitable for entrepreneurial and functional structures. Compare it with the USA in which, presumably, there are enough people with managerial characteristics for all types of structure, including CEs for multi-structures. There is at least a two-generation gap between the first country and the USA. It may take more than two generations before there are enough managers for more advanced structures, i.e. the decentralized and multistructures. It usually takes longer first, because, the environmental socio-culture and technology-educational systems may not yet have changed sufficiently for children to acquire leadership and followership characteristics for a more advanced structure. Secondly, there may be only a partial bringing up of managers with new characteristics. Therefore, for the country in the present example to have an ample number of people with 'decentralized leader' and 'multistructure leader' characteristics, one may have to wait more than two managerial generations. The managerial gap for countries like the UK and Canada may be up to one generation, for a country like the Soviet Union at least two generations, and for some of the developing countries it is at least three generations.

18 See note 2 to chapter 5.
19 See Harris (1973).
20 In the industrialized countries of the world management training philosophies are often contrary to management contingencies actually occurring in organizations. There are quite different management training philosophies to be found even within the USA which is the most advanced country, both in its industrialization and in its management education. Thus, for example, the management education philosophies of Harvard University and the University of Chicago business schools fundamentally differ from each other. Nevertheless, both of them believe that all kinds of organizations should have the type of managers graduating from their universities.

The only industrialized country which is an exception to these management training philosophies is Japan. There, the managerial training and development may differ according to the type of managers. For example, entrepreneurs and their aides would derive much more benefit from meeting each other outside their habitual milieu. It is likewise felt in Japan that such managers would 'recharge their batteries', innovating their thinking about methods, products, etc., while visiting other organizations in Japan and in overseas countries. When these visits are carried out by an entrepreneur together with his aides, and a brain-storming process is occurring at the same time as an eye-opening process, this experience can be even more enriching.

If, on the other hand, the same entrepreneurial managers had been sent to formal executive training programmes, they would be able to learn very little. In fact, the authors' own experience in this type of training implies that the restlessness of entrepreneurs makes it quite difficult for them systematically to attend and participate in long executive training programmes, i.e. longer than one or two weeks. Their dominating and domineering personalities induce them to impose themselves on the other participants and teachers. They are usually 'telling' rather than 'listening'. They try to run the show rather than participate in it. Those of the entrepreneurs whose education has been limited may also feel antagonistic towards the teachers and some of the other participants, and try to force a showdown between those who can *do* and those who can *teach*.

The Japanese make a distinction between managers with formal and those with informal managerial characteristics when it comes to participation in formal executive training programmes; this is something we could learn from them with regard to other training programmes. One cannot categorically establish that training managers to be more participative in their decision making is something that would be good for everyone. There are managers whose leadership and followership characteristics are completely unsuited to participative decision making.

Authoritative managers, like all other managers, should be trained to be aware of different types of managers and managerial styles. Thus, they should be helped to distinguish between those of their decisions which are suitably authoritative, and those which are not conducive to the survival of the organization.

21   I have used this example of India, because it was there that David McClelland carried out his famous experiment. He has claimed to have 'trained' a group of unsuccessful businessmen in India in need achievement (McClelland, 1961). I feel that he has actually enabled them to get some 'Japanese' type entrepreneurial training, advocated in note 19. It seems to me, in fact, that in having these Indian managers go through formal training, he limited the time they could talk with each other about business ideas and opportunities. Had they just all gone for a holiday, to have a good time together, they would have increased the contribution to their future achievements. Had they gone on a trip to a new environment in which they could learn new things, this would have been even better.

22   The 'action research' in which the researchers participate in the action of the operating organization, i.e. management and the workers, first appeared in, and is very much associated with the names of two famous research centres. The first is the University of Michigan, at Ann Arbor (Katz and Kahn, 1966); the second is the Tavistock Institute for Human Relations in London (P. A. Clark, 1972; A. W. Clark, 1976). This sort of participative research is not a so-called 'participative observer research'. This latter research is mainly associated with anthropological research, in which the researcher turns into a regular member of the organization for a prolonged period of time, usually not less than one year. As such he collects both his own observations and the perceptions of others as related to him for his research. The anthropologist, or any other researcher collecting data in this fashion, does not use his findings and conclusions in order to activate the members of the organization to behave differently from the way they have been pursuing their work.

23   There are those things in life which one usually likes to keep to oneself or share with only one other person. Such an intimate thing is love making. An aspect of love making is undressing. Therefore an orgy in which more than two people take part, or a strip-tease show, is considered as 'vice', or out of the ordinary. This is probably why some people refer to group exposure of innermost feelings as 'mental strip-tease'.

24   Even the best business games are much more removed from organizational reality and behaviour than case studies, especially those cases describing organizational reality and behaviour as they are seen from within. One cannot very well learn about the behaviour of one's colleagues and oneself, either from one's own involvement in real organizational behaviour or from involvement in business games, because once the participation is real, one's involvement is emotional.

25   This type of training has been incorporated in the management training advocated by Reginald Revans, who has devoted a large part of his rich life to management development (Revans, 1971). There is no doubt about the quality of the different types of training afforded to managers by Revans. On the other hand, this is a much

longer and costlier training. Those who went through it have, in certain cases, relinquished the practice of management, moving to teaching, research, and advisory roles.

26 Another analogy of innovation versus false 'innovation' could be found in the biblical prophet era. The Bible distinguishes between prophets of truth and prophets of untruth. The prophets of truth foresaw both encouraging and discouraging things which eventually turned out to be true. The prophets of untruth usually predicted a rosy picture which turned out to be false.

27 If an alternative cannot be implemented, it should be dropped, even without an *a priori* analysis of its suitability as a solution. This is reminiscent of an anecdote about Napoleon Bonaparte's advance on Moscow. There were several reasons for Napoleon's failure to bombard Moscow with 2000 cannons. First, it was night time and it was difficult to aim; secondly, it was raining and the cannons were wet; thirdly, the soldiers were very fatigued; and, finally, Napoleon had in his possession only 200 and not 2000 cannons!

28 A recent presentation of matrix structures and organizations discusses both their positive aspects, as seen by the authors, and some of their failures (Davis and Lawrence, 1977).

29 A description of Fredrick Taylor's 'Functional Experts' Structure' is given in the beginning of Brian Twiss's and Teddy Weinshall's book (1980).

30 It is interesting to note that those who developed the principles of a matrix structure were probably subjected to engineering influences similar to those evident in Taylor's 'machine model' of the organization (Taylor, 1911). Some of the original work on matrix organization was done at MIT (e.g. Galbraith, 1971). The engineering environment usually has an effect even on those who teach and research management in an institute of technology like MIT.

31 Frederick W. Taylor (1856–1915) started his working life as a patternmaker and machinist. Around 1880, when employed as a gang boss, his innovative thinking led to his important achievement in mechanical engineering (inventing a new method for tempering steel tools) and management. He introduced time studies and wage incentive schemes in his capacity as a consulting engineer in industry (Taylor, 1903; 1911). In 1911, the same year that his *The Principles of Scientific Management* saw print, Taylor appeared before the Interstate Commerce Commission. The counsel of this commission was Louis D. Brandeis, appointed a US Supreme Court Justice five years later. Brandeis established, on the basis of Taylor's evidence, that the railroads, which were asking for fare increases, could save $1 000 000 a day by the adoption of the principles of scientific management. Taylor was called in as an expert witness, since he was a management consultant. This was the first formal authorization for the profession of management consultancy.

32 Amazingly, very little research has been done on present-day scientific management consulting, while a lot of studies have been made on all kinds of OD (organizational development), combining the two types of cures which have been previously described: 'changing' managerial characteristics and 'innovating' managerial structures. One of the few studies made on scientific management consulting is Seymour Tilles's 'The consultant's role' (1961).

This research consists of twelve studies of consulting projects. Each case study describes the relationship between a consultant and a client for the duration of one project. All the consultants and clients are different in Tilles's studies, i.e. there are twelve consultants and twelve clients. Tilles found that only one such consulting project could be regarded as having succeeded in helping the client. This means that over 90 per cent of Tilles's small sample ended in failure.

33 The friends of Professor Bezeemer of Holland presented him, on his retirement from Erasmus University in Rotterdam, with a Dutch–English book on organizational theory and practice (Verburg *et al.*, 1976). In an illustrated summary, called

'visualization of thoughts', the concepts and ideas presented by the 35 contributors to this book were integrated. This was done by four of the contributors (F. J. Gossellink, J. Heijnsdijk, J. H. Huijgen, and F. Schippers), who opened the discussion of 'The first annual rings: scientific management and the right man in the right place', with the following passage (Verburg et al., 1976, p. 547):

> It is almost self-evident that in growing organizations, work-doing and work overseeing become problematic. This was the case in organizations at the turn of the century. Therefore at that time those topics were the main subjects of the first management studies. A school called Scientific Management emerged in the Netherlands in the first quarter of the twentieth century. That school considered the human factors as economic, motivated by financial incentives and as technical; i.e., man was seen as a means of production and was not integrated as a person in the work structure. Followers of this school of thought can still be encountered today.

34   The first author had a practice in what he now refers to as 'conventional management consulting' from 1950 to 1958. He believes that an important reason for the consultant's ignorance, in whatever degree, of the client's organization can be traced to the wrong assumptions conventional consultants make about clients. They presume that the higher managers are in the organization, the more they know about what is going on in it. We have already seen that the higher the manager is in the hierarchy, the less he knows about what the people at lower levels really think and feel.

When collecting his data in the organization, the conventional consultant rarely registers fully and precisely what the managers tell him. He usually notes down what he, the conventional consultant, feels and thinks about what he is told and what he sees. The way the consultant perceives the organization, its decision-making process, and its managers is to a large degree irrelevant to the organization, as he is not part of the management itself. The relevant things are the perceptions of all the organizational members (managers, workers, customers, etc.), even though they do contradict and disagree with each other. After all, the organization is the compilation of the subjectiveness and bias of all its members.

When the first author was a conventional consultant in the 1950s, he used to develop new trainees much in the way it was done elsewhere. 'The final report', he used to tell them, 'should be divided into two, the first part describing the present situation, while the second one is devoted to the proposed situation. The present situation should be as short as possible, because the manager (i.e. the chief executive) knows very well what the present situation is. If you tell him too much about it, he will feel offended. The part of the report which should be as long as possible is the one devoted to the analysis, findings and, especially, the recommendation, i.e. the proposed situation. This is what the client pays for.'

Such training was, and still is, based on the conventional consultant's ignorance of the partiality of the flow of information up and down the hierarchy. The most important thing the managers could get from a consultant is better information about what managers think and feel about their organization, their decision making, their communication, and their relationships with other managers. They rarely care and almost never could be helped by what the outsider feels and thinks about all these things.

35   The following is an anecdote of the first author's which occurred shortly after he was 'converted' from conventional consultancy to a consultancy based on the principle of an outsider helping his clients to help themselves. He was teaching at a seminar in the early 1960s, of which several of the participants belonged to the same management consultancy firm in which he had been employed before his 'conversion'. These students felt that in criticizing the consulting in which he had been involved several

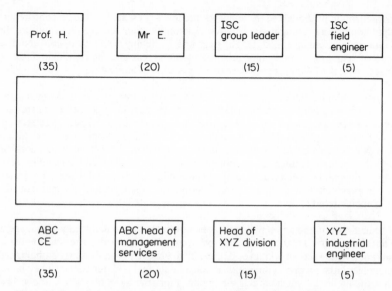

Figure 7.7   Confrontation between two management teams. In the upper seats on the end of the table are consultants for the Industrial Service Corporation (ISC). In the lower seats are executives of the ABC corporation and its XYZ division. The figures in brackets are the years of service in each of the organizations

years before, he was 'biting the hand that had fed him'. As they were newly involved in conventional consultancy, and quite enthusiastic about it, they could not understand what was wrong with the expert advice given by their firm, based on the long experience, knowledge, and know-how of its consultants.

He told them that he was both obliged to and appreciative of their firm, in which he had spent eight years. In fact, he had always been grateful to the person who headed it, who had been one of the best teachers he had ever had, and from whom he learnt most of what he knew about industrial engineering and systems.

He then gave them a hypothetical example using the actual names of the same head of their firm, referred to here as Prof. H, and the senior consultant and chief engineer of the firm (who was his successor in these roles), referred to here as Mr E; the firm is referred to as ISC (Industrial Service Corporation).

Assume that ISC is performing a consulting project in corporation ABC. The main focus of ISC is on industrial engineering areas of the largest division of ABC, Division XYZ. ISC assigns one field engineer to the task.

ISC is structured in groups of three to four field engineers, each headed by a group leader. The group leader divides his time roughly in proportion to the time invested by his engineers in the different projects (one project may have a full-time engineer, like the one at corporation ABC; there could, however, be another project in which only half of a field engineer's time is invested; or projects in which a team of two or even all the field engineers of one group are working).

So the ISC field engineer in the example often meets with his group leader who devotes about a third of his time to the ABC project. When they meet they analyse the situation in the XYZ division and together enrich the analysis of the project with their joint insights and ideas. From time to time the group leader will discuss this project with Mr E (the senior consultant and chief engineer); this is sometimes done in the presence of Prof. H, the managing director; in several of these meetings the group leader will have with him the field engineer working for ISC at the XYZ division. At least twice during such a period the whole vertical team—Prof. H, Mr E, the group leader, and the field engineer—will have a brain-storming session in order to contemplate the best solutions for the ABC corporation. One of these sessions takes place during the last stage of the preparation of the final report. (This is actually how ISC carried out its consulting assignments.)

Subsequently the report is presented to ABC corporation. A meeting is arranged between Prof. H of ISC and the chief executive of ABC. It is scheduled that those concerned at ABC will have ample time to study the ISC report and its recommendations. Prof. H brings with him the other members of the vertical team (Mr E, the group leader, and the field engineer), while the CE is joined by his head of management services (including industrial engineering), the head of the XYZ division, and his own XYZ resident industrial engineer. The two teams are seated at a table confronting each other as shown in Figure 7.7.

Assume that the length of their professional careers is equal for each of the ISC–ABC pairs confronting each other at the table. The length of professional career, in years, appears below each person seated at the table (e.g. Prof. H and the ABC CE each have a working career of 35 years). Thus the total professional career of the ISC, like that of the ABC team, is 75 man-years $(35 + 20 + 15 + 5)$.

The ISC report represents a pooling of the best contributions of the four ISC persons out of their combined experience of 75 years. Of this experience, less than 1.5 man-years were acquired in the ABC corporation (1 field engineer + 0.33 team leader + a little of Mr E's and a little of Prof. H's time).

However, the combined experience of the ABC team differs completely from that of the ISC team, although it is also 75 years long. The ISC experience is composed of a long chain of organizations in which the four consultants spent relatively short periods of time, usually up to a year, and rarely more than a few years in the same firm, if and when they were employed by one or more non-consulting organizations before joining ISC. The ABC experience was mostly acquired at ABC itself; say, 60 out of the 75 man-years, or 80 per cent of it.

The common experience grounds of the two teams may overlap only to a very small extent. The ABC managers may have difficulties in understanding the analytical approach and reasoning of the ISC consultants, and even fail to comprehend some of their terminology. The ABC managers will not easily admit these difficulties. The ABC subordinates, on the other hand, will not want to expose their shortcomings—which they feel may indicate ignorance on their part—especially in front of their superiors. The superiors, on the other hand, may feel that they are not, and should not, be aware of all the details which they believe are plain to their subordinates. Thus the ABC managers may express their appreciation and even their admiration of the ISC report and its recommendations.

The ABC managers may even believe and be convinced that the ISC report is absolutely clear to them and is 'brilliant', 'extremely useful', etc. However, they will discover the disparity between what the ISC consultants said and what they understood them to say if and when they try to implement the recommendations in their organization.

36 A more profound study of the development of management consultancy firms shows that with the passage of time they lose their knowledge advantage over their clients. The reason for this is that the clients, business and other types of organizations, are continually updating their knowledge by sending their managers on all kinds of courses. Some of these organizations will even have people go through university education for first, second, and third university degrees.

Rarely do management consultants send their people on any courses. Their people are always overloaded and generally do not have time even for private study. The reason for this phenomenon is that the demand for management consultants is cyclical, often with unforeseen ups and downs. The consultancy firms

380

cannot easily adapt their size of personnel to the demand for their services. They have, therefore, to decide at what level of demand to staff their organizations. Should they have enough people to satisfy the peak demands for their services? By following such a policy, they could use the slack, low-demand periods for retraining and updating their personnel. This would mean, however, a considerable rise in costs. Most consultants work closer to the other extreme: staffing their organizations according to the low demand for their services. This is why their people are always under pressure. It also means that in time the conventional consultants lose their relative expertise advantage in comparison with the knowledge level of their actual and potential clients' managers.

37 The comparison between the roles of consultants and experts in organizations is based to a large extent upon the pioneering doctoral research of Seymour Tilles (1961), described in note 30.

38 'Change agent' is used in this context in its wider sense. In the literature on change agents they are considered usually as actively involved in the change process. The writers whose work originates from Kurt Lewin (1974) first regarded change agents as people from outside the organizations, but eventually came to consider them 'almost as a helper'. This has developed into a recent definition that 'change agents are those people, either inside or outside the organizations who are providing technical, specialist, or consulting assistance in the management of a change effort' (Ottaway and Cooper, 1976). The latter definition fits any one of the previously discussed 'three cures which have only marginally helped', as well as the 'ways to help organizations' described in this section.

39 Data about chief executive interorganizational mobility appear in a text by H.-C De Bettignies and P. L. Evans in Weinshall (1977, pp. 277–292). The four countries where there is relatively more interorganizational mobility are the USA, the USSR, Germany, and Japan. The fact that these four also happen to be relatively stronger in their economies is not unrelated to their being able to have more suitable managements for their organizations in their different contingency situations.

40 Wilfred Brown (1960) points out that an *independent* analysis of the organization takes place when 'the person carrying out the analysis is not an employee and had no executive relationship with anyone in the company'. The Tavistock research team took up such a role at the beginning of their project at the Glacier organization, and Dr Jaques has continued in it since then. It involves:

(a) The completely confidential nature of all communications to the independent analyst, unless specific permission is given to make them public.
(b) The undertaking of analysis of work only at the request of those individuals, managers, or groups responsible for that work.

Given such circumstances, "unconditioned" views and feelings may become available. It has been our experience that this approach to the understanding of the way in which the company operates has permitted the emergence of data and ideas which would not otherwise have been obtained. (Brown, 1960, pp. 30–31)

41 Joseph may be considered the pioneer of psychoanalysis in his reading of dreams. He first analysed his own dreams, interpreting them in terms of his family relationships; he was already considered by his brothers a deviant, i.e. an outsider. Joseph subsequently interpreted the dreams of two of Pharaoh's ministers who were in jail with him; and finally he interpreted Pharaoh's own dreams. All this he did when he was an outsider in Pharaoh's court and, as such, people perceived him to be uninvolved in their organization, i.e. 'objective'. It is interesting to note that the moment Joseph became Pharaoh's viceroy and no more an

'outsider', he stopped playing the counselling and psychoanalytical role he had performed before. These and other aspects of Joseph's managerial behaviour (as well as that of Moses) are discussed in Weinshall (1972).

42 Mooney describes the significance of electing the members of the council of the general of the Society of Jesus in the following words:

> The counselors are chosen by the general congregation. They are not appointed by the General and they are not removable by him. They are literally imposed upon him. Here we have more than a compulsory staff service. We have another principal equally notable, that of staff independence. (Mooney, 1939, p. 121)

It is fair to assume that, as an individual can choose from among the clergy the person to whom he would confess, he would choose to confess to the counsellor he had democratically elected. Thus the Jesuit counsellors play similar roles to those of elected representatives to the assembly of a nation. The latter are chosen to legislate on behalf of the people. The elected delegates are, however, always available to listen to members of their constituencies or other members of the public. This process of approaching chosen representatives serves to keep the elected delegates informed of changing trends in popular political views and to update them about current local interests. As in the case of the counsellor in the Society of Jesus, they perform a cathartical role in their relationship with members of their constituencies.

43 Actually, there are other communities, outside Israel, where life, work, and sharing are quite reminiscent of the Israeli kibbutzim. Some of these communities have a longer history than that of the 70-year-old kibbutzim (the first kibbutz, Degania, was established on the banks of the Jordan river, where it flows out of the Sea of Galilee, in 1910). Thus, for example, in the US Mid West the Menomenees' social behaviour and customs were very similar to those of the kibbutz settlers (Ames and Fisher, 1958).

A recent comparison between kibbutzim and German-origin religious communities in the USA draws many analogies between the two types of organizations, in spite of the evident disparity between the two in religion, nationality, geographical environment, ethnic origin, and the like (Niv, 1976).

44 Unfortunately, we do not have a reference for this fascinating catharsis. Neither can we recall the name of the tribe.

45 One of these movements, which has derived its being from the human need for catharsis, is the so called 'Re-evaluation Counseling Community'. The original proclaimed objective of re-evaluation counselling was for the 'improvement of the individual'. However, in time Harvey Jackins, the originator and dominant figure in this movement, recommended 'that this community be thought of, primarily, as a network of local communities, groups and classes' (Jackins, 1971).

This movement, with its central figure and its evolving group therapy (developing into such things as 'express appreciation of each other, say loving words, embrace one another, link arms in a circle and look warmly at each other'), is just one of several such 'new' developments.

46 The transactional analysis was created by Eric Berne. Dr Thomas Harris, who presents the thinking of Eric Berne, the originator of transactional analysis, defines its purpose as follows: 'The purpose of the analysis is to discover which part of each person—Parent, Adult or Child—is originating each stimulus and response' (Harris, 1973, p. 62).

47 These foundations for counselling and psychotherapy have been laid down by Carl Rogers (1942).

48 Every 200 members in the Marks & Spencer organization have a so-called 'staff

manageress' overseeing them. These staff manageresses are not trained psychological counsellors, and perform a variety of roles. One of their prime roles is, however, to help the employees, many of them sales-girls, to open up and relieve their undisclosed feelings. Thus under the prevailing conditions at Marks & Spencer it was found that the roles performed by a 'staff manageress', including her personal availability to the individuals under her care, would enable her to be a sort of 'godmother' to 200 employees.

49 Indeed, we have rewritten large parts of this section on the basis of extracts from previous publications on case study and general organizational research. Thus the section which describes the main stages of action research is taken from a short book on organizational and case research, written several years ago (Weinshall, 1971).

50 It must be stressed again that 'action research' is used in different ways and contexts. It may mean different things to different people. Action research is described in this book in only one specific way: to help organizations overcome their ailments.

51 The terms 'consultant', 'researcher', and 'interviewer' are variously used for the same person. This is the person who conducts the action research and also the other people working with him. Any member of the action research team can be a 'consultant' (his role), 'researcher' (the way in which he conducts his role), and 'interviewer' (the main technique used in this clinical type research).

52 The CEs are physically surrounded by the operating organization most of their working time. Hence they are partially ignorant of the equal importance to the survival of the organization of the cooperation of factors other than the employees (e.g. customers, bankers, government, etc.). Because of this they are more aware of the problem of management and workers.

Chester Barnard (1938) was the first to present a systematic analysis of the equal importance of the cooperation of customers with the organization, and cooperation of workers.

53 A fascinating example of the differences between an organizational chart as it appears on paper and the formal organization as it actually works in the X-ray department of a hospital, is given by Roy (1958).

54 Researchers may encounter different degrees of difficulty in acquiring information about managerial remuneration. This depends primarily on the managers' country. There are many cultures in which information about financial remuneration is considered a personal matter. Revealing such information may be contrary to the norms of such cultures.

55 A more comprehensive description of the informalogram is presented elsewhere (Weinshall, 1973).

56 Extensive information about the communicogram is included in another book (Weinshall, 1979).

57 On the average, out of every 20 interviews for which permission to release has been requested, the following has occurred in our own action research studies:

—Sixteen interviewees did not mind the disclosure of extracts from their transcribed interviews, and did not suggest any alterations to them.
—Three interviewees suggested minor changes, e.g. one substituted 'Three years ago the organization was on the verge of collapse' for 'Four years ago the organization underwent a very grave crisis'; or instead of 'The Chief Executive is an unscrupulous bastard', one put 'The Chief Executive is completely insensitive and ignores the feelings and opinions of other managers'.
—One interviewee (or 5 per cent) refused to grant permission for the release of any part of his interview.

58 The researcher could, of course, try to persuade the one interviewee out of twenty

to release his interview or parts of it; after all, by that time the consultant may have acquired permission to release much more daring feelings than those expressed by the reluctant interviewee, which could be presented to this interviewee. However, such efforts are not advisable. The reactions of such a reluctant interviewee are often critical, accusing, and, even, belligerent. They may lead to a chain effect which could undermine the whole action research process.

The professional reputation of the researcher who respects the wishes of the interviewed managers, without appeal, would never be tarnished.

59 The distinction between 'scope' and 'structure' is clear and easy to make with regard to all factors outside the operating organization, i.e. customers, suppliers, owners, government, etc. The difficulty in distinguishing between scope and structure arises when dealing with the two factors belonging to the operating organization: management and the workers. This difficulty can be overcome if one remembers that everything which has to do with the attitudes of the employees towards the organization and towards other employees, as well as everything which concerns the relationships among employees of the organization, is part of the managerial structure. All the other things concerning the employees are part of the SDM. Thus, for example, the prevailing employment situation of the environment is part of the SDM. So are the personal characteristics of the organization's employees: their education, ethnic origins, family relationships, ages, salaries, etc. In other words, all things which are decided by the environment and by previous decisions of management are considered as 'scope', i.e. as part of the SDM, which the management has to cope with. *How* management organizes itself for handling this scope of decision making is found in the managerial structure which includes the relationships and attitudes of the management.

As the workers are the lowest level of the managerial hierarchy, and because it is sometimes difficult to distinguish between a worker and a manager, it is often preferable to include the attitudes and relationships of all the employees within the managerial structure.

60 The matching of mutual choices (when one participant mentioned another and one checks whether the other reciprocated) is done in the informalogram only once. In the communicogram the choices are matched hourly. There are about 100 working hours during the two weeks during which such a study is carried out.

61 In non-verbal cultures the total number of perceived interactions for a group of 30–50 participants for the duration of two working weeks does not exceed several hundred interactions.

62 As seen earlier in this book, the chief executive is the highest ranking executive in the organization, an executive being a person who devotes at least half of his working time to the organization. Thus, for example, a member of a board of directors who is fully and more or less equally occupied in the management of four organizations is *not* the CE of any of them. However, if he is a member of chairman of two boards of directors and devotes all his working time more or less equally to the management of both, he is the CE of both organizations, whether or not there exists a person bearing the title of 'general manager' in either or both of the two organizations.

63 Note 40 above presents what Mooney (1977, p. 121) calls the *staff independence* principle. Immediately afterwards he continues:

> The implications of this principle are tremendous in their possible implications of other spheres. The first necessity in sound line decisions is a complete knowledge of the truth. But the mere possession of such knowledge by the staff is not enough. The system must ensure that this knowledge shall

384

reach the line executive. This the Jesuit organization does, insofar as any system can. Under this system there is little danger that anything will be withheld from the General that he ought to know.

64 This was the US organization in which Weinshall carried out his doctoral research and which is presented as the Devon Corporation in the organizational example in chapter 3. One organization outside the USA with which one could compare Devon is the French Galvor organization (also a disguised name). The managers in this organization, which was described in a series of case studies (by Edward Learned of the HBS under the auspices of IMEDE, Lausanne), expressed their opinions about each other in quite candid and blunt language.

65 An example of this phenomenon appears in the Dashman Company, one of the earliest case studies in organizational behaviour (Glover and Hower, 1962). Shortages in materials early in the Second World War prompted Dashman's president to bring a vice president for purchasing into his decentralized organization, which was composed of 20 factories operating autonomously, i.e. independently of each other and of the president. The new vice president, Mr Post, subsequently sent the 20 purchasing managers of the decentralized factories a letter informing them of new purchasing procedures. This procedure compromised their autonomy. During the following two weeks replies came in from all except a few plants. Although a few executives wrote at greater length, the following reply was a typical one:

Dear Mr Post:
Your recent communication in regard to notifying the Head Office a week in advance of our intention to sign contracts has been received. This suggestion seems a most practical one. We want to assure you that you can count on our cooperation.
Yours very truly

This letter does not, however, mean that they actually reacted in their manifest behaviour differently from managers in other countries facing the same situation. In spite of the letter, these purchasing managers did not comply with the instructions given by Mr Post. Managers in other countries may have refrained from responding to Mr Post's letter, or turned to their immediate bosses, the factory managers, or tried to organize the purchasing managers in the other factories in order to obstruct Mr Post; they may even have openly opposed Mr Post, responding negatively to his letter. The US managers responded, superficially, in a positive and polite manner, but actually reacted in the same way as their counterparts in other countries would have done.

66 Appears in Weinshall, 1977, pp. 7–8.

67 The necessity for receiving data about the managerial income or remuneration brackets has been discussed earlier in this section on action research, when describing the informalogram. Regarding Figure 7.4, which presents an example of an informalogram chart, one can see that the visual comparison between the formal and informal structures could be achieved only by superimposing the MPWR diagram on to the formal grid. It is only by knowing in what income bracket every manager is, that one can place him in his formal unit-income square.

68 The organizations appearing in Table 7.3 (details of managerial research studies) include only organizations in which the action research incorporated also a managerial structure or communication study (through an informalogram or communicogram). This is why this military organization, as well as other organizations in which no simultaneous sociometric studies were conducted, is not described in Table 7.3.

The consequences of the consultancy rendered to this organization by way of action research were that the formal changes were introduced in the whole logistics branch of this specific army. It so happened that the army was involved in subsequent operations, in which the logistics branch demonstrated the adequacy of its revised managerial structure. This army logistics organization is presented as an organizational example in chapter 3.

69 Most of these studies using the communicogram or similar techniques are reported in a recent book describing the process of managerial communication (Weinshall, 1979). By 'process' is meant a study of *how* the communication flows through the organization and what are its effects, rather a study of the actual contents of communication. Studies of the contents of managerial communication deal with *what* the managers do and how much time they spend on their different occupations.

70 Weinshall's (1979) book on managerial communication discusses the contributions of the communicogram technique and findings to cross-cultural researches as well as to other managerial fields (e.g. power bargaining, managerial information systems, etc.).

71 One such publication presents some findings regarding counselling as part of the feedback process (Nadler, 1977).

72 All the CEs of organizations in which we carried out such action research agreed in advance to support the process *vis-à-vis* all the organizational human factors (managers, workers, owners, etc.) whenever such support would be necessary. However, the degrees of enthusiasm for plunging in (some perceived it as plunging into cold and unknown waters) varied. Indeed, the initiative for such studies varied, from the very few who had heard about this type of consultancy, and wanted to have it undertaken in their organizations, to the very few at the other end of the scale who were induced by others (usually the chairman of the board of directors) to go through with it. The majority of CEs were willing to try it, with varying degrees of interest, curiosity, and enthusiasm.

73 The relocation of CEs took different forms: two moved to other organizations, one got involved in new operations in other countries, and one plunged into regional and national politics.

I have known other cases of CEs who reached the conclusion that the only way to save their organization (usually which they owned) was by cutting themselves off from the organization. They did this in varying ways. One of them deliberately appointed very strong personalities to head all his six product groups—people who would prevent him from interfering in the organization. (Unfortunately, he eventually fired some of them and his organization collapsed once more!) A few others tried to detach themselves from their organization by becoming active in an international organization like the YPO (Young Presidents' Organization).

74 Two of them, belonging to larger organizations (of which the organizations they headed, were part), were transferred to higher positions just when the feedback reports were submitted to them. The transfers were not initiated by them and the decision by the heads of the larger organizations to transfer these two CEs had been made before they saw the reports.

SELECTED BIBLIOGRAPHICAL SOURCES

Ames, D. W., and Fisher, B. R., 1958. 'The Menomenee termination crises: Barriers in the way of a rapid cultural transition', *Human Organization*, **18** (3), pp. 101–111.
Barnard, C. I., 1938. *The Functions of the Executive*, Harvard University Press, Cambridge, Mass.

386

Beck, J., 1975. *How to Raise a Brighter Child: The Case for Early Learning*, Pocket Books, New York.

Bogen, J. E., 1975. 'Educational aspects of hemispheric specialization', *UCLA Educator*, **17**.

Brown, W., 1960. *Exploration in Management*, Penguin, Harmondsworth, Middx.

Christensen, C. R., 1953. *Management Succession in Small and Growing Enterprises*, Harvard University Graduate School of Business Administration, Boston, Mass.

Clark, A. W., 1976. *Experimenting with Organizational Life—The Action Research Approach*, Plenum Press, London.

Clark, P. A., 1972. *Action Research and Organizational Change*. Harper & Row, London.

Davis, S. M., and Lawrence, P. R., 1977. *Matrix*, Addison-Wesley, Reading, Mass.

Drucker, P. F., 1971. 'What we can learn from Japanese management', *Harvard Business Review*, March–April.

Galbraith, J. R., 1971. 'Matrix organization designs', *Business Horizons*, February.

Glover, J. D., and Hower, R. M., 1952. *The Administrator*, Irwin, Homewood, Ill.

Gouderian, J., and Cahen, J. F., 1932. 'The calculation of the necessary stock for producing and selling organizations', *Proceedings of the 5th CIOS Conference*, Amsterdam.

Harris, T. A., 1973. *I'm OK, You're OK*, Pan Books, London.

Helmich, D. L., 1974. 'Male and female presidents: Some implications of leadership style', *Human Resources Management*, Winter, pp. 25–26.

Jackins, H., 1971. *Revised Guidelines of Re-evaluation Counseling Communities*, Rational Island Publishers, Seattle, Wash.

Katz, D., and Kahn, R. L., 1966. *The Social Psychology of Organizations*, Wiley, New York.

Kelley, R. E., 1979. 'Should you have an internal consultant?', *Harvard Business Review*, November–December.

Krech, D., Crutchfield, A. S., and Ballachey, E. L., 1962. *Individual in Society: A textbook of social psychology*, McGraw-Hill.

Lewin, K., 1947. 'Groups decision and social change', in E. Maccoby, T. Newcomb, and E. Hartley (eds). *Readings in Social Psychology*, Methuen, London.

McClelland, D. C., 1961. *The Achieving Society*, Van Nostrand, New York.

Maslow, A., 1954. *Motivation and Personality*, Harper & Row, New York.

Mooney, J. D., 1947. *The Principles of Organization*, Harper & Brothers, New York.

Nachmias, M., Weinshall, T. D., and Etzion D., 1978. The communicogram as a change agent, presented at the XIXth International Congress of Applied Psychology in Munich, August 1978.

Nadler, D. A., 1977. *Feedback and Organization Development: Using Data-Based Methods*, Addison-Wesley, Reading, Mass.

Niv, A., 1976. 'A search for a theory about the survival of communes', unpublished doctoral dissertation, Harvard University, Boston, Mass.

Ottaway, R. N., and Cooper, C. L., 1976. 'Moving towards a taxonomy of change agents', *Management Education and Development*, **7**.

Revans, R. W., 1971. *Developing Effective Managers: A New Approach to Business Education*, Longman, London.

Roethlisberger, F. J., and Dickson, W. J., 1939. *Management and the Workers*, Harvard University Press, Cambridge, Mass.

Rogers, C. R., 1942. *Counseling and Psychotherapy*, Houghton Mifflin, Boston, Mass.

Rossi, E., 1977. The cerebral hemispheres in analytical psychology, *Journal of Analytical Psychology*, **22**, pp. 35–51.

Roy, R. H., 1958. *The Administrative Process*, Johns Hopkins University Press, Baltimore, Md.

Schank, R. L., 1932. 'A study of community and its groups and institutions conceived of as behaviors of individuals', *Psychological Monographs*, **43** (2).

Taylor, F. W., 1911. *Shop Management*, Harper, London.

Taylor, F. W., 1911. *Scientific Management (Comprising the Principles of Scientific Management and Testimony Before the Special House Committee)*, Harper, New York.

Tilles, S., 1961. 'The consultant's role', *Harvard Business Review*, November–December.

Twiss, B. C. and Weinshall, T. D., 1980. *Managing Industrial Organizations*, Pitman, London.

Verburg, P., Malataux, P. C. A., Halbertsma, K. T. A., and Boers, J. L. (eds), 1976. *Organisatiewetenschap en Praktijk*, Senfert Kroese, B. V. Leiden.

Weinshall, T. D., 1960. 'The effects of management changes on the organizational relationships and attitudes', unpublished doctoral dissertation, Harvard University.

Weinshall, T. D., 1966. 'The communicogram, a method for describing the pattern, frequency, and accuracy of organization and communication, in *Operational Research and The Social Sciences*, Tavistock Publications, London.

Weinshall, T. D., 1971. *Applications of Two Conceptual Schemes in Case Study and General Organizational Research*, Papers in Management Studies, Ashridge Management College, Hertfordshire, UK.

Weinshall, T. D., 1972. 'The Bible as pioneer in the fields of management and organizational behavior', mimeographed working paper no. 156/72. The Leon Recanati School of Business Administration, Tel-Aviv University, December.

Weinshall, T. D., 1973. 'The informalogram as an indicator of managerial structure', The Leon Recanati Graduate School of Business Administration, Tel Aviv University, working paper no. 167/73.

Weinshall, T. D. (ed.) 1977. *Culture and Management*, Penguin, Harmondsworth, Middx.

Weinshall, T. D., 1979. *Managerial Communication: Concepts, Approaches and Techniques*, Academic Press, London.

Weinshall, T. D., 1982. 'How chief executives may be helped by outside consultants', *California Management Review*, Spring.

Weinshall, T. D., Silver (Shaler) M., and Beal C., 1971. 'Patterns of communication and organization structure in a management training college', a mimeographed research report, Ashridge Management College, Hertfordshire, UK.

Weinshall, T. D., and Vickery, L., 1970. 'Some uses of communication pattern research in analyzing and influencing organizational behaviour', in Roig-Amat B., ed., *La Empresu Multinacional* (The multinational corporation), in Coleccion IESE, Serie AC-3, Ediciones Universidad de Navarra, Barcelona.

Selected TOS Bibliography*

Barnard, C. I., 1938. *The Functions of the Executive*, Harvard University Press, Cambridge, Mass.†

Brown, W., 1960. *Exploration in Management*, Wiley, New York.

Caplan, G., 1958. 'Some comments on problems of community psychiatry and technical co-operation in Israel'. Paper presented at conference on *Economic Planning and Social Policy in Israel*, Harvard University Center for Middle Eastern Studies.†

Chandler, A. D., Jr, 1962. *Strategy and Structure*, MIT Press, Cambridge, Mass.

Davis, S. M., 1971. *Comparative Management: Organizational and Cultural Perspectives*, Prentice-Hall, Englewood Cliffs, NJ.†

De-Bettignies, H.-C., and Evans, P. L., 1977. 'The cultural dimension of top executives' careers', in T. D. Weinshall (ed.), *Culture and Management*, Penguin, Harmondsworth, Middx.

Glover, J. D., and Hower, R. M., 1952. *The Administrator*, Irwin, Homewood, Ill.

Hall, E. T., 1970. *The Silent Language*, Fawcett Publications, Conn.†

Heller, F. A., 1971. *Managerial Decision-Making*, Tavistock, London.

Katz, D., and Kahn, R. L., 1966. *The Social Psychology of Organizations*, Wiley, New York.

Lederer, W. J., and Burdick, E., 1958. *The Ugly American*, Gollancz, London.†

Pugh, D. S., 1963. 'A conceptual scheme for organizational analysis', *Administrative Science Quarterly*.† Vol. 8, pp. 289–315.

Roethlisberger, F. J., and Dickson, W. J., 1939. *Management and the Workers*, Harvard University Press, Boston, Mass.

Stopford, J. M., 1968. 'Growth and organizational change in the multinational firm', doctoral dissertation, Harvard University (published by Arno Press, New York, 1980).

Vernon, R., 1971. *Sovereignty at Bay: The Multinational Spread of U.S. Enterprises*, Longman, London.

Weber, M., 1947. *The Theory of Social and Economic Organization*, Oxford University Press.†

Weinshall, T. D., 1960. The effects of management changes on the organizational relationships and attitudes', unpublished doctoral dissertation, Harvard University.

Weinshall, T. D., 1973. 'A study of organizational size and managerial structure', in Desmond Graves (ed.), *Management Research—A Cross-Cultural Perspective*, Elsevier, Amsterdam.

Weinshall, T. D., 1976. 'The Total Organizational System (TOS) and the interdisciplinary approach in management and organization', in P. Verburg, P. C. A. Malataux, K. T. A. Halbertsma, and J. C. Boers (eds), *Organisatiewenschap in Praktijk (Organization Science and Practice)*, Stenfert Kroese, Leiden, Holland, pp. 55–106.

Weinshall, T. D., 1979. *Managerial Communication—Concepts, Approaches and Techniques*, Academic Press, London.
Woodward, J., 1958. *Management and Technology*, HMSO, London.
Woodward, J., 1965. *Industrial Organization: Theory and Practice*, Oxford University Press.
Zwerman, W. L., 1970. *New Perspectives on Organization Theory*, Greenwood Publishing, Westport, Conn.†

* This bibliography contains all the works that appear in the Selected Bibliographical Sources following at least three chapters. It also includes works (marked †) which do not appear in at least three Selected Bibliographical Sources, because they are important for the following reasons:

(Barnard, 1938)	is the main origin of the TOS.
(Caplan, 1958)	is an exceptional insight into the problems involved in cross-cultural help, consulting, and technical aid.
(Davis, 1971)	is an excellent selection of case studies of management in differing wider environments.
(Hall, 1970)	is one of the most important contributions to interpersonal relationships and communication.
(Lederer and Burdick, 1958)	is a book which prompted an enormous change process in the American way of doing business outside of the USA, and contributed more than any other book to the creation of multinationals which do not carry the constraints of one country to others.
(Pugh, 1963)	is the first publication of the Aston group which was the basis for their whole organizational contingency research.
(Weber, 1947)	is the translated original presentation of the first theory of the bureaucratization (i.e. formalization) of organizations.
(Zwerman, 1970)	is a worthwhile contribution to those aspects of the TOS which are universal rather than culture-bound. This book shows that the relation between organization and technology first discovered by Joan Woodward in the UK holds true for the USA as well.

Author and Personal Index

This index is followed by a Geographical and Organizational Index and a Subject Index. The names of the authors do not appear in the Subject Index.

Geographical and Organizational Index

The index is preceded by an Author and Personal Index and followed by a Subject Index.

398

Shell (Royal Anglo Dutch), 31, 167, 231, 285
Senate Joint Armed Forces Committee (USA), 198
SHAPE, 287
Sheraton Hotels (of ITT), 124, 127, 140
Shiites (Islamic sect), 224, 284
Sicily or Sicilian, 198
Society of Jesus (*see also* Jesuits), 356, 381
South Africa, 90, 229
South Essex Industry (SEI, organizational example), 72, 91, 95, 130, 140, 199
Soviet Union (*see* USSR)
Spain, 201, 229, 271, 285
Spanish, Castilian, 288
Standard Oil of New Jersey, 13, 95, 371
Strategic Planning Institute (in Boston, US), 38
Students for a Democratic Society (SDS) (US student movement), 78, 202
Sunnis (Islamic sect), 224, 284
Sweden *or* Swedish (*see also* Scandinavian countries), 169–170, 184, 201, 240, 248, 263, 267, 280–281, 290, 361
Swissair (SA, organizational example), 35–37, 53, 134, 135
Switzerland, 184–185, 243–244, 248–249, 250, 252, 254, 263, 266–267

Tahiti, 141
Tavistock Institute for Human Relations (in London, UK), 94, 132, 200, 375, 380
Technical, efficiency and organization (TEO) product group, 175
Tel-Aviv, Israel, 127, 355
Tel-Aviv University, 91, 135
Tokyo, Japan, 215
Toronto, Canada, 200
(International) Transport Worker's Federation (trade union), 286
TRW (US electronics manufacturer), 199
Turkey, 280

UNESCO (United Nations Education, Science and Culture Organization, in Paris), 233, 239, 297
Unilever, 31, 285
United Auto Workers (US trade union), 286
United Kingdom (UK) (*see also* England, Scotland), 26, 28, 36, 87, 90–92, 108–109, 110–111, 129–131, 133, 142, 169–170, 182–185, 191, 194, 196–197, 200–201, 203–204, 212–213, 215, 226, 229, 234–237, 239–241, 247–249, 250, 252, 254–257, 262, 266–267, 271, 280–282, 285, 290, 294, 325, 353, 354, 358, 361, 365–366, 371, 374, 389
United States of America (USA), 18, 24, 26, 28, 37, 43, 54, 78, 86, 90, 95, 123, 130, 133, 138, 140, 142, 147, 153–156, 169, 170, 184–185, 188–189, 191, 195, 196–201, 212–215, 217–218, 221, 223, 225, 226, 235–237, 239–250, 252, 254, 255, 263, 266–267, 270–273, 277–278, 280–283, 285–290, 292–294, 304, 312, 323, 329–331, 340, 352, 357, 361, 365–366, 369–374, 376, 380–381, 384, 389
United States, Mid West, 381
University of Aston (Birmingham, England), 95
University of Chicago (US), 374
University of Michigan (US), 375
University of Navarra (Spain) (*see also* IESE business school), 285
US Army, 282
US Navy, 155, 156, 198
US Steel, 231
US Supreme Court of Justice, 376
USSR, 28, 172, 173, 198, 212, 213, 214, 215, 240, 243, 270, 271, 274, 276, 288, 293, 294, 340, 374, 380
Utah (USA), 226, 285

Vatican, 159
Volkswagen (VW, car manufacturer), 167, 201
Volvo (car manufacturer), 161, 199

Washington, USA, 78, 215
Weinshall-Raveh Ltd., 91
West *or* Western, 64, 100, 194, 234, 285, 358
Western bloc, 136
Western countries, 169, 190, 235, 274, 294, 340, 358
Western democracies *or* Western democratic countries, 138, 149, 233, 240, 276, 285, 294
Western Electric Company (*see* Hawthorne), 341
Western Europe *or* Western European (countries), 111, 173, 185, 191, 213,

Subject Index*

This Index is preceded by an Author and Personal Index and a Geographical and Organizational Index.

---

* The subjects may be listed in either their regular order (e.g. 'Administrative behaviour') or in reverse order (e.g. 'Behaviour, administrative'). Basic terms (e.g. administration, administrator, behaviour, corporation, management, manager, etc.) are usually not listed, unless in relation to additional words (e.g. 'Administrative behaviour', 'Corporate strategy', 'Managerial structure', etc.). Whenever the subject is synonymous or similar to another one, the words '*see also*' will follow, e.g. 'Stockholders (*see also* Shareholders)'. In cases where the same subject could be shortened by one word, this additional word is put in brackets. Thus 'Market (system), money', could indicate either 'Money market' or 'Money market system'; similarly, 'Structure, Entrepreneurial (Managerial)' could mean either 'Entrepreneurial Structure' or 'Entrepreneurial Managerial Structure'.

402